SISTER DOMINIQUE'S INCREDIBLE WAR

OTHER TITLES BY GERRY FELD

A Journey into War
Published in 2017

A Soldiers Final Journey
Published in 2019

Vietnam Honor and Sacrifice
Published in 2019

Sarah Rosenbaum's Dachau Redemption
Published in 2021

PT Boats; Terrors of the Pacific
Published in 2021

SISTER DOMINIQUE'S INCREDIBLE WAR

GERRY FELD

SISTER DOMINIQUE'S INCREDIBLE WAR

Copyright © 2022 by Gerry Feld

ISBN Paper Back 978-0-578-29131-4
ISBN E-Book 978-0-578-29130-7

All rights reserved. No part of this book may be reproduced or transmitted in any form or by any means electronic or mechanical, including photo copying, recording or by any information storage and retrieval system without permission of the copyright owner.

Sister Dominique's Incredible War is purely a work of fiction. Names, characters, places, and incidents are the product of the authors imagination or are used fictitiously. Any resemblance to any actual person living or dead, or events and locales is entirely coincidental.

Printed in the U.S.A.

Editing and proofreading by Lori Hawkins
Interior design and Typesetting by Roseanna M. White
Cover design and Art work by FrinaArt

Prologue

Throughout World War Two, there were thousands of women that quietly became heroes, for many varied reasons. Some served in the new military organizations created strictly for women, such as the Navy's (WAVES) Women accepted for volunteer emergency services, The Army's (WACS) Women's Army Corp, The Air Corp's (WASPS) Women's Air Force Services Pilots, or the Coast Guard's (SPAR) program.

Other women chose to work in defense factories, relieving men that were needed in combat roles. Many married women became both mothers and fathers to their children throughout long periods of time while their husbands were away fighting the war.

In Europe, many women took dangerous roles working with underground partisans that fought the enemy whenever and where ever they could, in order to disrupt their operations and destroy munitions and equipment.

No matter which role a woman decided to undertake, it is very clear that World War Two could never have been won without their significant effort and sacrifice.

Sadly, all too often, the sacrifices made by women during the war years are overlooked and sometimes nearly forgotten. We owe a large debt of gratitude to those women that broke through the glass ceiling, proving women were equal and just as vital as the men they replaced.

Today, women hold top jobs in industry, the military, academia, and medicine, because of these hero's that came before them.

Dedication

I would like to dedicate this book to all the unsung brave and courageous women like my mother, that worked tirelessly during the war years to assure victory was achieved. My mother left her parents farm to take a job in St. Cloud to replace a man that had been sent off to the war. These women are a shining example for all future generations of women and men alike.

As always, I would also like to dedicate this book to my wife JoAnn who spent countless hours discussing my story, and helping iron out problems that at times appeared insurmountable.

Contents

Prologue 5
Dedication 6
Chapter One – Sister Dominique 9
Chapter Two – The Furlo Valley 18
Chapter Three – Italy's New Realities 30
Chapter Four – Occupation 36
Chapter Five – The Raid at Pescate 47
Chapter Six – The Long Trip 59
Chapter Seven – Captain Paulo Trevisiani 76
Chapter Eight – A Beginning 90
Chapter Nine – Caught in the Middle 102
Chapter Ten – Destruction of the Abbey 130
Chapter Eleven – The Horrors Begin 143
Chapter Twelve – The Nogatu Maru 160
Chapter Thirteen – Decisions 183
Chapter Fourteen – Move to Japan 192
Chapter Fifteen – Who Lives, Who Dies 211
Chapter Sixteen – Prisoner Camp 216
Chapter Seventeen – A Bright Light 230
Chapter Eighteen – Camp 45 249
Chapter Nineteen – Vengeance 257
Chapter Twenty - Uncertainty 266
Chapter Twenty-One – Devastated 273
Chapter Twenty-Two – The Past is Present 292
Chapter Twenty-Three – Italy Once More 310
Chapter Twenty-Four – Lt. Charles Freeborn 322
Chapter Twenty-Five – Reunions and Good byes ... 333
Epilogue 341

Chapter One – Sister Dominique

The snow swirled around the courtyard at St. Benedict's Monastery in St. Joseph, Minnesota, as Sister Dominique slowly ran her frail, weathered fingers across the frost that had formed on the bottom of the window pane. She smiled slightly as she watched a bright red cardinal attempt to land on the bird feeder as it spun and tumbled in the powerful wind.

After shivering several times, Sister Dominique sat back down in her wheelchair and covered her still strong shoulders with a black shawl that had been given as a gift from a close friend. Turning the chair back toward a group of students that were sitting at a large wooden table, notebooks and recorders at the ready, she smiled.

"You all remind me of the days when I was still teaching. Ready to hear what I have to say, but not too sure you want to take on the project in front of you."

The students laughed as they watched Sister Dominique roll her chair up to the table. After taking a sip of hot coffee, she looked at the student directly across from her. "I'm sorry my dear, where did I leave off? Or did I actually get started?"

Smiling, a pretty blonde named Catherine, replied. "You started telling us the story about the day your father took you to the convent."

"Ah yes. I was distracted by the wind and blowing snow in the courtyard. Actually, it was a day much like today. Although my bones have become brittle, I get chilled easily, and my eyesight is not as good as I would like it to be at times, but my mind has never missed a beat. I can tell you where my spare glasses are, what I had for breakfast on Monday, and where I hid three cookies after dinner last night. I have no intention of sharing them with you or anyone else by the way. They have butterscotch chips on top, my very favorite."

Everyone laughed once again at the cordial polite old woman with a slight Italian accent that sat before them. After a moment of thought, she said, "But you see, I was not always this way."

You will find that no one gets to be one hundred years old without cultivating some special attributes. Yes, my hair has turned as white as the snow in the courtyard, the color in my eyes has dimmed, and my legs no longer carry me too far. But there was a time when I could run as fast as all of you, stand straight and argue like a United States Marine, and fend for myself in ways you cannot imagine, but you will hear all about that, since I promised Mother Superior that I would help all of you to write my story before I am gone from this world. By the way, I call her Mother Superior out of respect. She is but sixty years old, so what does she really know, she is way too young yet." After laughing at her own comment, Sister Dominique's demeanor shifted more toward the serious side. "Throughout everything I accomplished and experienced in my long life, the one thing I always took time to do was cultivate a clear mind that would hold all the memories of a life time, although I never expected to live quite this long. You really should all begin to do the same."

After taking another sip of coffee, Sister Dominique looked up at the ceiling for a minute before beginning. Here is what you all want to know about me."

Dominique Celina Margretta Trevisiani, the fifth child of Leopoldo and Maria Trevisiani, a poor farming family living near Acqualagna, Italy, was born in 1915. Although Leopoldo was a good farmer, the rocky soil he had to work with did not provide enough good crops to feed his family, much less the small herd of livestock he had built up over the years.

Moving was not an option, as the family did not have enough money to pay for a farm where with better soil. After a long and painful discussion over many weeks, Leopoldo and Maria made the heart wrenching decision to give up their youngest child to the sisters in the Benedictine Convent in the Abbey di San Vincenzo al Furlo. There, she could attend school, and not have to fight with her equally hungry siblings, brother Paulo and sisters Giana and Claudia, for the last scraps of food on the table. At the convent, she eventually would become a Benedictine Sister, and be able to help others in need.

On a very cold winter morning while the other children had gone off to school, Maria bundled up her youngest daughter and kissed her on the cheek for the last time, as tears rolled down her face. She looked at five-year-old Dominique, saying. "Cooperate well with the sisters, and they will be very good to you. Do you understand?"

Not understanding what was about to happen to her, Dominique looked strangely at her mother as she placed a little hand upon her cheek. "Mama, I am always good. You say I am your good daughter all the time."

Nodding her head in agreement as her heart continued to break, Maria replied, "Yes Dominique, you have always been an angel. And now you must be so for the sisters as well."

As Leopoldo wrapped his daughter in a heavy blanket, she looked up at her mother. "I will tell the sisters hello from you and see you when we get back."

Closing the door behind her husband, Maria sat down at the kitchen table and wept.

It took a good part of the day for Leopoldo to guide his horse drawn sleigh down the icy roads that eventually came to the treacherous mountain trail which led to the front door of the Abbey. All the while, little Dominique sang funny songs as she looked at the icy scenery, or studied a picture book of animals her mother had packed for her.

After knocking on the heavy wooden door, a tall straight woman of about sixty appeared in front of him and asked. "My name is Sister Santina, what do you ask of God this cold winter day, sir."

After looking down at the ground for a moment, Leopoldo raised his head while removing his hat. "I am a poor farmer that can barely keep food on the table for my family. We should not have had a fifth child, although we love her very much. It's becoming an increasing burden to feed and clothe her. We have no other family to turn to, so we would like to give her to you, so you can raise her to become a sister like you, it may be her only chance at survival."

Stunned by Leopoldo's statement, she looked intently into his face. "This will be a big task for us, but one we are most willing to do. Are you absolutely certain this is the only way?"

Nodding his head, Leopoldo looked forlornly at Sister Santina. "We have prayed for an answer, but this is all we have come up with. We do not wish her to die of hunger or illness. Please help us."

"Yes, yes bring her in so we can talk inside," the anxious sister replied, as she watched Leopoldo take the precious bundle from the sleigh.

With the heavy blanket removed, Dominique looked up at Sister Santina "My mama told me to say hello to you. Mama says I'm always a good girl, and I should be good for you, too. I'm not sure why I'm here, but I will be good while we visit."

Grasping her chest, Sister Santina took a step back, astonished that the child understood nothing about what was about to happen to her. She glared angrily at Leopoldo. "You have not made an effort to tell this child what is going on? How could you do this to your own flesh and blood?"

Once more hanging his head, Leopoldo replied, "No, no we could not. Maybe I am a coward, maybe I am not the strong man of character God wanted me to be, but Maria and I could not find the words to tell her. We thought it was best for you to explain, once I have gone," Leopoldo responded, as he turned to leave.

"This is not the way, sir, she is not an orphan," Sister Santina responded, feeling somewhere between anger and shock. "You are her father, you must try and explain in words she can understand. You must be honest, or she will never get over what you are doing to her. She must be told so that years down the road she will have a chance to understand."

Leopoldo stood motionless for a moment, before kneeling by Dominique. "Your mother and I love you with all of our hearts. But like your brother and sisters, and the animals in the barn, we can no longer feed everyone. We have brought you here to live with the sisters, where you will always be warm, have clothes to wear, and have food to eat. They will teach you in their school, and one day, you will be a sister just like Sister Santina. You will have a good life here, Dominique."

Jumping forward, Dominique threw a strangle hold around her fathers neck. "No Papa, no! You cannot leave me here, I want to play with my sisters and brother, I want to ride the horses, I want to play in the meadow with our dog in the spring. I want to watch him jump and try to catch butterflies. I will be a better little girl; I am sorry for everything I have done wrong. Please take me home to Mama. Please Papa, please!"

After kissing Dominique on the cheek, Leopoldo stood up. "It's the only way child, it's the only way."

Dominique stood motionless for a moment near Sister Santina, letting everything her father told her sink into her young brain. Suddenly, she raced toward the door, screaming, "No father, no! Come back, I do not want to be here!" She slammed her little fists against the heavy wooden door, over and over as she wailed in agony. Slowly, she slid down to the cold tile floor where she curled up in a fetal position. As she continued whimpering, she called out, "No Papa, no! Papa please, I'll be good and I'll eat less."

Each time Sister Santina or another sister would come near, Dominique would scream for her Papa and kick at their legs. Near night fall, one of the young novices named Agnesia, walked over, placing a plate of warm food on the floor in front of Dominique.

"You should eat, little one, this has been a long day for you. Then we can talk and I will help you through this. I was young when I was brought here myself, and I know what you are going through. Please eat, Dominique."

After Agnesia had left the foyer, Dominique sat up, placing her back against the door. Picking up the plate, she began to eat the dumplings and small pieces of chicken and carrots. It was not like her mother's cooking, but it satisfied the pains in her stomach.

Standing up, she turned and looked at the heavy wooden doors. Maybe her Papa was just outside, waiting to see if she passed the test of being good. Maybe he was just going to buy oats for the horses and would change his mind and come back before it was too late. But maybe what he had told her was the truth. Maybe this was to be her new home and she would never see her family again.

Not wanting to think of that prospect, Dominique walked around the foyer, looking out the windows at the blowing snow, and examining the elegant statues that adorned the room. As she sat down in a large red velvet covered chair with ornately carved arms, the door on the east side of the room opened.

Agnesia slowly walked over to Dominique and sat down beside her. "My name is Agnesia, and I am thirteen years old. I have been here since I was six. One winter my parents died in an avalanche and no one else in the family wanted to raise me, so the sisters took me in. I don't know what happened to my two brothers, I never heard from them again. I know you are still grieving over what happened today, and it will take time to work through it. But everyone here will do what they can to help you. Mother Superior whom, you have not met yet, has asked me to spend as much time as I can with you, so we will become good friends. If you wish, I will be your big sister, you can tell me all your secrets, and no one will know but me."

For the first time, Dominique smiled a bit as she leaned over against Agnesia.

"Tonight, I really need a big sister since I have lost both of mine. Giana is three years older than me, and Claudia nearly five years older. Giana always looked out for me, and sometimes took the blame when I did naughty things. She was really good with our two horses, and taught me how to ride. I loved feeding the animals with her. She always talked to them, and they almost seemed like they understood her. I shall miss her most." With that she cried bitterly as the faces of her sisters danced back and forth in her mind.

After rocking Dominique for several minutes, Agnesia asked, "And what of your brother, you haven't mentioned him at all."

"Paulo is almost seven years older than me. He always seemed to resent having me around. We never really played together and in some ways he bullied us girls a lot. But he is my brother and I will always love him for that, but I shall not miss his taunting and slapping. He could be very mean at times.

Agnesia gave Dominique a squeeze as she replied. "You must forgive Paulo. He was the only boy in a family of girls. I am sure he had a tough time dealing with that. I am certain that he misses you very much.

It was nearly midnight before Dominique's eyes became too heavy to keep open, no matter how hard she tried. Agnesia picked her up and carried her to her small bedroom on the third floor of the Abbey. After tucking her in, Agnesia kissed Dominique on the forehead. "Sleep well, little one, you will be alright here, I shall look after you."

When they arrived home from school, Leopoldo and Maria explained to their children that Dominique had wandered off during the snow storm while they were attending to the animals in the barn, and they were unable to find her. Paulo jumped up from his chair, pointing to the window. "It's still light out there and the storm stopped hours ago. Why are you not out searching with the neighbors to find her? She could be hurt and she must be freezing out there. We must do something to try and help her!"

Leopoldo placed his large hand on Paulo's shoulder. "She is lost by now, there is nothing more we can do for her. The wolves may have found her already. We must accept that she is gone."

Pushing his father aside, Paulo replied, "I shall look for her until dark, then I will look some more in the morning. I will not go to school until I find Dominique. I shall not give up until I can bring her home. I am not weak like you are father, a man who would give up on his own daughter and not care if she is in trouble."

Cold and tired, a dejected Paulo entered the small farm house about eleven o'clock that night. Although he was tired and emotionally drained, he planned all night where he would search the following morning. As dawn broke over the valley, Paulo was already searching to the east of the farm where the foot hills began to rise up into the mountains. He felt safer today carrying the pitch fork from the barn, in case he ran into hungry wolves. Carefully, he searched each cave for any signs of his sister, but all he found was wolf tracks, along with bones and fur from small animals. After following a set of wolf tracks for several hours that led him higher into the mountains, the sun was beginning to set, and he grew frightened. Slowly he began retracing his tracks back to the last cave he had inspected. As he turned back toward the west, he heard a noise behind him. Placing his back up against a large boulder, Paulo peered into the gathering darkness for any sign of what was behind him. It did not take long before a rather large wolf appeared out of the darkness and began to growl. Although Paulo was frightened, he felt more confident that there was only one wolf to contend with. The hungry animal paced back and forth, each time closing the distance with Paulo.

As the wolf hunched its back, Paulo brought up the pitchfork ready to strike. Suddenly, the animal lunged forward, sinking its teeth into Paulos large coat. At the same moment, Paulo thrust his pitchfork into the neck of the wolf. The animal howled in pain as it stumbled back away from Paulo. Immediately, Paulo charged forward, thrusting the pitchfork into the chest of the injured animal. Once, twice and a third time, the pitchfork's tines were thrust deep into the dying animal. Standing over the wolf with his pitchfork raised in the air and ready to strike again, Paulo realized he had won the battle. Blood covered the heavy gray coat of the wolf, as the terrifying green eyes were now closed forever.

Backing away, Paulo quickly scanned the area for signs of any more wolves. Seeing nothing, he hurriedly retreated down the mountain toward home where he would be safe. Entering the house, Maria gasped as she looked at her son.

"Paulo, are you alright?"

Taking off his coat, Paulo was surprised to see how much blood had sprayed all over him during the battle. "I am fine, mother. I killed a wolf tonight. I'm no longer afraid of the dark, or what haunts it. I shall keep looking for Dominique as long as I am able."

Maria took the bloody coat and washed it, knowing everything that Paulo was going through was for nothing. She felt like she should explain what they had done with Dominique, but then the children would apply pressure on them to get her back.

Paulo continued searching for his sister from dawn until well into the dark night for two more weeks, until a huge snow storm dumped nearly a foot of snow on the area. He knew he had covered far more miles than Dominique could ever have traveled, and was confident her little body would never be found. No matter what his parents said to him, Paulo could not forgive his father for giving up on his little girl so easily. It was a wound that could never be healed.

Day after day for the first week, Dominique and Agnesia explored the old Abbey with all its strange corridors, odd shaped rooms and ramparts that over looked the steep valley below. Soon, she came to know all the sisters and novices by name, and ate in the large dining room with them. She began attending daily prayer and bible reading sessions with Agnesia, and loved practicing with the choir.

But at night when she was all alone in her small room, her heart ached, and she continually felt her family pulling her back, regardless of what her father had said about her being a burden. She knew very well that the sisters in the Abbey had come to love her very much, but the need to be with her family was becoming stronger by the day.

One night as she sat by the window looking out over the Furlo Valley, she wondered which was the right way to travel home. For the next two weeks,

Dominique studied the valley from every outlook in the Abbey, searching for anything that looked familiar or promising, but saw nothing.

The one thing Dominique was happy about was that Agnesia had shown her a scary passage that led to a large door that exited out onto a stone outcropping. From there, Agnesia said a person could find their way down into the Furlo passage without anyone seeing them leave. After giving her plan consideration for nearly a week, Dominique decided to set out and find her family.

Chapter Two – The Furlo Valley

With an old back pack stuffed with a good supply of food, a large knife and a ten-foot rope she had found in the basement, Dominique was ready to begin the search for her family.

Around two in the morning, she quietly slipped out of her bedroom and made her way toward the west entrance to the sub-basement. After walking down the first twenty steps, she came to the large wooden door that led to the passageway. Using the knife to help pry open the door, Dominique observed the lantern and matches Agnesia had left on a small shelf.

With the lantern lit and the door closed solidly behind her, Dominique started her way down the narrow corridor that had been hewn out of the rock centuries earlier, by the monks using the Abbey. The farther she went in the tunnel, the more she felt the eyes of those long dead monks watching her every step. Looking up at the walls of the tunnel, she could see where many of them had carved their names into the rock. Some places had memorials written that said things like, 'In memory of John killed in cave in 1659.' She wondered if John's spirit still lingered in the tunnel, and if he minded her passing the place where he had died. As she approached the end of the tunnel, the sounds created by the whistling wind around the old door frightened her even more. At one point she stopped and looked around the tunnel and called out.

"John, is that you? Please don't hurt me, I'll be out of here shortly and you can rest again."

Dominique stood totally still for a moment, as if waiting for John to reply. With everything remaining quiet except for the wind, she slid open the latch, used the knife to help pry the door open, then finally stepped out onto a narrow rock ledge.

Dominique set the small lantern off to the side as she prepared to close the heavy door. She knew she would need it to light the path down to the road. Once the door was closed, Dominique stood nearly breathless as she peered into the night sky. From nearly two thousand feet above the Furlo Valley, never before had Dominique seen so many stars covering the night sky in every possible direction. As the wind gave her a chill, Dominique picked up the lantern and began her descent down into the dark valley below.

The path twisted and turned, often times passing major drop offs where a wrong step could send a body hurtling down hundreds of feet into a rocky abyss. Several times Dominique placed her back up against the rock wall as she slid her feet carefully past the ledge. Just as daylight was beginning to break over the mountain peaks to the east, Dominique finally entered the valley. The path exited down onto a dirt road that appeared as if it had not been used in a very long time.

Blowing out the lantern and hiding in the brush near the trail, Dominique pondered which way to go. Something told her that following the direction of the sun's path over the earth was her best bet. So, without hesitation, Dominique turned west and followed the road to wherever it would lead her.

Up in the Abbey, the sisters were assembling for morning prayers, and all of them wondered where Dominique was. So Agnesia ran up to her room to get her. After knocking on the door twice and calling out for Dominique, Agnesia opened the door and peered about the room. It was evident that Dominique had not slept in the perfectly made bed, and she noticed that most of her clothing was missing from the small chest of drawers.

Running back down to the chapel, Agnesia announced that Dominique had vanished during the night. Immediately, all the nuns made a quick search of the Abbey to confirm that she was not hiding anywhere.

Approaching Mother Superior, Agnesia knelt down. "I fear that Dominique escaped through the monks tunnel. When I gave her the tour, she asked if there were ghosts here. I told her there were not, but she wanted to see some creepy areas, so I showed her the tunnel."

Minutes later, one of the caretakers arrived back at the chapel. "The small lantern is missing and I found small foot prints leading all the way down to the exit door. It was unlocked, but I did not see any signs of Dominique or the lantern. She must have used the light to find her way down from the mountain. I will take the old truck and check out the road."

About ninety minutes later, the caretaker arrived back at the monastery, carrying the lantern. Nodding his head, he stated, "She hid the lantern in the bushes and started walking west. I drove quite a way until I found the spot where she left the road and began following the rock path that leads down toward the river. There are several paths she could have taken from there. We will need a search party to find her."

Arriving at a small stream, Dominique knelt down to get a drink of water. After realizing how cold and invigorating it was, she splashed it all over her face and giggled. Sitting down on a boulder, she opened the back pack to get something to eat. Just as she removed a hard dinner roll from the pack, she heard noise in the brush around her. She hadn't considered the possibility of wild animals when she planned her escape. Standing up, she held the knife firmly in her hand and yelled out.

"Go away! I am not afraid of you!"

Before she could say another word, a small spotted puppy walked out into the open and sat down about four feet from her. Laughing, Dominique sat down on the boulder and started eating the roll. Slowly the pup moved closer as it whined and scratched with its front paws.

"You just want my food, but I don't have enough for you and me both, so go away and find your own breakfast."

The pup whined all the more as it stood up on all of its legs. Reaching down, Dominique picked up a small stone and tossed it at the pup, striking it on the side. The pup backed away several feet and let out a sad yip. As the animal would not leave and it was getting on her nerves, she yelled, "I said go away, and I mean it!"

Cautiously, the pup walked forward and laid down by Dominique's feet. It laid it's head down on her shoes and whined all the more.

Slowly, it raised its head and looked up into Dominique's eyes but didn't make a sound. Taking a deep breath, Dominique said, "You're hungry, aren't you? When was the last time you ate anything?" Reaching down, Dominique picked up the pup, placing it on her lap. Immediately, the pup licked her on the face before placing its head against her chest.

Tearing off part of the roll, Dominique placed it in front of the little dogs mouth. After sniffing it for a second, it began to eat. Before she realized what she had done, she had fed the rest of the roll to the hungry little dog.

"I'm sorry to say that's all you are going to get for now. We need to make the rest of what I have last until I can find our farm. Then there will be plenty for you to eat."

Picking up the pup, she walked over to the creek and set it down. Without hesitation, the little pup lapped up more water than Dominique had ever seen a dog drink before.

Reaching into the backpack, Dominique pulled out the rope she had taken from the basement. After making a splendid loop, she placed it over the pup's head, so she had a leash. The pup struggled for several minutes trying to remove the rope, but quickly decided it would be alright.

Sitting back on the boulder, Dominique smiled at the dog. "What shall we call you, everyone needs a name. My name is Dominique, and I will be your master, at least for now. What do you want to be named?"

The animal sat quietly in Dominique's lap, looking up at her as she spoke. Laughing, Dominique said, "I guess you can't answer me, but it sure is nice to have someone to talk with. After petting the pup several times, she said, "With all the different colored spots on your coat, I think I'm going to call you Checkers. That will be a good name for you, because you certainly have a lot of colored spots. What do you think of that? Do you like Checkers?"

She was surprised when the dog barked and licked her on the face. "Alright then, Checkers it is!"

Dominique and Checkers followed the stream downhill for several miles, until it came to a macadam surfaced road that was busy with traffic. They hid in the brush for several minutes until there was a break in the traffic, then Dominique quickly picked up the dog and ran across the road, straight into a wooded area. After taking a break along the stream, once more they began walking west.

Hearing the sound of rushing water, Dominique looked at Checkers. "I bet that is the Candigliano River that my father used to talk about. We must be close to the farm."

Walking about a hundred yards they came up to the wide rushing river. Dominique was excited, but was not sure her parents lived on the west side of the river. If they did she knew she was in trouble because she was on the east side.

Sitting on the bank of the river, Dominique shared another roll and a few small pieces of cheese with her new best friend. Looking north, then south, she wondered which way her father had come from. Turning back toward the east, she could see the Abbey sitting majestically on the side of the mountain. It towered above the valley and the sun made the windows sparkle like diamonds.

Finally, Dominique decided to walk toward the north, thinking that the farm could not be too far from the Abbey. Walking along the river bank she saw many small farms, but something appeared to be wrong. After she tied Checkers to a small tree, she climbed a larger tree to get a better look across the river. Seeing a small farm house with lights shining through the window, she realized that their farm was certainly on the west side of the river with the mountains behind the house. Her little heart sunk, but she was determined to find their farm.

Climbing down from the tree, Dominique felt crushed. Picking up Checkers, she said. "We need to get across this river, Checkers. That's the way home." As darkness began falling over the Furlo Valley, Dominique took refuge in an old barn as rain began to fall. Curling up with Checkers in some soft hay, Dominique began to cry. She wanted to find her family, yet the sisters had taken good care of her. She was confused and scared as thunder echoed through the Furlo Valley, but at least she was not alone.

As the rain continued throughout the next day, Dominique and Checkers played in the barn and watched several small barges navigate the river heading south. They ate sparingly of the food Dominique had packed into the backpack, as she hoped it would last until they arrived home.

The next morning broken clouds appeared over the Furlo Pass. Feeling ready to search again, Dominique continued following the river, looking for a place to cross. About two hours later a rather large town appeared in front of them. She was stunned when she read a sign saying it was Acqualagna. She knew that was where the Abbey got most of its supplies. The sisters went there at least twice a week to pick up items they needed, or to see Father Moretti.

Dominique had never been there, but she could see the town covered both sides of the river, so there must be a bridge she could cross somewhere ahead.

No one in the town appeared to make much of a little girl with a backpack walking her dog. They were all busy setting up their carts in the town square, where city folks and sisters from the monastery would come to buy their groceries. As they passed a vendor selling homemade breads, Dominique stopped to sniff the air. The smell of fresh baked goods reminded her of the small bakery in the Abbey.

Moments later an older man walked up to her, "Ah, there is nothing like the smell of fresh baked goods in the morning, don't you agree?"

Smiling, Dominique replied. "Yes, they smell so good, you are a wonderful baker."

The man laughed as he patted Dominique on the head. "To be honest, my wife is the baker of the family, and yes she is very good." Looking over his shoulder, he said, "I do not see my wife, so here, take one of these biscuits and go over to the park by the bridge and enjoy it."

Dominique's spirits rose immediately. First, she was getting free food, plus she now knew where the bridge was located.

After sharing the wonderful bread with Checkers, Dominique walked across the busy bridge along with many residents of the city, and no one paid them any attention. Standing at an intersection on the east side of the bridge, she read a road sign pointing out which way to go for all the neighboring towns, but none of them sounded familiar to her. She thought the city of Fossato sounded like it might be something she had heard of before, but it was nearly fifteen kilometers away. She couldn't be sure, but she did not think her father had driven the sleigh that far the morning he took her to the Abbey.

Once again, she read the names of the towns, but nothing stood out in her memory. As she stood up, trying to decide what to do, a chugging police car pulled up on the sidewalk. A short funny looking police officer walked up to her.

"Signorina, you have stood here a long time. Are you lost? Can I help you in any way?"

Dominique was scared that the police officer would take her to the station and they would find out who she was, so she said, "No, I am not lost. My parents are over on the other side of the river in the piazza selling their goods. I always wanted to see what was on this side of the bridge, so I took my dog for a walk."

The officer laughed as he bent down to pet Checkers "Do you want a ride back to the piazza or are you going to continue your sightseeing?"

Smiling, Dominique replied. "I think we are through sightseeing today. We will walk back to the piazza and help my father sell his goods."

The officer tipped his hat slightly and walked back to his smoking patrol car. As he drove off into the traffic, he watched Dominique and Checkers turn and walk back across the bridge.

Arriving in the park, Dominique sat down on a bench with Checkers. "Checkers, I do not know which way to go. I do not know where our farm is, other than it's on the west side of the river. Tonight, we will cross the river and begin to search.

Late in the afternoon, the bridge was crowded with vehicles and carts as the vendors began their trip back home. It was easy for Dominique and Checkers to join the crowds without attracting any attention. This time, Dominique continued straight west without reading the road signs. The farther they walked from town, the road became narrower and more poorly maintained.

Walking off the road, Dominique found an old horse barn that was now used for miscellaneous storage. There was a buggy in the middle of the building that would be perfect for sleeping, so Dominique covered herself and Checkers with empty grain bags and they drifted off to sleep.

The following morning, Dominique back tracked toward Acqualagna, then took a larger and better maintained road toward the west. Dominique had no idea how far they had walked, but every farm they approached appeared to be where she grew up, until they got close. It was heartbreaking each time she realized it was not her parent's farm. Storm clouds gathered in the west as the sun began to set, and Dominique had no idea where to go to find shelter. She had not seen a barn in nearly an hour. As rain drops began to fall, Dominique observed a huge tree that had recently blown over. Knowing it would provide decent shelter, Dominique picked up Checkers and ran for the tree. Crawling under the heavy branches, Dominique found the ground to be dry and sheltered from the strong winds that were beginning to blow.

Checkers whined and cried every time a large clap of thunder rolled across the valley. To make sure Checkers did not run away, Dominique tied the rope to a strong branch near her head. After a bolt of lightning struck the ground about fifty yards from the tree, Checkers tugged with all his strength and broke free of the branch. In a heartbeat, he ducked under several branches and ran up the hill. Dominique retraced her steps out from under the downed tree and took off after the frightened pup. She called out over and over, "Checkers, come back, Checkers, where are you?" But by now he had disappeared into the blackness of the forbidding forest before her.

For several hours, Dominique searched in and around the forest for any signs of Checkers, but came up empty. Soaked, tired and disheartened Dominique began heading back toward the tree where she had left the back pack. As she began descending the hill just a hundred yards from the tree, she heard a snarling sound behind her.

Looking over her shoulder, she could see a large wolf walking back and forth on the ridge line. Each time he made a turn, he appeared to be getting closer and it frightened Dominique terribly. She knew breaking to run for the tree and taking her eyes of the wolf was the worst thing she could do. So, slowly she backed away, hoping to get to the tree where she might avoid getting killed.

As she took her next step back, her foot rolled over a stone, causing her to fall and roll partway down the hill. Immediately, the wolf charged forward, opening its mouth preparing to strike at Dominique's throat. Suddenly, Checkers appeared out of the darkness, clamping his jaws down on the wolfs rear leg. The wolf howled in pain as it turned to attack his small opponent.

Just as Dominique stood up and reached for the rock that had tripped her, the wolf once again turned its attention back to her. As the wolf dove forward, Checkers charged after it chomping down on the predators left ear. The wolf howled as it shook it head violently, but could not get Checkers to let go. With a quick spin, the wolf threw itself to the ground and rolled over the small dog. With a lightning turn, the wolf grabbed Checkers by the throat and shook the small dog violently.

Dominique screamed as she saw the now lifeless body of Checkers hanging limp in the jaws of the massive wolf. Without a moment of thought, Dominique charged forward, striking the wolf on the top of the head with the rock. As the wolf staggered back, attempting to regain its footing, Dominique continued slamming the rock onto its head until the animal collapsed and lay dead on the hill.

After tossing the rock, Dominique hurried over to Checkers. Picking him up, Dominique knew he was still alive but was in tough shape. She sat down on the hill, holding Checkers tight as she continued petting her best friend. Looking up at Dominique, Checkers struggled to move forward and licked her several times on the face before closing his eyes for the last time.

Dominique screamed out in pain as tears rolled down her face. Now she was totally alone and had no idea where she would go or what she would do. Several times she shook Checkers and cried out, "Don't leave me! Everybody I love leaves me. Come back, Checkers, please come back!"

The following morning as a young farmer drove his buggy into town, his wife pointed up the side of the mountain, and said, "Good Lord, is that a little girl?"

Stopping the buggy, the farmer ran up the hill while looking over the bloody situation. Kneeling down by Dominique, he said. "Girl, are you alright, you are just covered in blood."

Turning back toward the buggy, he yelled out to his wife, "Come up here quick and bring the shovel."

When his wife arrived, the farmer went to work burying the dead wolf, then prepared another hole for Checkers. All the while his wife attempted to get Dominique to talk, but all she did was stare down at the lifeless body of the little dog.

With the hole ready, the farmer walked over to Dominique. "Sweetheart, it is time we bury your friend. There is nothing anyone can do for him now." As he reached out to take Checkers, Dominique turned away, clutching her savior even tighter.

The wife ran her hand over Dominique's dirty wet hair and said, "It's time, honey. Let my husband bury your friend properly. Everyone deserves a decent burial, even your puppy."

Slowly, Dominique handed the lifeless body of Checkers over to the farmer, and watched as he placed the dog into the hole he had prepared. As the farmer filled in the hole, his wife took Dominique over to a patch of wild flowers and knelt down. "Don't you think your friend would like to have some flowers on his grave?"

Nodding her head, Dominique picked out the largest and most colorful flowers in the patch. When the farmer was finished packing down the wet earth, she knelt down placing the flowers on the grave. "Sleep well, Checkers," she whispered. "I will never forget you."

When she stood up, she reached out her hand to the wife, but said not a word. Slowly, the couple walked Dominique down to the buggy and helped her aboard.

Arriving in Acqualagna, they drove straight to the small hospital near the center of town. Seeing so much blood on Dominique, they immediately began removing her clothing, looking for where it may have come from. After finding just several deep scratches on her shoulder, the farmer said, "I'm guessing the bulk of the blood came from the wolf she killed, and the little dog she was holding. No one but her will ever know what happened up there, but she went through hell, that's for sure."

After giving Dominique a bath and dressing her in a set of hospital pajamas, a nurse brought her a bowl of oatmeal. As Dominique slowly ate the cereal, one of the nurses kept trying to get her to talk, but Dominique sat quietly, not uttering a word.

Finally, an older nurse said, "I heard the other day that a small child disappeared from the Abbey. The police and several other people have been looking for her. Let's summon one of the sisters down to see if this is the child.

About an hour later, Mother Superior and Sister Xavier arrived at the hospital. The moment Sister Xavier laid eyes on Dominique, she raced across the room grabbing hold of her, and hugged her gently. "Where have you been, child, we have all been so worried about you."

Dominique looked up at Sister Xavier, saying, "Checkers is dead, he left me just like everyone else, has. But he saved my life and I loved him."

Not sure what to make of what Dominique said, she looked up at the doctor and the farmer, hoping to get an answer.

The farmer related what he had seen on the mountain side and said, "This is the first time she has spoken. I'm guessing Checkers was the small dead dog she was holding when we arrived. He was pretty torn up by the wolf, but the wolf's left ear was almost torn lose, and there were other injuries. I'm thinking the dog did that trying to save the girl. That is the best I can tell you."

Sister Xavier nodded her head as she looked back toward Dominique. "You said that Checkers left you like everyone else, but we did not leave you, Dominique. We have been searching ever since we found out you were gone.

We have all been praying so hard that you would be found safe and sound, and we never gave up on God sending you back to us. Dominique, you have a family in the Abbey that will love you forever, and do nothing but the best for you. But now is the time for you to make a decision. Do you want us, or do you want to leave the Abbey?"

As tears flowed down Dominique's face, she threw her arms around Sister Xavier's neck and said, "Take me home, I will never leave you again, I promise. I want to live with you forever." After taking a look around the room, Dominique asked, "Where is Agnesia, I thought she would come looking for me."

Mother Superior knelt down by Dominique. "Poor Agnesia felt it was her fault you ran away. She has taken your disappearance harder than anyone, and has barely left her room since you disappeared. Come with us back to the Abbey now, child, and you will see how much your family has missed you."

After thanking the farmer and his wife, Sister Xavier led Dominique out to the small old carriage the sisters used for traveling.

Arriving in the foyer of the Abbey, Dominique was greeted by every sister that lived in the Abbey. When they were finished hugging her, Sister Xavier led Dominique up to Agnesia's room. "Go to her child, let her know that none of this was her fault. This you must do!"

Nodding her head, Dominique pushed open the door to Agnesia's small room. She observed Agnesia kneeling beside her bed, praying from a large book. Taking a deep breath, Dominique said, "You can quit praying now, I am back."

Agnesia spun around as tears rolled down her face. "Dominique, Dominique where have you been. I should have never showed you the passage way. I'm so sorry, please forgive me."

As Dominique hugged Agnesia, she said, "I was afraid of John. I did not see him, but I knew he was there watching me. I think he followed me the entire time."

Laughing, Agnesia said, "I will have to thank him for watching over you." After looking into Dominique's eyes, she asked, "Are you here to stay now, or have you found a life somewhere else?"

Sitting down on Agnesia's bed, she said, "I am here to stay, I missed you very much. But let me tell you about Checkers."

Later that evening as the sun was beginning to set, Dominique walked to a glass door that led to a small sitting area up on the fourth floor of the Abbey. Sitting down on one of the chairs, she watched the stars begin to shine as a light wind whistled around her. Looking beyond the river, Dominique said quietly. "Mother and Father, I tried to find you, but I did not know where to look. But I found a little friend that gave his life to save me. I guess this is where I belong, so here I shall stay. I do not know what life has in store for me, but I will accept each day as a new challenge. Please know I will always love you and never forget you."

That night as Dominique pulled up her covers and closed her eyes, she was sure she heard Checkers barking somewhere off in the distance, letting her know that he was just fine.

Although returning to the Abbey made Dominique feel safe and loved, she still missed her family very much. Slowly, Dominique let go of the idea that one day her Papa would return to take her back to her family. No matter how she felt about her new life, it was still a bitter pill for her to swallow. There would be many long nights when she would cry herself to sleep, thinking about the joy and fun she was missing playing with her sisters and brother.

However, as the days turned into weeks and the weeks into months, Dominique began to place her former life behind her, and grasp the life the sisters were offering. Throughout her novitiate, the biggest challenge she faced was her iron will, and the desire to control her surroundings.

Many times, she was given extra responsibilities as a penance, or sent to her room by Mother Superior to pray and ask God for his help in relieving her of this imperfection. The problem was, Dominique liked being in control of her life as much as she could, especially after what her parents had done to her. She felt having that powerful personal will was a gift from God that could be used for good, if controlled, and that was something she would need to work on.

Chapter Three – Italy's New Realities

In 1919, an angry leftist by the name of Benito Mussolini founded the National Fascist Party, with intentions of overthrowing the Unitary Parliamentary Constitutional Monarchy of King Victor Emmanuel II. However, he was not able to gain a foothold in the government until 1922. By 1925, he had obtained enough followers, forcing Victor Emmanuel to abdicate the throne.

Immediately, the parliament filled with fascist representatives appointed Mussolini as Prime Minister. Without hesitation, Mussolini dismantled every aspect of democratic rule and appointed himself as dictator, calling himself IL Duce, (leader).

Attempting to model himself and his form of rule after Adolph Hitler, Italy and Germany quickly became aligned, allowing the Italian Secret Police, called the Ovra, to form a solid bond with Germany's Gestapo. Later, the alignment would allow German S.S. units to operate freely in Italy as they sought out and captured 46,000 Jews for deportation.

While living in the Abbey, Sister Dominique had been separated from politics, but was well aware of the political upheavals in Italy. She had been in the foyer when representatives of the new Fascist Government came to the Abbey to let Mother Superior know what was expected from her and the sisters in the future. If there was one thing Dominique learned early on about the fascists, is that they were arrogant and lacked any type of tolerance toward the problems or suffering of other human beings. Mother Superior attempted to steer clear of political entanglements, but made it very plain to the women in the convent that the fascist government was evil, and that everyone should limit contact with them.

Nevertheless, throughout all her struggles and early fears, on her eighteenth birthday, Dominique professed her final vows and became a Benedictine Sister. Her first assignment was to a school in Milan, where she worked with kindergarten age children, and began learning how to teach first grade students. She loved both jobs, and quickly settled into a daily routine that lasted two years.

As Mussolini and his fascist government continued tightening their control of Italy, many Catholic and private schools were closed, all the books were burned, and anyone continuing to teach in secret was jailed. With Italy becoming a signer of the Tri Partite Pact with Germany and Japan in 1940, it did not take long for the German Gestapo and S.S. Officials to take a more proactive position on how Mussolini's fascist government operated within their own borders.

On several occasions, Sister Dominique complained to the local compliance officials that what they were doing to the children was wrong. Each time she was rebuffed and told it was the law and if she did not like it, she could give up her job in the school and return to the Abbazia di San Vincenzo.

After her third meeting with the local officials, Sister Dominique was approached by three men from the local underground. They explained that her protestations were bringing more heat on the area by the gestapo and Italian authorities, and she might want to back off.

She could have cared less regarding their concerns, and continued teaching as best she could without proper text books. One afternoon, several gestapo agents walked into her classroom and sat down at the back. All of the children quickly jumped up from their seats and fled the room without saying a word. Once the room was empty, one of the men walked to Sister Dominique where she stood by her desk. He picked up the Catholic Catechism that was laying on the desk and threw it on the floor.

"Have you not been told this type of instruction is contrary to good order and discipline within Italy and the Third Reich? Have you not been ordered to stop these instructions immediately, Sister Dominique? Do you think prison time could help you remember these things?"

Glaring at the agent, Sister Dominique replied, "I am just doing the work of my God. His word and his orders supersede any and all decrees put out by Mussolini and your Third Reich."

"Ya, there you go with this God thing again, and it does not impress me." Pushing his riding crop into Sister Dominique's chest, the agent continued. "If I'm informed again that you are teaching this rubbish to the children, we shall have another talk, and I assure you it will be most unpleasant for you and the rest of the sisters assigned to this so-called school. Do I make myself clear!"

Feeling like her heart was about to beat out of her chest, Sister Dominique replied. "Very clear, sir. I will abide by your rules, I do not wish to see anyone get hurt."

Nodding his head, the agent smiled. "Now see how easy it was to come to an agreement. I think school is out for the day as your students seem to have vanished. That will give you time to remove the rest of these books from your classroom."

After the three men left the room, Sister Dominique sat down before her legs became any weaker. She had never come face to face with the gestapo before, but now believed all the stories she had been told about them.

That evening, as Sister Dominique sat alone on a bench on the school playground, a man by the name of Lorenzo Seneca, who owned the carpenter shop in town, approached her.

Looking up at Lorenzo, Sister Dominique said. "So, it must be all over town by now."

"Yes, when the gestapo comes to town, everyone knows who they talk to and usually why. It was not a big secret why they spoke to you. If you do not follow the directions of the Third Reich on what is allowed to be taught, you will simply disappear one night. They do not care that you are a sister. If they had their way, the entire Vatican would be done away with," Lorenzo said, as he sat down next to Sister Dominique.

"He angered me so badly, I literally wanted to slap his smirking smile. I wanted to rub it in the dirt on the floor and kick all of them out of my room," Sister Dominique replied, as she looked up at the stars. Laughing, she continued. "That is quite a confession for a sister to reveal to a carpenter."

Nodding his head, Lorenzo said. "Nothing more than most people in Milan feel any time the gestapo shows up. They are pigs."

After a moment of silence, Sister Dominique looked over at Lorenzo. "Why is it I feel you did not come here tonight just to talk about what I teach. What is it you really came for?"

"Yes, you are right, sister. I came here tonight to see if you are interested in joining our small underground unit. I need influential people to join our cause if we are going to be able to make a difference. You as a sister and teacher here in Milan, would be a good asset for us. You see—"

Sister Dominique held up her hand. "No, that is not possible, I cannot join such a group where violence may be the last resort. It is out of the question. I ask you to leave now and never approach me about it ever again. This must end here!"

Standing up, Lorenzo looked up at the stars. "I have enjoyed talking astrology with you, Sister Dominique. I hope that maybe we can do it again." As Lorenzo walked off, he whistled the former Italian National Anthem, sending shivers down Sister Dominique's spine. She knew she had not seen the last of Lorenzo Seneca.

Several weeks went by without any major problems in or around Milan, allowing Sister Dominique to feel more relaxed as she put the visit from the gestapo out of her mind, however, that was not to last for very long. On a cool Saturday morning, Sister Dominique, Sister Margaret and Sister Willamette all went to the local market to pick up the order that had been called in by Mother Superior. Once everything was loaded and Sister Willamette was about to pay for the food, two gestapo agents wearing the typical black suits walked up to the counter. One of the men pulled his Luger out of his holster, aiming it at the store owner.

"You will come with us, let someone else run the store!"

The store owner frowned. "I have done nothing wrong. I work twelve hours a day and then go home to my family. Tell me what I have done?"

The second gestapo agent walked around the counter and began placing handcuffs on the man, when a young girl stepped from a side door holding a shotgun.

"Let him be or I will shoot. Get out of our store and go back to Germany where they put up with bastards like you!"

The agent with the pistol laughed as he glared at the girl. "Put that gun down and put your hands in the air. You're also going to be arrested for getting involved!"

"Not today!" the girl yelled, as she turned the weapon toward the agent that had just finished cuffing her father. A second later, a blast from the shotgun sent the agent flying out through the plate glass window onto the street in front of the shop. Before the girl could swing her shot gun toward the agent carrying the pistol, he grabbed Sister Willamette and pulled her in front of him as a shield.

As he backed toward the door of the shop, the young woman followed him yelling, "Let her go, she is not a part of this!"

Shaking with fear and realizing he was in a bad situation, the agent looked at the determined girl. "Put down your weapon, let me go and everyone here shall live. There is no reason we all must die."

Laughing, the girl responded. "No. You will just come back with more of your men, and you will kill my parents and me. As of today, we have lost everything, so what does it matter?"

Taking a moment to process what was happening, the agent shook his head and said, "The hell with you." Pushing Sister Willamette toward the ground, the agent fired several shots at the girl before being struck by a blast from the shot gun and several bullets from a man standing in front of a floral shop across the street. As the agent spun around, bouncing off his car, he fired several bullets from his Luger wildly into the shop, before falling to the pavement.

Immediately Sister Dominique and Sister Margaret ran to check on Sister Willamette. It was instantly obvious that she was never going to move again. One of the bullets from the Luger had struck her in the chest, while the other bullet had hit her in the forehead. The two sisters dropped to the ground crying as they clutched one another. Over in the doorway of the grocery shop, the owner knelt on the ground holding the lifeless body of his daughter who had also been struck by the ricocheting bullets.

Three days later after the funeral of Sister Willamette, Lorenzo Seneca approached Sister Dominique. "We are all sorry for what happened. It was all so tragic. We have moved the store owner and his wife to a safe location where the gestapo will never find them."

As Lorenzo turned to leave, Sister Dominique took hold of his hand. "The gestapo and Mussolini's government have brought the war to this convent. Whatever I can do to help you, I will do. Sister Willamette cannot have died for nothing."

Chapter Four – Occupation

After the death of Sister Willamette, Mother Superior felt it was best that Sister Dominique and Sister Margaret should return to the monastery for a while. However, Sister Dominique's anger continued to boil under the surface and she was ready to do whatever she could to help the partisans.

Although Hitler and Mussolini shared many of the same dreams of world conquest, they differed in the ways they carried out their plans. There was no doubt that Hitler's Nazi Germany could gain anything they wanted through the use of brutal force, while Mussolini's less brutal form of fascism created more problems than it solved.

With Italy now a partner of the Axis alliance, Hitler's military expected Mussolini to begin ruling with a solid iron hand, and put an end to the regional factions that failed to cooperate. However, it was evident Italy was never going to be united under Mussolini, and a more powerful force was going to be needed.

As German forces began to spread out over Italy, they began treating it like just another occupied European country. They took what they wanted and used force wherever necessary to achieve their goals. The government in Rome would protest, but would never go beyond that, as they knew they existed strictly because Berlin allowed them to exist.

Every day trains loaded with tanks, artillery and trucks rolled south, heading for the ports of Rome and Naples where it would be used for the invasion of Sicily and Corsica.

All along the rail lines and highways heading south, German engineers searched for areas that would give them full command of valleys, bridges and damns that could be used to slow allied opposition in the future.

Such was the case with the Furlo Passage near Acqualagna. The Furlo passage was the only major transportation route on the east side of Italy. On the west side of the passage was a major rail line and a north-south highway. Across the Candigliano River was another highway that distributed traffic toward the towns on the east coast of Italy. The mountain ridge on the east side was much broader and higher than that of the west, and included a large Benedictine monastery named the Abbey di San Vincenzo. From its large balconies, terraces and rock cut outs, the Furlo passage could be viewed both to the north and south, covering a distance of nearly twenty miles. It was a perfect place to install a major communications headquarters, and heavy antiaircraft weapons that could wipe out any Allied bombers attempting to destroy roads and rail lines that snaked through the valley below.

Many Italian military forces stationed near the valley were anything but sympathetic to the German cause. Several units that chose to cease backing the German backed Italian government either joined underground units or turned their weapons over to well established groups.

The sisters in the Abbey had a front row seat as resistance units battled German forces in the valley below. Train tracks and bridges would be blown, creating tremendous explosions, and German tanks would rumble forward firing their large cannons at resistance positions, shaking the walls in the old monastery. The most frightening part of these battles was when German fighter aircraft attacked resistance forces on the mountainside with machine guns and bombs. Several times bullets had struck the Abbey, breaking windows.

One afternoon as the battle raged, several resistance fighters were brought to the Abbey for medical attention. Although Mother Superior could not turn away the wounded men, she realized if the German's found out the Abbey was being used as a hospital, it might very well be destroyed.

Sister Dominique and several other sisters worked diligently, bandaging the wounded men and splinting broken bones. She even removed a few bullets that were not too far under the skin on legs or arms. But they all knew the day would come when a doctor was going to be needed, and the closest one was down in Acqualagna. One evening, after a German Messerschmidt attacked a resistance unit that had dug in on the side of the mountain, several fighters arrived with abdominal injuries that required a surgeon. After much discussion, Sister Dominique agreed to go down the back of the mountain with a resistance fighter to fetch the doctor and all the supplies he might need.

The resistance fighter was Stephano, and while he was not more than sixteen or seventeen years old, he already looked older than his age. He carried a British Sten machine gun and wore a back pack that must have weighed all of sixty pounds, yet he was nimble on his feet, and knew how to move carefully over rocky outcroppings without losing time.

The entire way down the mountain he pointed out dangerous places and helped Sister Dominique with her balance and footing. Arriving near the bottom of the mountain, Stephano pushed Sister Dominique down behind several large boulders. "You must wait until I can figure out the best way to go from here. Please stay down and be quiet."

Before Sister Dominique could say a word, the young man was gone, disappearing into the darkness. The night was cool with a northerly wind and it did not take long for Sister Dominique to get cold as she listened to the battle raging somewhere deeper in the valley. About fifteen minutes later, Stephano returned with another resistance fighter. "This is Salvo, he will take us to a safe place where we can cross the river."

Salvo smiled as he slightly bowed. Reaching into his jacket, he pulled out a pistol, handing it to Sister Dominique. "You may need this if we run into Germans. In the dark they will not be able to see who they are killing."

Handing it back, Sister Dominique replied. "I am killing no one. I am on a humanitarian mission to pick up a doctor. I shall not carry any weapon!"

Smiling, Salvo replied, "Of course you won't, but I had to ask. Now come, we must get moving as the bridge is still in our hands tonight.

Salvo led Stephano and Sister Dominique down deeper into the valley, where the fighting was not far away. It was evident the battle had moved back and forth across the valley, as bodies of German and Italian forces lay dead among those of resistance soldiers. Nearing the river, Sister Dominique was stunned to see two smaller boys pulling a cart filled with weapons, ammunition, coats and boots they had removed from the dead.

Grabbing hold of Salvo, Sister Dominique said, "They're nothing more than boys! They should be home with their parents. How can you make them do this?"

Glaring at Sister Dominique, Salvo replied. "Boys today. Tomorrow they will be men fighting for Italy. We need all the hands we can get. And if they do not steal from the dead, where will they get their equipment? For your information, my own younger brother is out there fighting right now. He killed his first Nazi three days ago, on his tenth birthday. He may not see twelve, but he will die fighting as a man of thirty."

Sister Dominique felt sick when she thought about what Salvo had told her. She turned and looked up river where the heavy fighting was taking place. She could see muzzle flashes in every direction as grenades exploded all along the side of the mountain. Out there was a ten-year-old boy who should be home taking care of the farm animals, or maybe even preparing for tomorrows school lesson. Instead, he was killing men and trying to stay alive himself. Trying to rationalize all the killing, she began walking down the river bank toward a large wooden boat that was already riddled with bullet holes.

As Salvo took up the oars, Stephano pushed Sister Dominique to the floor. "Keep your head down, Sister. I will cover our crossing if necessary." Stephano sat down on the floor of the boat, aiming his machine gun over the side, preparing to fire if necessary.

Reaching the west bank, Salvo turned the boat over to three resistance men that were taking grenades to the east side of the river. Once again, Sister Dominique took a good look at the soldiers and shook her head. Grabbing the arm of one of the soldiers, she said, "How old are you?"

Smiling, the boy replied, "Thirteen, but I have already killed three Germans over the last few days. We will throw the pigs out of Italy, one way or the other."

As he placed a case of grenades in the boat, Sister Dominique asked, "How old are the other two boys, they must be younger than you."

Nodding his head, the boy replied. "They are ten and eight. Their families were killed by the Germans up north. We are the only family they have now. They know what they must do to keep the German's nervous until the American and British armies arrive. Then we will win the war, Sister. Do not worry about us, we are strong!"

Salvo grabbed Sister Dominique by the arm, "Come quickly, we must get moving, those boys will be just fine. They are true heroes."

After walking several miles, Stephano walked up to a house and knocked on the door. A man of about forty opened the large wooden door. Peering out into the darkness he said, "Stephano, I told you, I simply cannot do this anymore, you must find someone else. I have to think about my wife and my children. The Germans will kill them if they know I am helping you."

Sister Dominique stepped forward. "Please doctor, we have two badly wounded men in the Abbey. Without your help they will surely die."

Stepping forward, the doctor looked at Sister Dominique. "Do you mean to tell me you came all the way from the Abbey to talk to me? Stephano should have known better. I'm no longer involved in this war. I quit."

"Quit? You quit when your countrymen are dying? There are eight and nine-year-old boys fighting out there tonight, and you quit? Tell me, doctor, what kind of example are you setting for your children? Without you, we have no one else to contact. Will you let those men die so you can be safe? I ask for mercy on your soul." Sister Dominique replied angrily.

"Sister, my family… we are Jews. If the Germans catch us, we will be deported to God knows where and never be heard of again. I have heard what is going on all over the occupied countries. I have heard about deportations from Trento and Padua already. An S.S. Captain named Barbie has already signed a decree authorizing the deportation of all Jews in Italy, and Mussolini is doing nothing to stop it. No, Sister. I cannot help you. I cannot even help my family anymore," the doctor angrily explained, as he glared at Sister Dominique.

Without saying a word to Stephano and Salvo, Sister Dominique replied. "Go get your wife and children and pack a quick bag. We will take you to the monastery and hide you there until we can find a safe place for you."

Salvo grabbed Sister Dominique by the arm. "We cannot do that, you saw how small the boat is, we will sink carrying everyone across the river."

Pulling her arm away from Salvo, Sister Dominique replied. "Then we will make two trips, but we are not leaving these people to the Germans." Turning to the doctor, she continued, "Pack all the medical equipment you can into your bag, and all the medicines and supplies you can. You will not be coming back here anytime soon."

The doctor nodded his head. "I packed all of that last night because I knew we were going to have to run. We will be ready in a few minutes."

Salvo angrily paced back and forth behind the house as he waited for the family to exit the house. When everyone was ready, Stephano led them back to the river bank under the bridge where the boys were just preparing to tie up the boat. Looking at Sister Dominique, the thirteen-year-old boy said, "You will need to make two trips. I will help paddle the second trip as the Nazi's are getting closer. You must move now."

As the first trip started across the river, the doctor's wife looked at Sister Dominique. "I am not so brave. I do not know if my children and I can do what you are asking us to do."

The ten-year-old boy spoke up. "This is called life now, ma'am. If you want to live you must fight any way that you can. I'll help get you across. Then listen to Salvo and Stephano, and you'll be fine, trust me."

When the boat returned, the two boys helped load everyone on board and began rowing back to the east side of the river where Salvo and Stephano waited with the doctor. Without hesitation, Stephano led everyone back toward the Abbey where the number of wounded men was growing rapidly.

Climbing the rugged trail with two small children and the extra belongings and supplies was not what Stephano had in mind when they left the Abbey. But now, Sister Dominique was insistent they all stay together and help one another so nobody would get lost or fall to their death in the dark.

Stephano sighed a feeling of relief when he reached the large wooden door that led to the subbasement of the Abbey. Before he could say a word, Sister Margaret and two other sisters pulled the heavy door open. As Sister Dominique walked in, Sister Margaret said, "Where have you been? We expected you back much sooner." Looking at the woman and the two small children, she inquired, "Who are these people? We were just expecting a doctor?"

Taking Sister Margaret by the arm, she said. "The doctor and his family are Jews. He would not come without them. They are very fearful of the Germans."

Sister Margaret placed her hands on top of her head. "Do you know what Mother Superior is going to say about bringing Jews into the Abbey? What are we supposed to do with them? What if the Germans come and want to search? We will all be doomed."

Over hearing part of the discussion, the wife of the doctor walked over to Sister Margaret. "It was not our intention to come here, sister. Your people needed a doctor and chose my husband. We could not afford to be separated for a long period of time in case we were captured. Tell me, what else were we supposed to do?"

Feeling somewhat ashamed, Sister Margaret shook her head. "This war, and all the fighting, it has everyone on edge, I'm sorry. Believe me, we will do whatever is possible to keep you safe. For right now, let me take you to a more comfortable area where you can rest until your husband is finished."

In a large room just off the main entrance, the doctor operated on several patients throughout the long night, removing shrapnel and sewing up wounds. Regrettably, it was impossible to save everyone that was placed on his makeshift surgical table. Two men had such serious internal injuries that there was nothing he could do for them except administer morphine and keep them comfortable until they died.

As dawn began to break over the Furlo Pass, the Germans began retreating toward the north to regroup. With the fighting dying down, quite a few young patriot fighters arrived at the Abbey to have minor wounds treated. One of them was a complete surprise to everyone in the Abbey.

An American Army Lieutenant by the name of Danny O'Brien had a large cut on his upper left arm that needed ten stitches. Walking out of the treatment room, he walked up to Salvo. "Your men fought well tonight and the Krauts weren't expecting such a battle. But we all know they will be back later today. You must regroup away from the Pass so enemy aircraft will not be able to attack. You also might want to bring up those two mortars that arrived yesterday and place them in the rocks above the highway. It will give you good coverage for the start of the battle.

Salvo nodded his head and departed the Abbey with some of the men that had been treated and were ready to rejoin the fight. Mother Superior walked up to Lt. O'Brien. "You are an American, so where is the rest of your army? Will we be liberated shortly?"

Shaking his head, the Lieutenant responded. There is only one other man with me. We are part of the OSS. We were sent here to help organize and equip patriot groups such as the ones that fought here last night. I'm afraid that liberation is still sometime in the future. We just don't want the Krauts to get too comfortable while they are here."

"Comfortable you say, Lieutenant. What are we supposed to do with the men that were operated on last night that cannot travel? Do you think they will be comfortable when the German's decide to take this monastery. Do you think my sisters will be comfortable in a prison camp? No, I don't think they will be. You need to take all of your people and leave at once."

Knowing this was a poor time to get involved in the conversation, Sister Dominique walked up to Mother Superior. "There are men that will not survive a trek down the back of the Abbey. Trying to move them will kill them as sure as another bullet will. We must wait until they are stronger."

Turning toward Sister Dominique, Mother Superior replied, "Sister, I believe you actually enjoy this war. Just be careful as to how far you go and get involved. Once you are in the hands of the Germans, it will be too late to walk away!"

The lieutenant looked at Sister Dominique. "I have been told you brought the doctor's family along for the ride. Good on you, Sister, we were not sure how to handle them. This is a good place to hide them until a new plan can be assembled."

Mother Superior looked first at the lieutenant and then at Sister Dominique. "Do you want to tell me what Lt. O'Brien is talking about?"

Before Sister Dominique could respond, the doctor walked forward. "Mother Superior, my wife and I are Jews. We were planning to run last night but were not sure where to go with the fighting. When I was asked to come here, it was like a sign from Yahweh. So, I said I would not come unless my wife and children were allowed to come with me. It is not Sister Dominique's fault."

"Children you say. This situation gets more untenable as the story goes on. Does anyone have a plan for how we are to get these people out of the Abbey safely?" Mother Superior inquired as her voice began rising to levels Sister Dominique had never heard before.

After a moment of thought, Lt. O'Brien said, "There may be a way, Mother Superior, but it will take a few days to work out the specifics once we decide what we are going to do when the Krauts return. For the time being keep them under wraps, and if the German's do come to the Abbey, do not let them search the place. You will be fine, I promise."

Walking across the large foyer Mother Superior waved her hands over her head. "Keep the Jews under wraps, do not let the German's search the Abbey.

Do you know how ridiculous that all sounds!" Walking back to Lt. O'Brien, she said. "This OSS you belong to, it is a clandestine operation, I presume?"

Nodding his head, the lieutenant said, "Yes ma'am, it is. We are attempting to—"

"Attempting to, attempting to. All I hear is attempting to. No one is sure how they will accomplish anything, and the Germans will continue occupying Italy one way or the other. I am sick of this already. Between you, the underground, and my own Sister Dominique, my Abbey has been turned into a military target, with the rest of my sisters caught in between. I never wanted to have anything to do with this war, and now look where we are."

The doctor looked down at the floor for a moment. "I will get my family ready, and we will be out of here tonight. We do not want to be a burden, we will leave."

Mother Superior closed her eyes as she placed her fingers on her forehead, "Doctor, you cannot go running off into the night without a plan. Not with two little children. We will take care of you until the lieutenant can work out a new plan. To be honest, we owe you that much for what you did for the underground last night. I do not like this war, but I know the underground is fighting for Italy, and that cannot be overlooked."

Stephano smiled as he looked at Mother Superior. "You were all we had left last night. Without the Abbey and your help, many good men would have died."

Turning to face Sister Dominique, Mother Superior asked, "Child, are there any more surprises I should know about?"

Shaking her head, Sister Dominique replied, "There is nothing else."

Late in the afternoon, a large German force began rolling into the Furlo Pass as fighter aircraft covered their movement. The partisan forces retreated to the south, unable to hold off such a massive assault. Before pulling back, Stephano and Lt. O'Brien made one last quick visit to the Abbey. Any man that was capable of walking was taken down the back side of the mountain where trucks were waiting to move them to safety.

Stephano looked at Sister Margaret. "The local underground will help get these other men out when they are ready to go. We thank you for your help."

Lt. O'Brien went to the main floor to speak with Mother Superior. "I do not have all the issues worked out yet, but there is an Italian politician living in Chiaravalle that happens to be a Jew. The Allies want him rescued before the Germans capture him. So tomorrow night we will take the doctor and his family along with the politician and get them out of Italy."

Mother Superior looked at the young Lieutenant. "I have lived through several wars, and I do not understand them. So many young people must die. But I am proud of men like you that fight for those of us who cannot. May God be with you."

As promised, the following evening, Lt. O'Brien and Salvo arrived at the Abbey ready to take the doctor and his family out of Italy. Sister Dominique helped get the children down the rocky mountain trail and loaded into the truck. As Salvo drove off into the night, Sister Dominique wished she could be going with them. At times like this, she wondered if her skills could be better served in the underground than in the Abbey. Nevertheless, she climbed the rocky path back into the Abbey without looking back.

That night, as fighting once more raged down into the pass, Sister Margaret came running for Sister Dominique. "Come quick, Stephano and two other partisans brought another young boy up the back trail and he's hurt bad.

Running down to the subbasement, Sister Dominique recognized the boy from the trip she had taken to get the doctor. Looking at Stephano she inquired, "What happened to this boy?"

Stephano shook his head as tears ran down his face. "We were trapped on a ledge by the Germans, but they didn't know we were above them. Without saying a word, he grabbed a grenade and ran down the path to where the Germans were setting up a machine gun. As he jumped in behind them, he pulled the pin. He was thrown back into the rock face of the dugout. When I got there, all the Germans were dead, but you can see what the grenade did to him. We patched him up as good as we could and brought him here."

Tears rolled down Sister Dominique's face as she began trying to stitch up some of his massive injuries. Just as she pulled out another piece of thread, the boy reached out and grabbed her arm.

"Mother, I have missed you. I'm sorry it took so long for me to find you. Now we can be together again. Hold me, Mother, hold me tight. It hurts so bad," he pleaded as he cried."

Dropping the needle and thread, she grabbed hold of the boy and held him tight. He continued to cry as his hands clutched tightly onto her already bloody habit. Slowly his breathing began to fade as his pulse weakened. Looking up at Sister Dominique, he said, "Mother, Mother, here I am." After releasing his last breath, his head turned to the side as his dark brown eyes closed.

Laying him back on the table, Sister Dominique brushed his dark hair off to the side. "He was just a baby, only eight years old. My God, what a terrible waste."

Stephano dropped down onto a chair and sobbed as he crushed the black beret belonging to the boy in his hands. The other two boys hugged each other as tears of anguish flowed freely.

Sister Margaret stood near the stairway leading up into the Abbey as she looked at the sorrowful scene playing out in front of her. Suddenly, a hand appeared on her shoulder.

"Get a blanket and help me wrap the boy for burial. Sister Dominique told me about him last night. He has no family so we must do what is right for him," Mother Superior explained, as tears rolled down her face.

With the help of the two boys and Stephano, the boy was buried under a starlit sky near the back garden behind the Abbey. As they finished raking over the dirt, Sister Dominique looked up at the bright starry sky. "There is one more star shining down on us tonight. May his little soul find comfort with his mother, and may he rest in peace."

At the very same time, a rubber raft pulled up alongside a large black British submarine about two hundred yards off the coast of Senigallia. With the help of the crew, the Italian politician and his wife, along with the doctor and his family all scrambled aboard the half-submerged vessel. As Lt. O'Brien and one other partisan paddled back toward shore, the captain of the submarine opened the ballast tanks the rest of the way, allowing the sub to slowly submerge below the surface of the Adriatic Sea, away from the prying eyes of the German Navy and S.S.

Neither Sister Dominique or Mother Superior had any idea whether or not Lt. O'Brien's mission was a success that night, but the families that were now safely cruising toward England would always be eternally thankful.

Chapter Five – The Raid at Pescate

Several months later, Sister Dominique requested she be sent back to Milan where she could be closer to the underground. Mother Superior was unsure if that was the right decision, but she knew the convent at Milan was certainly in need of help. So, after admonishing Sister Dominique regarding her need to be involved with underground activities, the assignment was made. It did not take long for word to reach Lorenzo that Sister Dominique was back in Milan. He was uncertain if she was interested in working with the partisans, but he felt the need to contact her and find out.

Nearly a month went by before Lorenzo sent word to Sister Dominique regarding a secret meeting that was taking place in a barn just north of Milan. Arriving at the barn with Lorenzo, Sister Dominique was inspired to see over thirty heavily armed partisans waiting to hear the latest news.

A few minutes later, a tall man of about forty years old stepped up onto an apple crate and raised his hand. Once the room was quiet, he began. "For the first time since we contacted the British offering our services, we have an important mission. I will not tell you what it is now, in case you are captured. However, I will tell you that British commando forces will be sent to us in about a week or so, and we will help them with their assigned task. This is big my friends and we will all be needed."

When the man that had spoken to the group was finished, he walked over to Sister Dominique. "I am glad to have you here, sister. Lorenzo told me why you decided to help us, and I am sorry for your loss. I can assure you that nearly every man and woman in this building has suffered at the hand of the gestapo or Italian secret police at one time or another. We will need your help to pick up the British commandos the night they are dropped. We will furnish you with civilian clothing to wear and a pistol for your own protection."

Immediately, Sister Dominique shook her head. "I am willing to help you, but I cannot go out in the countryside at night in civilian clothing picking up commandos. That is just not something I can do. And I will not carry a pistol or any firearm ever!"

Looking dejected, Lorenzo said, "Sister, when you agreed to help us, we figured you were a full-fledged partisan. We already have two priests and a deacon that are solid members. All we want you to do is drive the truck while we pick up the six men."

Sister Dominique looked down at the floor, realizing she was in deeper than she had ever planned to be and was seriously scared. Looking up from the floor, she could feel the eyes of Lorenzo and the leader of the group boring into her as they waited for an answer. Realizing she was putting her entire life as a nun on the line, she nodded her head. "I shall drive your truck."

Eight days passed before Lorenzo contacted her. He sent a message with one of the students, taped to the inside of his shoe. The note simply said, "1900hrs. Playground."

It was nearly impossible for Sister Dominique to think straight the rest of the day, but she knew she had to act as normally as possible so the children would not know anything out of the ordinary was taking place.

At 1830hrs, Lorenzo and a young woman named Amara arrived at the school with a bag filled with civilian clothing and a solid pair of hiking boots. Without question, at 1900hrs, Sister Dominique slid in behind the steering wheel and started the truck. She headed north out of Milan where she pulled into an apple orchard, allowing four more men to jump onto the truck.

Amara climbed into the cab of the truck, taking up a position in the passenger seat next to Sister Dominique, holding on tight to her German Mauser. She was quiet for the first few miles as she checked and rechecked her rifle. After being sure her weapon was ready to fire, she said. "I admire you very much, Sister. What you are doing for our cause is wonderful. The gestapo killed my father and brother for no reason whatsoever. Since then, all I have thought of is revenge. I will fight until the war is over or the bastards kill me, too. But I will never quit!"

About an hour later, Lorenzo poked his head through the tarp covering the back of the truck. "Pull off the road at the next left. Follow the trail until it comes to an end by the orange grove."

Sister Dominique froze when she saw several shapes moving inside the orange grove. She was just about to alert Lorenzo, when Amara jumped from the cab and waved at the four men that were staying partially hidden in the evening shadows. Carefully Sr. Dominique drove deeper into the grove parking the truck where she was directed.

Exiting the truck, Sister Dominique followed Lorenzo toward the men. After shaking hands with the man that appeared to be the leader, Lorenzo said. "Did you get the box to work?"

Smiling, the man replied, "It works as if it were brand new. Now let us see if it does what it's supposed to do.

Walking part way out into the open field next to the grove, everyone sat on the ground being very quiet. About five minutes later, the drone of an aircraft could be heard approaching from the west. The man holding the box, flipped on a switch then placed it on the ground. Operating a lever on the side of the box, he opened and closed a series of slats on the top of the box that allowed the red light to be seen from above. As the plane circled overhead, Sister Dominique could see a red light flashing from the side of the plane. Moments later, four dark shapes appeared to be falling toward the ground as the plane turned back toward the west, disappearing into the gathering clouds.

Sister Dominique watched intently as four men hanging from dark green parachutes landed in the field just yards from where the group was waiting. Lorenzo jumped up. "Everyone, gather up the chutes and harnesses and throw them in the truck, we must get moving. Leave nothing behind!"

Within five minutes, Sister Dominique was back behind the wheel of the truck driving south back toward Milan. Using instructions supplied by Amara, Sister Dominique drove the truck into a garage near the grounds of the old Castello Storzesco near the center of Milan.

Immediately, Lorenzo ran up to Amara. "As we planned, take the sister back to the convent at once. Then go home, I'll talk to you tomorrow."

Without questioning a word Lorenzo said, she took Sister Dominique by the arm, leading her to a car parked along the wall. Within minutes, they were heading away from the castle, down streets Sister Dominique had never seen before.

Driving into the courtyard of the convent, Amara said. "We will contact you, go now!"

Walking into the darkened convent, Sister Dominique was frightened when she heard the voice of the convent's abbess calling out from the dark near the rear of the kitchen. "Where have you been, child? Are you putting all of us in the convent in jeopardy?"

By now, Abbess Costanza was standing just a few feet in front of her, looking rather grim. Before Sister Dominique could say a word, Costanza sat down at the large wooden table and said, "Sit with me for a while, Dominique."

The room was silent for a moment before Costanza spoke. "You have several sisters here in the convent, including me, scared regarding your activities. And there are at least two more sisters that want to join you in whatever you are doing, and I cannot allow that. You are a remarkable woman that I like very much, but I am not sure I can trust you anymore. What am I to do with you?"

Taking a deep breath, Sister Dominique replied. "I am sorry for all of that, but I'm afraid I am in far too deep now to back away. I know there is a big mission coming up, and they are going to be counting on me to help get it done."

The Abbess shook her head. "This is not the way a catholic sister is supposed to behave. I know I cannot lock you up here in the convent, but if you bring the gestapo or the Italian security service down upon us, we will all be lost. So tell me, what am I supposed to do?"

Sister Dominique looked firmly at her friend and supervisor. "I shall move out of the convent. I know a woman in the underground I can stay with. That will relieve you of all responsibility for my actions. I can contact her tomorrow and have her pick me up."

Abbess Costanza shook her head. "I will need to think that over. Go to your room now and pray for an answer to our dilemma."

The following morning very few words were exchanged between Sister Dominique and Costanza, but none of them concerned the conversation of the past night. Just as school was about to wrap up for the day, Sister Dominique observed Amara walking through the garden looking at the roses. Walking up to her, Sister Dominique said, "Ah, I see you like the pink roses, they are my favorite as well. These bushes are said to be two hundred years old, and yet they bloom every year like magic."

Amara smiled as she sniffed one the flowers. Looking up at Sister Dominique, she said, "You must come with me now, and not return to the convent tonight or tomorrow night. The mission time table has moved up and we must prepare. Get your things and come with me quickly."

Arriving at a small brick house west of the castle, Lorenzo walked up to Sister Dominique. "Is all well with you and the sisters in the convent?"

Shaking her head, Sister Dominique replied. No, and I fear after being away for two nights, Abbess Costanza will ship me off somewhere far away. But I am here now because I choose to be, and I wish to do what I can to help you, regardless the consequences to my own situation."

Giving Sister Dominique a reassuring smile, he led her into the living room where the four British paratroopers stood drinking tea. When everyone was assembled, the leader spoke up. "I am Major Cyrus Burton of the Kings Fifth Fusiliers. We are all assembled here because we are going to take on a very tough nut to crack." Walking up to a map that was hanging on the wall, he pointed to the Adda River just north of Pescate. "Our bombers have attempted to collapse the tunnel for several weeks now, but have only done slight damage, I'm afraid. We must collapse the tunnel and take out the bridge to the south. The problem is, the jerries have anti-aircraft batteries all along this escarpment, giving the Hun a clear view of the road below where we will be coming from. We will send a flight of Lancaster's over at 2200hrs. tomorrow evening that should keep the bastards busy while we run in and set our charges. Lorenzo and his team will set the charges on the bridge at the same time. I plan to send it all to hell at 2245. Sister Dominique, you are not only the driver again, but you will be the time clock for the boys mining the bridge. You must get them up and away from the monster by at least 2235 or they will get caught up in all the explosions. As you can see, this means we must work fast, silently, and avoid all contact with jerry until after we have pulled it off. It's a sticky wicket to say the least."

Sister Dominique realized she was now in deeper still, but there was no turning back. As she studied the map, one of the Fusiliers walked up to her. "Ma'am, if I may say so, I admire your courage and determination to help us." Reaching into his waistband, he pulled out an American .45 semi-automatic pistol. "Sister, I want you to take this with you tomorrow night. I do not expect you to fight jerry with it, but if everything goes south, use it to shoot yourself. You do not want to be captured after what we are going to do."

Never had she considered the need to kill herself, and the thought of it made her physically sick. Sister Dominique was unsure whether or not she could pull the trigger to end her own life, knowing it was against the teachings of the church. But then again, being involved in killing Germans was not among the teachings of the church she had received, either.

After taking the weapon in her hand, Sister Dominique replied. "As you say, I shall not kill the Germans, but you are totally correct, I do not wish to fall into the hands of the enemy. May God understand and have mercy on my soul."

The following evening, standing next to the truck loaded with explosives, British Commandos and underground heroes, Sister Dominique looked at the pistol in her hand for a moment before looking up at Amara who was clutching her rifle. By now, she had resigned herself as to what she had to do, and to the consequences of failure. As she turned to enter the truck, she moved the safety switch on the side of the pistol to off, and slid the weapon into the waist band of her pants.

A minute later, Lorenzo jumped up on the running board of the truck and looked at the two women. "Are we ready to do this?" he inquired, as he took a long look at Dominique and Amara.

Both of them nodded and replied very firmly, making Lorenzo feel a bit more comfortable.

There was very little traffic on the streets as Sister Dominique drove out of the city of Milan. Before the war it had been a beautiful city, where the many fountains were bathed in colored lights and the gas street lamps shimmered like diamonds. It wasn't hard to fall in love with such a beautiful city. But now, with the harshly imposed blackout, as in all of occupied Europe, the city took on a somber disagreeable tone that reflected the negative attitude of its residents.

Approaching Highway 36, Sister Dominique watched for the small turnout where the British saboteurs would jump out. If she went too far and crossed Highway 83, she would have to turn around and risk being seen by the German soldiers in their anti-aircraft batteries. Luckily, there was not a vehicle to be seen anywhere along the road. Her heart was pumping like a race horse galloping at full speed, while sweat rolled down her face, even though it was a cool and mild evening. Suddenly, there was the small turnout on her right. Dropping the transmission into neutral, she turned the wheel slightly, allowing the truck to slowly and quietly roll into the narrow turn out. When the four men had left the truck, Lorenzo rapped slightly on the back of the cab. With even precision, Sister Dominique pushed in the clutch, slid the transmission into first gear and pushed down lightly on the throttle, allowing the truck to accelerate back onto the road without jerking or making any noticeable noise.

Amara smiled and winked as Sister Dominique drove on to her next turning point that would take her down into a ditch just fifty yards from highway 83. This turn would be harder to see, as the blackout lights on the truck did not spread wide over the opposing lane. Luckily, a partisan with a red flashlight was standing nearby, to give Sister Dominique a signal to turn, after Amara flashed him two red blinks of her light. Just like clockwork, Amara flashed her light twice, and the man returned with a wave of his arm. Turning the wheel to the left, Sister Dominique drove the truck down the small path until she could turn around, keeping the vehicle clear of view from the road.

Instantly, everyone jumped from the truck, preparing to begin their mission. Amara led the team to a large culvert that ran under the road, directly to the base of the bridge. Kneeling down next to Sister Dominique, Lorenzo made sure their watches were perfectly synchronized.

Like a bunch of trained chimpanzees, Lorenzo's team swung from girder to girder, setting charges and running wire that led back to the timer Amara was holding. Sister Dominique kept a close eye on her watch as it ticked off the minutes, faster than she had ever seen a clock do before.

As the men worked, a large flight of British Lancaster's flew overhead. Every German anti-aircraft battery began throwing up flak, hoping to bring down one or more of the enemy bombers. The pounding of the guns was so intense, Sister Dominique could feel it reverberate off her chest. Standing on the ground looking up at the flak explosions was like nothing Sister Dominique had ever seen before, or for that matter, ever wanted to see again.

One by one the men returned to the base of the bridge, pulling wires behind them. When Lorenzo dropped back down on the ground from the bridge, he looked at Sister Dominique. "How much time do we have left?"

"A minute, fifteen seconds," Sister Dominique replied, with a mouth so dry she felt like she had been gargling with sand all night. After setting the timer, everyone but Amara and the signal man with the flashlight ran for the truck. The two of them kept an eye on the road to make sure it was clear before signaling Sister Dominique to drive out. With the road clear, Amara waved her flashlight. Sister Dominique pushed down hard on the throttle, attempting to get up enough speed to climb the ditch without having to take a second run at it. Amara jumped on the running board and pulled the door open as the truck began to enter the highway. Sitting down, she looked over at Sister Dominique and smiled. "That was magnificent, Sister."

Sister Dominique could not help but smile back at Amara, knowing what the success of the mission would mean to the young girl.

Approaching a small turn in the road, Sister Dominique identified the four British saboteurs running out of the brush. Slowing slightly, the men in the back of the truck pulled the Fusiliers over the top of the tail gate and yelled at Sister Dominique to get the hell out of there. The truck had just cleared Pescate when a tremendous explosion roared through the sleepy valley. In the rearview mirror, Sister Dominique could see two massive fireballs rise from the river valley.

As the second explosion in the tunnel detonated, the entire first anti-aircraft battery that sat on a rocky outcropping, broke loose from the mountain, sliding down over a hundred feet to the road below.

In the second battery, two of the firing team were struck and killed by huge shards of steel flying up from the bridge. A German staff car that was just approaching the bridge when it blew, was pitched skyward before it dropped down into the river upside down.

Cheers went up from the back of the truck as everyone patted each other on the back for a job well done. Tears rolled down Amara's face as she nodded her head. "We have taken the fight to the bastards, and now they know what it's like to lose. And that we'll be back, again and again!"

Arriving back at the garage near the castle, several underground members were waiting to talk to Lorenzo. After hearing what they had to say, he was furious. Running back toward the truck, he pulled Amara out of the cab and told Sister Dominique to drive. Following Lorenzo's directions, Sister Dominique drove as quick as she could without drawing attention. Seeing a large crowd on a street corner, Lorenzo told Sister Dominique to park the truck.

Approaching a woman, Lorenzo asked, "What is going on here this late at night?"

The woman shook her head in disbelief. "There was a meeting here between German and Italian security people. Apparently, several underground men stormed the room, killing five German officers and one Italian officer. You know all of Milan will pay for this one way or the other."

Nodding his head, Lorenzo replied, "I am afraid you are correct."

Just as Lorenzo and Sister Dominique were about to leave, several gestapo agents came walking past the crowd. The leader of the gestapo team was a Captain Rochefort, a very dangerous man with no qualms about killing anyone that crossed him. He took a good look around the crowd as Sister Dominique slowly walked down the street, away from the crowd and the truck. Lorenzo walked across the street and continued walking until he came to an alley. Ducking into the alley, he ran until he came to the next street. Coming back down to a casual walk, he turned back toward the street where the truck was parked. He observed Sister Dominique standing in the shadow of a doorway, watching the crowd begin to disperse. Realizing the gestapo men had gone inside the restaurant, Lorenzo grabbed Sister Dominique and walked quickly toward the truck.

Stepping out of the truck back at the garage, Lorenzo walked up to the three men that had assassinated the high-ranking officers. "Do you know what you have done?"

One of the men said, "Lorenzo, you did not need us on your mission, and we wanted to make you proud of us, so we decided to put together an attack of our own."

After thinking for a minute, Lorenzo said. "Take the truck, pack your bags and get out of Milan tonight. I would drive to Genoa. Maybe you can escape to Corsica to live out the war. No arguing, now go and never let me see you in Milan again, you are now like poison to all of us."

Amara drove Sister Dominique back to the convent the next morning, and told her to stay away from meetings for a while as it would not be safe.

Although she understood the consequence of being captured, after staying away for several months, Sister Dominique once more began attending meetings whenever possible. The day after attending her last meeting, a massive round up of underground members was ordered. After a large part of the Milan group was raided by the gestapo, Sister Dominique immediately requested a transfer back to the Abbazia di San Vincenzo al Furlo, above the town of Acqualagna.

Everyone in the Abbey, including Mother Superior, was well aware of Sister Dominique's connections with the underground, but had no idea of the extent of her work. They knew nothing about the attack on the bridge and tunnel, or the gun running she had been involved in. Nobody in the convent had been aware that it was members of Sister Dominique's underground unit that had attacked the planning session in the restaurant.

After settling back into the daily operation of the Abbey, Sister Dominique attempted to steer clear of underground members in Acqualagna whenever her duties took her into town. However, it was totally impossible to stop the notes that were passed to her when food was delivered to the Abbey. She would read them, then burn them in the courtyard to keep secret whatever the underground was up to. She knew that the mayor of Acqualagna was an ardent fascist and a man to be avoided, although his wife Anastasia, was a member of the underground, and controlled an information pipe line south to Naples. Everything was complicated in the world of the partisans, and no one was ever safe.

From time to time as repair work needed to be done in the Abbey, Leandro Folliero, an all-around handyman from Ponte di Ferro, would complete the work. He also was a member of an underground group controlling about thirty members that harassed the Italian and German military as much as they could. Whenever he visited the Abbey, he would fill Sister Dominique in on everything his group was up to. Although she enjoyed hearing what her countrymen were doing to fight the fascists, she was aware of what could happen if she were overheard talking with Leandro. After all, the safety of the sisters in the Abbey had to be the most important factor to consider, and Mother Superior in the Abbey di San Vincenzo al Furlo was much less forgiving than the Abbess in Milan.

Realizing her activities with the underground might one day catch up with her, she knew she was an outright risk to all the members of the Abbey.

After much prayerful thought, she finally decided to ask Mother Superior for an assignment that would take her away from the Abbey and even Italy, if that were possible.

After hearing Dominique's request, Mother Superior sat down behind her desk. "There is an owner of a banana plantation in the South Pacific that lives in Naples. The plantation is on the island of Nusa Simbo in the Solomon Islands. He has inquired as to whether or not we would like to send some missionaries and a priest to his island to start a school to teach his children and the natives. Father Renaldo from Rome has volunteered to be the priest, and he would like three sisters to work with him. I was going to ask for volunteers tomorrow morning after breakfast. But I think this is a job you may be interested in, and we could get you out of the country safely before you are captured, which is imminent I am afraid."

Surprised by Mother Superior's last words, Sister Dominique swallowed very hard.

Mother Superior looked seriously across the desk. "Did you not think that word regarding your experiences with the underground would come to my attention? If I had known about all of that I might not have allowed you to transfer back here in fear of what could happen to the rest of us. I have been thinking about asking you to transfer out, I was just not sure how to approach you. But now you have made it simple for me, for you, and everyone living in the Abbey. What do you think of moving to a mission in the South Pacific, Sister Dominique?"

Smiling, Sister Dominique replied. "I will go without question. It sounds like a job that I would be good at, and it is best I disappear from Italy for a long time, if not forever."

Nodding her head in agreement, Mother Superior stood up from her desk. "Good, I shall put your name down as one volunteer. We will see who decides to go with you in the morning."

The following morning, Mother Superior explained about the missionary work and had two instant volunteers. Both Sister Margaret and Sister Veronica jumped at the chance.

Sister Dominique was extremely happy with the volunteers, as they were close to her age and were both hard workers and fun to be around. Before anyone could say another word, Mother Superior explained that Sister Dominique would be in charge of the day-to-day operations of the mission and the sisters, but work hand in hand as need be with Father Renaldo.

As she packed her few belongings for the long trip, Sister Dominique realized that the strong will that had been such a problem when she was younger, had now nearly cost her life and that of those around her. She hoped now that she could use her strong will to make the mission on the island of Nusa Simbo an ideal place to live, work and serve the people, as she had been trained to do. She hoped for a much simpler life that was free of fear and war.

Chapter Six–The Long Trip

In some ways loading onto the old bus for the long road trip to Naples, was much like when her father had dropped her off that cold winter morning. The Abbey had been the only home she had known for nearly twenty years, and she had come to know the place like the back of her hand. She had come to know the tunnels beneath the Abbey where many monks had lived, prayed and died for hundreds of years. She had enjoyed walking among the countless large frescoes that decorated miles of walls throughout the Abbey, and wondered how they had been constructed. She had become good friends with the elegant paintings created by many of the master painters of Italy throughout the last few centuries, that hung in so many rooms and corridors. She would sit near them as she prayed, always discovering something new in each one of them.

Most of all she had built a family, a real family that cared about her. She had experienced the deaths of many older sisters, and had helped new members adjust, just as sisters now long gone had done for her. The Abbey had its own cycle of life, one that could never be appreciated unless you experienced it from the inside. All these years later, Sister Dominique could still remember the painful day she had been left by her father, but what she had gained spiritually from living in the close knit environment of the Abbey was beyond anything she could ever have imagined when she first arrived.

But now this was her time to go out into the world and give back for all the blessings she had received, and she knew she was ready for the challenge.

Although Sister Dominique had come and gone from the Abbey several times over the last two years while teaching in Milan, she seldom paid much attention to the surrounding area. But now, she was totally unsure when or if she would ever see her beloved Abbey and the beautiful countryside again, so as the bus drove down the highway, she kept to herself, taking in every aspect of the gorgeous river valley.

Off in the distance she observed several small farms, and wondered if any of them could still be owned by her family. Suddenly, she realized that although it had been decades since arriving in the Abbey, the pain of that moment when she realized she was not returning home with her father, still hung heavy in her heart, and she realized it would always be there. But now all was forgiven and she was happy.

As the bus crossed over the Furlo River, Sister Veronica turned around in her seat. "I cannot believe I'm out in the countryside again. Since I took my vows eight months ago, I have not left Acqualagna. Now it's hard to believe we are going to an island in the South Pacific. What an incredible life. I am glad you are in charge, Sister Dominique. I trust your judgment very much."

Sister Margaret laughed as she looked over at Sister Veronica. "So, you will be alright if you are assigned to peel potatoes every day for the next six months?"

Shaking her head, Sister Veronica smiled. "Then I guess I would need to add that Sister Dominique's decision making might be slightly flawed."

The three women laughed as the small bus was waved through an Italian Army checkpoint. However, Father Renaldo made the sign of the cross, as he knew their trip could be derailed at any checkpoint for no special reason. The German soldiers did not need a reason to confiscate everyone's documents and place you in custody until they were positive you were not on their watch list.

Hours later, as they approached the outskirts of Rome, they ran into a large German checkpoint where several gestapo agents paced back and forth, waiting for their next victims. A soldier carrying a Schmeisser machine gun directed the driver to turn off into a parking area.

A Gestapo agent stepped onto the bus wearing the typical long black leather overcoat, and his black hat pulled down close to his eyes. Holding out his hand to the driver, he said firmly, "Travel documents, please!"

As he looked over the documents, he said. "So, you are taking the priest and three sisters to Naples. What are they going to be doing there?"

Father Renaldo stood up quickly walking up to the agent. "We shall be catching a ship to the South Pacific where we will be doing missionary work."

"Missionary work! Blah! Do those natives not know that there is no God? Are you going to fill their heads will all kinds of false promises, then pull the rug out from under them when you leave? If I had my way, you would all be thrown in prison, but as you are leaving the Third Reich, we will all be better off."

Stepping down the aisle he asked the sisters for their individual papers. When he looked over Sister Dominique's papers, he frowned. "Have we not met before Sister Dominique, you look very familiar."

Everyone in Italy already understood that lying to a Gestapo agent always came with a severe penalty that needed to be avoided at all costs. Sister Dominique shook her head as she replied. "I do not believe we have ever met, but I taught school in Milan for two years before the schools were closed, so you may have seen me around there."

"Ja Milan, it has been a hotbed of anti-government activity since I arrived here. Did you take part in any of the street protests? Don't lie to me, we have hundreds of photos I can look at to see if you are telling the truth."

Sister Margaret was scared, as she knew exactly how Sister Dominique felt about Mussolini and the German occupation. There was little doubt in her mind that it was possible she may have attended the illegal rallies.

Shaking her head, Sister Dominique replied. "Check your files. You will not see my face on any of those photos. I was a teacher in a Catholic grade school. I would never have done anything wrong and give my students a bad example."

Giving Sister Dominique a cold sneer, the agent replied. "So, you acted as a saint setting good examples and never speaking out against the government, did you?"

"Why yes, that is what being a woman of the cloth teaches us to do. And I am surprised you know about saints, since they have no place in the Third Reich."

Father Renaldo cringed when he heard Sister Dominique's last comment. He was waiting for the agent to pull her off the bus and arrest her.

Laughing, the agent handed Sister Dominique's papers back to her. "As a sister of your God, isn't it wrong to falsely judge a man? My parents were devout Lutherans, and I grew up being taught all that false dribble about saints, Moses and rising from the dead." Placing his hand on the butt of his pistol, he continued. "Believe me, Sister, when I shoot someone, they will not be rising from the dead."

Just before he was going to leave, he looked back at Sister Dominique. "Living in Milan, you must have known a man by the name of Sebastian Andorle. He had quite a reputation in the city."

This was going to be a tough question to answer, as she knew Andorle supplied hundreds of weapons and explosives to the underground, and some had been stored in the basement of the church, as the local priest was completely involved with sabotage in and around Milan. Plus, she had met him several times as she had taught one of his daughters. Nodding her head, Sister Dominique replied. "I did not know him well. I taught his daughter for the first year I was there. Several times he came to pick up Lucinda early and took her out of class." Now she hoped the nervous agent would walk off the bus and allow them to continue their journey.

"Ja, he has children, what a shame. When he is caught, they will suffer also." Nodding his head, he turned forward and walked off the bus, signaling the driver to continue.

When the bus was a good quarter mile down the road, Sister Margaret looked across the aisle. "May I breathe now? I thought for sure you were going to be arrested, and all of us would be sitting in jail for a few days. What were you involved in while you were in Milan? Did you know the officer before today? He sure appeared to have recognized you to some degree."

Father Renaldo looked back from the front seat. "Sister Margaret, at this time in history, it is not a good idea to know what everyone else is involved in. That way, if you are taken in for questioning, you can honestly answer that you haven't a clue what a certain person is doing. That alone may save your life. I do give you permission to ask her that same question when this awful war is over. It will make for good conversation over a cup of coffee, or maybe even a Cognac."

The sisters all laughed as Sister Margaret understood exactly what Father Renaldo was speaking about. But now she realized why her good friend had volunteered for the job in the South Pacific so fast. The more distance she could get from the Germans increased her odds of living a long healthy life.

It was apparent that the driver was not very happy with the conversation that had just taken place on his bus. The sisters heard him tell Father Renaldo several times that he was going to need to take a longer route home to avoid contact with the Gestapo, and his wife would not be happy.

The port of Naples was a busy place when the bus turned on to the street above the wharf an hour and a half later. Seeing the tramp steamer, *Rose of Italy,* tied up a mere twenty yards away, smoke already rolling from its stack, Sister Dominique was more than prepared to climb aboard and escape from Italy forever.

Stepping from the bus, the driver took her by the arm. "When you mess with the gestapo you take your life into your own hands, along with everyone else you know. You are either an ignorant woman, or a very uncaring and careless person. I do not wish to have you on my bus ever again, and I hope your friends know what they are getting into with you. You are a very poor risk to be around!"

Pulling lose from the driver's grip, Sister Dominique replied, "Someday, you too may have to get involved to save your Italy from destruction. I promise not to judge you."

Climbing aboard the steamer, the captain greeted them and escorted them to their cabins on the top deck near the rear of the ship. The sisters were berthed together in a large room with two sets of bunk beds, while Father Renaldo was across the corridor in a room containing a nice standard size bed.

Thirty minutes later, the *Rose of Italy* backed out from its berth and began a slow trip through the busy harbor. Leaving the breakwater, the captain threw the throttles forward as the five-hundred-foot steamer began crashing through the waves on the open ocean.

Sitting down on her bunk, Sister Dominique was quiet for a moment. After gathering her thoughts, she looked at her friends. "I apologize for the scare I put you through with the gestapo today, I had no right to do that. I did not want to get involved in the things that were going on in Milan, but when I arrived there, several other sisters in the convent were already heavily involved and it appeared the gestapo had them dead to right. I needed to work hard with Abbess Costanza to get them transferred out of Italy, or they would surely have been tortured and killed. Had the gestapo broke them, many more people would have been killed. But in the end, I too became far too heavily involved. What Father Renaldo said was accurate. What you do not know about someone is a good thing."

Sister Margaret sat down beside her friend. "I do not care what you may have done, I will always be your friend, and I trust you with my life."

Standing over in the corner, Sister Veronica said. "Just help me find the dining room, I am starved. Leave the world to fend for itself right now, as long as my stomach is filled soon."

The three women laughed just as there was knock on their door. Standing in the corridor wearing khaki-colored shorts and a bright yellow button-down shirt, was Father Renaldo. "Please tell me you ladies are as hungry as I am. I found a short cut to the dining room, anyone interested?"

The food on the ship was better than they had expected it to be, and it appeared that most of the passengers were either business men or families. Everyone appeared to speak freely and look relaxed, which gave the missionary crew a sense of relief.

Making a wide turn past the toe of Italy into the wide Mediterranean, the ship began to roll much more than it had as it sailed down the west coast. Standing out on deck on the rear of the ship, Sister Margaret spoke up. "Is anybody getting off the ship at Alexandria when we stop in Egypt?"

Sister Dominique shook her head. "No, too many Germans and British military in the area. I think the place is best left to the sturdy and brave of heart."

Nodding her head, Sister Veronica agreed. "No, I'll just walk around the ship and see whatever I can see from the safe decks of the *Rose of Italy*."

Father Renaldo shook his head. "Well, I shall go ashore for a short walk. I need to pick up several things the Moretti family needs for their short-wave radio at the banana plantation. Things like that are readily available here, and it should not take me long to get them.

The following afternoon, the *Rose of Italy* was carefully nudged into its berth in Alexandria, Egypt. After the ship was tied down, Father Renaldo walked ashore, disappearing into the large crowds of people moving about the pier. The sisters sat on the foredeck drinking lemonade and conversing with several women that were married to business men.

It was evident that one woman was of Jewish decent. She and her husband had been able to get false documents for themselves and their two small children, allowing them to travel. Arriving in Rome, they had spent a fortune getting all new passports and more travel documents, allowing them to get on board the ship, then debark once they arrived at Suez. From there, her brother-in-law would take them cross country to Palestine where they could live in peace without fear of deportation by the Germans. She stated that the trip cost them every penny they had, but they would start over again when they were safe.

Sister Dominique's heart went out to the woman, realizing what an impossible task it must have been to make all the arrangements while living in fear the entire way, until they boarded the ship. She felt a kinship to the Jewish woman, but was still not ready to let anyone know what she had hidden in her past. Not even Mother Superior back at the Abbey had any idea of what had happened to her before she made her final escape from Milan.

About two hours after leaving the ship, Father Renaldo returned, carrying several boxes of radio equipment, and a few special candy bars Mrs. Moretti wanted for her children. As dusk settled over the gritty Mediterranean City, traffic near the port died down to a mere trickle, including several British military patrol vehicles that stood watch over two British destroyers that had docked late in the afternoon.

About midnight, the tugs returned once more, pulling the *Rose of Italy* clear of her berth. After turning the ship toward the north, the captain sailed out of the congested harbor before turning east toward the Suez Canal.

Every ship had to have a set time and date to pass through the canal. If you missed your time, you could be delayed as much as a week before you could get back into rotation once again. The captain of the *Rose of Italy* was keenly aware of the rule, and had his ship properly in line when it became his turn to enter the canal at 0300hrs. local time. Both Sisters Dominique and Margaret were excited about watching the ship pass through the canal, so they found a safe quiet area under some spot lights on the rear deck to take up a comfortable viewing position. Although very few passengers were on deck to observe the passage through the canal, Sister Dominique noticed quickly that the Jewish family was on the foredeck with their bags, ready to depart as soon as possible.

Arriving at Suez, Sister Dominique watched the family depart the ship, shake hands with their relatives and climb into a small truck for the first leg of their trip to Palestine. She was happy they had fled the torture of Nazi Germany, and said a prayer for them as the truck left the harbor.

That evening during dinner, the captain reminded everyone that their next stop in Mumbai, India, was the last stop before the *Rose of Italy* turned around. After discussing several important reminders about the port of Mumbai, the captain stated, "Mumbai has become a dangerous place over the last few years. The city is occupied by German, Japanese, British, American and Russian spies, along with government operatives. India does not care who is operating out of the port, as long as they keep their issues out of public scrutiny. So, be careful who you talk to and what you say."

A heavy rain was falling over the dreary city as the *Rose of Italy* entered the port. Slowly the ship was guided to its berth by a large tug boat. From his room with a small pair of binoculars, Father Renaldo could see their next ship. The *Port of Jakarta* was already in port, preparing for its turn around voyage. They would only need to walk about seventy-five yards to the boarding station.

After turning over their luggage to a pier worker, Father Renaldo led the sisters off the ship and down to the busy cobblestone street that connected the busy pier to the old city. What the captain had told them the night before about foreign agents was very clear to see. All along the busy street were German and Japanese officers, stopping people to check their travel documents and identities.

When Father Renaldo reached the boarding station, a German captain named Rochefort watched him hand over their travel documents and speak in Italian to the Indian processor that had a tough time understanding everything being said. Reaching over to the desk, the captain picked up the documents and read them over carefully. Looking at the processor he said, "Three of these are just fine, but the one for Sister Dominique is questionable. I will need to take her to my office for questioning!"

Father Renaldo immediately began to argue with the captain, until two more German soldiers arrived to see what the problem was. Holding up his hand, Father Renaldo bowed slightly. "Herr Captain, there is nothing wrong with these documents, and I can assure you they are not forgeries. I do not—"

Before he could finish, Captain Rochefort looked sternly at the priest. "If I say there is a problem, there is a problem. If you wish to continue to argue,

I will have you and the good sisters escorted to the Japanese jail, to be held there until I am ready to have you released. That could take days, and by that time your ship will have sailed."

Sister Margaret placed her hand on Father Renaldo's shoulder. "Father, I'm sure it's a minor mistake that the captain can iron out quickly. I think the rest of us should board the ship now and clear the area for other passengers."

Realizing that several other men from other countries had now taken interest in what was happening, Father Renaldo nodded his head. You are correct, Sister. We should allow the captain to go on with his business, so he can get it cleared up before the ship sails."

He was about to say something to Sister Dominique, but the two soldiers had already taken hold of her and were leading her over to a black Mercedes.

Arriving at the German headquarters, Captain Rochefort removed his long raincoat as he glared at Sister Dominique. "So, we meet again, Sister. Did you ever imagine the two of us would meet so far away from Milan? Don't act timid now, Sister. You know exactly who I am."

Sister Dominique looked up at the officer and shook her head. "Yes, I was in Milan as a teacher until the schools were closed. But you, I do not remember."

Shaking his head, he pulled up the right sleeve of his tunic to uncover the scar from a six-inch gash on his forearm. "And now you will tell me you have no idea how I received this wound?"

"That is correct, Herr Captain, I know nothing of it," Sister Dominique replied, getting more nervous by the minute. "As I said, I was a teacher of small children and I lived in the convent. I had nothing to do with the uprising or underground activities. It was horrible what happened to some of those people. Yes, I saw the gallows from the upstairs window of the convent. It was ghastly!"

Nodding his head, Captain Rochefort paced the floor. "Perhaps you should have taken the a position on the gallows instead of those poor peasants. Am I right, Sister?"

Looking up at the captain, who was now standing directly in front of her, she replied. "Your people arrested anyone they felt was involved without provocation. I can tell you there were two innocent people hung that morning. Their blood is on your hands!"

Reaching down and grabbing Sister Dominique by the throat, he yelled, "If that is so, why did you not step forward and confess your crimes to save those so called innocent people. Why Sister? Why did you not step forward? I think their blood is on your hands!"

Sister Dominique was about to pass out when the captain removed his hand from her throat, pushing the chair over on its side. Removing his pistol, he placed the barrel directly on the side of her head. "Do you wish me to be judge and jury right here, Sister?"

Sister Dominique closed her eyes, waiting for the bullet to end her life as she silently prayed, saying nothing to the angry officer.

Reaching down with his other hand and placing it on her shoulder, he shook her violently. "Tell me what I want to hear. Tell me what I know is the truth. I can save your life and have you live out your life in prison back in Germany in a place called Dachau. Now speak!"

"I prefer you use your pistol and get it over with. You would never believe anything I say, so this is fruitless." Though Sister Dominique spoke calmly, she was beginning to believe her life was about to end.

Stepping back and holstering his weapon, he looked down at Sister Dominique. "Get up, get off the floor and sit back in that chair!"

Picking up the chair, Sister Dominique readjusted her veil and sat down. "What's the matter, Captain? You could kill those innocent people in Milan, but you can't kill an innocent woman here in Mumbai? Or are you afraid there may be some honest civil authorities in this town that may object to a nun being executed by a foreign official for no reason!"

Stepping forward, Captain Rochefort struck Sister Dominique across the face, hard enough to knock her back off the chair. As blood ran from her bottom lip, she shook her head. "Mark my words, Captain, the day will come when the likes of you will be shunned by the people of the world, and there will be no place for you to hide. Then there will be true justice, and you will be made to pay for your sins by man and by God. Believe me Captain, it will happen."

Walking over to his desk, he picked up the phone. "Albrecht, come in here."

Instantly, a tall sergeant walked into the room. "Stop the bleeding, wash her face and take her back to the ship." Stepping up to Sister Dominique, he once again grabbed her by the throat. "Let me see you again and next time I will do as you asked and put a bullet in your head. Get out of my sight!"

Pushing her backward, into Sgt. Albrecht, Captain Rochefort grabbed his raincoat and hat, then walked out into the damp evening.

Arriving back at the ship, Sgt. Albrecht opened the door of the black Mercedes for Sister Dominique. "Listen to what I am about to tell you. Do not come back to Mumbai ever again. He will be watching for you to pass back this way. He will kill you like a sick old dog and think nothing of it. Never, and I mean never cross the captain again. Now go, get on the ship. Remain in your cabin until you sail. Do not be out on any of the decks. Do you understand what I have told you?"

Nodding her head and shaking with fear, Sister Dominique replied. "I do. Thank you, Sergeant. Now you must go and save yourself. Do not let that awful man defile your soul."

Without another word, Sister Dominique charged up the gang plank into the waiting arms of Sister Margaret. "Come sister, let me take care of your injuries, we were so worried, then relieved when the sergeant called the boarding station to inform us you were on the way back. We sail in two hours, let's get you out of sight now."

For the next two hours, Sister Dominique held her breath and paced the room in fear of the captain returning to the ship to arrest her. She knew full well that if that happened, she would disappear from the world, never to be heard from again.

Once the tugboat released, the *Port of Jakarta*, allowing it to set sail for the Arabian Sea, Sister Dominique collapsed into a large over-stuffed chair in the corner of the room and closed her eyes. Several minutes later there was a knock upon the door. Sister Veronica walked over, looked through the viewing hole and smiled. Looking very concerned, Father Renaldo walked into the room and sat down on the edge of one of the beds.

"Sister Dominique, we do not wish to live through another night like this one. There is no other choice, you must tell us what happened in Milan. We have been and are continuing to put our lives on the line being with you, so we have the right to know!"

Nodding her head, Sister Dominique replied. "Yes, you do. I thought once we left Italy, I would never see any German officer that had been stationed in Milan, and the nightmare would be over forever. But now I realize that this war that is just beginning has tentacles reaching halfway around the world. A very dangerous world at that."

Standing up from the chair, she paced the room several times before sitting down next to Father Renaldo. Looking over at Sister Margaret and Sister Veronica, she took a deep breath. "I am sorry for having kept this in for so long, and for not trusting you enough to share what happened. Please forgive me."

Taking another deep breath, Sister Dominique continued. "I had only been in Milan a short time when the father of one of my students came to me, asking if I wanted to be part of the underground, saying that I could use the children's work assignments to pass messages. I was shocked that anyone could even ask such a question, not to mention put their own small children at risk. I declined and asked him to never bring it up again.

About two months later, Sister Agnes and I went to a theater to watch a movie on a Friday night. When we came out of the theater, there was a large anti-Nazi protest going on near the city square. We were both taken back by what was going on, so we hung around and listened to several speakers. Suddenly, about thirty German soldiers on horseback rode into the square, shooting into the air and killing some of the protesters at the same time. Sister Agnes and I fled down an ally and ran back to the convent as fast as we could.

I was saddened to see innocent people being slaughtered in the square, and it made me sick when I thought about it. A few days later I was contacted by the city administrator, who had seen us listening to the speeches. He came to me and asked if I would like to help pass out leaflets and let citizens know when there would be gatherings. I said yes. Maybe wrongly or foolishly, but I agreed.

Over the next eight months, I spent a lot of time working with the administrator and I felt that everything was fine. Well, it wasn't, it wasn't fine at all. One evening when we were making up pamphlets in a store basement, the gestapo and the Italian police raided the building. I ran through a narrow passage into the next building, but the lights were not on. After I dashed up the stairway to the main floor, someone put their arm around me and yelled, "You are mine!" Struggling, I was able to get my right hand free. I grabbed for a large metal yard stick that was laying on a table, and swung with all my might. The ruler slashed the man's arm, sending blood everywhere. As he slipped and fell, I noticed he was a captain in the Wehrmacht, the same captain that grabbed me tonight, Captain Rochefort.

He came to the school on several occasions, looking over the sisters in the classrooms, which told me he had no idea of exactly who had struck him, which relieved me very much. Then about two weeks later, a gestapo agent was killed outside the school as he attempted to arrest the city administrator as he picked up his children from school. As the argument turned into a pushing match, the agent pulled his gun and shot one of the children in the leg, missing the other by inches. The city administrator grabbed for the gun, trying to protect his children, but was beginning to lose the fight.

Sister Agnes and I yelled for the agent to stop, but he would not. We stupidly grabbed hold of the agent, struggling with him in the hope of getting the gun away before anyone else was shot. Horribly, moments later the gun discharged, striking the agent in the chest. With the amount of blood I saw, I am positive he was dead before he hit the ground. We all ran in different directions, not knowing who else was in the area. Later that evening, Sister Agnes and I washed out our habits in the basement of the convent, and promised never to tell anyone what happened. I have no idea who actually had their finger on the trigger, but I am ninety-eight percent sure it was not me.

The gestapo arrested nearly twenty people for the murder, hanging ten of them on gallows built specially for the occasion several days later. I watched the hanging from the top floor of the convent, realizing several of the people that were hung never had any contact with the underground. It was all so ugly and disgusting. I confessed what had happened to one of the parish priests, but as I could not be sure who pulled the trigger, he absolved me of my sins, and told me to have no further contact with anybody involved with subversive activities. There was no doubt there would be retribution for the killing of the innocent people, but I never knew to what extent. The school was closed about a week later which worked out well, and I left Milan in a hurry, hoping to never return. But I did return, becoming heavily involved after the death of Sister Willamette. My involvement consisted of many things, including sabotage. I was instrumental in blowing up a bridge and rail tunnel."

Father Renaldo looked over at Sister Dominique. "That is quite the story, and I realize why you have kept it to yourself. I have no worries about being with you. You tried to keep children from being shot, and that alone tells me of your virtues. The shooting was an accident, and God knows that. Your other activities have merit, and may have been ill advised, but it no longer matters."

Before Sister Dominique could stand up, both Sister Margaret and Sister Veronica walked over to give her a hug. After sharing a meal in the dining room, Sister Dominique stood on the deck looking out over the dark waters of the Arabian Sea, as it was bathed in the brilliance of a full moon. Looking up at the stars that covered the sky like a silver blanket, she began to cry. She had never cried that hard since being dropped off at the Abbey as a child. Tonight, it felt like her soul had finally been cleansed, and she was ready to take on her new responsibilities on Nusa Simbo, whatever they may be.

About an hour later, Father Renaldo walked up to Sister Dominique. "You are a courageous woman. I don't know if I would have had the courage to jump into a fight like that, even though the lives of children were at stake. I must confess that I'm not a brave man and never have been. But standing up for God is an attribute that has worked out well for me. We shall make a good team, Sister Dominique."

Sometime during the long conversation, the ship turned southeast after rounding the southern tip of India, sailing deep into the Indian Ocean, on course for Jakarta, Indonesia, which was their second to the last stop before arriving at Nusa Simbo.

The evening before they docked in Jakarta, Father Renaldo and the sisters ate dinner with a business man from India. He described how friendly the people in Jakarta were, and how they would do anything to help a person, especially if it meant making some money. Regrettably, he added, most Indonesians in the island chain were fearful over Japan's intentions for expansion. Everyone knows Japan has few natural resources, such as oil, tin and bauxite, all necessary materials to build weapons of war. Indonesia, however, was blessed with these materials, making them the perfect target for an ambitious Japanese military. The people felt it was not a matter of if the Japanese attacked, but when.

Arriving in Jakarta, the captain of the ship told the passengers they would have about two hours to check out the nearby shops as they refueled the ship. It did not take long for Sister Dominique and Sister Margaret to find a small shop that sold many kinds of incense at a very good price. Father Renaldo purchased several brands of cigars, and a pipe tobacco he was not able to procure in Italy. Sister Veronica spent nearly an hour bartering with an older woman over a set of sheets she thought would come in handy when they arrived in the islands. The people in Jakarta were very friendly, and treated Father Renaldo and the sisters like royalty, a far cry from what they had experienced in Mumbai.

The sun was about to set as the *Port of Jakarta* headed back out to sea, following the south coast of Java into the Timor Sea. By morning, they would dock at Port Moresby on the southern side of New Guinea, before sailing on to Nusa Simbo.

Port Moresby had pretty much been taken over by the Australian military over the last six months, in the hopes of stopping a Japanese drive into New Guinea. The last thing the Allies wanted, was for the Japanese to gain a foot hold in Australia. Once that was accomplished, the entire southwest Pacific region would be lost, possibly forever.

The ship stayed just long enough to drop off freight and a few passengers before heading out into the Coral Sea, where passengers spotted several Japanese destroyers cruising among the islands. Several hours later, the ship sailed into the Solomon Sea where hundreds of islands dotted the ocean surface. The sisters stood on the open deck, staring out at the palm covered islands in awe. It was as if all the books and magazines they had read about the enchanting South Pacific were coming to life right in front of them. The small island of Nusa Simbo is located slightly southwest of the larger Ranongga Island, the primary island on the southeast side of Wilson Passage.

A half hour later, the *Port of Jakarta* slid slowly into a cove on the south coast of Nusa Simbo. There were two large piers built out into the cove, where young island natives ran to attach the mooring lines of the steamer.

As the crane whirled back and forth unloading wooden cases from the hold of the steamer, Father Renaldo led the sisters down from the ship onto the sturdy pier, then onto the island, where they met a large white man with a full dark beard that covered most of his face.

After shaking hands with Father Renaldo, the man spoke loudly. "I am Pierre Duncan, manager of the Bertusconi Banana Plantation here on Nusa Simbo. The plantation itself is located to the south on Simbo Islet near Ove.

Our office and living quarters are located right here in Mengge. The Bertusconi family has built a church, a school, and nice living quarters for you and our workers. I am sure you will find everything to your liking, although it's not comparable to Naples, I'm afraid."

The sisters laughed as Mr. Duncan led them to a small old bus that took them to the Bertusconi compound on the south side of Mengge, closer to the cove.

Arriving at their quarters, five island women dressed in black dresses greeted the sisters, insisting they carry all their luggage. Sister Dominique refused, telling the women they were strong enough to carry their own belongings.

Before they could get unpacked, an island man of about fifty years came and knocked on the door to the small dormitory. He bowed as Sister Margaret opened the door. "I am sorry to disturb you, as you have just arrived, but things on the island are not what you are used to. The women that greeted you are responsible to keep the church and your area clean. They are to do your laundry and help you with other matters that you need assistance with. You must respect them."

Sister Dominique smiled at the bald man. "We did nothing to disrespect the women. We just felt we could carry our own luggage."

Shaking his head, the man responded. "That is part of their job, Sister. They felt offended that you refused to allow them to do what they are paid to do. You should apologize to them and make it right once you are unpacked. It will make life easier for everyone if you do."

Sister Dominique nodded her head and smiled. "Then that is exactly what we shall do. Tell me, sir, what is your name? And what is your job here?"

"I was born right here in Mengge nearly fifty years ago, but it has grown somewhat, thanks to the plantation. My native name is Ozamis, and that is what I prefer. I am a master of many trades that I have learned over my years. Mr. Duncan is good to me, and gives me many responsibilities. If you need something the women cannot help you with, just call for Ozamis." The man replied with a huge smile.

After the sisters were unpacked, Sister Dominique called the working women together and apologized for being rude to them. After a long conversation about their duties, it was clear to see that all fences had been mended and peace had been restored.

Besides the island natives that numbered about three hundred, there were about a hundred white and Spanish workers and their families that occupied the island. Everyone appeared to get along well, and Mr. Duncan was always quick to step in if there was a disagreement that needed to be settled.

For the first time in a long while, Sister Dominique felt totally at peace. She was thousands of miles away from the prying eyes of the German and Italian armies, there was total peace on the island, and the island natives from Ranongga easily traded goods with the people of Nusa Simbo and had a good time doing it. Since the other islands in the Solomon Island chain were far away, the natives from Ranongga were the only other native people to stop by and visit.

Chapter Seven – Captain Paulo Trevisiani

You could not have asked for a more beautiful day in Livorno, Italy as Captain Paulo Trevisiani prepared to do his morning inspections. A slight breeze was blowing off the ocean as light cirrus clouds drifted off to the northeast, and temperatures were predicted to be about seventy-five degrees. Before the war, a day like today would have brought out hundreds of people to enjoy a perfect day along the coast. But now, sharp concertina wire, gun emplacements, and large wooden posts containing mines kept everyone away from the pristine beaches. This was all part of Hitler's fortress Europe, and there was no way he was going to allow the allies to spoil his new bastion.

Two busy ferry docks operated out of Livorno. One smaller craft went to the island of Corsica, and a larger tender type vessel crossed the Ligurian Sea to Nice. Since the war started, getting passage on either of these vessels had become quite a task. You could no longer walk down to the pier and purchase a ticked for the next ferry. Everyone had to apply a week in advance, so German and Italian security people could check on your status to see if you were allowed to leave the mainland.

Anyone attempting to apply with false papers was putting their lives on the line. Yet there were days when the Gestapo or German S.S. would arrest someone for violating the strict orders. Rarely would they be seen or heard of again.

So, on this splendid morning, Captain Paulo stood on the pier checking travel documents for passengers heading toward Nice. Frivolity and friendly greetings among travelers had become a thing of the past. Now, everyone stood quiet in a long row, holding their papers in their hands without saying a word unless spoken to by the soldiers.

As an old couple approached that Captain Paulo had seen several times before, he smiled at them as he reached for their documents. "It shall be a nice day to cross the sea, I hope all goes well for you."

The old man looked at the captain. "You should be ashamed of yourself working with the Nazis. They are ruining our country and you allow this to happen. You are a disgrace to Italy."

This was nothing new to Captain Paulo as he had heard it many times before. He simply looked at the couple and replied. "I simply do my job. If it is not me, it will be someone else."

The old man sneered as he took back his documents. "Captain, someday the Nazi's will turn on you, too, no matter how much you do for them. You will see."

With the last of the passengers on board, Paulo waved at the security officer who closed the fence to the boarding ramp. "Walking back to the ticket office, Paulo looked at the gestapo man standing behind the desk. "Sixty-five ticket holders accounted for."

Although Paulo enjoyed being in the Italian Army, he despised the German Gestapo and S.S. soldiers that dictated policy to the Italian government. They were arrogant and had no respect for the Italian people, or for life in general. They simply were not the type of people you wanted to cross.

That evening after Paulo was relieved, he walked down to a small restaurant near the waterfront that he enjoyed. He had barely sat down at a table when an attractive red-haired woman sat down across from him, holding a drink in her hand.

Looking at the woman, Paulo stated firmly. "I do not believe I invited you to join me, and I would appreciate it very much if you left!"

"Captain Paulo Trevisiani, are you not?" The woman inquired as she sipped from the drink.

Always being aware of gestapo agents that could cause someone serious problems, Paulo replied, "You can tell your superiors that you found me, that I am having the ravioli for my dinner with a red wine, and I am eating alone. Now that you know all of that, please leave me alone."

Smiling slightly, the woman responded. "I am not associated with the gestapo or S.S. I am here because your sister may be in serious trouble."

Paulo frowned as he shook his head. "My sister Claudia is a Benedictine Sister down in Naples. What kind of trouble could she be in?"

After taking a quick look around the room, the woman replied, "I am talking about your sister Dominique. She is the one you need to be concerned about."

"Dominique! She died during the winter of 1920. We searched for her in the mountains most of the winter and into the next summer, but never found her remains. Father figured wolves pulled her up into the mountains somewhere," Paulo replied, almost angrily.

"I don't believe that was the case, Captain. When the Germans threw the sisters out of the Abbey, they were not allowed to take much with them. However, Mother Superior took a large box of files with her that the Germans never went through. One of the documents explained how a poor farmer named Leopoldo Trevisiani from Acqualagna dropped off a five-year-old girl, stating he and his wife Maria could no longer care for her. The child's name was Dominique, and she stayed in the Abbey to become a Benedictine Sister. Are those not the names of your parents, Captain?"

Captain Paulo nodded his head. "Yes, those are the names of my parents, but that could never be. My parents would never have given away their youngest daughter, we all loved her very much."

Reaching into her large purse, the woman pulled out several sheets of paper and handed them to Paulo. "Read for yourself, Captain. I received these documents from a sister that had helped Mother Superior set up her new office after leaving the Abbey."

Slowly, Paulo read through the paperwork before looking back at the woman. "Our Dominique is alive? Why? Why did our parents not tell us. If this is all true, it's abhorrent, it's maddening, and should never have happened. But how do I know this is all true?"

Dominique taught school in Milan for a little over two years. During that time, she became involved with the Italian underground. She had no idea what some of the more ruthless members were up to. One night they attacked a restaurant where high-ranking German and Italian officers were meeting. When it was over, five German officers and one Italian officer were dead.

It did not take long for Major Schneider and his group of gestapo thugs to find out which underground people were involved. Some were killed instantly, but others were tortured for information. Throughout the process, they learned that a priest by the name of Father Alessi was the leader of the group in Milan. Realizing the gestapo was coming for them, Father Alessi warned everyone in the group to scatter. A woman by the name of Carmelo told Dominique to change clothing with her, hand over her documents, and leave Milan immediately. She was not happy about it, but did comply after Father Alessi urged her to do so. The group that escaped with Father Alessi was found in Turin. After a heavy gun fight, the gestapo threw several grenades into the building which caused a fire.

All the bodies were badly burned, including that of Carmelo. However, the gestapo found Dominique's documents on her and were satisfied that they had all the culprits. However, if your sister is ever recognized by any S.S. or gestapo agents, her life will have a very sad and terrifying end. You must find her and get her to safety as soon as possible. We no longer know what happened to her."

Before Paulo could say another word, the woman stood up and laughed. "Thank you for the drink, Captain. It was so nice to see you again. Next time I hope my husband can join us, he always enjoys your humor." Moments later, she stepped out of the restaurant and was gone into the night.

Paulo contemplated everything he had been told and it intrigued him very much. If Dominique were alive, he had to do everything in his power to keep her that way, but finding her was not going to be easy, since he was certain the sisters in the convent would do all they could to keep her away from a snooping Italian captain.

The following morning, he drove his staff car to the convent of Ponte di Ferro, just north of Acqualagna, where the sisters had moved to after being driven out of the Abbey. He was not sure what kind of reception he was about to get, but finding Dominique was all that was on his mind.

Stopping near the front gate to the sprawling garden that surrounded the convent, Paulo observed an older sister sitting on a bench reading from a book. As he entered the courtyard, the sister looked up from her book. "What can I do to help a captain in our Italian army this morning?"

Smiling, Paulo snapped to attention before bowing respectfully. "My name is Captain Paulo Trevisiani. My parents, Leopoldo and Maria delivered my sister…"

Before he could finish, the sister raised her hand. "Oh, so you want to see Bishop Barone. He just arrived last evening. Come I will take you to the church next door, he is staying in a back room."

All of a sudden, Paulo realized he had crossed a serious line and was not sure how this was going to end. Still, he was not about to walk away if he could help it.

Once the huge wooden door to the church slammed shut behind Paulo, the sister turned around to face him. "What are you trying to do, get us all killed? Have you no idea what kind of problems you may create by asking questions like that out in public? Why would you even come here looking for your sister?"

Shaking his head, Paulo looked at the nervous woman. "I apologize, I should not have been so blunt with you in the courtyard. Through my job, I heard the sisters from the Abbey came to Ponte di Ferro after being forced from the Abbey. I just figured Sister Dominique would come back here if she were in some sort of trouble, thinking that you would be willing to help her."

Placing her arms across her chest, the sister said quietly. "You are Sister Dominique's actual brother?"

Nodding his head, Paulo replied. "Yes. I did not know she was alive until just last night. I was told she might be in trouble and may need my help. I lost her once, and do not intend to lose her again, especially to the gestapo."

The sister looked at Paulo intently, and shook her head. "She is in trouble, but Mother Superior has worked out a plan to help her. Wait here, and I shall be back in a few minutes."

Five minutes later, the sister arrived with another sister, about fifty years of age. She looked at Paulo for a minute before asking, "Why should we believe anything you have to say? Did not the Italian army help the Germans in moving us out of our home? Did they care that the Germans are turning our beautiful Abbey into some sort of a massive anti-aircraft and artillery battery? Should we even believe who you are? We may all end up in prison just for talking to you."

"Every concern you have is accurate, Mother Superior. None of us know who we can trust anymore. However, what I have said is the truth as I know it. Dominique is my sister and I must do what I can to save her life, even if it means losing mine."

Mother Superior walked over to the last pew in the church and sat down. After Paulo was seated, she said. "I had been asked repeatedly to supply several of my sisters for a mission in the Solomon Islands, but had always refused. However, with Dominique's life being in jeopardy if she is recognized, I felt this may be the only way to protect her. I asked if she would want the assignment and she agreed. Sister Margaret and Sister Veronica volunteered to go with her to an island called Nusa Simbo. I received a cable when they arrived in Naples from Father Renaldo, the pastor of their mission group. They were to sail from Naples at the end of the week, but that was nearly a month ago. Sorry to say, I have not heard another word since. I just pray they have made it."

Paulo nodded his head. "The gestapo and S.S. have long tentacles, just like an octopus. They will reach out and find their enemies anywhere they can. She will never be truly safe as long as Hitler is in power. I shall go to Naples to see if they left alright."

Reaching over and taking Paulo's hand, Mother Superior said, "Paulo, I understand how important it is for you to find your sister, but you must be more discreet once you leave here. There are too many ears listening to every word being said, and you truly can trust no one."

That evening, Paulo followed the tight twisting highway into the deep Candigliano River gorge west of Acqualagna. Finding a large truck turnout, he parked the car and set it on fire. After changing into civilian clothing, he placed his uniform jacket on a large fence post, along with a hastily written note.

"We have captured the captain and are charging him with war crimes. If you want him back you must deliver two million Lira to the train station in Smirra tomorrow by noon. You will find further instructions there. Signed, la Resistenza."

Paulo ran off into the foothills, heading for the town of Naro where he hoped to find another car that would get him to Naples. Around midnight, he slipped behind the wheel of an old French Peugeot that was parked near a school. Moments later, he was motoring toward Citta di Castello, where he could catch the main highway to Rome and then Naples.

Arriving at Naples, Paulo removed his inspector's uniform from his bag. Walking briskly, as if he were in a hurry, he entered the port office. "I have been sent to inspect your travel vouchers to make sure everything is in order. I am looking for paperwork on a ship that left here about a month ago, heading to an Island named Nusa Simbo."

The agent behind the desk shook his head. "Captain, none of our ships go to the South Pacific islands. Our last stop is Jakarta, and from there passage must be booked on a smaller vessel."

Paulo nodded his head. "I am looking for a ship that sailed from here with a priest and several sisters going to set up a mission on this Nusa Simba."

The agent jumped up from his desk. "Ah yes, I remember that well. The group was led by a Father Renaldo from Rome." After searching through a file cabinet for a moment, the agent pulled out a file. "Here it is. They sailed on the *Rose of Italy*. After handing the file over to Paulo, the agent walked over to pour himself a cup of coffee.

Paulo wasted no time flipping through the documents. Coming across the passenger manifest, he slid his finger slowly down the list until it stopped on a Sister Dominique, Sister Margaret, Sister Veronica and Father Renaldo. Closing the file, Paulo handed it back to the agent.

"Was there a problem, Captain? We pride ourselves on doing the best job we can under these difficult war time issues."

Smiling, Paulo bowed slightly. "No, the paperwork is fine, as I was sure it would be. Thank you for your help."

Walking out of the office, Paulo was delighted to know Dominique had made it out of Italy without a problem, though now he had to figure out how to track her the rest of the way. As a slight drizzle was beginning to fall, Paulo pulled up the collar of his uniform jacket and stepped under a large passenger canopy that led down to the ship that was being prepared for an evening departure. Heavy in thought, Paulo was not paying proper attention to his surroundings. Suddenly, a voice broke the silence.

"Paulo Trevisiani, is that you?"

Turning to his left, he observed a former classmate of his from the Officer's Academy. Trying to act nonchalant, Paulo smiled and shook hands, hoping all was going to go well.

"Paulo, it has been too long. What brings you here to Naples? I figured you had a nice little thing going up in Livorno as you are once again on the promotion list," Captain Bironi said with a smile

Nodding his head, Paulo forced a smile. "Yes, things are well, my friend. I just came down here to Naples seeking a friend of mine that was going to Jakarta. I wanted to visit him before he sailed, but alas, he had already gone."

"Ah, that is great!" Captain Bironi replied. "Then you can join my wife and I for dinner tonight. We will have a great time sharing old stories from our days at the academy."

Although Paulo felt trapped, he knew being at a quiet dinner party with friends was better cover than wandering the streets of Naples, so he heartily agreed.

After a great meal and several bottles of wine, Paulo knew his friend was just slightly more drunk than he was. Leaning forward, Paulo said. "I see you are in the Air Ministry now. What base are you assigned to these days?"

Smiling, Captain Bironi replied. "My wife and I have the best assignment. We are stationed at the huge airfield at Reggio Calabria, directly across from Messina in Sicily. The sands are warm, the temperatures are so mild, and the beaches are glorious. You must come and spend a week with us when you can. I assure you that going back to Livorno will be sorrowful.

Paulo laughed as he slapped his friend on the shoulder. "So, tell me my friend, is there a Portuguese Consulate in Reggio Calabria?"

Captain Bironi's wife laughed. "You mean the Portuguese travel agency? That place is so busy handing out travel documents and Visa's, there is no way they can keep everything straight. We all know that Portugal is the capital of spies, and the largest hub for information traders north of the Mediterranean. Almost anyone can get travel documents, especially if they are wearing a uniform of one of the warring countries."

Paulo smiled, as he had another sip of wine. "Yes, I have heard those stories, but I'm surprised the gestapo hasn't put a stop to it."

Laughing, Captain Bironi replied, "Why would they do that, my friend, when their own people use it more than anyone else."

After leaving the restaurant, Paulo went back to the small room he had rented in the dock area of Naples. Pulling out a road map of Italy, he determined he could make the trip to Reggio Calabria in two days, if he left early the following morning.

Although he had a terrible headache from the wine he had consumed the night before, Paulo was on the highway in his stolen Peugeot by 0400hrs.

Paulo drove around the Portuguese Consulate several times looking for German staff cars before he decided it was safe to go inside. Walking up to a desk where a young woman was working, Paulo sat down.

"Miss, could you help me get travel documents to Libya before going on to Lisbon?"

Looking up from her work, she said, "You are a naval officer. You don't need paperwork to travel to Libya where we have ships at Tripoli. Just go down to the pier and they will let you on any freighter heading in that direction." Removing some documents from her desk, she handed them to Paulo. "When you are ready to go on to Lisbon, fill out these forms and take them to the Consulate, they will get you a ticket."

After thanking the woman several times, Paulo left the consulate and drove down to the pier. Walking up to one of the ticket agents, he said, "I need to go to Tripoli to check on damage to one of our ships, and I cannot wait for one of our naval ships to pick me up."

The man nodded his head. The *Star of Magic* will sail in two hours. As you do not require a cabin, you can board at any time. Good luck, Captain."

Paulo looked back, watching the coast of Italy fade into the distance. He was not sure what would become of him, now that he had left his home and was running from his military responsibility during a time of war, but finding Dominique was now his main priority.

The Port of Tripoli was busy with ships from Italy and Germany bringing much needed war supplies to the German Africa Corp. So Paulo went to a bathroom, and quickly changed from his uniform into civilian clothing.

The sun was setting as the *Star of Magic* settled into its pier. Waiting for a group of passengers to unload, Paulo walked into the middle of the group and quickly made his way down the gang plank. The following morning, he strolled along the pier looking for a ship that was heading farther east. By mid-morning he observed a combination freighter-passenger ship called *The Far Seas*, preparing to leave at noon. Walking into the office, Paulo asked, "How far does *The Far Seas* travel before it turns back?"

The agent looked irritated by the question, but replied. "How many passengers?"

"Just me," Paulo replied, hoping he could still book passage.

"*The Far Seas* only goes as far as Port Suez. Will that work for you?" Taking out a copy of the manifest, he frowned. "Let's make it quick, I must get these documents to the captain in the next half hour!"

Paulo smiled, as he nodded his head. "My name is Lorenzo De Cippio."

After the man scribbled the name on the manifest, he said, "That will be three thousand Lira, and you have cabin number 22. Now go, as I have to lock up the office and deliver the manifest."

As the ship slipped from its berth, Paulo laid back on his bunk and fell asleep. He was closer to Dominique, but there was still a lot of the world to cover, and a good part of it was at war.

Port Suez was a bustling harbor city at the south end of the Suez Canal. There were people there from all over the far east, trading goods and operating steamers to every exotic port a person could think of.

For two days, Paulo searched for a ship that could take him at least to Jakarta, Indonesia. Sadly, he came up empty. Finally, on the third day he observed a smaller ship called *The Jakarta Moon* pulling into the harbor. Instead of going to the port office, Paulo walked up the gang plank of the ship where the captain was making notes on a clip board.

"You need to get off my ship, or I will have you arrested," the captain barked as he pointed back toward the pier.

Seeing the pistol in the captain's waistband, he realized this man meant business. Pulling out his billfold, Paulo said. "I need to go to Jakarta, what will it cost me?"

"I do not deal with traitors, spies or the like. Go buy a ticket like everyone else. If you can get one, I will let you on my ship. Otherwise, you must leave. By the way, Jakarta is not a great place to go now. The Japanese are causing great distress for everyone," the captain replied as he placed his right hand on the butt of his pistol.

Understanding this man could not be bought at any price, Paulo left the ship and found the booking office. After hearing Paulo's request, the clerk shook his head. We no longer book passengers to Jakarta because the Japanese will no longer allow it. Go back to where you came from."

Returning to the ship, Paulo found the captain standing on the dock, drinking a cold bottle of beer. Looking at Paulo, he said. "I hear you are out of luck, passengers can't be ticketed for Jakarta."

Paulo nodded his head. "That appears to be a fact. Look, I really need to get to Jakarta to find a family member, it is very important."

After taking a large swallow of beer, the captain said, "The ship lines force me to make decisions on my own, so I can keep making money. For five thousand Italian Lira, I will take you."

That amount really hurt, so Paulo countered the price. "I will give you forty-five hundred Lira, and that is all."

The captain laughed. "You can have cabin ten. We do not sail until morning, so get on the ship and stay there. We do not wait for anyone, and Port Suez can be a dangerous place."

Just as the sun was rising over the horizon, *The Jakarta Moon* sailed into the Gulf of Suez on a southerly course. Paulo was not sure as to what he would run into, but for the first time he took his German Luger out of his suitcase and placed it in his waist band, under his extra-long shirt.

The five-day voyage was excruciating as the seas were rough and storm clouds dumped heavy rain and hail, day after day. Arriving in Jakarta, the harbor was filled with several types of Japanese war ships. All along the pier, armed Japanese soldiers patrolled, keeping a close eye on everything and everybody. Throughout long evenings of conversation and wine, Paulo had built up a good relationship with the captain, and now was the time to use it.

The captain had stationed himself near the gang plank, exactly where Paulo had first seen him. Walking up to the officer who was wearing a highly starched set of uniform whites, Paulo inquired. "Sir, how do I get to Port Moresby from here?"

Turning toward Paulo, he said. "Port Moresby is under control of the Australian and American Forces. Only military supply ships can sail into the harbor now. And that is if a Japanese submarine does not sink you first. No captain worth his salt will sail into those waters, and yes, that includes me! I will not sail back to Port Suez for two days. You are welcome to stay on board until then if you like."

The day before *The Jakarta Moon* was to sail, Paulo found a small steamer that was carrying supplies to several islands west of Port Moresby. The skipper of the vessel was Australian, and had two of his crew disappear so he was willing to take on anyone that would work. Paulo took the job, hoping to make the best of it. Although they were tailed by a Japanese destroyer all the way to Tenggara, Paulo felt quite comfortable as the skipper assured him they were not carrying any military contraband. Their next stops were small islands named Wetar and Banda Neira. From there they turned north to Maluku where they unloaded in the harbor of Piru, Indonesia. The harbor was under control of the Japanese and they watched each worker like a hawk.

After all the supplies were unloaded, Paulo walked up to a Japanese sailor who was patrolling the pier. "Do you know of Nusa Simbo Island?"

"It is west of the main Solomon Islands. There is nothing there but a banana plantation. Why do you ask?"

Paulo shook his head, "No special reason. A friend of mine was going there to work. I thought I might try and visit him."

"The island is all but blockaded. Only the supply ship can get there, and that is only if we allow it to travel there. You are already in the war zone, so you can go no farther," the sailor replied, as he stared at Paulo, unsure whether he should be trusted or not.

The morning his ship was to sail, Paulo walked up to the skipper of the ship. "Take me to Thursday Island!"

"No can do, mate, Thursday is controlled by the Australian Navy and Air Force. They will sink us before we get close to the island."

"Then take me to Darwin, Australia!" Paulos demanded, unsure of how the skipper and the rest of the crew would respond. He was happy to find out three of the crew were more than happy to end up in Darwin, so the skipper gave in, knowing he would have problems with the Australian Navy.

About two hours out of Darwin, a Japanese submarine surfaced and ordered the ship to stop for inspection. The skipper looked at Paulo who was standing next to him on the bridge. "We have no load for Darwin, and we have no documents allowing us to sail into Darwin. I'm telling you we are in serious trouble, and may well end up in a Japanese prison camp before this day is over."

"Then we run, Skipper. Put the engines in high speed and make a run for Darwin," Paulo directed, as he held his pistol on the skipper.

"Run? Are you crazy? We can't outrun that sub, they'll blow us right out of the water!"

Stepping forward, one of the other men wanting to go to Darwin said, "You heard Paulo. We run, now let's go!"

As the skipper watched Japanese sailors climb out onto the deck of the submarine, he threw his throttles forward. The Japanese sailors stood in disbelief as they watched thick black smoke billow from the smoke stack of the old freighter.

Immediately, the captain of the Japanese submarine ordered men on the bow to fire a shell across the bow of the freighter. Seconds later, a shell exploded about fifty yards off the port side of the old ship, sending a geyser of water into the air.

The skipper of the freighter looked at Paulo, "The next one will be nearly on top of us, and the one after that will blow us out of the water. We need to cooperate before we're all killed!"

Paulo shook his head, "Continue running, Skipper. Get on the radio and call for help from the Australian Navy."

"Do you see any Australian war ships on the horizon, Paulo? This old scow will be at the bottom of the Arafura Sea before any friendly war ships can do us any good," the skipper yelled as he watched the Japanese sailors load another round into their cannon.

Seconds later, the bow of the freighter was awash with water as the shell exploded a mere ten feet from the ship. The sailors on the bow of the sub wasted no time loading a third round as they were sure now the skipper of the freighter was not going to stop. A moment later, a five inch round slammed into the fore deck of the freighter, blowing a large hole into the hull on the port side. Immediately, water rushed into the hold, causing the bow to begin to drop down into the ocean.

The skipper pulled back on the throttles, bringing the ship to a stop. "It's over, Paulo. Now let's see if they rescue us, or let us float off to our deaths."

The captain of the sub brought his vessel up close to the freighter as the crew was already boarding life boats. To his surprise, the captain of the submarine allowed the crew of the freighter to sit on the aft deck as he began a northerly turn. In the distance, the old freighter slowly rolled over on its port side, as broken steam pipes hissed, and steel girders bent and groaned under the weight of the sea water that continued to pour in. Soon, all that was left was the bubbling churning water where the ship had disappeared under the waves.

Several hours later, the crew of the freighter were back on Maluku, but this time under guard of Japanese soldiers. For nearly ten days, the crew stayed in what had been an old warehouse used for storing sugar cane before the war. Finally, a Japanese landing ship arrived in Piru, Indonesia. The prisoners were loaded aboard the vessel and taken to Japan for the duration of the war. They originally spent time in a camp near Tokyo, until American aircraft began bombing raids. They were then transferred to a several other camps where they were used as slave labor to cut down trees, work in mines or build miles of new railroad tracks that fed the war factories.

Paulo felt bad when the skipper of the freighter was killed in a mining cave in about a year after they arrived in Japan. Several more crew members were also killed in different types of work-related accidents.

Eventually, Paulo and seven other crew members were assigned to a new prisoner of war stockade, Camp 45, about fifteen miles from Hiroshima. By this time, it was clear the tides of war had begun turning against Japan, and they wanted to have as many prisoners to swap with the allies if negotiations for peace began. There were two other large camps in the area, one strictly for military prisoners, and another camp like the one Paulo was in, for political prisoners or captured civilians. It was called Camp 46.

Chapter Eight – A Beginning

It did not take long for all the residents of Mengge to find out three sisters and a Catholic Priest were once again on the island. The sisters were inundated by requests from parents to get their children back into some type of school, and many island natives wanted their children to learn how to read and write. So, schedules would need to be created by the sisters to accommodate everyone that wanted to attend school. Knowing the temperature and humidity in the tropics was going to be unbearable for the sisters with their long habits, Father Renaldo had a seamstress in Italy make knee length brown dresses, including a short veil that could be attached to their hair with bobby pins. When the crate was opened displaying their new wardrobe, the three women were ecstatic, as they were already getting a taste of what life would be like under the heavy brown habits they traditionally wore.

It was clear that the church was far too small to hold everyone that wanted to attend services again, so Father Renaldo needed to add a second service on Sunday mornings, a problem he was all too happy to solve.

Once a month, a smaller inter-island supply ship arrived from New Caledonia, dropping off everything that was requested the month before, along with the regular food, medicine, and supply shipments. It was always a big day when the ship arrived, and Mr. Duncan supplied trucks from the plantation to help get the goods from the ship to where they belonged.

Fishing played a big part of the food supply on the island, as there was a small fishing fleet that went out each morning to see what they could catch. As there was a strong current surrounding the island, many types of fish rested in the small coves on the north side, allowing the crews to bring in a bountiful catch. However, as Simbo Islet was separated from the rest of the island by a deep and narrow channel, sharks loved to feed on the smaller fish that sought refuge there. People that chose to swim in the channel were frequently attacked by the hungry predators, which all too often ended in death.

The islet was connected to the main island by a hundred yard long heavily constructed log bridge at the west side of the channel. Most often, the only traffic that crossed the bridge was concerned with the banana plantation.

A week after arriving on the island, Sister Dominique was sitting in prayer on a hill above the village, when she observed an Australian destroyer sailing slowly up the south coast of the island. She watched curiously as several men crawled into a life boat before it was lowered into the water. Quickly, Sister Dominique ran down to the village, calling for Father Renaldo who was working in the small vegetable garden with the other sisters.

Looking up, he called out, "What is it, Sister? What is going on?"

"Come, you must come with me, all of you!" She called out over her shoulder, as she raced toward the cove where the lifeboat was about to enter.

After several sailors jumped from the boat and secured it to the pier, three officers disembarked and walked onto the island. Sister Dominique had barely stopped running when the officers approached her.

Smiling broadly, a lieutenant held out his hand, "Lieutenant Billingsly, Australian Royal Navy at your service. Can you tell me who is in charge here?"

Sister Dominique, neither offering her hand or smiling, replied, "You may leave, Lieutenant. We will not be a part of this evil war that appears to be taking over the world. You can turn around and march right back onto that boat and depart Nusa Simbo. We are neutral now and shall remain so. I have had my fill of the belligerent parties in this war, and want nothing more to do with any of you!"

Father Renaldo stepped forward, holding up his hand. "Wait one moment, Sister Dominique. Before you single handedly throw these men off the island, I think it's fair to see why they have come here to speak with us. Don't you agree, Sister?"

"No, I do not. They represent the warring parties, and their presence here will signal the Japanese that we are taking sides. They must leave!" Sister Dominique said angrily, as she glared at Father Renaldo.

Before either of them could say another word, Lt. Billingsly spoke up.

"We are here representing the Queen of England. It is essential that we place a coast watching station on the Mountain overlooking the north side of Nusa Simbo. The crown will pay you a stipend if you shall allow it. There will only be two men, a large tent, and a small, but powerful radio. Their presence shall also be an early warning system for you if the Japanese approach your island."

"We do not need your stipend or an early warning system, Lieutenant. As far as approaching Japanese ships goes, the ocean belongs to no one, and they are as free to sail on it as you are. So now go back to your ship, pull up your anchor, and leave us alone. This is not our war, nor shall it be!" Sister Dominique replied as she began to shake in anger.

Father Renaldo remembered mother superior had placed Sister Dominique in charge before they left the Abbey, but he was not sure if that authority gave her power to control diplomatic relations with other countries. After all, Sister Dominique had never been one to be very diplomatic about much of anything. He wanted to discuss it with her, but also realized she did make some good points regarding their neutrality and desire to stay out of the war. In the end, he looked up at the angry lieutenant and said, "Please give our regards to the Queen, but also tell her we are turning down her request to place a coast watcher station on Nusa Simbo. Maybe our neighbors to the north on Ranongga Island may take up your offer."

Taking a step forward, the officer glared at Sister Dominique. "The day will come when the war will overtake Nusa Simbo, and you will find yourself right in the middle of it with no one to defend you. Believe me, Sister, it will happen!"

Not being intimidated, Sister Dominique also took a step forward and glared right back. "If the war does come here, we will have God to defend us. He is much more powerful than your Royal Navy. Now please get off our island before the Japanese see your ship."

Turning toward his fellow officers, Lt. Billingsly nodded his head, "Our business here is completed, let's return to the ship."

Once the lifeboat had left the cove, Sister Dominique was overwhelmed. As she turned to return to her hut, she found that nearly a hundred island natives and plantation workers had assembled behind her. As she began to walk, the crowd let out a whoop and cheered as they all approved of her showdown with the Australian Navy.

Several weeks later, as school was over for the day, Sister Dominique spied a small native boy that had been absent all day long waiting for his sister. Walking up to him, she asked, "Anaru, where have you been all day? If you do not come to school, you will not learn how to read."

Anaru stood motionless as he looked down at the ground. Sister Dominique knelt down in front of Anaru, placing her hand under his chin. Raising his head, she looked into his eyes. "Anaru, tell me what is going on with you. I can sense fear, and I sense it in you right now."

Placing his arms around Sister Dominique's neck, he began to cry. "I went to the mountain this morning to pick flowers for my mother's birthday. When I neared the highest peak, I was grabbed by a man. He told me to leave and never come back, and not to tell anyone he was there. He scared me, Sister. He was carrying a big rifle and a machete."

Brushing back Anaru's dark black hair, Sister Dominique asked, "What else can you tell me about the man? What was he wearing, was he Japanese?"

"He spoke like the men that came on the boat a few weeks ago. He has skin like yours, and was wearing clothes that looked like jungle leaves," Anaru replied.

Not quite sure of what to make of it, Sister Dominique replied, "Can you take us there?"

Anaru shook his head. "I do not want to go back there. They will harm me or throw me over the cliff to the sharks. They are scary men!"

Realizing Anaru had been somewhat traumatized by his experience with the man, she replied, "You only have to show us from a distance, and then you can hide and we will do the rest. Can you do that for me?"

Nodding his head, Anaru replied, "You should not go alone, they may hurt you, too."

Smiling, Sister Dominique replied, "No, we will not go alone, we will have plenty of help."

After informing Father Renaldo, the other sisters, and the tribal leaders of what she had learned from Anaru, a group of twelve men, along with Sister Dominique and Sister Margaret, would go to the mountain hide out.

They were nearing the point on the north coast where the mountain dropped off toward the ocean, when Anaru stopped them. "There by the two big rocks where the flowers bloom is where the man grabbed me. We must be very close."

Sister Margaret was about to take Anaru by the arm to lead him safely back into the jungle, when she pointed out a large black pipe with an antenna on top of it near the rocks.

Working their way quietly around the rocks, the tribal leaders found two men laying on the ground behind a log, peering out into the ocean with binoculars. In the corner of the make shift tent behind them, Sister Dominique saw a radio in a canvas satchel that said, "Property Australian Navy."

Carefully picking up a small rock, Father Renaldo tossed it right between the two men. They spun around quickly as they attempted to grab their pistols. Seeing the natives around them with spears and a World War One British Enfield rifle, they dropped their weapons.

With everything under control, Sister Dominique walked forward. "I told Lt. Billingsly the Australian Navy was not welcome here on our mountain. So, please tell me how you got here, and I want to know now, or our men will toss that radio set off the cliff."

Shaking his head and holding up his hand as if to surrender, the older of the two men stood up. My name is Staff Sergeant Willy King, His Majesties Royal Fusiliers. We arrived six days ago by submarine on the south side of the island. As you are now well aware, we were told to watch the straits below this cliff for Japanese air or ship movements. Lt. Billingsly said that once we were actively involved on the island and caused no problems, you would eventually agree to leave us alone. That attitude has worked well on many other islands where there are missionaries."

Father Renaldo stepped out of the shadows. "Threatening a young boy collecting flowers for a birthday bouquet for his mother, doesn't sound like causing no problems."

Folding her arms across her chest, Sister Dominique asked, "Who threatened the boy?"

Looking down at the ground for a moment, Sergeant King replied, "That would have been me, Sister. I'm sorry."

"So, you are nothing more than a bully. I do not believe your King would appreciate having bullies in his vaunted Fusiliers. So. Sergeant, if you are a big bad bully when it comes to children, do you think you can bully a poor little charitable sister?"

Knowing he was going to lose this argument anywhere it went, Sgt. King took a deep breath. "No, Sister. And I don't even wish to attempt it. If you will allow me to do so, I will radio HQ and have them send out a sub to pick us up later tonight. We will have them send a raft into the cove and be off your island well before dawn."

Nodding her head. Sister Dominique smiled. "That would be splendid, Sergeant. And give my best to Lt. Billingsly."

The two men went to work breaking down their tent and packing up their equipment without saying a word. When they were ready to move down the mountain back toward the village, Sgt. King walked up to Sister Dominique. Handing her a commando knife, he said. "Please give this to the young scalawag as a peace offering. I never meant to scare the boy."

Taking the knife, Sister Dominique replied, "Understood. Stay safe, Sergeant."

About 0130hrs., a rubber raft being paddled by two men arrived in the cove. Without saying a word, the Fusiliers climbed on board and took up two more oars. Moments later, the raft disappeared into the darkness of the ocean. About ten minutes later everyone near the cove could hear a large hissing sound as the submarine flooded its ballast tanks and once more slipped beneath the surface of the ocean.

Once more, Nusa Simbo returned to normal, although Father Renaldo spent countless night time hours monitoring the short-wave radio to see if there were any messages regarding Nusa Simbo on the Japanese frequencies.

The only message he received was concern from a meteorologist on the island of New Caledonia, about fourteen hundred miles to the southeast, regarding a typhoon that was roaring across the Solomon Sea from the Bismark Archipelago at about forty miles per hour. His estimate was that it would reach Nusa Simbo in about four days.

The following morning, Father Renaldo called a meeting to inform them all of the approaching storm. Everything that couldn't be tied down was taken to several caves in the mountain where they would be safe from the destructive winds.

Most of the natives began taking cover in the caves two days before the storm was to hit, as heavy wind and driving rain were already striking the island. Father Renaldo, the sisters and many of the plantation workers, took cover in the basement of one of the processing plants near Ove. Although

Sister Dominique felt she was mentally prepared for what was to come, it quickly became obvious that there was nothing that could prepare a person for the horrifying experience that was about to ravage the island.

The typhoon howled and roared like a prehistoric monster determined to rip the roof off the shelter. Wind driven rain began permeating the shelter from every small crack, scaring the children as well as many adults. As a large palm tree was twisted lose from its roots, it slammed into the roof of the building, creating a tremendous crash. Children screamed and huddled close against their parents, screaming for the storm to stop. However, one little girl named Sophia bolted from her mother's arms and ran toward the steel door at the far end of the basement. Before anyone could grab her, she slid open the bolt and pushed the heavy door open. As she disappeared into the pitch black stormy night, windswept rain and debris flew into the basement, creating mass hysteria.

Before Father Renaldo and several other men could grab the heavy door to secure it once more, Sister Veronica charged out into the eye of the storm in search of the child.

Sister Dominique screamed as she rose from the floor in an attempt to stop the young woman from fleeing the safety of the basement. It took Pierre Duncan and several other men to hold her back before she too disappeared into the dangerous night. Sister Margaret ran over, taking hold of Sister Dominique as she wept and called out for Sister Veronica, over and over.

With the door secured, Father Renaldo took Sister Dominique over to a large unoccupied bench and sat her down. "There is nothing you can do for Veronica now but pray she will be alright. If you go out there, you too will be lost forever and we cannot afford that. Pray with me, Sister. Pray with me."

Sister Dominique shook her head, "I was not to lose any of my charges, this was not supposed to happen, Father. I have failed the ones that were given to me by Mother Superior."

Placing Sister Dominique's head on his shoulder, he replied. "It was God's will that she went after the scared girl. Did not God talk about the shepherd that left his flock to search for the one lamb that was missing. Likewise, Sister

Veronica went in search of a lost lamb. You must accept that there was nothing you could have done to stop her. Just pray that she is found alive."

By mid-afternoon the following day, the storm had moved on out over the Pacific and small shafts of sunlight were beginning to shine down on Nusa Simbo. After pushing hard on the steel door that had been blocked by debris, the men were able to allow the fresh air to flow into the basement.

Everyone paused as they stared at a new landscape they had never experienced before. Most of the banana trees near the coast were gone, along with countless palm trees. Several of the processing and packaging buildings were totally smashed. Small lakes of water occupied low spots around the plantation, where dead birds and other jungle creatures floated.

Turning to Father Renaldo, Sister Dominique said, "Where do we start looking for Sister Veronica?"

Over hearing the question, Pierre Duncan walked over. "In all truthfulness, Sister, she may have been blown out in the ocean along with the child. We may have to set our minds to the fact that neither of them will ever be seen again."

Looking very angry, Sister Dominique replied, "No, I cannot accept that attitude. We must search the island. We must look for her. Surely, she took cover somewhere, now it is our job to find her!"

Father Renaldo shook his head. "Look around you, Sister. Some of the downed trees are stacked two and three high. We do not have the equipment to move such heavy monsters. What we must do now is go back to the village and attempt to rebuild our huts, and see what condition the church and school are in. God will provide for Sister Veronica.

Surprisingly, as the village was down in a depression, most of the huts had sustained little damage, except for missing palm branches on the roofs, which were easily repaired by the native men.

However, each evening Sister Dominique and Ozamis searched a new part of the island, looking for the remains of Sister Veronica and the little girl. It was tough going as many of the trails were washed out by the tremendous rainfall, or were now blocked by fallen trees.

When the next supply boat arrived from New Caledonia, Sister Dominique handed the captain an envelope. "Please make sure this gets in the mail as soon as you can. My Mother Superior in Italy will want to know what happened to Sister Veronica."

The captain nodded his head. "Consider it done, Sister. Again today, we searched along the west coast where it's rockier and a body could get caught up, but we saw nothing but logs and banana trees."

It was nearly a month after the storm had passed that two boys out collecting coconuts discovered the remains of the girl under a fallen tree. Just about everyone from the village searched the area for the next three days, looking for some sign of Sister Veronica, but always came up empty.

As normal, Sister Margaret walked down to the pier with many of the children as the supply ship arrived from New Caledonia. She never knew what might be unloaded, and she enjoyed keeping the anxious children out of the way of the workers, as the ships crane set down the heavy pallets on the pier. But today was going to be different from any other supply ship that had arrived in a long time.

As the crane whirled and men attached ropes and chains to the massive hooks, the skipper of the boat everyone knew so well escorted a woman dressed in a dark brown habit up to the crowd of excited children.

"I think she belongs to you, Sister Margaret. I didn't know until we were about to sail that we were bringing her along." Turning to the new missionary, the skipper said. "Best of luck, Sister. I hope all goes well for you."

While shaking hands, the new sister said. "I am glad to meet you, Sister Margaret. I am Sister Claudia from Naples. I had wanted to be assigned to a foreign mission for a long time, so when I heard what happened to Sister Veronica, I immediately volunteered to come and replace her. Your Mother Superior was most gracious in allowing me to fill the vacancy."

Sister Margaret smiled, "Welcome to Nusa Simbo, Sister. Yes, we had a very serious storm come through here and create a lot of damage, but Mr. Duncan, the manager of the plantation, has many contacts around the Pacific. With material and equipment arriving quickly, things are getting back to normal sooner than we could ever have expected. Now, come with me, I will introduce you to Sister Dominique and Father Renaldo."

Approaching the school, Sister Margaret laughed. "When the skipper of the supply ship blows his whistle, the children run to the pier, there is no holding them back. Once the boat leaves, they will all return to their classrooms like nothing ever happened."

Sister Claudia was about to laugh at the story, but froze solidly in her tracks, unable to speak. She watched in complete disbelief at the woman walking toward them from the school. Gasping, she took hold Sister Margaret's arm as she felt as if her knees might buckle. She couldn't breathe, and her heart felt as if it were going to explode as tears flowed down her cheeks. Gathering every ounce of energy she could muster, she yelled out, "Dommy, is that you? Are you a ghost?"

Sister Dominique had not heard the word Dommy since the day before her father had taken her to the Abbey. It was the pet name her sisters had always called her since she was born. Shaking uncontrollably, Sister Dominique ran and stumbling the last few feet, she grabbed her sister and held her tight in her arms. As tears rolled down her face, she struggled to speak. "Claudia, my sweet Claudia. Where have you come from? Is this some sort of an evil joke?"

Kissing her sister on the cheek, Claudia responded. "God has sent me here, and I was not sure why. But now everything is clear, for he wanted me to find you."

Although Claudia had never been happier, a sense of anger welled up deep inside of her. Realizing she and her siblings had been lied to their entire lives, the pain was excruciating. Here in front of her was the sister she had searched for with her brother Paulo on so many cold winter nights. Here was the little sister she thought she had heard calling for help so many nights that her mother wouldn't allow her to sleep alone, fearing Claudia would wander out into the cold black night searching and be lost forever. Here on this island was the thread that had held their family together through many bad times. Dominique's disappearance had broken that thread and thrown the family into a chaos that could never be repaired. It was clear to her now. All the lies, pain and distrust had turned their parents against one another, draining them of all love and spirit, leaving them nothing more than cold empty shells that would never find peace the rest of their lives.

Looking down at the table in the conference room, as tears flowed down her wrinkled, weathered cheeks, Sister Dominique forced a smile at the students that were hanging on every word she had told them. After drying her eyes, she looked over at the window where the gathering dusk was beginning to draw the long day to an end. After recomposing herself, Sister Dominique said. "Here is where we end for today. I must go back to my room and prepare for evening prayers. Sister Constance will contact you when I am ready to continue. Tonight, I must deal with these emotions I have suppressed for such a long time."

As sister Constance led the students out of the conference room, Sister Dominique rolled her wheel chair over to the window once more. Now all was quiet in the courtyard, as all the birds and squirrels had retreated to their shelters for the long cold night that was upon them. But once again, for Sister Dominique, the cold winter that still lingered in her heart was almost more than she could bear.

Staring up at the heavy leaden clouds that began to cover the night sky, Sister Dominique took in a deep breath. As Sister Constance reappeared, Sister Dominique pointed toward the dark, wind driven clouds. Looking over her shoulder, she looked up at the young sister that stood beside her.

"They hide the grandeur of God's creation of the moon and countless stars that cover the heavens, but still, they serve a purpose in the plan of our unending universe. Sister, do you think those clouds are anything like the pain that blotted out the love my parents lost after they gave me away? There was always an opportunity to change what they had done, what kept them from changing their course and rebuilding our lives? Was it human pride? Was it the shame of what they had done? Could they not face up to it with their children, for fear of being rejected?"

Sister Constance sat down in a large black leather chair that sat up against the wall. "I did not know your parents of course, but it took incredible strength to make the decision to bring you to the Abbey. The unanswered question is whether the decision was made with mutual consent. Did the light go out in their hearts because they agreed they had to give you away, or did the light go out because of pure animosity towards one another that could never be repaired.?"

After rolling the wheelchair partly across the room, Sister Dominique turned once more to face Sister Constance. "You have a degree in psychology, Sister. Which of the two do you think it was? I like to think that my mother was not in agreement with this plan to let me go, and that my father persisted until she caved in, but I can never know for sure. They were both strong willed people."

Sister Constance stood up, walking slowly toward the wheelchair. When she was in front of Sister Dominique, she knelt down to face her. "Ninety-four years later, your heart is still unsettled and your soul searches for the truth, a truth you may never find. It appears that Claudia was never able to shed light on the facts that keep you from finding the answers you most desire. I fear you may never find those answers in this mortal life. God has kept those answers from you for a reason, and we cannot question what his plans for you were then, or now, or why this all happened. Like all things in his creation, we must accept his judgment and understand he has done what was right."

Placing her hand on the young woman's cheek, Sister Dominique smiled. "You are a smart young woman, and possibly understand this entire world better than I do after a hundred years of bumping into the ghosts that haunt this old soul. I quit with the students today because I was troubled, but now I am ready to proceed with my story. Let's meet again on Monday before I am brought home and am never able to finish."

As Sister Dominique turned her wheelchair back to the courtyard, she shook her head. "And today, once again we opened the story of Sister Veronica. I have always wondered what happened to her, why was she swept away from me, why was her brilliant light snuffed out without a trace. Was her death painful, or was it quick? I have always prayed she did not suffer. I was sure we would find her body so she could be given a proper burial, but that was also never meant to be. So many things, never meant to be."

Chapter Nine – Caught in the Middle

Monday afternoon, Sister Dominique rolled her wheelchair into the conference room where Sister Constance and her students had gathered once again. After setting the brake on her chair, Sister Dominique said, "Well, it's nice to see you all again, and I thank you for being here and being patient with me. Now, can anyone tell me where we left off on Friday, as my mind was in a bit of a blur when we departed."

A senior by the name Anna, who was in charge of the project, spoke up. "You had just met your sister after she'd walked off the supply ship. I have thought about nothing else all weekend. I can only imagine what kind of a shock that must have been."

Nodding her head, Sister Dominique smiled. "That is a wonderful place to start, as life began to change on the island shortly after her arrival, and sorry to say, it was not for the good."

The evening Claudia arrived, the two of us spent several hours together, catching up. She told me that my mother had passed away during the flu season of 1937, and my father dug deeper into himself, and became even more withdrawn and angry.

Paulo left the farm during that time and much to my regret, joined the Italian Army. It was apparent to me before I left the Abbey, that Mussolini was not the man you wanted to follow, but millions of young men decided he was the man that would make Italy great again. The last time Claudia received a letter from him he was a sergeant leading an infantry platoon in North Africa.

My sister Giana had run off before my mother died and married a doctor in Sicily she had met while in school. Apparently, they still live there and have several children. She has never contacted Claudia since then.

My father was shot and killed by an underground team when he attempted to inform the German Gestapo of their activities near Acqualagna. The farm was seized by the government and resold to the highest bidder about a month after his death.

Claudia was going to follow Giana to Sicily, but became very sick with the flu and was taken care of by the Sisters in Naples. After recovering, she decided to join their convent. So now you know what happened to my family. A family that was once filled with love and caring, ended up being separated by anger and mistrust.

Well, let me see, Sister Claudia quickly filled the shoes left vacant by the death of Sister Veronica, and was willing to take on any mission Father Renaldo handed to her. We once again became good friends and loved being with one another.

Early one morning while the children were having their recess time, we heard the sound of an aircraft engine circling near the island. Using our binoculars, Father Renaldo identified the aircraft as a Japanese float plane. Every day over the next several weeks, the plane would circle the island slowly from an altitude of about a thousand feet. Both Father Renaldo and Mr. Duncan figured the man in the back seat was taking reconnaissance photos of the island. When the supply ship arrived a week later, the captain told us they had been followed by a Japanese submarine for two straight days and nights, but the sub never surfaced or caused them problems.

The worst thing that happened that day, was that one of the native men on the island traded a crew member of the boat two gold coins for a dreaded German Schmeisser machine gun, and several loaded magazines. He was proud of his purchase and carried it around the island day and night, pretending to be our protector. In the end, it would be our downfall.

No one on the island had been using the radio for several days, so there was no way anyone could have heard the news regarding the attack on Pearl Harbor on the island of Oahu in the Hawaiian Islands. We did not know until the tenth of December that Japan, the United States, England, Italy and Germany were all at war. The second world war was well underway, and the

Japanese were trying to decide if they should invade us, or just keep an eye on our quiet island.

Soon, the Japanese planes began flying directly over the island at nearly tree top level, with the co-pilot photographing our every move. When we heard the planes were coming, we would have the children run out of the school, stand on the playground and wave and cheer at the pilots. We figured a sign of good will could go a long way with the Japanese commanders at Truk and Rabaul that were monitoring everything that happened in the Solomon Islands.

One morning in January, a worker for Mr. Duncan claimed he observed an American aircraft carrier and its escort ships south of Nusa Simbo, sailing on a westerly course. We figured it was either headed for Port Moresby, New Guinea Brisbane, Australia, or searching the waters deeper in the South Pacific to map out Japanese ship movements.

Although Mr. Duncan now kept up round the clock watches on the high ground on both ends of the island, we did not see another American war ship until May of 1942. During the night of May first, from the high points of the island we could see large flashes of light on the water south of Nusa Simbo, and once in a while, we could hear the rolling thunder of large naval guns. There were some days we could hear the report of large explosions during the day, and the nights were very quiet.

According to short wave radio broadcasts from Australia, the United States and Japan were having an all-out battle in the Coral Sea, in an attempt to protect the sacred supply lines from the United States that were keeping Australia in the war.

On May 8, 1942, when the battle supposedly ended, we observed three American destroyers sailing toward the Solomon Islands from the south. They sailed into a large rain squall near Wilson Passage and we never saw them again. But by late summer, Australian Radio was reporting the United States had invaded an island named Guadalcanal in the southeast Solomon Islands, and it appeared the Americans were here to stay.

Although Nusa Simbo did not have enough flat land to build an auxiliary airfield like the Japanese enjoyed building throughout the islands, we had the deep cove on the south side of the island that was perfect for Japanese float planes to operate from. Plus, the island had a good look out position on each end of the island. We were certain it was just a matter of time before we had a visit from the Japanese military, and we were right.

In late May, two Japanese destroyers and an amphibious landing ship arrived near the island. The destroyers dropped anchor off the southern coast, as the landing ship slowly made its way into the cove. With the ramp down, a large contingency of Japanese Marines made their way ashore, driving back everyone that had approached the pier. Finally, a very distinguished looking colonel walked forward with his body guards. Stopping in front of one of the native men, he asked. "Who is in charge here? Where are the missionaries. Get them now!"

Quickly, the native ran toward the church where Father Renaldo and Sister Dominique had already gathered. It was clear to see the officer was impatient and that his marines were liable to shoot anyone they felt were a hazard to their operation. To avoid any problems, Sister Dominique ran down toward the pier, as Father Renaldo took off to find the chief who usually worked at the banana plantation.

Approaching the colonel, Sister Dominique bowed respectfully. Standing straight, she said, "I am Sister Dominique, a Benedictine Sister. I am in charge of the mission here on Nusa Simbo. What may I do to help you?"

The colonel looked disapprovingly at the woman standing in front of him wearing such a shabby brown dress. "I am Colonel Mizawa, territorial governor for the empire of Japan." Pointing back toward the church, he asked, "Who was the man in black that ran away when you came to see me? Is he a combatant?"

"Oh no, that was Father Renaldo our priest. He went to get the island chief that works up at the plantation. They should be back here in a few minutes," Sister Dominique responded, feeling they were off to a good start.

Turning his head from left to right, the colonel inquired. "How many Australian Coast watchers are on the island and where are they set up. We will remove them today."

"There are no Australian Coast watchers on the island, although Pierre Duncan, the owner of the plantation, has set up watching stations on both sides of the island so we know who's in the area. I assure you they are not for military purposes," Sister Dominique replied, fully realizing their happier days on the island were about to come to an end.

Finally, Father Renaldo and the chief walked up to the colonel and bowed. Nodding his head in approval, the colonel began, "As of today, Nusa Simbo is under protection of the Imperial Japanese Navy. We can either occupy your island, or we can take your word that you will comply with all Japanese Military dictates without question. If you harbor any American, Australian, British or New Zealand forces on the island, you can be shot for disloyalty. We will make intermittent inspections to assure you are cooperating. Do you have any questions?"

Father Renaldo stated, "Our supply ship has different crew members on it each time it visits. We do not know them or from what countries they come. How are we to deal with that?"

"As long as they do not stay here, or are used to transfer military information during their visits, you have nothing to fear from us. But Father, do not attempt to deceive us. We stop the supply ships and search them regularly," the colonel responded coldly.

Looking over at the chief, the colonel said, "Take my men to your look out points so we may know where they are."

As the chief led the Marines up into the hills, Sister Dominique offered the colonel a cup of tea as she was just brewing some hot water. There was clearly a moment of mistrust on the part of the colonel as he hesitated to reply. Finally, he nodded his head, and followed Sister Dominique and Father Renaldo over to the church.

As Sister Dominique filled the officers cup, she said. "We have to drink what the supply ship brings us. I preferred the tea in Italy, as it was of better quality."

The colonel nodded his head after taking the first sip of the hot liquid. "This is acceptable, and I appreciate your hospitality." He was quiet for a moment before looking up toward the sky. "You must remember, we cannot have any discipline problems within the islands or we will need to occupy them and send you all off to a prison camp, and we do not wish to do that. Marshall law is now in effect everywhere in the Solomon's, and anyone choosing to cause us problems may be executed on the spot. You must understand these rules for your own safety." After placing his empty cup on an old packing crate, he stood up. "I thank you for the tea, and hope we have all come to an understanding."

Father Renaldo smiled as he stood up. "I assure you, Colonel, we do not wish to have problems with you. We wish to continue to lead the quiet life we have here on Nusa Simbo."

Smiling, the Colonel waved for his guards to lead him back toward the ship. Moments later, his men that went to check on the watching stations returned to the pier. After speaking to the men, the colonel turned to Sister Dominique. "Everything appears to be in order and is satisfactory. My sergeant says he saw the plantation's short wave radio and feels it is being used properly."

Without another word, the colonel returned to the landing ship with his men. Moments later, it was easy to hear the sound of anchor chains being lifted from the sea as the destroyers prepared to sail on to their next destination. According to the watching point near the plantation, the ships sailed off toward the northeast in the direction of Blackett Straits.

To say the least, it had been a very unnerving day for everyone on the island, especially Sister Dominique. It was evident there was no place for airfields to be constructed, but she had watched several men near the ship making drawings of the cove, and pointing out areas among the village while notating them on the rough map they were making. With the plantation and high observation points on the island, she was certain it was only a matter of time before the Japanese decided to occupy Nusa Simbo.

From that point on, low flying Japanese float planes made daily passes over the island at varied times of the day, keeping a close eye on activities. Several times, spotters on the north side of the island reported Japanese aircraft carriers sailing in the channel between Nusa Simbo and Ranongga Island. Every time they were in the channel, the float plane patrols were replaced by carrier based Zero fighter bombers, ominous reminders as to why they needed to cooperate with the Japanese dictates.

Being able to see as far north as Blackett Straits with the high-powered binoculars Pierre Duncan had purchased, it was clearly evident at night that battles were being fought between the Japanese and American naval forces. Flames from burning ships could often be seen on the horizon for many hours before the vessels finally went to their final resting place on the bottom of the Solomon Sea. Many nights, the rolling thunder of explosions kept

Sister Dominique awake. She knew the war was slowly closing in on Nusa Simbo and there was nothing they could do to stop it.

Over the next month, Father Renaldo spoke of leaving the island on the next supply ship, but always changed his mind when the ship arrived. But now, a feeling of impending doom made him more uncomfortable, filling him with a desire to leave Nusa Simbo. Late one evening, as Sister Dominique and Sister Margaret remained seated near the campfire, Father Renaldo approached them.

"Sisters, I have a serous feeling of dread that something bad is going to happen and that we need to get out of here as soon as possible."

Sister Dominique was taken back by Father Renaldo's fears. True, he had spoken of them before, but this was different, this time the dread that he was feeling came through quite clearly in his voice. After giving his comments a moment of thought, Sister Dominique replied, "Father, where shall we go, every island in the Solomon's is now controlled by the Japanese. The only thing we can do now is ask to be taken to Australia or New Caledonia, and that is only if the Japanese would allow us to go."

Shaking his head, Father Renaldo said, "I have spoken to a coast watcher on Ranongga Island just across the channel to the north. Their island is still controlled by the Australian Army, and the Japanese have not attempted to land there. We must pack up and go on the next supply ship, or surely, we will all be doomed. We cannot stay here and become prisoners or slaves of the Japanese empire."

Sister Margaret stood up and paced near the fire for a moment before speaking. Turning toward Pierre Duncan, who had just come down from the plantation to join them, she said, "The supply ship arrives in two days. Why don't you and Sister Dominique go along with the supply ship to Ranongga and check things out with the Australian commander, then report back to us. With that information, we could make a good decision as to what is best for everyone."

Sister Dominique nodded her head. "That sounds like an excellent plan. Looking over at Father Renaldo and Mr. Duncan, she said, "What do the two of you think of that idea?"

Smiling at Sister Margaret, Father Renaldo replied. "We shall do just that.

My heart already feels like a weight has been removed from my shoulders. We shall look for a way out. Pierre, where are you at with this plan?"

Pierre puffed on his pipe for a moment before replying. "I hate to leave my plantation, as my family has owned it for a very long time. But I fear the Japanese will destroy it one way or the other. I am most willing to go along with Sister Dominique, to check out an escape route."

As Sister Margaret had said, two days later the supply ship arrived at Nusa Simbo. Once everything was off loaded, Father Renaldo approached the skipper of the vessel. "Sir, I know you do not carry passengers often, but would you be willing to take Sister Dominique and Pierre Duncan over to Ranongga. We want to speak with the Australian commanders there. The fast current makes it very unsafe to try and cross the channel between the islands with a small boat."

The skipper smiled. "Of course, Father, have them climb aboard and we will shove off in about fifteen minutes. We even have a few cases of rum to turn over to the Aussies. Maybe they will let Pierre crack a bottle with them tonight."

Father Renaldo laughed as he patted the young skipper on the shoulder. Turning toward Sister Dominique, he signaled for them to get on the ship. Father Renaldo stopped Pierre and said, "If they don't offer you a drink, remind them that you know they have a new case of rum."

The skipper laughed as he helped Sister Dominique climb up the rickety loading platform. Reaching the main deck, Pierre and Sister Dominique sat down on a wooden bench, waiting for the small ship to set sail.

Forty-five minutes later, the rusty old vessel pulled up along a sturdy dock that ran nearly ten yards out into the sea. It was made of massive coconut logs lashed together by large ropes that had survived years of tropical sun and monster waves.

Walking ashore, Sister Dominique stepped up to a sergeant holding a British Sten machine gun. "Can you tell me where we could find the island commander or governor."

Nodding his head, the sergeant replied, "Here on Ranongga, Colonel Joseph Winslow has the job of both. You can find him in the third Quonset hut on your left, ma'am."

Arriving in the hut, they found the colonel speaking with two of his officers. Looking up from the conversation, he said, "Well, no one told me I was to expect distinguished visitors today. I am Colonel Winslow of the Australian Royal Army. What can I do for you, and where did you come from?"

Pierre Duncan smiled. "Well, Colonel, I do not believe we are distinguished guests, just a few nervous missionaries looking for some serious advice."

Pointing toward several chairs, the colonel led them over to his desk and sat down. "Now what kind of information are you looking for?"

Sister Dominique leaned forward in her chair and said, "We have come from Nusa Simbo. The Japanese placed us under their protection about a month ago. So far, they have left us alone, although air patrols fly over usually twice a day. We were wondering about moving our mission over here so we would be safe from the Japanese."

Standing up, the colonel looked over a map of the Pacific that hung on the wall. Pointing to the island of Ranongga, he said. "For some odd reason the Japanese have left us alone, as well as Baga Island just to the north of us. However, I suspect that will change as they continue to build their base at Rabaul on New Britain. They won't leave us here for long, I suspect. We will give them a good fight and call home for more help if need be. I have two thousand men under my command here on Ranongga, and another five hundred men on Baga. We have artillery and tanks dug in from Emu Harbor in the north, all the way down to Pienuna in the center of the island. As the sandiest beach is located on Wilson Passage, that is exactly where I would attack from."

Pierre frowned, as he listened to the Colonel. "So, what you are telling us is that you expect Ranongga to be invaded in the near future."

After looking down at the floor for a moment, the colonel responded. "We are actually surprised they have not hit us yet, to be honest."

Sister Dominique looked seriously at Mr. Duncan. "Then we would be no better off here than at Nusa Simbo, at least there the island was taken peacefully without a shooting war."

Turning toward his visitors, Colonel Winslow replied. "I'm afraid you are right Sister Dominique. The Japanese are still rolling up islands to fulfill their dream of being Pacific conquerors. The Americans are going to have a tough job of wrestling those islands back. I am seriously thinking your best bet now is to make a run for Australia on the next supply boat. However, I believe the Japanese may shut down that supply line in due course, just as they have done to air traffic."

Pierre looked curiously at the Colonel. "What do you mean by that?"

Pointing toward a map of just the island of Ranongga, the colonel replied. "We had two airfields, here and here. Not quite a month ago, Japanese bombers hit those fields, putting them out of commission. Every time we try fill the holes on one runway, they come in at night and make new craters. I have given orders to stop working on the airfields. A better use of the equipment is to help build more defensive positions on the coastline to hinder the Japs when they come ashore."

After a moment of silence, Sister Dominique said, "Colonel, how can you get us to Australia?"

Shaking his head, the colonel responded. "When the supply ship comes back in two weeks, be on it with all your people when it pulls out. I can't whistle up a destroyer or landing ship to get you out of here. In fact, my patrol boat was sunk last week by Japanese Zeros flying off Vela Lavella. We are pretty much locked in now. But as I said, we will give them a black eye before they take control of Ranongga. The best we can hope for is American air power to mess up their landings."

Sister Dominique stood up and paced the floor for a minute before turning back to the colonel. "Sir, do you mean to tell us we are here on Ranongga for two weeks before we can get back to Nusa Simbo?"

Nodding his head while folding his arms across his chest, Colonel Winslow responded. "That is exactly what I'm telling you. It is perfectly fine to use the radio to inform your people on Nusa Simbo about your situation. At the same time, you can tell them to get packed for the next supply ship."

Pierre looked up at Sister Dominique, "I'm afraid Father Renaldo's fears are becoming a reality, Sister, and I do not like this at all. The Japanese have us over a barrel and there is nothing we can do to change it."

Colonel Winslow took a deep breath. "I have very nice quarters for you to stay in while you wait for the supply ship. Why don't you follow my corporal down to the hut, freshen up, and then join me and my staff officers for dinner. It will take your mind off everything that is going on."

After dinner, Sister Dominique used the short-wave radio to inform Father Renaldo of their situation. After leaving the communications building, Sister Dominique walked over to the pier where Pierre was sitting on a fifty-five gallon drum, observing the sunset that was beginning to form.

"Looks like we'll have another memorable sunset tonight, Sister. I have a feeling that will be the only good thing I will remember about the South Pacific.

The following morning, Colonel Winslow took Sister Dominique and Pierre on an inspection tour of the installations along the north coast of Ranongga, and the many anti-aircraft batteries constructed around the island. There was no doubt that all the installations were well built, and would be deadly to the invading Japanese and their pilots. But there was also no doubt in Pierre Duncan's mind that the Japanese would invade with a lot more than two thousand men. Ranongga was a large island and it would take a lot of troops to secure it.

Throughout the first week, everyone on Ranongga appeared to be relaxed and in a good state of mind as all was quiet out in Wilson Passage, and there were no Japanese planes attacking from the air. Colonel Winslow did everything he could to make Sister Dominique and Pierre as comfortable as possible, although he knew they wanted to leave before anything went horribly wrong.

The day before the supply ship was scheduled to arrive, Colonel Winslow convinced Sister Dominique and Pierre to climb into his jeep and take a ride along the north coast. He told them the view into Wilson Passage from the top of the small mountain was breath taking. After a moment of thought, Sister Dominique smiled and said, "Colonel, you have been most hospitable to us. We appreciate all you have done to make us comfortable. Driving to the mountain would surely take my mind off of what is all happening. Yes, we would be happy to ride with you."

Colonel Winslow had been completely accurate. The ride up the back side of the mountain allowed some wonderful vistas of Wilson Passage, Gizo Island and the large volcanic cone located on Kolombangara. They had been stopped only a few minutes when the sounds of naval guns pierced the majestic silence.

Quickly the colonel put the jeep in gear and continued around toward the northwest side of the island. Slamming on the brakes and coming to a dead stop, the colonel gasped at the sight he saw below him. Down in Wilson Passage were three heavy Japanese cruisers and fifteen destroyers lobbing high explosive shells into the Australian's prepared positions. Smoke was rising from fires, and shells fired from the embedded field artillery that was blasting back at destroyers that cruised in close to shore, attacking targets. It was evident the plan to use the artillery was paying back dividends, as one destroyer was sailing north past Gizo Island with a major fire burning near its engine room.

Coming down the from Vella Gulf, they could see four large troop transports and three landing ships that would bring the troops ashore once the prepared positions were destroyed. Watching the entire operation unfolding in front of them, no one saw or heard the two Japanese Zero's that were dropping down from about 10,000 feet. As they leveled off, the pilots began to strafe the mountain top where the jeep was parked. Not wasting time, the driver attempted to back the vehicle into the thick jungle just off the road. Nevertheless, both tires on the right side of the jeep were blown out, the windshield exploded and the radio sitting next to Pierre was torn to pieces as bullets ripped through it. As the planes passed over head, Colonel Winslow grabbed the Thompson machine gun by his feet and yelled.

"Get out and duck into the jungle, Sister, the bastards are coming back!"

As Sister Dominique jumped from the jeep, she realized the driver was not going anywhere. He had two machine gun bullets in his back and one through his helmet. Grabbing hold of Pierre's hand, they ran as fast as they could into the dense jungle, dropping to the ground just as the planes began their second attack. As machine guns clattered, the jeep exploded in flames, sending it rolling sideways down the road toward the landing beach.

With the jeep gone, the pilots began strafing the Aussie positions and dropping their hundred-pound bombs on an anti-aircraft emplacement. The stored shells behind the gun instantly exploded, sending a large orange ball of flame skyward. Moments later, one of the artillery pieces was struck by a naval shell, sending a tremendous volume of deadly shrapnel across a large section of the beach as flames erupted from the ammunition pit. All around the beach, fires roared and explosions tore apart huge sections of log barriers intended to slow down the Japanese invasion. It was becoming evident the infantry that was to fight off the invading Japanese could not hold up to such a tremendous onslaught. After each explosion, the colonel could see his men grabbing their weapons and retreating back into the jungle.

About forty-five minutes after the ships had begun firing, the landing ships raced toward the beaches, as Japanese troops climbed down the sides of the transports into waiting landing craft. More planes began streaming into Wilson Passage from Rabaul, dropping high explosive shells on the retreating soldiers. The island shook as the massive bombs detonated on the hard packed corral rock and sand that made up the base of the island.

Luckily, one of the 105mm howitzer artillery pieces that been dug into the sand and fortified with coconut logs survived the initial attack. As one Japanese medium class tank came rolling off the landing ship, the driver attempted to drive over a log emplacement, fully exposing the soft under belly of the machine. Instantly, the crew of the 105 fired a round point blank into the bottom of the tank. Seconds later, the machine exploded as all the fuel and ammunition went off at one time. The shrapnel from the explosion cut down thirty Japanese Marines that were using the tank for close cover as they came ashore.

The driver of the tank that was next to the exploding vehicle turned toward the east to avoid the log emplacement, allowing the 105 crew to have a full side shot. A moment later the second tank was turned into a burning hulk as the turret rose ten feet into the air before falling to the ground.

Reloading quickly, the 105 crew fired a third round that struck a truck just coming off the ramp of the landing ship. The vehicle exploded, blocking the ramp of the ship while killing a large number of infantrymen that were scheduled to follow the truck ashore.

Before the crew of the 105 could do any more damage, a Japanese Zero dropped a hundred-pound bomb on the concealed position, destroying the weapon and wiping out the valiant crew.

The Aussie troops that had retreated into the jungle dropped down into prepared positions and began fighting back with sheer determination.

Colonial Winslow stopped a jeep heading for the mountain and told the driver to turn around. Quickly, Sister Dominique and Pierre Duncan jumped on the jeep as the driver drove like a man possessed toward the island headquarters.

Entering the communications hut, Colonel Winslow was overwhelmed with radio messages that had come in since the invasion began. He called out orders and sent runners toward the front to get the latest information, since some of the infantry radios had now been destroyed.

Everyone in the headquarters hut was totally dismayed when they heard two light cruisers, two more destroyers and another landing ship were heading south out of Vella Gulf into Wilson Passage, but there was nothing Colonel Winslow could do to stop the enemy reinforcements. He knew the end of the defense of the island was inevitable. The question was, how long could they hold out?

Throughout the long night, Aussie defenders threw back several Japanese attacks that had been costly to both sides, but the Aussie troops had not given an inch of territory. Around midnight, a coast watcher reported a destroyer dropping Japanese troops along the southeast coast across from Emu Harbor. Immediately, Colonel Winslow sent out a patrol to find them, but somehow, they had disappeared into the thick jungle.

Several times during the night, Japanese float planes attempted to bomb the Aussie command center with incendiary bombs, but each time were shot down by anti-aircraft batteries set up near the loading pier. These were not big victories, but it gave the soldiers a moment to whoop it up and pat each other on the back. Just the type of morale boost that Colonel Winslow and his troops desperately needed.

At 0600hrs, the commander of the resupply ship reported his vessel had been attacked by two Japanese Zeros and he was taking on water about a hundred miles southwest of Ranongga. He stated his crew was working on damage control, but he was not sure they could save the old vessel. At 0620hrs, the skipper reported the resupply ship was going down by the stern and they were evacuating the stricken vessel.

Sister Dominique and Pierre Duncan felt totally sick, as they understood their only chance of leaving the island had now gone to the bottom of the Solomon Sea. Walking out of the communications hut, Sister Dominique looked at Pierre. "What are we to do now? I have a bad feeling the Japanese are going to be angry for the losses they are taking and will kill every survivor."

Pierre Duncan looked intently at Sister Dominique. "I fear you are accurate. The Japs never counted on such a stiff costly fight for this island. They will want revenge. We must stay together and remain unarmed when the end comes. Maybe they will allow us to surrender. That is our only hope."

Much to the surprise of everyone in the command center, at 0715hrs, three American PT Boats slid quietly along the south coast of Gizo Island using a fog bank for cover. When they broke into Wilson Passage, they unmuffled their engines and attacked at full speed. One of the boats fired two torpedoes at a destroyer that was moving slowly behind one of the heavy cruisers. The ship shuddered as the blast ripped open one of the fuel bunkers, nearly tearing the vessel in two. Another PT Boat fired several torpedoes at one of the light cruisers that had just joined the attack group, striking it near the engine room. Within minutes, flames roared from the ship as it began to take on water and slowed to a stop in the dangerous channel.

The third PT Boat went after the landing ship that had the truck explode on its ramp. As the ramp had been bent and did not close well, sailors had set up pumps to keep the ship afloat as repair crews worked on the ramp so they could finish unloading. The twenty-millimeter gunner opened fire on the ramp, killing most of the repair crew while punching massive holes in the weakened steel plating. The skipper of the PT Boat circled the ship as his machine gunners ripped up everything they could. After making a sharp turn, he fired one torpedo into the engine room of the ship. The torpedo ended up being a dud, but it severed three hull panels, allowing sea water to pour into several holds. Severely damaged but still afloat, the skipper turned his vessel north, attempting to escape into Vella Gulf.

As the skipper of the third PT Boat played cat and mouse with one of the destroyers, the skipper of one of the heavy cruisers was in no mood to play. He anticipated the next turn the PT Boat would make, and fired two of his heavy fourteen-inch guns in its direction. In a blinding flash, the wooden PT Boat disappeared from the face of the earth. All that was left were small floating shards of wood and other light debris as the high-grade aviation fuel burned on the surface of Wilson Passage.

Beginning to run low on fuel, and not wanting to sacrifice another boat to the skipper of the Japanese heavy cruiser, the skipper of PT 262 led PT 289 circled around the northwest corner of Ranongga.

Getting on the radio, the skipper of the 262 boat called Colonel. Winslow. "Ranongga Island, this is blue Blue Chip One. We have done about all we can do and are heading back to the wedding chapel, anything we can do before we go?"

Grabbing the handset, Colonel Winslow replied. "I have two packages that need to be mailed to Nusa Simbo promptly, can you take them?"

Lieutenant Earl Stoneman, Skipper of PT 262 replied. "Have them on the end of the pier in fifteen minutes, we'll take them with us."

Throwing the handset to his radio officer, Colonel Winslow ran from the communications hut with a corporal. He found a dejected Sister Dominique and Pierre Duncan sitting on a bench near the small infirmary. Running up to them, he said, "There will be an American PT Boat arriving at the end of the pier in fifteen minutes. Get down there and get on it, they won't have time to wait!" Turning toward the corporal, he continued. "Go with them and keep them alive."

Turning back toward Sister Dominique, the colonel took her by the hands. "Sister, I need you to pray for me and my men, for I fear the worst. I do not believe there will be any prisoner taking when this is over. I am certain that by nightfall we will all be dead. I'll do all I can for my men, but I know some of them will lose faith and run." As tears ran down his face, he kissed Sister Dominique on the cheek. This is my moment of deliverance that I feared would come one day. Pray for me so I may measure up to the task at hand, and then humbly join God in paradise when this battle ends."

Tears streamed down Sister Dominique's face as she looked up at the strong, yet terrified officer who stood humbly before her. Placing her hand on his forehead, Sister Dominique said, "As Jesus told the robber crucified next to him on Calvary, 'today you will be with me in paradise,' so today, Colonel, you shall also be with Jesus in paradise, you have humbly served him well."

With that said, the corporal took hold of Sister Dominique's arm and began pulling her toward the pier. The corporal had just set foot on the pier when four Japanese soldiers climbed up from the rocky shore line. Before they could fully react, the corporal fired a long blast from his Thompson, killing two soldiers, sending their bodies back down into the rocks below, and wounding a third.

Sister Dominique and Pierre Duncan threw themselves onto the wooden pier as bullets flew over their heads. Seeing the corporal killed by the fourth Japanese soldier, Pierre rolled across the deck, scooped up the Thompson machine gun and let go another long blast. The soldier stumbled forward a few feet, before falling to the deck, As the injured soldier attempted to reach for his rifle, once more Pierre pulled the trigger on the machine gun, sending the man back off the pier as blood sprayed from his chest.

Jumping to his feet, Pierre grabbed Sister Dominique by the arm as he yelled, "Run Sister, here comes the boat!"

Just as PT 262 slid up alongside the dock, PT 289 stopped a few feet away, sitting parallel to the shore line. Instantly, every .50 caliber machine gun, and the 20mm cannon on the stern of the boat opened fire. Looking back toward the island, Pierre could see the fifty Japanese soldiers the destroyer had dropped off the night before moving along the rocks, attempting to attack the command center from the rear. In a matter of minutes, they all lay dead on the rocks as the rising tide began pulling them out to sea.

Reaching the 262 boat, one of the crew members grabbed Sister Dominique and shoved her to the deck aside the number one torpedo tube. After handing the Thompson to the sailor, Pierre Duncan dropped down over the top of Sister Dominique, covering her head.

In mere seconds, the 262 boat was reversing away from the pier into the deeper water where the skipper of the 289 boat was covering the withdrawal. With the 262 boat once again pointed toward the northeast, both boats screamed across the Solomon Sea at full speed.

Several minutes later, Pierre stood up, helping Sister Dominique up from the deck of the boat. She looked at the plantation owner and smiled. "Pierre, I had my questions when I first met you, but I have come to learn you are one hell of a man."

Pierre laughed as he shook his head. "Someday you must tell my daughter that. It would be good for her to hear that her old man is not just a money-grubbing bum."

Patting Pierre on the shoulder, Sister Dominique replied. "That young lady has a tremendous amount to learn about her daddy."

As Sister Dominique walked up to the cockpit, the sailor handed Pierre the Thompson machine gun. "She is a nice piece and rather new. Take care of it, she will treat you well."

Handing the weapon back to the sailor, Pierre responded, "Please keep it on your boat for protection. I do not wish to keep it. I saw what it is capable of, and I never wish to use such a weapon ever again."

The young sailor smiled. "I'll clean it up later and put it in the lock box. It will be a nice addition to our weaponry."

As Sister Dominique walked into the cockpit, she took a moment to look up at the night sky. "Even though the mountains are high in Italy, you never see stars like you do out here in the pitch-black darkness of the ocean."

Lieutenant Stoneman smiled. "You are so right, Sister. I have been out here for almost ten months now, and some nights I'm still amazed at the stars. Writing letters home, I have peaked my wife's interest in the ocean and stars. She says when the war is over, I will need to bring her out here to see this for herself. I just hope I can bring myself back out here after everything we have gone through. It's been an ugly war, Sister."

Staring off into the distance, Sister Dominique asked. "How far away is Nusa Simbo? It did not seem to take this long when we came over on the supply ship?"

The lieutenant smiled. "When we left Ranongga, we went deeper out to sea to make sure no one was following us, but we have been slowly making our way back. If you look at our eleven o'clock, you can just make out the shadow of the west coast line. We'll be there in about twenty minutes. When we hit the pier, you and Duncan jump off as quick as you came on board, so we can get the hell out of there."

Sister Dominique smiled "No time for a cup of coffee, I suppose?"

Lieutenant Stoneman laughed. "Well, I'm sure it would be better than the mud our so-called cook concocts down in the galley, but no, we need to be on our way. We need to refuel and rearm for our mission later today, so it will be a long night yet."

As the island came closer into view, Sister Dominique said, "What do you think the fate of the men on Ranongga is going to be?"

Shaking his head, the skipper replied. "If those were Americans or British, the Japanese would allow them to surrender, although they would be treated badly. But knowing how the Japanese hate the Australians, I wouldn't give you a plug nickel for any of them to walk off that damn island."

Sister Dominique walked from the cockpit to meet Pierre as they neared the entrance to the cove. The only light visible was the burning embers from the evening bonfire.

As the 262 idled up to the familiar wooden pier, Sister Dominique and Pierre Duncan jumped clear of the wooden war ship. As Lt. Stoneman threw his boat into reverse, the sailor that helped them on and off the boat called out. Remember, your welcoming committee was Torpedoman Second Class Quincy from Amherst, Wisconsin. A second later, he snapped off a perfect salute as the 262 backed out into the darkness of the Solomon Sea.

As the sound of the PT Boats heading back to Rendova reverberated off the hills, Father Renaldo led a welcoming committee down toward the pier. Quickly, several of the natives rekindled the bonfire and several women brought out pineapple snacks and fresh juice.

Sister Dominique cried as the other Sisters took turns hugging her and telling her how much they missed her. Many of the little children took turns crawling up into Sister Dominique's lap, wanting her to tell them stories about her travels. Although it was good to be back on Nusa Simbo with the people she loved, her heart was breaking for Colonel Winslow and the Aussie soldiers she had left behind. She knew nothing good was going to happen on Ranongga this night.

Sitting down on the edge of her bed, Sister Dominique felt emotionally drained. Not since being dropped off at the monastery had she felt such empty sadness. In the Abbey, she knew the sisters would teach her a new way to live, and help her to build a life she could be happy with. But this was a situation no one could help her with. She knew that sometime in the next few days, Colonel Winslow and his men would be slaughtered by the Japanese, and there was no one that could stop it. Every time she closed her eyes, she could see the fearful face of Colonel Winslow looking back at her. There was no doubt it would haunt her for a long time to come.

Over the next few days, Sister Dominique and Pierre filled in everyone regarding what they had seen and learned while being on Ranongga island. They were all dismayed to hear the resupply ship had been attacked and sunk. Father Renaldo spent several days on the shortwave radio, attempting to find out who was going to perform that important task. After the loss of Ranongga, it was evident no one in Australia wanted any part of the job. Luckily one of Pierre's contacts in New Caledonia decided he would take on the job if the Japanese allowed him into their waters.

With Ranongga and Baga Islands both now in the hands of the Japanese, no one will ever know where the Australian medium bomber came from that bright January morning of 1943, but it changed the quiet existence on Nusa Simbo forever. One Sunday morning as Father Reynaldo had the duty on the high point of the island near the plantation, Sister Claudia and Sister Dominique made him some sandwiches, and delivered them in the school's dilapidated pickup. While he was eating his lunch, Sister Claudia picked up the binoculars to begin scanning the Solomon Sea toward the northwest. All of a sudden, she observed an Australian bomber drop down from a cloud bank heading in their direction.

Since it was obvious there were no Australian or British airbases on any islands north of New Guinea, the plane must have come from an American base somewhere near Rendova or another island to the east. What had been a light stream of greasy black smoke emanating from the right engine bonnet, quickly became a torrent of flames and smoke as the engine began to sputter, and lighter parts fell from the plane, revealing a hundred-pound bomb still precariously dangling from its rack under the fuselage.

In order to give himself a chance to survive bailing out of the stricken aircraft, the pilot raised the front of the plane, attempting to gain altitude, but that just increased the flames roaring out of his engine bonnet. After gaining about five hundred feet, the misfiring, disabled engine cut out completely. As the nose began to drop over toward the sea, the pilot opened the canopy, stepped out onto the wing and jumped clear of his doomed aircraft.

What the pilot was not expecting, was a very strong trade wind aloft that drove his parachute farther away from the main Solomon Islands, and deeper out into the Solomon Sea, near Nusa Simbo. As the parachute headed southwest at an incredible speed, the bright silver aircraft detonated as it struck the surface of the sea. The sound of the heavy explosion reached the radio position near the plantation in a very short time as everyone watched the massive fire ball climb several hundred feet before settling down over the gas and oil spread out on the surface of the water.

Father Renaldo turned and yelled. "Go find him, find that parachute, it's most likely on the cliffs down toward the southeast and can be seen for miles from a plane, ship or submarine. It's an invitation for the Japanese to come visit us!"

Climbing into the truck, Sister Claudia and Sister Dominique grabbed several workers from the plantation that were carrying machetes. After explaining the situation, they jumped into the back of the truck. They followed the road until it came to an end, then hiked a foot trail along the cliffs until they spotted the large white canopy draped over some low hanging branches of a palm tree. Like a couple of squirrels, the men climbed up the tree and began hacking at branches until they were able to lower the pilot and the parachute down to the ground.

The pilot was still somewhat dazed as the sisters gently lowered him to the ground. The right side of his face had several cuts and abrasions from the tree trunk as it had stopped him mid-flight. It had to have been a very sudden stop.

Quickly, the men gathered up the parachute and the harness and tossed them in the back of the truck. What could not be used at the plantation, was buried in a large hole behind the warehouse.

With the pilot regaining consciousness, the sisters took him down to the church where they cleaned and bandaged his wounds. When he was his fully awake, they explained to him where he was, and told him that the Japanese were watching the island very closely. They asked him to stay out of sight because of the over flights, and do nothing to alert the Japanese by accident.

When Sister Dominique inquired about his name and where he came from, the pilot shook his head. "Sister, I don't know you, and I'm sure you have a transmitter on this island that the Japanese may be monitoring, and I don't trust you enough to give you any more information than I would to the Japs if they captured me."

Nodding her head, Sister Dominique responded, "I am good with that and will respect your desires and not ask any more questions. Please just honor us the same way and cooperate with what we have asked of you."

Somewhat angered by Sister Dominique's reply, the pilot stood up and said, "Sister, there is a war going on out there whether you like it or not, and I'm part of it. My job as an Australian Officer is to return to my squadron and take the fight back against the Japs. I am sure you have heard the bastards attacked Pearl Harbor and killed thousands of American service people without a declaration of war. This is no game, Sister, and men are dying all over the Pacific." After a moment of silence, he glared at Sister Dominique. "Yeah, and that accent you two have is Italian, isn't it?"

"Yes, it is, we were both born in Italy as was Sister Margaret and Father Renaldo. What difference does that make?" Sister Dominique responded, knowing where the pilot was going.

"Come on, Sister, you're not stupid. Italy and Germany have been allies with Japan since something like 1940. Now you expect me to trust you and ask me to give in to your considerations, when I'm not even sure you're not planning to turn me over to the Japanese to be shot? Does that make sense to you?"

Getting angrier by the moment, Sister Dominique pointed her index finger in the direction of the pilot's face saying, "We are sisters of St. Benedict, not members of the Axis nations. We want no part of this war, and what has been thrust upon us already is not to our liking. You must—"

Before she could finish, Father Renaldo walked into the church. "I have been hearing what has been said between you. You want us to accept the credo of an Australian war pilot, but you refuse to accept the simple rules we have laid out to you that will assure us of our lives. I would think that after we cut you down, hid your parachute, doctored your face and fed you, that everything we've said would surely make a difference to you. Do you know that two Japanese patrol boats already arrived over the area where your plane crashed. They searched through the debris, then worked their way south past Nusa Simbo, in search of your parachute. Had we not plucked you from that tree, you would already be in the hands of the enemy you hate so much." Walking up to the pilot, Father Renaldo pulled the man's pistol from its holster. "Now that I see you cannot work with us, I do not trust you with this weapon."

The next supply ship will be here in two weeks. After it drops our supplies, it will sail back to New Caledonia, where you can rejoin the Australian or British Navy. I think that should be to your liking."

The pilot shook his head. "Two weeks on this hell hole is bullshit, I need to join my squadron now." After a moment of thought, he looked at Sister Claudia. "Can you tell me where I can sleep?"

Without saying a word, Sister Claudia led him down to a small hut near the pier that was empty. "You can sleep here while you are visiting, no one will disturb you, and we will let you know when it's meal time."

Without saying a word, the pilot walked into the hut and laid down on the heavy mat.

Back in the church, Father Renaldo paced back and forth as he shook his head. "This man can cause us many problems over the next two weeks. We will need to have someone watch him around the clock. I will have the natives keep an eye on him.

The following evening, one of the natives appointed to watch the pilot came running to find Sister Dominique. "The pilot is dragging dried palm branches over to the cliff near the bridge. I think he wants to set a signal fire there tonight."

Jumping into the pickup truck, Sr Dominique raced over the bumpy dirt road until she was near the point where the branches were being stacked. Jumping from the truck, she kicked the already assembled stack over the cliff as the pilot was dragging more from the jungle.

"What the hell do you think you're doing, Sister. I'm getting off this island one way or another and I am ready to try tonight." The pilot yelled angrily.

"Who in God's name do you think is going to come and investigate the fire other than Japanese? Then they will know someone is on the island that does not belong here, and we all shall pay the price," Sister Dominique screamed as she shook with anger.

"You're wrong, Sister. Tonight, when I light off this fire, American PT Boats operating in Blackett Straits will come to investigate, and I'll be out of your hair by morning. You want me gone, believe me, that will do the trick. That's what we're taught in survival school." The pilot replied as he once again began to arrange the new palm branches."

Closing her eyes and shaking her head, Sister Dominique said angrily. "You don't know if those PT Boats are going to be in Blackett Straits tonight or anywhere else out there. You don't know if they are going to run into rain squalls or if clouds will cover the island tonight blacking out your fire. What we do know is some Japanese craft will see the fire and we will be doomed!

About that time Father Renaldo arrived on a rickety bicycle that had somehow survived the storm. Throwing it to the ground, the priest reached into the waistband of his slacks and pulled out the pilot's pistol. "You will come with me back to your hut, I will not allow you to jeopardize the good people on this island."

The pilot laughed as he looked at the priest. "Give me that thing before you hurt someone, Father. You don't have a clue what that thing can do."

Firing a round into the dirt about three feet from the pilot's foot, Father Renaldo replied. "You see son, I was not always the priest I am now. I have been a man of many talents in my lifetime. I can tear this weapon down, oil it with coconut oil, and have it spic and span in under thirty minutes. Care to time me or are you willing to trust me on that?"

Looking down at the ground, the pilot said, "Fine, whatever Father."

During the next few days, the pilot either slept much of the day, or sat on the pier pitching stones into the water. He knew every native on the island that was diligently going about their work was also watching him like a hawk. Every time a spotter observed a Japanese plane coming close to the island, they would hustle him back into his hut.

However, that kind of surveillance began to wear thin on the angry pilot. Two days later the man assigned to guard him was the islander that always carried the German Schmeisser. About two in the afternoon, as the sound of the Japanese float plane making its late day run over the island could be heard, the pilot jumped from his mat. He punched the man in the face, grabbed the machine gun and ran from the hut. Just as the Japanese pilot neared the pier, the pilot stepped clear of the hut, opening fire with the automatic weapon at the low flying aircraft.

Blood splattered all over the side window of the plane as the pilot pulled back on the stick trying to climb out of harm's way. The Australian pilot ran out along the shore of the cove in time to see the plane crash into the Solomon Sea shearing of its floats, and sinking away out of sight.

Jumping up and down that he had taken out some revenge on a Japanese aircraft, his heart sank quickly, as he turned sideways to see another Japanese float plane flying off to the southeast. He realized his position had just been given away as the Japanese pilot was already radioing his superiors on Truk or Rabaul.

Walking back toward his hut, Sister Dominique stood silently shaking her head. As the pilot stopped in front of her, he said, "What do you want me to say, I'm a naval officer, I was just doing my duty, as you do with the children every stinking day on this God forsaken island.

Staring at the pilot, as she shook with anger, she replied. "We teach, we teach these people to love one another. Just forty years ago they were head hunters, today they see the natives on the other islands as their neighbors, their friends, their trading partners that treat them with respect and without fear.

Now the Japanese will come in force, they will kill whoever they wish, and destroy all we have built here, all because you wanted revenge. There is no place to hide anymore, and no place to run for your help. In the next few days, you will suffer with the rest of us I am afraid."

"No, Sister, you are wrong, there is still the radio. I can still call for help, and you will not stop me," he replied, as he held up the machine gun.

Within an hour, seven Japanese Zero's rolled out of the clouds, attacking the island with machine gun and cannon fire. Natives and plantation workers screamed as bullets and shrapnel ripped into their bodies. The normally clean community area outside the huts and school was littered with bodies of the dead and wounded as the church and several storage buildings burst into flames. Three of the planes carried hundred pound bombs that were dropped on the area around the plantation, setting everything on fire.

After the raid was over, Father Renaldo came back into the village on the old bicycle. Stopping in front of Sister Dominique, who was covered in the blood of the wounded, he said. "He never made it."

Frowning at the priest, Sister Dominique replied, "I don't know what you are talking about."

"The pilot, he never made it to the radio shack. Several workers fought to stop him from using the radio, but ran off when the planes arrived. The bullets from the planes tore up the radio shack knocking down the antenna, and exploding the gas tank for the generator. After they flew off, I looked inside the shack. The pilot was laying over the desk with several bullets in his chest. All of this for one man's hatred."

As he turned to walk away, he removed the pilot's pistol from his waistband and threw it on the ground. Walking over to the dejected priest, Sister Dominique took hold of his arm.

The night he was going to set the fire, you threatened him with his pistol.

You talked about cleaning it and putting it back together, did you mean all of that?"

"In another life I was involved in the Sicilian mafia. I carried a similar pistol every day, just to make me look bad. One day I was involved in a gun battle with a rival gang. I moved pretty good in my younger days, and killed two of them before the others ran off. Scared for my life, I quit the mob I was with and two days later sailed from Messina and traveled to Naples. After thinking about taking my life, I met a priest that talked me into a monastery. So, now you know who I really was, but none of that will save us tomorrow."

Early the following morning, several Japanese Zeros circled the island as a large Japanese assault ship slowly entered what had been a picturesque cove, something you might see pictured in a National Geographic photo lay out of the South Pacific. But today, the cove appeared dark and forbidding, as two destroyers stood off the coast, ready to use their fire power to wipe out every living soul on the island.

Quickly, most of the natives began running into the hills, after hearing stories from other islanders of the brutality of the Japanese Marines. Employees from the plantation sat huddled on the ground near the school, terrified as to what was about to happen to them.

As the ramp dropped down onto the island, three small Japanese tanks rolled ashore, followed by several hundred battle hardened combat Marines.

As the tanks rolled through the village, then up the muddy road to what was left of the plantation, the Marines rounded up everyone they could find in the huts and delivered them to the school where the sisters called out for them to quickly assemble.

A short time later, the tanks and Marines returned from the plantation after setting everything on fire, with about twenty more prisoners being led by Pierre Duncan.

With the round up completed, a Japanese Major escorted by his body guards slowly strolled off the ship. After looking over the empty huts and the terrified people huddled tightly with their children, he shook his head. He looked over at Father Renaldo and the sisters.

"I am Major Ouichi of the Imperial Japanese Navy. Tell me who is in charge here."

A moment later, the chief and his wife walked forward, bowing down in homage, which was the custom when greeting a Japanese Officer. Looking up at the angry officer, the chief spoke. "I apologize for any wrong doing that has angered the Japanese government. But you must understand it was not anyone that lived on this island. The problem came from a downed Australian pilot that—"

Before the chief could finish, the major yelled, "Where are your children!"

After two young girls stepped forward, the major nodded his head toward a lieutenant standing nearby.

"Take them over to the jungle and shoot them!"

Once the mother had gathered up her daughters close to her body, the lieutenant gave two of his men holding machine guns orders to fire. In seconds, the chief and his family lay dead on the ground.

Sister Dominique ran forward, yelling, "What is wrong with you!"

Before allowing Sister Dominique to get much closer to the major, a Marine struck her with the butt of his rifle, knocking her to the ground.

Looking down at Sister Dominique, the major yelled, "Do you also wish to die? Were you not told by Colonel Mizawa that you would suffer the consequences for harboring enemy combatants? Were you not told the simple rules you must follow to get along with the Japanese Military? And now you protest and feel you will not have to pay a price for your arrogance!"

As Sister Claudia helped Sister Dominique back to her feet, the soldier that struck her placed his barrel against the side of her head. He held the rifle steady as Major Ouichi walked up to her.

"Sister, are you now in charge since the chief had been neutralized?" The major inquired as he glared angrily at her.

After taking a long breath she replied, "I am Sister Dominique, I am responsible for the missionaries. What the chief told you about the Australian pilot was the truth. No one here on Nusa Simbo did anything to offend the Japanese Government or military. I assure you; we were doing everything the colonel asked us to do."

Spitting on Sister Dominique's shoes, Major Ouichi replied. "The truth! How do you expect me to believe anything you say is the truth. You and your kind come to these islands and fill the heads of the natives about some person named God that is all perfect and the one holy deity. There is no God other than our sacred emperor! Each time you teach these people otherwise you commit a sacrilege that is blasphemy. You foul the minds of these people with your lies and degrading teachings!"

After slapping her across the face, he yelled at his marines. "Round them up!"

Immediately, the marines began to push everyone still standing near the school toward the ship, yelling and pushing them forward with their sharp bayonets.

As Sister Dominique stood on the ramp of the ship with Sister Margaret, she said. "So now the war every one dreaded has come to Nusa Simbo, and we are all lost. This is all my fault, and now everyone shall perish. We should have helped the pilot get off the island one way or the other."

After hearing what Sister Dominique had said, Sister Claudia took hold of her long-lost sister's arm and replied. "No, Sister Dominique, you could not have prevented what happened here. Everything was out of your hands."

Before Sister Dominique could respond, the soldiers began pushing them onto the ship toward the aft storage hold. Taking one last long look around Nusa Simbo, tears ran down her face.

With the prisoners firmly sealed in the storage hold, and the tanks and Marines back aboard, the ramp slowly raised up off the beach. As the ship slipped from the cove, a large group of natives and a few employees from the plantation that were able to avoid capture, silently walked up to the pier as they cried. None of them understood what was going to happen to them now, as they were sure the Japanese would stop all the supply ships that had serviced the island for many years.

Chapter Ten – Destruction of the Abbey

Two months after Sister Dominique left the Abbey for the South Pacific, a German Kubelwagon drove up to the front door of the castle like structure. A tall, straight as an arrow major by the name of Gerhard Jung stepped from the vehicle. After taking a quick look around, he spoke to his aide, Lieutenant Hans Vogel. "Ya, this is everything you explained to me and more. This will work out just fine. Good job, Lieutenant. Now let's inform the occupants that they must leave."

Walking up to the large wooden front doors, the corporal driving the Kubelwagon pounded his fist hard against the old wood as he yelled. "Open up immediately!"

A moment later, Mother Superior opened the door as several other sisters stood in the foyer, more frightened than they had ever been in their lives. Looking at the tall officer, Mother Superior asked, "What can we do for you, Major, we are just simple sisters doing the work of God."

Brushing past Mother Superior, the three Germans walked into the foyer. Taking a long look around, the Major said, "Yes, this will do nicely, very nicely." Turning toward Mother Superior, he continued. "There will be three trucks here on Monday morning to move you and the rest of your sisters out of here. The German Army will be taking control of this Abbey. There will be no arguing and there will be no changes in our plan. Be ready by 1000hrs. Monday!"

Mother Superior's heart sank as she looked at Major Jung. "Herr Major this Abbey dates back to the 1200's. It has always been the home of Franciscan monks or now Benedictine sisters. It is a blessed place, not a place for war. Please, can you not consider another location for your command post?"

The major smiled. "I expected arguments such as this, so here is the alternative. If you refuse to leave, I will get trucks up here right now with a platoon of soldiers. We will force you onto the trucks and take you out of here with nothing. Which way do you prefer?"

Closing her eyes for a moment as she shook her head, Mother Superior replied. "We shall be ready Monday as you originally requested. We do not want any trouble."

"Ya, that is good, Sister. The less trouble we have the less amount of pain everyone feels. It is a win, win situation all the way around. Now, be aware, we will begin bringing equipment up to the Abbey over the next few days. We will have soldiers bivouacked with the equipment, so there will be no sabotage. They will not enter the Abbey or cause you any problems I assure you. Leave them alone, and they will leave you alone. Do I make myself clear!" The major replied as he glared at Mother superior, awaiting her response.

"It shall be so," Mother Superior replied quietly with a nod of her head.

Over the next three days, trucks grunted and groaned as they made their way up the steep drive to the Abbey. Some of them dropped loads of artillery and anti-aircraft weapons, while others dropped off boxes of ammunition and other field equipment. The soldiers slept in the back of the trucks or in tents pitched near one of the large flower gardens the sisters loved to work on.

By Monday morning, the entire area around the front of the Abbey was piled high with every type of military equipment possible. As scheduled, at 1000hrs. several trucks backed up to the front door of the Abbey. Soldiers assisted loading everything the sisters wanted to take with them. Before climbing onto the last truck, Mother Superior walked up to Major Jung.

"We have done as you asked without argument, so I ask you one favor now. We have taken many ancient pieces of furniture and art work to the lower basement and wrapped them in blankets so they will remain safe. Promise me they will be left alone so they can survive this war."

The major looked seriously at Mother Superior. "All I can tell you is this. The Third Reich has a director of antiquities. I will inform him of what is here. He will make the final decision as to what stays and what may need to go. That is the best I can tell you."

Shaking her head, Mother Superior said. "In other words, everything will be lost. I feel sorry for what you are about to do to this Abbey. I have heard stories about your so-called treasure hunting."

Waving at the driver, the major said. "Start the engine and take them down the hill, we are finished here." After one of the groundskeepers helped Mother Superior onto the back of the truck, he stepped aside and watched the sisters disappear down the steep driveway.

As the last truck disappeared from sight, Major Jung turned toward one of his sergeants. "You may call Field Marshall Goering now and tell him the sisters have been moved out. Tell him to bring a convoy of trucks as there will be much to be removed."

Over the next few days, the artillery and anti-aircraft guns were dug into place, heavy machine guns were installed in windows and on ledges below the Abbey walls. A powerful transmitter was placed in what had been the library, and tons of ammunition, hand grenades and other explosive devices were stored in secure sites in the sub-basement. Within a week the Abbey had become a fortress, complete with a hospital surgical ward and mortar tubes in the courtyards. Every ornate wooden door had been reinforced to prevent easy access to the structure.

Now the Germans had full control of anything that moved in the Furlo Valley, and artillery pieces were arranged so they could hit enemy targets nearly five miles away in any direction.

Field Marshall Goering was in awe of the wonderful construction of the Abbey. What he found inside pleased him even more. By the time he was finished marking everything he wanted to take, the Abbey had been pretty much stripped of anything of value. As he climbed into his black Mercedes to leave, he followed the twentieth truck full of well cased plunder down the rough road on its way to Germany. Some of the plunder would eventually be found in his residence near Berchtesgaden after the war ended, some would never be recovered.

After American forces destroyed German and Italian forces in Sicily and Corsica, allied aircraft based on the islands began attacking every enemy strong point they could find on the mainland.

It soon became evident that the Abbey di San Vincenzo above the Furlo Valley would need to be dealt with. The anti-aircraft guns that were strategically placed on the mountain sides were taking a serious toll on bombers and fighter aircraft as they attempted to strike at targets in the valley below.

The Mayor of Acqualagna begged General Mark Clark, the overall commander of the Italian campaign, to not destroy the Abbey, but to find a peaceful way to convince the Germans to leave the structure.

General Clark was not inclined to deal with the German's, as their ability to be honest and keep up their end of bargains was not at all reliable. However, after what had happened at Monte Casino, he felt that making an attempt to save the Abbey might be in everyone's best interest, but it had to be done quickly before Major General Ira Eaker, Commandant of the Eighth Air Force, became involved.

Through sensitive Swiss diplomatic channels, General Clark contacted Major Jung regarding the use of the monastery as an anti-aircraft battery or defensive position. Clark stated boldly that neither the Italian authorities or the Allies wanted to see the Abbey destroyed.

Several days later, a Swiss courier arrived at Clark's headquarters. When he was ushered into the General's office, he handed over an envelope. "My superiors want me to wait and see if you have any response you wish to have delivered back to Major Jung."

Nodding his head, General Clark pointed toward a large chair in front of his desk. After tearing open the envelope, he sat down to read the Major's response. Throwing the letter down on the desk, General Clark rubbed his forehead. Looking at the Swiss courier, he said, "You can tell your superior's there will be no response. The Abbey will need to be destroyed."

Standing up, the courier bowed slightly and said, "I have been there, this will be such a shame. However, I understand the spot you are in." Turning quickly, the courier left the office.

General Clark stood up, pacing his office for a moment before coming to a stop in front of a large map of Italy that stood on an easel. He stood motionless at first, as if he was memorized by what he was seeing. Finally, he raised his right hand and rubbed his chin several times before shaking his head. Turning to his aide Lt. Orton, he said, "Get General Eaker on the phone, and scramble the call."

About ten minutes later, Lieutenant Orton walked into the office. "General Eaker, line two."

Picking up the phone, General Clark said, "Ira, how the hell are things going for you down there in Rome? Have you spoken to the Pope lately regarding our entrance into heaven?"

General Eaker laughed as he replied. "Well Clark, I think Pious the Twelfth will certainly not give the Lord a glowing recommendation on either of us. Every time his people show up at my door, I can see my heavenly entrance disappear farther into the rearview mirror. So, what can I do for you today, General. Any news on the Furlo Valley?"

General Clark smiled at the last question. "Sir, I was wondering how many of those B-24 Liberator's you brought back from Africa are still sitting on the tarmac over in Sicily?"

Removing the smile from his face and leaning forward toward his desk, General Eaker replied. "I have about twenty, but only have crews for about a dozen right now."

Nodding his head, General Clark asked, "Do you have any British Lancaster's you can whistle up in a hurry?"

"Six for sure. Most of them were in pretty tough shape when I received them. Give me a month and a ship load of parts, and I'll have about twenty more ready to fly." So, what are you looking for, General?"

Without hesitation, General Clark replied. "I'll take the six Lancaster's, along with the dozen B-24's you have ready to go. Set up a mission for tomorrow night to strike the mountain sides around the monastery above the Furlo Valley."

General Eaker was quiet for a moment before he replied. "Clark, I cannot guarantee, even with precision bombing, that some of those hundred pounders won't fall on the Abbey itself."

"The only occupants of the Abbey are German. We will send them straight to hell if that's what it's going to take to guarantee the safety of our fighter bombers!" General Clark responded angrily.

Nodding his head, General Eaker responded. "We'll hit them at dusk, that will make it a bit tougher for the gunners to see them. I'll send you a bomber report as soon as I can."

At 2030hrs the following evening, the airfield near Messina, Sicily was a beehive of activity as the last B-24 roared down the runway carrying a bomb load of 5,000 pounds. Next in line were the British Lancaster's, carrying their typical bomb load of 14,000 pounds.

The flight crews watched anxiously as their planes flew a northeasterly course out over the Straits of Messina. In just a short time the bombers began flying up through a large cloud bank to an altitude of 20,000 ft.

Five miles out from the target, the planes readjusted their formation and opened the doors to the bomb bays. One by one the pilots turned control of their aircraft over to their bombardiers as they studied the terrain below through their Norden bomb sites

No doubt the German anti-aircraft crews had been notified to the flight of bombers headed their way. Every gun on the south and west slopes of the mountain began pouring flak into the evening sky. Despite the rocking of the planes, the bombardiers kept their planes on a perfect heading until they were over the target. With bombs away, the aircraft turned hard toward the south to avoid flak from the northern side of the mountain.

Explosions rocked the mountain as the bombs detonated in a cascade of steel and fire. Large secondary explosions sent more shrapnel flying through the air as ten anti-aircraft batteries took direct hits. It appeared as if the entire west side of the mountain was on fire.

Deep down in the subbasement of the Abbey, Major Jung listened to the switchboard as damage results were called in. He stomped his foot and swore as he realized how many of his guns were taken out, while not one Allied bomber was shot down.

Arriving back at Messina, the ground crews began checking over their aircraft and pulling shrapnel out of the skin of the bombers. They were in a hurry to get their planes repaired, as General Eaker had already announced they were going back the next day.

The following evening as the bombers approached the mountain, fires in gun pits that had been hit the night before continued to burn, giving bombardiers a much better aim site. However, at the last minute, the B-24's did a mid-course correction, so they could drop their bombs on the south side of the mountain. Half the Lancaster's attacked the south side of the mountain while the other half attacked the north side. The flak on the south side of the mountain was much more accurate than the night before. One Lancaster suffered a catastrophic blow after releasing its bombs. Its port wing was smashed by a direct flak strike, causing the entire wing to be ripped from the plane. After the crew bailed out, the injured pilot aimed his stricken bomber directly toward two German Tiger tanks that were parked on the road leading up to the Abbey. The impact and explosion sent one burning tiger rolling down the side of the mountain, while the other tank exploded, creating a massive crater in the narrow dirt road that led to the front of the Abbey. An anti-aircraft battery dug into the side of the mountain a short distance away exploded, as gallons of burning high octane aviation fuel poured down on the gun pit, detonating shells standing out in the open.

General Eakers and his staff went over photos of the bombing mission with great satisfaction as they looked over the damage their crews had created, with the loss of just one plane.

As bad weather was moving into the area, a third attack was called off until the storms cleared. Meanwhile, in the Furlo Valley, units of the underground worked feverishly attempting to find the six surviving members of the Lancaster before the Germans did.

After crawling out of the cold water of the Candigliano River, Second Lieutenant Adkinson observed a group of men running toward his position. Recognizing the outline of the helmet, he realized he was about to be taken prisoner. As he began to raise his hands, one of the soldiers fired a blast from his Mauser. The lieutenant flew back into the river, where more bullets began striking the water all around him. Diving toward the bottom of the river to escape the bullets, the Lancaster navigator was in tremendous pain and losing blood rapidly. Reaching over to his left side, he pulled out his .38 pistol and swam toward shore. Pushing himself out of the water, he began firing at the German soldiers that were walking the shore line. After he had shot two of them, a soldier with a Schmeisser let go a long blast from his weapon, killing the lieutenant.

Later that night, men from the underground recovered his body from the river and gave him a proper burial in the nearby forest. The other five crew members were eventually transported back to Corsica, where they were reunited with American forces.

A week later, a third raid was planned against the mountain, but this time the Abbey itself would be targeted. Each aircraft bound for the Abbey was carrying five-hundred-pound bombs. When they reached the Abbey, four

B-24's would strike the east side of the mountain, four would strike the west side and four would strike the south side. Four of the Lancaster's would bomb the Abbey directly, while the fifth attacked positions near the north side. It would be the last attack before the Tenth

Mountain Division and units of the 504 Airborne Brigade assaulted the monastery two days later.

With very few anti-aircraft batteries left on the mountain, the bombers swept in at 15,000 feet, and began their assigned attacks.

The first five-hundred-pound bombs from the Lancaster's, tore through the roof of the Abbey, detonating on the fourth and fifth floors. Several other bombs tore through the roofs of the far east wing, detonating on the first and second floors. Major Jung lay on the floor of the foyer with his mouth wide open, as he watched plaster fall from the ceiling and light fixtures tumble to the floor where they shattered.

Picking himself up, he yelled at Lt. Vogel. "Get in the basement, the barbarians are going to tear this place apart!"

Explosion after explosion rocked the monastery, collapsing walls and caving in floors, while blowing out windows in every room of the fortress. Running to the radio room, Major Vogel attempted to radio his superiors in Berlin, but was unsuccessful, as the massive twenty-foot antenna was now so much twisted metal, nearly fifty feet below the roof it had been attached to.

As the bombers turned west, soldiers returned from the basement, attempting to fight the fires that were raging inside sections of the Abbey. Major Jung walked through what had been a very ornate foyer and kicked at the rubble. Yelling, he said, "Look what they have done to my home! They will pay a price for what they have done, they will pay a price!"

Two days later, at 2345hrs., thirty C-47 Dakotas dropped 840 men from the 504 Parachute Regiment into the Furlo Valley near the west side of the mountain. Immediately, the men began to climb into the foothills, establishing a foothold for the Tenth Mountain Division that was scheduled to arrive around 1200hrs. There was little resistance as most of the German gunnery units had either been wiped out, or had already abandoned their wrecked guns. At dawn, a dozen P-51 Mustangs roared in over the valley, attacking remaining German strongholds, that were well marked by the paratroopers.

Inside the monastery, Major Jung attempted to organize the troops inside the Abbey to drive off the attackers. He still had heavy machine guns and mortar tubes that could rain death down upon the Americans as they struggled up the mountainside.

With P-51 Mustangs and P-38 Lightening fighter bombers continuing to strike German targets on the mountain side, a heavily armed battalion opened a path for the Tenth Mountain Division that arrived nearly an hour earlier than expected. They wasted no time following paths set up by paratroopers, as they worked their way up the rocky face of the mountain.

The Germans were successful in turning back two attacks by American forces that could have breached the north road, giving the allies access to the front of the Abbey. As night fell over the mountain, the Tenth Mountain Division retreated back to safety as their commanders figured out another avenue of approach for the following morning. The paratroopers held their line, refusing to take a step back in hopes of creating a hole sometime during the night, but the opportunity never existed.

With more German troops arriving from Milan overnight, the belt had been tightened and every attempt by American troops to break through the next day was turned back.

Bloodied and tired, the men from the Tenth Mountain Division resupplied overnight and prepared for a third day of bitter fighting. However, a platoon of paratroopers stumbled on the door that Dominique had used to leave the Abbey years earlier. As the heavy door had been sealed from the inside, the paratroopers used several pieces of well-placed plastic explosives to blow it from its hinges. When the smoke and dust settled, nearly a hundred paratroopers began the assault up the tunnel, past John's inscription and right up to the second heavy door.

Once again placing charges on the hinges and the heavy sliding bolt, the paratroopers withdrew down the tunnel, waiting for the door to be blown to bits allowing them into the subbasement. German troops that had been sleeping in the basement jumped to their feet, unsure of what had just taken place. By the time they could get organized, paratroopers were streaming into the subbasement firing at anything that moved. Bodies of German soldiers fell to the floor as blood splattered on the walls and massive stone support columns. Screams echoed off the stone as the pride of the Wehrmacht raced for the exits leading to the basement overhead where their headquarters was located.

By now, nearly a hundred Mountain Division men were streaming in through the tunnel, as more congregated outside the tunnel waiting to join the attack.

Major Jung was terrified when he was told what was happening two floors below him. He knew beyond a doubt that the monastery would fall to the Americans before the day was over, but he and his men were not going to quit without a fight. Several Mountain Division men carrying a bazooka, charged up to a stairway leading to the main basement. After the loader placed the round into the weapon, the gunner pulled the trigger. The heavy antitank round destroyed the door while killing ten German soldiers that were standing on the other side. Once again, paratroopers raced up the undefended staircase to begin battling more bewildered Germans that were attempting to make a determined stand against overwhelming odds.

Hand grenades were tossed by both sides, and explosions rocked the room, sending massive amounts of shrapnel in every direction. As the second stairwell was breached by paratroopers, the Germans found themselves caught between two advancing units, that now numbered nearly three hundred well-armed soldiers. Attempting to climb up the wide twisting staircase to the foyer was becoming an act of suicide, as bodies covered nearly every step leading to the centuries old ornate brass covered door.

Watching the bloody hand to hand combat taking place near the second stairwell, a young Wehrmacht Lieutenant became sick and vomited in a closet near the front of the room. Realizing any attempt to escape the onslaught of American forces was purely impossible, he jumped up on a chair, waved his arms and yelled, "Comrades, cease fire, everyone cease fire, it is over. No more killing!"

Looking at their blood covered officer, one by one the Germans laid down their weapons and raised their hands above their heads. The paratroopers pushed back the remaining enemy soldiers to the back wall so they could not pick up the weapons laying on the floor.

With that completed, Captain Studdard from the Tenth Mountain Division walked over to the scared German officer. Reaching out his hand, he said. "Lieutenant, hand me your pistol, do it carefully."

With his hands shaking, the lieutenant looked down at the captain that was firmly pointing a semi-automatic pistol toward his chest. Fumbling with getting the weapon out of his holster, he said, "Do not shoot, please do not shoot. I surrender, do not shoot."

After taking possession of the Luger, the captain backed away. "Come down from the chair, let my medics look you over, then we shall talk."

Several German soldiers helped their wounded officer down from the chair and set him on the ground. Immediately, a medic ran forward and knelt down to look at the lieutenant's injuries. As he poured sulfa into the wounds and began wrapping them, the medic said. "You'll be fine, sir."

Already, the paratroopers were escorting the prisoners out of the basement and into the tunnel, where more Tenth Division soldiers waited to take them down to a hastily built POW cage. After the bodies had been removed from the stairs leading to the foyer, Captain Studdard walked up to the lieutenant. "In your estimation, how many more men are still above us in the Abbey?"

Shaking his head, the lieutenant replied. "I cannot be sure. Maybe another two hundred, maybe more. They are all heavily armed and well experienced. Major Jung will not be taken easily. He is a true Nazi."

Reaching down to help the lieutenant from the floor, the captain walked him over to the stairwell. Pointing toward the door, he said. "There is a slot in the door for communication. Go up to that slot and ask to speak with the major. Tell him there is no way to escape and it would be best if he surrendered his men."

Nodding his head, the lieutenant climbed the stairs and asked for Major Jung. A soldier from the Tenth Mountain Division that was fluent in German stood near the middle of the stairwell listening to the conversation. Turning to the captain, he said. "The major wants a minute to think it over." He had barely turned back to face the lieutenant, when a German Panzer Faust was fired through the heavy door. The explosion knocked him back down the stairs, while ripping the young German lieutenant to shreds.

As the door hung in shambles, a German heavy MG 34 began firing around the basement. Everyone dove for cover as the captain looked over at one of the men holding a bazooka.

"What the hell are you waiting for?"

"My loader, my loader is dead, the machine gun got him." The bazooka man shouted.

Quickly the captain slid across the floor, picked up the rocket and loaded the weapon. When he was done, he slapped the gunner on the helmet and yelled. "Make it happen!"

The bazooka roared and the machine gun ceased firing. Instantly, paratroopers streamed up the stairs into the foyer, not allowing anyone to surrender. German soldiers ran up the stone stair case to the top levels of the monastery, firing down at the advancing paratroopers. Hundreds of bullets ricocheted off the marble floor, creating a deadly no man's land for the paratroopers, until another well-placed bazooka round cleared the stairway.

As the misty dawn broke under a cover of heavy clouds, the Tenth Mountain Division had encircled the monastery and finally gained control of the mountain. But now, the remaining sections of the Abbey would have to be taken room by room, until the structure could be considered secure. Fighting raged on for the next two days as American soldiers chased down German soldiers in a game of cat and mouse, using grenades, machine guns and more bazookas to finally bring peace to the devastated monastery. Some prisoners were taken, some died from their wounds as medical care could not reach them, and the rest were either killed or committed suicide.

On the last day of fighting, Major Jung and his aide Lieutenant Vogel sat in what had been a large bedroom overlooking the valley when a sergeant walked into the room. "Herr Major, we are all out of food, we are down to three bullets per man, the machine gun ammunition is gone, and we have no more grenades. It is hopeless. I have seriously wounded men next door that will not survive without a doctor. May I have your permission to surrender, we all knew it was inevitable. We must save the lives of those that can still walk out of here."

Lieutenant Vogel looked at the trusted sergeant. "How many men are you talking about?"

Looking down at the floor for a moment the sergeant replied. "I am afraid there are only twenty of us left, Herr Lieutenant."

Standing up from the chair he had been sitting in, the lieutenant said, "Twenty, that is what we have left as a fighting force?"

Nodding his head, the sergeant responded. "Ya Herr Lieutenant, the balance of the two hundred fifty are all gone."

As tears filled the lieutenant's eyes, he said. "They were all so brave, how can this be, how can this be. Where are they all at?"

"Sir, they fill the corridors and rooms of this Abbey where they died. They fought bravely, but there was no way we could fight off such an attack. Sir, may I surrender?"

Nodding his head, the lieutenant took out his pistol, handing it to the sergeant. "Give it to the American officer in charge, and have our men leave all their weapons behind and go with you. The Major and I will follow."

Holding on to a piece of white cloth, the sergeant walked down the corridor with his hands in the air. Looking down the connecting corridor he yelled out. "Captain Studdard, we wish to surrender. Here is the lieutenant's pistol as a peace offering. My men are behind me with their hands in the air. Will you let us surrender?"

Leaning against a bullet riddled wall, the captain looked at Lieutenant Coppecio, an Italian born American. "What do you think, Coppecio?"

After giving it a moment of thought he replied. "We want Major Jung, ask him where he is."

Smiling at his lieutenant, Captain Studdard yelled out. "Where is Major Jung? There will be no surrender without him!"

A moment later, Major Jung stepped out into the corridor with his hands in the air. "I am here, Captain. We shall surrender without causing you any more problems."

Stepping over his machine gunner that was laying on the floor behind his weapon ready to fire, the captain replied. "Lead your men over to us, but if anyone fires or tosses a grenade, so help me God, Major, every single one of you will die right here. I have lost too many good men taking this Abbey, and I will lose no more!"

Slowly with their hands over their heads, the remaining Germans left the monastery and were driven to the POW stockade. Captain Studdard felt heartbroken as he walked past the bodies of his men and those of the German defenders. Several times, he repeated, "Such a damn waste, such a waste."

Chapter Eleven – The Horrors Begin

With a near gale force wind of over fifty miles an hour blowing out of the northwest, the Solomon Sea was a very dangerous place to be. Unlike most oceans in the world, the Solomon Sea had many uncharted sand bars, rock piles and reefs lurking just under the surface. In a storm like this, it was possible for a ship to strike one of these obstacles and rip the bottom out of their vessel before the crew even knew what was happening. However, the skipper of the Koshiro Maru felt it was safer than traversing the narrow passages of the Solomon Islands, where running into a squadron of American PT Boats was always a possibility. Consequently, the flat-bottomed assault ship and its two destroyer escorts, were not making very good time on the voyage to the island of Choiseul, where the prisoners would be added to an already over-crowded camp. The dark damp hold on the assault ship did not have any windows and was lit by just two medium sized incandescent light bulbs People screamed each time the boat slammed down onto the surface of the sea after dropping down from a large wave, as it felt as if the vessel were going to break in two.

Although it was impossible to know what time it was in the hold, by late evening the wind was beginning to subside, but the constant rain continued to fall in torrents. The five-foot waves and the cover of rain allowed a lurking American submarine to get a fix on the slow-moving ships just rounding the west coast of Vella Lavella. Killing a destroyer was always a good target, since it was a combat vessel, but taking out a landing ship with infantry and field equipment was an important target here in the Solomon's, and was exactly what the high command in Hawaii wanted to be sunk.

Lieutenant Sam Kirksy, skipper of the submarine U.S.S. Rockfish, watched carefully out of his periscope until he had a clear view of the landing ship. Turning to his executive officer, he said, "Dave, she's not riding very low in the water, so it does not appear to have a big load on board. But taking out a landing craft is still a strong kill. Make ready tubes one and two."

Moments later, Ensign Dave Collins called back, "Tubes one and two at the ready, Skipper!"

"Wonderful, Mr. Collins, stand by for my order." Lieutenant Kirksy replied waiting for the transport to drop off the edge of a large wave before calling out, "Fire one and two!"

Seconds later, Ensign Collins replied, "One and two away, distance three thousand yards, both fish running hot and true, sir."

Knowing that sometimes a kill on a semi-loaded assault ship was a tricky business, Lieutenant Kirksy stayed glued to the periscope in order to see what was going to happen. At 1905hrs, two miles off the northwest coast of the island of Vella Lavella near Liangai point, two large explosions nearly ripped off the front half of the north bound attack transport.

Slamming the handles of the periscope down, Lieutenant Kirksy called out, "Dive! Dive! Dive! Take us down to six hundred feet, make a course for 340 degrees, engines all ahead full."

The veteran crew was following the orders to escape the destroyers, before Ensign Collins could repeat the order back to his skipper.

On the landing ship panic raged through the cargo hold, as sea water began to enter the compartment from buckled and torn bulk heads.

Sister Dominique slammed her fists against the water tight door as she screamed for help. Above her on the main deck, sailors were preparing to abandon ship, as they began lowering life boats into the water. Once every sailor and marine had found a spot in the life boats, two marines ran down the deck firing holes into the bottoms of the remaining life boats, making them unusable.

The last marine to shoot holes in the boats then charged down into the hold and unlocked the water tight door. Looking at Sister Dominique, he called out. "Let your God save you now!"

Running back up the stairway, he jumped in the life boat and disappeared over the side of the sinking ship.

As the water in the hold was now nearly waist deep, everyone scurried up ladders to the main deck where they watched the motorized life boats sailing off into the gathering darkness.

Pierre Duncan and a couple of his men found some more primitive life rafts stacked next to the main superstructure of the ship. After cutting them lose, they began placing them into the rising water that was quickly reaching the main deck. However, as the ship began to list to port, two of the battle tanks being carried in the cargo hold slammed into the outside wall, causing the vessel to begin to capsize.

Mothers and fathers held on to their children, especially those that had not learned to swim yet. There were many people that had been injured during the torpedo attack that were not sure of what to do. Not wanting to go down with the ship, they began jumping into the swirling water, not knowing what awaited them. But soon, sharks that had been attracted by the blood began attacking the swimmers. The cries of swimmers that had already been attacked by the sharks echoed out across the storm-tossed sea. Men in the small rafts worked as hard as they could, pulling people out of the water before they could be attacked by the growing number of sharks.

As Pierre Duncan reached for Sister Dominique to pull her onto a raft, she quickly pulled free from his grip while screaming. "The children, save the children, Pierre!"

Realizing the ship was beginning to roll over and would suck anyone nearby down with it, Sister Dominique yelled for them to swim away from the wreckage as quickly as they could. Grabbing onto a little girl, Sister Dominique yelled. "Dog paddle, kick your legs, help me get away from the ship, but the girl did not respond. Looking closer at the child, she observed a large piece of shrapnel sticking out of her throat. Crying, she let go of the child and watched her sink into the abyss.

Moments later, the colder water of the sea surrounded the boilers on the transport, causing them to explode along with several tons of ammunition that were stored near the engine room. Thousands of pieces of shrapnel roared across the ocean surface, striking survivors in the water as well as those in the flimsy life rafts. It appeared as if the devil himself had reached out across the ocean, tearing souls from the wretched survivors.

The screws of the ship were clearly visible as flames now roared through the massive hole in the bottom of the hull. With the front end of the landing ship already gone, the massive engines began pulling what remained of the landing ship to the bottom of New Georgia Sound. The boilers hissed as steam escaped into the night sky from broken pipes. Large iron girders groaned before snapping as the heavy internal machinery broke loose from their mountings. On the surface near the dying vessel, unaware of what was about to happen when the landing ship made its final dive, many prisoners of European descent, unaccustomed to naval tragedies, clung together in a circle and prayed. Moments later, the tremendous suction of the sinking ship sucked most of them down, never to be seen again. However, other survivors who were able to escape the sinking of the ship, were still at the mercy of the ravenous sharks.

Then suddenly, there appeared to be a calmness over the water as the ship had disappeared, and those that remained alive were shocked into silence. Rolling over onto her back, Sister Dominique looked up into the carpet of stars that blanketed the night sky. As the waves pushed the bodies of dead and dismembered victims into her, Sister Dominique looked up at the Southern Cross Constellation.

"Why, what did these poor people do to deserve any of this? Answer me, damn it, I want an answer. Were their sins so terrible, were they not worth saving? How could you allow this to happen?"

After sobbing uncontrollably for several moments, Sister Dominique was brought back to the reality of the situation when she observed a large shark attack the remains of a child less than ten yards away from her. Suddenly, she realized the ocean was alive with more sharks coming to join in the killing feast.

Filled with utter terror, Sister Dominique was uncertain whether she should stay quietly in one place, hoping the sharks would overlook her, or attempt to swim away as fast as she could. Before she could make the decision, something large bumped into the back of her neck and shoulders. Closing her eyes, she waited for the painful end to come.

However, before she could realize what was happening, two sets of strong arms from the raft began plucking her from the bloody water. Nevertheless, before they were able to get her into the raft, a shark clamped down on her right forearm. The pain was indescribable as razor-sharp teeth sunk into her flesh as the determined predator attempted to pull her back into the water. Sister Dominique let out a blood curdling scream she was sure could be heard all the way back to Nusa Simbo. Instantly, one of the men in the raft holding an oar, slammed it down onto the shark's eyes with every ounce of energy he could muster.

Releasing Sister Dominique's arm, the vicious killer slipped back down below the surface of the sea, as the men struggled feverishly to complete the rescue. One of the men removed his shirt and began binding up the bleeding wounds the hideous teeth of the shark had left behind.

Sister Dominique drifted in and out of consciousness throughout the remainder of the long night, as several people in the raft worked together to stop the horrible bleeding from her arm.

As a drizzly dark dawn broke over the Solomon Sea, several black shapes appeared out of the growing fog. Sailors standing by the rail were stunned, as they looked down at the blood covered men, women and children that packed the over loaded sinking life rafts.

Immediately, the skippers of the two Japanese patrol boats brought their vessels to a stop, as life rafts were dropped into the sea. Crew members from the patrol boats quickly began delivering the survivors to the main deck so they could be treated by their medical staff. Other members of the crew shot sharks that continued to get in the way of the rescue operation. Within two hours, one hundred fifteen survivors had been taken aboard the two vessels.

A young medic placed sulfa on Sister Dominique's arm before wrapping it with a clean white bandage. When he finished his work, he took out a morphine syrette and stuck it into her upper arm. Looking over at Pierre Duncan, the medic asked. "How did you end up in this situation?"

After Pierre and Sister Claudia explained what all had happened, the medic bowed down feeling ashamed. "To many of my brothers have become cold and callous already, and I fear for them. But I am one man, what can I do?"

Sister Dominique looked up at the medic, and said, "I'm afraid that before this war is over, we will have many things to hang our heads over. Do nothing that will cause you disgrace. You must find ways to do the right thing and save your own soul."

One of the patrol boat's officers walked up to Father Renaldo. We heard you were to be taken to Choiseul to a prison camp near Kakasa. We cannot continue taking you there, so we will take you to Liangai on Vella Lavella where there is a small port. We will turn you over to the Japanese base commander until other arrangements can be made to transfer you. I am sorry, but that is the best thing we can do for you now."

Father Renaldo nodded his head. "We appreciate your help in getting us out of the water. We are not about to argue with where you need to drop us."

As the patrol boats turned toward the southeast, Sister Claudia and Father Renaldo walked among the survivors. Shaking his head, Father Renaldo said, "We lost over a hundred souls last night, and some of these still may not survive. My question is this, Sister. Were these people saved just so they can go through another hell with the Japanese? These Japanese sailors have compassion for victims lost at sea, and they understand the horrors of surviving a sinking ship. But I'm afraid the Japanese marines like those that took us off Nusa Simbo will care less about us. To be honest, I'm worried about going to Vella LaVella where there is no camp prepared for us."

Sister Margaret was changing compresses on Sister Dominique's forehead when Father Renaldo and Sister Claudia arrived. Kneeling down, Father Renaldo asked. "Is she any better?"

Smiling Sister Margaret replied. "Her temperature is way down and she has taken some broth. She even spoke for a few minutes while I checked her dressing. The bleeding has stopped, so I think she will be better by morning."

Sister Claudia sat down on the teak deck beside her sister. "Go get yourself something to eat, Sister Margaret. I will take over for you. The people I have been working with are all doing well."

Standing up, Sister Margaret looked at Father Renaldo. "Do we know where we are going?"

Shaking his head, Father Renaldo replied. "Somewhere on the island of Vella LaVella. I had hoped we would be taken to either Truk or Rabaul, where they have camps for people taken off the islands that are noncombatants. It really didn't matter which one, it would have only been a stopover point until they move us to a prison camp well behind their lines. But now I have no idea what will happen to us."

Opening her eyes, Sister Dominique replied in a shaky voice. "We must have faith that they will treat us properly, after all we are noncombatants."

Smiling, Father Renaldo knelt down and kissed Sister Dominique's cheek.

"Only God can help us now, I'm afraid. But you must get some rest so you will be ready to walk when we reach the shore."

About a half hour later, the two patrol boats arrived in a small inlet near the town of Liangai. on the island of Vella LaVella. The survivors were placed in an empty ammunition storage bunker until dawn.

As the sun rose over the western Pacific, a Captain Kimura, along with twenty marines arrived at the bunker. After ordering everyone to step out into a fenced area, he looked over the survivors. Walking up to Father Renaldo, he inquired. "Why are there natives with you?"

Before Father Renaldo could respond, Sister Dominique stepped forward. "I am in charge of the missionaries, you shall address me, please."

Angered by Sister Dominique's abruptness, the captain walked toward her. "And what happened to your arm?"

"I was in a wrestling match with a shark, and I came out on the winning side. So, now I have nothing left to fear from man or nature." Sister Dominique responded, realizing she was about to catch the wrath of the angry officer.

Walking directly up to Sister Dominique, he looked her in the eye. "Sharks can bite, they can do no more. You have no idea what a Japanese officer can do to you for being so arrogant! You may wish to think twice in the future when you speak out and disrespect an officer of the Japanese empire!"

Before another word could be spoken, the captain struck Sister Dominique across the face, knocking her to the ground. As Sister Claudia stepped forward, he yelled. "Do not help her, she has brought this on herself!"

Sister Claudia stepped back as she watched the captain pull his pistol and aim it at Sister Dominique. "So, now let us try this again. Why are their natives with you? Are they your slaves?"

"No, they are not slaves, they lived on Nusa Simbo. When we were loaded on the transport, Major Ouichi's marines pushed many natives on the ship with us. These few are all that survived our ordeal at sea," Sister Dominique replied, trying to sound respectful.

Placing his pistol back into its holster, he looked at his sergeant. "Have the natives taken to the work crew. They will remain here and work for us unloading ships. I do not care where they came from."

Immediately, several Marines pushed the natives out of the fenced area, marching them down a dirt road toward the harbor.

Turning back toward the dirty scared survivors, the captain said. "We were not expecting nearly a hundred survivors last night. We have no place to keep you, and we do not wish to tie up marines to watch you, as this is a forward combat base. We will transfer you over to a warehouse where we have about thirty more prisoners to be sent to the rear. Once we get a ship ready to sail, you will be on it."

The prisoners were marched about a mile to a concrete warehouse that had clearly already been damaged by a bombing attack. Inside were thirty prisoners that had come from various islands the Japanese had overrun. Two of the prisoners were British missionaries from Bougainville Island, named Henry and Evelyn Baker. Evelyn told horrific stories of Japanese atrocities toward natives and white plantation owners. She told Sister Dominique to be very careful in the future, as the soldiers did not always punish the perpetrator. They were very good at having the perpetrator watch as they tortured and slaughtered other innocent victims, especially natives.

The second day they were in the warehouse, a flight of carrier based American fighter bombers attacked, dropping bombs and incendiaries in the warehouse area. One bomb exploded against the corner of the building, collapsing part of the wall and ceiling where some of the survivors had been sleeping. Quickly, Father Renaldo and the men began digging through the rubble attempting to extricate those that were still alive, before removing the dead.

Three badly wounded people had just been laid out in the center of the warehouse as Captain Kimura and his men arrived. Pushing the sisters out of the way, Captain Kimura took a machine gun from one of his soldiers and shot the victims. "We have no medical supplies to treat these people. But we do have shovels so you can bury them."

With the burial detail completed, Sister Dominique walked up to the sergeant who was standing by the door. "I would like to see the base commander. We have not been treated properly, for we are not combatants."

The sergeant laughed as he looked Sister Dominique face to face. "Our base commander is an Admiral. He does not even live on this island, and surely does not know you even exist. Captain Kimura is the highest-ranking officer you will see while you are here. You have already seen what he can do, and I assure you if a ship does not come soon, you will all die. We have much work to do here as the Americans are moving toward us every day. To be honest, you are just in the way."

That night as Sister Dominique attempted to sleep; she heard in the distance the sound of airplanes approaching Vella LaVella. These were not the type of fighter bombers she had become accustomed to on Nusa Simbo. She knew these were large American bombers coming out of Port Moresby with tons of high explosives. The sound of the engines rose to a crescendo as the concrete beneath her began to vibrate. It was almost as if she could pick out each plane by the vibration of their massive engines.

By now, everyone in the building was awake and screaming as the heavy bombers crossed over from the Solomon Sea onto the island of Vella LaVella. Bombs began to whistle and whine as they left the bomb bays of the B-17 bombers. In the pitch blackness, the ground began to shake as if a giant earthquake were about to swallow them up. Loose material from the damaged ceiling began to fall down upon the survivors, creating shear panic. Women and children screamed, as men attempted to pry one of the steel doors open with several shovels left behind by the guards.

Suddenly, a bright light filled the room, seconds before the sound and shock wave of the exploding bomb threw everyone against the back wall.

There was no way of knowing who was next to you, under you, or on top of you, when the wall stopped the mass of humanity that had been tossed into the air like so many stuffed toys.

Feeling the solid floor under her left foot, Sister Dominique was attempting to get a foot hold and stand up, when another bomb struck the corner of the building that had been damaged earlier in the day. Once again, the shock wave threw her sideways, where she tumbled across screaming bloody bodies that had no way of escaping the pure hell that had been dumped upon them.

Finally, the roar of the massive rotating engines disappeared into the night, as the bombers were once more out over the ocean, heading back to their base in Australia.

The silver light from a brilliant full moon shown through a gaping hole where the entire corner of the warehouse had collapsed. Though her ears rang from the explosions, from somewhere off in the distance, Sister Dominique could hear Father Renaldo calling out. "Make your way to the corner and crawl out before the rest of the building collapses!"

Slowly, the wounded and bleeding survivors began the arduous task of crawling up over the sharp broken concrete and shredded steel sheeting that had fallen in from the roof. Once they reached the top of the pile, Father Renaldo and several men from the plantation help them down to the ground.

Although it was still very dark, several Japanese marines came running up to the building shooting into the air, demanding everyone crawl back into the damaged structure. Struggling to make it to the top of the rubble pile past the last few survivors, Sister Dominique pushed one of the soldiers to the side. As she watched him slip down the debris, she called out. "I am here to save these people, not kill them. You must let them pass before the building caves in and crushes them all!"

As the final survivors reached the ground and ran away from the angry marines, Captain Kimura ran up to Sister Dominique, pushing her down onto the rubble. Pulling his pistol, he fired a shot toward her head. Due to the fact that his hand was shaking with anger, the bullet struck a brick and shattered, sending several pieces of shrapnel into her cheek.

Completely sure the angry officer was going to fire again, Sister Dominique rolled the rest of the way down the rubble pile, attempting to cover her head. Realizing he had completely lost control of the situation, Captain Kimura fired once more at Sister Dominique as she scrambled toward a truck the marines had arrived in. The headlight on the truck shattered, as Sister Dominique raced past the grill, dropped to the ground and crawled around to the driver's side, of the truck looking for cover.

Before Captain Kimura could fire again, Pierre Duncan ran over to the truck, throwing his body over the top of Sister Dominique, as Sister Claudia and Sister Margaret placed themselves between the captain and his target. Slowly, Pierre raised his head while holding up his hand. In a very calm voice he said, "It is finished, Captain, let it go!"

Slamming his pistol back into its holster, he yelled at his sergeant. "Put them in the small warehouse, and make sure they bury the dead tonight!" Still filled with rage, Captain Kimura walked off toward his staff car, swearing every epitaph he had probably ever learned.

It was evident to the survivors that the sergeant wanted to fulfill the request of his commanding officer to bury the dead, but he appeared to be a reasonable man that did not want any more killing tonight.

While undertaking the grizzly task of removing the fifteen sets of remains from the warehouse, twenty more prisoners were being marched down the dusty road from the wharf by Japanese guards. Without saying a word, they all pitched in to dig the graves and finish the work.

Father Renaldo was interested to see another priest and two more catholic sisters in the group, however, they appeared to be very standoffish, and did not want to speak with the others.

As dawn began to creep over Vella LaVella, Father Renaldo walked over to the new priest who was sharing his meager breakfast with some children. Sitting down on the concrete floor, Father Renaldo said, "So, what island did you come from, Father "

"Omana Island, just north of Santa Isabel. We had escaped from Santa Isabel when the Japanese invaded, and really had nowhere else to go. They burned the mission and killed several of our members. We escaped across the channel with the help of some of the natives who were still very loyal to us. We survived for about three months, before we were spotted by a Japanese pilot. When they came looking for us, there really was nowhere to hide. By the way, I am Father Martin, and the taller sister is Sister Josephine and the shorter sister is Sister Henrietta. We are all from the United States, so we were more than scared to be captured by the Japanese. But so far, they have treated us fairly well. I am not sure why they brought us here to Vella Lavella, but it's good to be with other prisoners."

Leaning back against the wall, Father Renaldo asked, "Do you happen to have an alter set in your belongings we could use to say Mass for the people?"

Shaking his head, Father Martin replied. "No, they took everything from us that was worth a plug nickel. I was surprised they let me have this prayer book and Rosary."

Nodding his head, Father Renaldo replied. "Yes, all of my things were taken, as well. But at least you can help me hear confessions. Many of the people here want to have a confession service, so it would be nice to have you help me with that."

Instantly, Father Martin stood up. "I do not believe that is something I would like to get involved in. No, Father Renaldo, you will need to do that yourself, I am sorry."

As the young priest walked away, Father Renaldo instantly realized something was not right, but was unsure what it could be. Walking to where Sister Dominique and the others were seated, Father Renaldo explained the conversation he had with Father Martin. "There is something strange going on there, and I have a feeling the good Father Martin may not be a priest at all. Talk to the new sisters, and see what you can find out."

Father Renaldo was about to stand up when Evelyn Baker approached. "I did not mean to listen in on your conversation, Father, but I can tell you for a fact that Father Martin is not a priest. My husband and I were hiding out from the Japanese on Papatura Faa Island just east of Omana. We heard from the natives that were protecting us, that Father Martin had been killed by a squad of Japanese soldiers during a night raid on the mission. The sisters managed to escape into the jungle and hide for a while. When the natives moved them across the channel, there was Father Martin again. I assure you he is neither a priest or a man of the cloth. He is an impostor that will need to be dealt with before the Japanese figure out what is going on."

As she finished speaking, Henry Baker approached. "Evelyn, I have told you to stop with that story. We do not know who the man is, all we know are the rumors from the natives, and all too often they are not reliable. However, the sisters have been doing what they can to protect him, so we must protect their privacy!"

Angered by his comment, Evelyn Baker turned and walked away. Shaking his head, Henry Baker said. "She is scared, as is everyone. She is right in believing the Japanese cannot be trusted, and will take out their anger on all of us if something happens. But it is wrong to put that man's life in jeopardy if we are not sure what he is all about."

Several days later, Captain Kimura came to the warehouse with the evening meal. After looking around the room, he said, "In several days you will board a ship for a prisoner camp at Rabaul where you belong. There are already several hundred prisoners being held there where you will live out your miserable lives until the Japanese military reigns over the Pacific. Then you may be allowed to return to your homes, if the emperor chooses to allow it."

After the captain and his marines left the building, Evelyn Baker looked at her husband. "That man pretending to be Father Martin must be dealt with. If the Japanese come to find out he is not who he says he is, we will all suffer the consequences."

Taking hold of his wife's arm, Henry Baker replied. "Evelyn, we all want to live. There are other people in this warehouse we know nothing about, but we must trust them also. We must trust that the sisters would not put us in danger."

Pulling away from her husband, Evelyn Baker replied. "You are wrong, Henry. We must find out who he is, and we must find out before they put us on that ship. Our lives depend on it, and I plan to see our children back in London when this war is over. I have no intentions of dying because of your misguided intentions. We have a family back home that needs us, and we must survive at all cost!"

Henry knew his wife was a headstrong woman, and that had worked well for them working in the missions. But now they were in a delicate situation, and he didn't trust her one bit. About midnight, Evelyn laid down next to her husband. "I told you the man was not a priest and he could get us all killed. One of the women that arrived with them says he's an American pilot that was shot down over Santa Isabel. The sisters have been trying to protect him so the Japanese don't kill him. Henry, we must tell Captain Kimura who he is!"

Sitting up, Henry looked angrily at his wife. "Evelyn, they will kill him and the nuns he has been staying with. God will provide for us if we pray. We have no right to take the life of that man into our own hands, it would be wrong!"

Glaring at her husband, Evelyn Baker replied. "Be assured, when the guards bring us breakfast in the morning, I will tell them who the man is. Then they will know we are willing to work with them, and they will leave us alone. That is the only way, Henry, and you must agree with me."

Without saying another word, Evelyn laid down on the damp floor and closed her eyes. Her decision was final, and now she felt comfortable sleeping with it.

Henry sat against the wall, sickened by what his wife of nearly thirty years had just said. There was no doubt her desire to survive this war was foremost in her mind, but how she could decide so quickly to turn her back on another human being bothered him greatly.

Around midnight, Evelyn woke up and looked at her husband. "You still feel I am wrong, don't you."

Nodding his head, Henry replied. "We are missionaries that teach the word of God. Over the last two years how often we have instructed natives to love and trust one another, and to forgive each other when times are bad. And now you are willing to turn your back on all of that."

Grabbing her husband by the shirt, Evelyn raised herself up and said, "You have always been the weak one. If it had not been for me, we would probably have died more than once since we began this journey. You are a pathetic man, willing to get all of us killed because you are too weak to stomach what must be done!"

As Evelyn turned away from her husband, Henry reached out from behind, placing his hand over her mouth as he pinched her nose shut. As she began to struggle for air, Henry placed the weight of his body on top of her, in order to keep her from creating a disturbance that would wake the others. Slowly, the strength began to slip from her body as he gripped her mouth tighter and tighter.

There is a point in time when a person's soul slips free from its earthly body and rejoins the creator that placed it on this earth. All time stands still as the doors to the kingdom of heaven close, and never again allows the power and sheer determination of human life to reenter the vessel from which the soul has finally departed. And so it was with Henry. He could not be exactly certain when his wife passed from life into death, but he felt a limpness overtake the taut struggling muscles that had fought him so valiantly minutes earlier. Evelyn's brown eyes looked dull and empty as he removed his hands from her face. No air flowed from her mouth as her jaw was seized tight by the muscles that had fought for a living breath just moments earlier.

Hanging his head, Henry felt the spirit of his wife somewhere above him looking down as if to ask why. But there would never be a sufficient answer that would satisfy their children back home, or the others in this wretched warehouse that had already survived so much.

Leaning back against the wall, Henry cried harder than he had ever cried in his life. He had made the decision to exchange one life for another, but now he could not be sure he had really made the right decision. Now all he could do was ask for redemption, but how and if it may come was something he could never be sure of.

As the marine guard slid open the heavy steel doors to pass out a hunk of bread and a container of warm water to each prisoner, Sister Dominique observed the lifeless body of Evelyn Baker on the floor. Walking over, she looked at Henry in disbelief.

"Why Mr. Baker? Why did you give in to your fears? You are a missionary, but do you not believe that God will come to you in your time of need?"

Looking empty and sick he replied. "Evelyn was right about me, I am a weak man, and I will have to answer to God for that. But I could not allow her to do what she was determined to do. No matter who Father Martin really is, he has the right to live."

When the marines had finished handing out the bread and water, Pierre Duncan and several of his workers buried Evelyn Baker near the edge of the jungle where the others had been laid. No questions were asked by Captain Kimura. One more dead missionary was no concern of his.

The following morning, as everyone walked around the fenced enclosure trying to get some exercise, Father Martin walked up to Henry Baker. "I know you have been avoiding me since yesterday morning, and I understand why. There is no way I can thank you enough for protecting me, but I never expected things to happen as they did. I know Sister Josephine and Sister Henrietta are heartbroken, but they still feel protecting me was the right thing to do, and they would do it all over again. Believe me or not, Mr Baker, I will never understand all that happened yesterday between you and your wife, nor will I ever forget it. You and I have a bond now, and we must look out for one another. Evelyn would want it to be that way."

Before Henry could respond, Father Martin placed his hand on Henry's shoulder and just nodded his head before walking off to join the sisters who were praying together with some of the prisoners.

Over the next few days, several flights of American F6F Corsair fighter bombers flew low over the island but never attacked or fired a shot.

It gave hope to the prisoners that they would be rescued in short order by American Marines that would storm the beaches and defeat the Japanese. But it was clear the Japanese were not going to be intimidated by flights of

American fighter bombers. During the night, three flak trucks were brought into the base and camouflaged near the end of the jungle.

The following day as a smaller fight of Corsairs approached the base, all three flak guns opened fire. The planes quickly turned north out over the slot, gaining altitude before disappearing into a cloud bank.

The prisoners could hear the drone of their engines as they flew around overhead, preparing to attack, but what would be attacked was anyone's question. The shrill scream of a diving aircraft sent all the prisoners running for cover near the damaged building. One by one, the Corsairs dropped down from the cloud bank with machine guns blazing. One truck stopped firing as its crew was killed, the second truck exploded as a hundred-pound bomb dropped from the third Corsair landed just feet from the truck. The crew of the one remaining truck ran as fast as they could, knowing they were now going to be the target of every aircraft. Moments later, the truck appeared to rise up about four feet in the air and explode as it was struck by two hundred-pound bombs from the fifth plane.

The two lead planes circled back toward the inlet, where one of the patrol boats had arrived a few hours ago. They strafed the pier and dropped their remaining bombs, destroying the patrol boat and a large tank holding marine engine fuel. A massive ball of fire and smoke rose up over the pier as the Corsairs once more grouped up and flew off toward the east.

Although the prisoners were happy to see American air power destroy Japanese assets, they understood that cheering would only aggravate the situation and could have catastrophic consequences for them. For Sister Dominique, it was incredibly hard to believe that she could see the young faces of the pilots as they dove low over the island to attack, but could not reach out to them to get away. Each time the planes came, they were so close, yet so far away.

Over the course of the next several nights, everyone could hear the scream of shells as they left the huge guns of the American war ships heading into the island to destroy Japanese positions. The ground shook with each hit, and the large plumes of fire and smoke could be seen for miles as fuel and ammunition dumps exploded.

After the third night of intense shelling, six trucks arrived, along with thirty Japanese marines and Captain Kimura, who no doubt had been wounded the night before, as he had many scratches on his face and his left arm was in a sling.

Once the marines had opened the gate, the captain walked in. "We can no longer keep you here. A landing barge will arrive in about an hour to take you to Rabaul. We will need to truck you over to the port as our facility has been destroyed as you well know. So, load up and let's get this finished."

Sister Dominique charged forward toward the angry officer. "Just leave us here for the Americans to rescue. Give us some water and we will not cause you problems."

The captain glared at Sister Dominique. "If I had my choice, I would rather shoot all of you right here, right now. You have been nothing but trouble for me. But I will do as my superiors tell me to do. So, you will get on the trucks as I have ordered!"

Sister Dominique was about to say something, when Father Renaldo grabbed her from behind. "Do not antagonize the officer, Sister. I do believe he would shoot us all if he had his way."

Without another word being said, the prisoners began moving onto the trucks. When everyone was loaded, the drivers set out for the town of Iringgila where there was a flat beach for the landing ship to come ashore. After what had happened to the *Koshiro Maru*, nobody wanted to step foot aboard the ship, but it was clear the Japanese marines were not going to put up with any dissension.

Once the ramp was pulled up, the landing ship backed off the beach and turned toward the northwest where the skipper joined up with his escort ships.

Chapter Twelve – The Nogatu Maru

The *Nogatu Maru* was an old Japanese trade ship that had been constructed in 1920. She had sailed all around the Pacific, hauling merchandise of every possible nature throughout her long life. Now that the Japanese command had decided to cut the ship apart and use the steel to build new fighting ships, there was just one last voyage left for the ship and crew to make.

She would deliver the civilian prisoners from the island of Vella LaVella to a large prisoner stockade on the island of Rabaul on the northern coast of New Britain. With one engine completely out of service, it would take two and a half days to make the voyage.

The commander of the ship was a recent graduate from the Japanese Etajima Military Academy named Lieutenant Hinata Matsuda. His descendants were all men of the sea, and most had served in the Japanese navy at one time or another.

One thing that had been pounded into Hinata at the academy was the Bushido Moral Code that had been written by the ancient Samurai's. Believing in the code, he despised the passengers he was about to transport to New Britain. He felt it was their duty to kill themselves instead of becoming prisoners of the Japanese Empire, even though they were civilians. He protested loudly to any senior officer he could find that he was responsible to feed them twice a day. He would have rather tossed them overboard and continued on to the ship works at Yokosuka where the ship could be dismantled.

However, he would never disgrace himself or his family name by failing to follow orders, no matter how disgraceful they might be.

Walking down the pier toward his ship, he noticed a large white flag flying directly below that of the rising sun. Turning toward the pier master, he inquired about the flag.

The pier master placed his hand on Hinata's shoulder. "All weaponry has been removed from your vessel, and you will not be carrying any military supplies. You are simply a prisoner ship, so you will display a white flag at all times, allowing aircraft and submarines to know you have no combatants on board."

Hinata shook his head. "I am a graduate from Etajima, and this is how I am to be treated by the high command? I am a loyal officer, a combat officer. This assignment is below the dignity of a dog catcher in Tokyo! I shall not sail this ship!"

Happy that no other men were on the pier at the time, the pier master replied. "It is just a two day voyage, and then you will sail the *Nogatu Maru* into the history books. Then I am sure you will be given a command worth your place in our magnificent navy, as they will understand the good job you have done."

Hinata smiled and nodded his head. "I think you may be right. This is just a test, and I shall pass it with flying colors, you will see." After looking over the rusted hull one more time, Hinata asked. "Is everyone on board and sealed in the holds?"

The pier master replied. "Your ship is ready to sail when you are. Now go, deliver your load to New Britain."

After the two men shook hands, Lieutenant Matsuda walked up the gang plank and saluted his first officer.

Minutes later. Lieutenant Matsuda signaled with his ship's whistle that they were ready to cast off. Quickly, pier workers ran to the ropes disconnecting them from the pilings. As the ship began to sail slowly out of the harbor, an old chief petty officer limped onto the pier and bowed to the pier master.

"I see you had a long and somewhat angry talk with the young Lieutenant. I take it he was not happy with his first command."

Nodding his head, the pier master replied. "Like all our young officers, he is in a hurry to die in combat and become an immortal God. Unfortunately, what he does not realize, is that his wish may come true all too soon."

The petty officer nodded his head. "Yes, we should have never started this war we cannot win. We are already cutting up ships to make new one's that will soon end up at the bottom of the Pacific. I am happy I can no longer go back to sea. At least I will survive this war."

As the *Nogatu Maru* began its voyage across the Solomon Sea, the passengers in the two holds sat quietly, not sure of the fate that awaited them. Sister Dominique visited and prayed with the passengers, attempting to keep them calm, however, the heavy seas, howling winds and severe rocking of the empty ship kept most of the passengers on edge.

Two thousand yards to the stern of the *Nogatu Maru*, the submarine U.S.S. *Eagle Ray* had just come to periscope depth, as the midday sun was beating down on the old transport, making temperatures inside the holds unbearable. Ensign Craig Spriggs was searching the horizon through the periscope when he observed the slow-moving ship off of his port beam.

Looking over his shoulder, he called out, "Captain, I have a Japanese transport running on one engine flying a white flag below the rising sun."

Walking over to the periscope, Lieutenant Commander John Greenway took a long look at the ship. "White flag, and she is riding high on the waves. I would guess she is carrying a load of prisoners to a camp on New Georgia or New Britain. It's rumored they have several camps for political prisoners there. Let's tail her and see where she drops her load."

For the next twenty-four hours, the *Eagle Ray* maintained radio silence, following the rusty cargo ship at a distance of three thousand yards off the rear starboard quarter. The navigator continued plotting the course of the ship, until he was positive the destination was New Britain.

When the *Nogatu Maru* was about three miles from the entrance to the harbor, Commander Greenway sent a message to Allied Command in Sydney Australia regarding the prisoner ship. He then dove to a depth of five hundred feet, making a course for the open Bismark Sea.

A long line of open cargo trucks sat on the pier at Rabaul, waiting for the prisoners that were in the process of being unloaded. Getting out into the fresh air was a major relief for the passengers, as they were covered in sweat from the unbearable heat of the cargo holds. The drive through the bumpy streets to the prison camp took about a half hour.

As the vehicles came to a stop, Sister Dominique and Sister Margaret were the first prisoners to jump to the ground. Looking around the base,

Sister Dominique observed a large crowd of people standing beside rather new looking wooden barracks, waiting to see who these new prisoners were.

Japanese guards pushed and prodded the new arrivals to stand in three long lines in front of what appeared to be some type of command building. Shortly, a tall officer walked from the building and stood just a few feet in front of his new charges.

"My name is Commander Ossani. I will be your lord and master, as long as you are here, and that may very well be until the war is over. I expect your cooperation with every rule that has been established for the operation of this camp. If you do not cooperate, you will find out quickly that I will not put up with disobedience. I was trained as a combat soldier, not a warden of a jail for cowards or missionaries. You will find your quarters here adequate, and your two meals a day plenty to keep you alive. You will be given seeds to grow vegetables to supplement our rations, and I recommend you follow through with our request.

Anyone trying to escape will be shot. I do not believe in torture or brutal punishment. Disobey the rules and you will be shot. It's just that simple."

Pointing to the guards, he called out "Take them away!"

The sergeant of the guard escorted the sisters and priests over to a barracks where three other sisters were already living. The sergeant looked at Father Renaldo. "We wish to keep all our trouble makers together in one spot."

During the long night, Sister Annuncio and Sister Perpetua from New Zealand explained the rules of the camp to their new house members. After about an hour of talking, Sister Annuncio leaned against the wall. "To be sure, Commander Ossani is just what he said he was. He is a ruthless, cold-blooded killer. The cemetery down the road is full of bodies of prisoners that he felt broke the rules. He will shoot you faster than ordering a guard to do it. He hates this place, he hates us, and would rather die in combat than ever be taken prisoner himself. Never doubt his word!"

The following morning as Sister Dominique was standing outside the barracks helping to do laundry, a woman approached her from the barracks next door. Would you like to participate in this morning's official count?" The women around Sister Dominique laughed as they all suggested she take part on her first day there.

Nodding her head, Sister Dominique replied. "Just tell me what I need to do."

Smiling, the woman led Sister Dominique out toward the center of the compound. "In about a half hour, an Australian fighter will circle the camp and then dive low overhead. There will be no shooting so you have nothing to worry about. But we will be telling him how many people are now in the camp. We do this twice a week. Now that you arrived with one hundred and twenty people, our count is now three hundred thirty-two. Three of us will stand in the middle of the camp, then thirty women will stand near the wash lines, and two will be near the shower hut, and one of them will be you today. The pilot will count us up and report back to Port Moresby. We need to gather at the last minute, and disperse as soon as the plane is out over the POW camp next door. So far, the Japs have not figured out what we are doing, and we've been very good at it for nearly a year.

When the British Spitfire began circling the camp, Sister Dominique walked over to the shower hut and began talking to the other women. Seconds later, the aircraft screamed overhead and was once again climbing up to nearly ten thousand feet over the Bismark Sea.

Walking back to the woman that had given her the job, Sister Dominique asked. "How far are the Australians from here?"

The woman shook her head. "A mile, ten miles, ten thousand miles. What difference does it make? The Aussies have to fight their way over the Owen Stanley Mountain range, and the only way to do that is by way of the Kokoda Trail. It crosses over from Port Moresby in the south and ends near Popondetta in the north. From there it is about a hundred miles to Lae. Then they have to cross the channel between New Guinea and New Britain to make an invasion of the island. We are more likely to be rescued by Eskimo's from Alaska to tell you the truth. We hear rumors all the time that we will be rescued by the Australians, but so far it has been nothing but sickening rumors. Coming after Rabaul would be like cracking a ring of steel. The Japanese made this base to last forever, and I don't think even the best American units can crack this tough nut. But we keep doing the head count so they know how many of us exist here. We just don't want to be forgotten."

Arriving back at the barracks Father Renaldo looked at Sister Dominique. "Did you get any information that might be useful?"

Shaking her head, she replied. "Everything here is against us and we will be here a long time, I'm afraid. They do a morning count pretty much to keep up moral. Other than that, what you see is what you get."

Father Renaldo took sister Dominique by the hand, leading her away from the others. "Last night, three POW's escaped from the military camp. Rumor has it they were helped by a guerrilla team from the town of Driwata, about fifty miles west of here. Rumor has it General MacArthur is going to make a landing near there in the future and needs good information about the island. The escapes were needed to give him the lay of the land when he arrives. Be patient sister, we may not be here as long as the commander believes."

A long hot month passed with everything in the camp continuing on just as it had the first day they arrived. Each day guards walked the perimeter of the camp, checking the tall fence for any signs of tampering, as the soldiers in the towers watched over the prisoners like a starving hawk.

The morning count flight continued, but now at least two more aircraft circled above the camp, making the Japanese soldiers more nervous than normal.

Although American forces would still need to capture several islands before they could attempt to assault the island of New Britain, the Japanese realized they had to continue fortifying the island, and not have marines guarding prisoners.

Tokyo decided they would send all the prisoners to a camp on the North Coast of New Guinea, near the town of Bunabufi, just a full day of sailing away.

Once again, the prisoners found out that believing all the scuttlebutt that ran through the camps was extremely tough on their moral. Father Renaldo began to believe that rumors had to be started by the Japanese just to keep the prisoners off guard. Nevertheless, once again everyone was loaded aboard the *Nogatu Maru*, which had remained berthed in the Rabaul harbor for just such a situation.

By noon the following day, the rusty old ship dropped its loading ramp on the beach near the pier. Luckily, the camp was only about four miles from the pier as there were no trucks to transport them. With so many people in tough medical shape, the trek to the camp took about two hours. Two prisoners were shot along the way, as they had a hard time walking on their own. Their bodies were tossed into the ditch like so much trash, providing the rest of the prisoners an idea of the mind set of their captors.

Arriving at Bunabufi the prisoners were trucked to the camp where they would live. The section of the camp the prisoners were being placed was a new addition to the original camp that had been built several years earlier. What no one had counted on, was the fact that Commander Ossani had been flown to Bunabufi on a cargo aircraft, so he and his staff would be prepared when his prisoners arrived. It was clear he was no happier to see them than they were to see him.

For the first three days they were in Bunabufi, the guards were brutal and sadistic. They tore up the thin mattresses looking for contraband and escape materials, and dumped several meals of watery soup on the ground, instead of feeding the hungry prisoners. Over in the adjoining camp they shot several prisoners for no apparent reason. Sister Dominique quickly realized that things were not going well for the Japanese and they were acting out accordingly. She warned everyone not to antagonize the commander or his men, as torture or death could quickly result.

As there were many children in the two camps, the sisters set up a small school in an empty hut. Each day they held classes, a soldier stood in the doorway, listening to everything the sisters were teaching. Some days he would limit how many students could attend, while other days he refused to allow the school to operate at all. It was all a game for many of the soldiers, as they knew the prisoners were no threat to them.

Many days the prisoners could see ragged, sickly Japanese soldiers marching past the rear of the camp. They were the lucky ones that had been able to survive the escape down the Kokoda trail to safety. Now they would have to rejoin defensive forces farther to the west. As there were not enough trucks to carry them, many of the sickest soldiers would die before arriving at a base where some type of medical assistance was still available.

However their presence was well known to the Allied forces. Several times a week either American or Australian aircraft would fly low overhead, keeping an eye on the escaping Japanese to see where they were regrouping.

One morning as Sister Dominique was sitting on the edge of her bunk praying the Rosary with Sister Claudia, an explosion tossed her to the floor.

Before she could get up, there was a second followed by a third explosion that appeared to come directly across the compound.

Running to the door of the barracks, Sister Dominique could see prisoners running through two large holes in the fence that had been caused by aerial bombs.

Screaming at the others, Sister Dominique grabbed hold of Claudia and raced toward the open fence and a collapsed tower about a hundred yards away. However, by now the guards were beginning to run from the safety of the bomb shelters, and fire at the escaping prisoners, but that did not deter Sister Dominique who was running at break neck speed, pulling Sister Claudia behind her.

As they cleared the fence, Father Martin knelt down, pulled the pistol from the holster of one of guards and returned fire, striking one of the advancing soldiers in the leg.

By the time the guards were able to stop the prisoners from escaping, over a hundred had made it into the jungle and were continuing along the west coast.

Dropping down behind several fallen trees, Sister Dominique looked over at Sister Claudia and Father Renaldo, who were all but out of breath. She was about to speak when Father Martin, Sister Margaret and Sister Henrietta dropped to the ground nearby.

Looking completely terrified, Sister Henrietta grabbed hold of Father Martin's arm. "What have you done? The Japanese will kill you for sure when they get their hands on you. A Catholic priest would not have done what you did. We may all pay for your thoughtlessness!"

Seeing the Japanese pistol in Father Martin's waist band, Sister Dominique said, "We have all been covering for you since we were joined together. Now that you have decided to take sides against the Japanese, you must tell us who you really are!"

"He is an American pilot, we pulled him from the wreckage of his plane before it sank. He was the same size as the real Father Martin, who had died from dengue fever several months earlier, so we gave him the father's clothing and attempted to keep him safe," Sister Henrietta explained angrily. "Now he has slapped us in the face and thrown away all our trust."

When Sister Henrietta finished speaking, Father Martin said. "My real name is Naval Lieutenant Charles Freeborn. I was flying off the *Enterprise* with my squadron to attack a Japanese airfield on Santa Isabel. I was at a pretty low altitude when my engine took a direct flak hit and I came down like a rock. Luckily, the plane skidded on the water for a short distance before striking some rocks. I hit the instrument panel with my forehead and was dazed. Thanks to Sister Henrietta, Sister Josephine and several natives, they were able to pull me free from the wreckage. I was not sure how or when I could rejoin the fleet, but the good sisters took good care of me." After a moment of thought, he continued. "I will stay with you as long as possible to protect you, but if capture becomes imminent, I will run off, so you are not blamed for what I did. Will that work for you?"

Sister Dominique shook her head, as she clearly remembered what had happened with the Australian pilot back on Nusa Simbo. "You pilots are all the same. Your desire to kill the enemy outweighs the safety of everyone around you, and you just proved that. I prefer you leave us now so the Japanese will never see you with us. You are trouble, Lieutenant Freeborn, trouble we cannot afford!"

Sister Claudia took a deep breath as she stood up. "I'm sorry Lieutenant, but I also feel you must go. I wish you well, and hope you find your way back to your ship, but for now we're better off without you."

Nodding his head Lieutenant Freeborn removed his Roman collar and buried it under some leaves. "Best of luck to all of you, stay safe," Lieutenant Freeborn said, before running off to the south.

Shots could be heard all around the jungle as the Japanese guards chased the terrified prisoners. Father Renaldo led the four sisters toward the southeast, deeper into the jungle as they climbed the foothills, not knowing at all where they were headed. By evening, they had arrived at the Ramu River which blocked them from going any farther south as the river was deep and flowing downhill at a good speed toward the coast.

After meeting up with Henry Baker and Sister Perpetua, they came across an abandoned hut that would allow them to sleep undercover before deciding what their next move was going to be.

As a slight mist covered the terrain the following morning, Henry Baker thought it would be best if they followed the river bank as the footing was much better. However, they had only gone two miles when the river bank began to parallel a well-traveled north-south road. They were just about to turn around, when a small armored vehicle and several trucks carrying Japanese infantry arrived from the south. The soldier manning the machine gun on the turret spotted the group and immediately opened fire, spraying the trees several feet above their heads.

As shredded branches fell to the ground, everyone quickly dropped to their knees, placing their hands over their heads.

A young Lieutenant stepped from the cab of the lead truck. Walking up to Father Renaldo, he said, "You chose the wrong way to go, Father. Ahead of you are two of our major bases at Lae and Finschhafen, where there are about twenty thousand battle hardened marines. My men and I were on our way to Bunabufi to help round up the remaining escapees. So now you may join us in our trucks."

Father Renaldo felt dejected, realizing he had led his little party right back into the hands of commander Ossani, who would be angry and want blood for what had happened in his camp.

About an hour down the road, the convoy was reaching the town of Madang where another large Japanese garrison was located, and a ship servicing pier had been constructed. The armored vehicle had just begun to slow down for all the traffic on the highway, when a tremendous blast destroyed a large combat tank coming in the opposite lane. Both vehicles burst into flames as shrapnel screamed in every direction. The three men in the cab of the first truck were instantly decapitated, allowing the truck to continue forward like a blazing coffin. Soldiers in the back of the truck began to jump for safety, just as another major explosion slammed into a destroyer tied up to the pier. The ship appeared to rise up from the pier for a moment before dropping back down into the water. The front of the ship had completely disappeared as flames roared from the ruptured fuel bunkers.

The driver of the second truck threw the transmission into reverse while slamming his foot down on the accelerator. A soldier sitting in back with the prisoners yelled, "Run, run for your lives! There's an American battleship over the horizon firing at us. You must run!"

Once the truck stopped, everyone jumped clear of the vehicle and ran toward the safety of the jungle. By now, the fire coordinators on the battleship had secured the range, and began firing the massive sixteen-inch shells one after another. The sound of the three-thousand-pound shells whistling through the air was enough to scare the bravest of men.

Being tossed into a dry drainage ditch by an explosion, Sister Dominique placed her hands over her head as she waited for the one that would end her life. Flames and large plumes of smoke rose from the pier as thousands of gallons of oil burned out of control, blotting out the afternoon sun. Cases of ammunition that stood ready to be loaded onto trucks went up in one massive explosion, killing any workers left on the pier that had not already been severely wounded.

As the naval gunners raised the azimuth of their gigantic weapons, the heavy explosives began raining down on the garrison compound. Barracks, warehouses, and office buildings disintegrated as parking lots filled with vehicles quickly became massive infernos. Men that were not killed by the massive explosions ran down the streets screaming with their clothing on fire, attempting to avoid the ongoing salvos.

A Japanese sailor with his right arm radically amputated near the elbow, and a huge piece of shrapnel sticking out of his left hip, dropped down into the ditch beside Sister Dominique. Grabbing her with his left arm, he called out, "Make it stop, make it stop!"

Trying to comfort the man, she threw her left arm around his neck and said, "Pray, pray as I am, so it may stop."

But at that point in time, all the sanctified war gods of Japan could not stop the hell that was being unleashed upon them by one battleship in preparation for the assault that was going to come in several days by one General Douglas MacArthur.

Nearly a half hour later, the roar of a thousand freight trains came to an end, as the wind created by countless fires burned everything in its path.

The sailor painfully rolled over on his back as his eyes kept a close watch on Sister Dominique. "Do not leave me here to die all alone, Sister. Help me find my way to Ame, what you call heaven. I cannot do it by myself, I have been an evil man and—"

With that, his head rolled to the side as he breathed his last. Still shaking from the massive barrage, Sister Dominique raised her right hand and drew out the sign of the cross on the sailor's forehead. Seeing what appeared to be a billfold in his pocket, Sister Dominique slid it out. Inside were several photos of the sailor with a very attractive Japanese woman and a small child of about two years old. Another photo was of the sailor and two older people, that were probably his parents, standing on a train platform with a sign overhead reading Nagasaki.

Closing the leather billfold, Sister Dominique placed it in the front pocket of her dirty well-worn brown dress. Looking down at the dead sailor, Sister Dominique said, "Somehow, I shall return this to your family. I shall tell them you died bravely and were not afraid."

Standing up, Sister Dominique's legs continued to shake as she looked around the scorched landscape, as fires still roared all around her. Looking down at the pier, all that was left of the destroyer was the mast as it poked out of the water at a curious angle. The patrol boat that was berthed next to the destroyer was all but gone, as just the front fifteen feet of its bow now sat on the sandy shore. Five landing craft that had been sitting so stately along the beach were jagged shards of steel and barely recognizable. Amazingly, all that remained of the three massive yellow cranes used to load ships, were the bottom four feet that were still embedded in concrete.

All around her the road had been pulverized into disuse, as huge craters had replaced what had been a busy two-lane highway. It was impossible for her to believe that any man-made weapon that could not be seen could cause this type of destruction in such a short period of time. What was more surprising, was the lack of human beings wandering among the ruins. Those that had survived, staggered aimlessly about saying nothing to one another as they passed like two ships in the night.

After taking a huge breath of the foul smoke-filled air, Sister Dominique slowly made her way toward the safety of the shredded jungle palms, where she could hide for the long night to come.

Reaching the edge of the jungle, Sister Dominique stepped over countless body parts that appeared to have been tossed about by some large giant as it made its way toward the mountain.

Arriving at the Ramu River, things were not much better. The water ran red with the blood and body parts of soldiers and sailors that attempted to take refuge in the water, only to be blown apart when the large shells struck the river.

Turning north following the river, Sister Dominique soon came to areas completely untouched by the massive sixteen-inch shells. Severely wounded shell-shocked Japanese marines walked aimlessly or sat quietly under the large palm trees, unsure of what their next move might be. By now all discipline had broken down, and they seemed completely unaware of who was walking among them.

Finally, the familiar face of Father Renaldo stood directly in front of Sister Dominique. Looking very concerned regarding her condition, he said, "Sister, where are you going? Are you alright?"

Sister Dominique continued stumbling forward, not responding to what he had asked her. Realizing Sister Dominique was not in much better shape than the shell-shocked Japanese marines, Father Renaldo and Sister Perpetua led her toward a small grove of palm trees where the other sisters were seated.

Once again, Father Renaldo inquired, "Sister, where are you headed?"

Instead of answering, she gave him a bewildered look as she shook her head. "What are you saying? I can't hear anything."

Nodding his head in understanding, Father Renaldo leaned close to her right ear, saying, "You have temporarily lost your hearing from the explosions. You should be better by morning. We are going to spend the night here and move on tomorrow. Did you hear any of that?"

Attempting to smile, Sister Dominique nodded her head. "Yes, yes, I could hear you, but not too well. The ringing is terrible."

Looking over at Sister Claudia, she inquired. "Are you alright, my sister?"

Nodding her head and smiling, she leaned over saying, "We lost you when we jumped from the truck. Father Renaldo made us run north for the river. We were knocked down a few times, but we just jumped up and ran. We all figured you were dead."

Sister Dominique smiled as she looked at the students across the table. "I never really thought of dying out there. I always thought I would survive the war for some reason. But after that attack, I felt like a cat that had used up at least six of its nine lives."

After a moment of silence, Anna, one of the students spoke up, "How long did it take for you to get your hearing back?"

"Actually, I was surprised when I woke up the next morning. I still had some ringing, but nobody had to yell for me to hear them anymore. And I can't say when the ringing quit, because all of a sudden later in the day, I realized it was gone," Sister Dominique replied with a pleasant smile.

"With all the destruction, what did you do the following morning? Where did you go?" Donald inquired, as he looked intently at her face.

Quickly, the smile disappeared from Sister Dominique's face. "Ah, the following morning. After having a breakfast of coconuts, we decided we had to keep going west and find a place to cross the river. There were too many Japanese coming from Lae and Finschhafen, so heading east was out of the question. The only problem going west was the angry guards from the prisoner camp. We were sure they would shoot first and ask questions later. We all wished we would have gone with Lieutenant Freeborn, but by now it was impossible to know whether he was dead or alive."

After looking at each of the students for a moment, Sister Dominique continued. "Father Renaldo was quite sure the battleship attack was a prelude to an invasion of the New Guinea coast, and there would probably be more over the next few days. He called it a softening up attack.

We found a good place to cross the river about an hour later, but it was evident the Japanese also knew about the spot. We had only been across the river fifteen minutes when we ran into a Japanese patrol made up of soldiers from our camp, and the POW camp."

Marching Fr. Renaldo and the sisters back across the river, the soldiers pushed and prodded them with their bayonets until they walked directly back into the camp. One of the sergeants checked off their names from a list of escapees before allowing them back into their barracks. One of the women in the barracks that had been unable to escape, warned them that Commander Ossani was waiting for the captures to be completed before the punishments would begin.

Two days later at morning roll call, Commander Ossani walked up onto a new wooden platform that had been constructed in the yard. Looking down on the women, he said, "There were 332 prisoners in this camp before the escape. Only 160 of you managed to get out, and we killed 75, so we now have 257 of you left to pay the price for the problems you have caused me."

Somewhere in the crowd, a child began to cry as the commander was speaking. Stopping his speech, he directed two soldiers to bring the mother and child to the platform. Minutes later a pleading woman and her frightened child sat on the ground below the platform. Looking down at the woman the commander yelled out. A Japanese mother knows when to control her child, it is clear you do not. Pulling out his sidearm, the commander fired two shots into the mother's head, and one into the child. So, now I have 255 to deal with. Pointing to several men in the front row he yelled. "Bury them, I do not wish to see their bodies in my camp!"

Quickly, four men picked up the corpses and ran toward the back gate where soldiers were waiting with shovels.

Over the next few days, everyone in the camp was on edge as rations were cut in half, and water became a rare commodity. On warm beautiful days everyone was confined to the barracks and the windows were shuttered. However, on stormy rain-filled days, they were forced to march in a large circle around the camp, as Commander Ossani sat on his covered porch, drank hot tea and yelled insults at them.

After being confined to the barracks on extremely hot days with the windows closed, it did not take long for a serious case of dysentery to begin making rounds of the camp. Sister Dominique pleaded with the guards to allow them to do laundry, take showers, and get more clean water to drink, but her requests fell on deaf ears. After fifteen prisoners had died from the ravages of the disease, Sister Dominique demanded to speak with the commander.

When she arrived at the office, Commander Ossani held up his hand. "You may not come inside, Sister, you have a foul odor of body excrement. Tell me, is this how Catholic sisters are taught to live?"

Attempting to avoid the cruel statement, Sister Dominique replied, "The water we are given is filthy, there are worms in our food, the rat population has gotten out of control and more people are being bitten every day, spreading the disease. Either you do something soon, or the last 240 prisoners you have will soon be gone. We have not seen a Red Cross inspector in months nor have we received any Red Cross packages. How will you explain to the Red Cross or the Geneva representatives that all your prisoners have died!"

Stepping forward, the commander slapped Sister Dominique across the face, hard enough to send her flying off the porch. "I shall not be threatened by a woman, I think you need some discipline so you remember your place in the world."

Turning toward his sergeant, he said. "Tie her to the platform. I think after a hot day in the sun, the good sister will once again learn her position in life."

Quickly, the guards tied Sister Dominique to the platform in the middle of the yard, with her arms out stretched. Being it was only nine in the morning and the sky was a brilliant blue with not a cloud in sight, Sister Dominique realized by night fall she could very easily be dead.

About midday, Commander Ossani strolled up to the platform, as one of his guards held a large umbrella over his head. After taking a sip from a large glass of iced tea he said, "So tell me sister, how is your day going? Have you learned anything yet?"

Looking down toward the ground, Sister Dominique refused to answer, not wishing to give the commander any sort of satisfaction.

"Sister, the day is only about half over, and the sun will get much hotter, probably near one hundred degrees, and there is not a cloud in sight. Do you not wish to end this foolishness?"

Knowing if she broke, the commander would become a hero to his men, and a man to be feared by the prisoners. So, it was clear in Sister Dominique's heart that her death would give the prisoners strength, while it would only embarrass the arrogant officer. Raising her head and opening her swollen eyes, she replied in a raspy voice. "May God forgive you."

Enraged by her response, Commander Ossani pulled his riding crop from his belt and struck Sister Dominique twice across the top of her head. As blood ran down her face, the commander took a step back, placed the riding crop under Sister Dominique's chin, and raised her head. Looking eye to eye with her he yelled, "Before this day is over, you will understand why the Japanese are a superior race!"

Around four in the afternoon, Sister Dominique looked up into the sky where the sun appeared to be spinning in circles, and the sound of her beating heart became a deafening roar in her ears. Looking over toward the enclosed barracks, she whispered, "I tried Father Renaldo, but I have no more to give." Dropping her head to her chest, she said, "Father, I am ready to come home." With that, her tortured body slumped forward.

Around six o'clock, as dark clouds began to appear in the sky, Commander Ossani called his sergeant to his office. "Cut her down and have some prisoners bury her with the others before it rains."

After retrieving four men from the barracks, the sergeant's men cut the ropes lose that held Sister Dominique to the platform. They all jumped back as she moaned softly as her body collapsed on the ground. Without saying a word, the sergeant ran to the commander's office. He burst into Ossani's office and said, "Commander, she lives!"

Rising up from his chair, Ossani looked out the window to see Sister Dominique crawling slightly across the ground. Shaking with rage, he pushed his sergeant out of the way and walked out to the platform with his pistol in his hand. "Look at me!" He yelled as he stood over Sister Dominique, but she refused to comply with his demand. After kicking her in the ribs hard enough to roll her over, Commander Ossani yelled, "Woman, I order you to look at me."

Pulling the trigger on his pistol, a bullet struck the ground inches from Sister Dominique's head. "The next one shall not miss, now look at me when I speak to you!"

Sister Dominique was now positive the commander would kill her, so she silently began reciting the Catholic prayer, The Act of Contrition.

Slowly, Commander Ossani lowered his pistol and shook his head, "Woman, it is not worth all of this. Take her to the barracks!"

Quickly the burial detail dropped their shovels and picked up Sister Dominique. Neither Father Renaldo or Sister Claudia her own sister, could recognize the swollen, blistered, blood covered face of the woman they knew so well. It took nearly two days before enough swelling went away so Sister Dominique could once again open her eyes. Although her sight was blurry, it was once again nice to see friendly faces.

Father Renaldo sat down on the corner of Sister Dominique's bunk and shook his head. "Sister, was it worth what you went through?"

Taking his hand, she forced a slight smile, "Would you have done any less?"

"Whether you know it or not, you accomplished more than you know. The guards have been killing the rats, we have clean water once again, and they have increased our food allotment a little. We have not seen the Red Cross packages yet, but some progress is better than none at all."

Nodding her head, Sister Dominique asked, "And the commander?"

Standing up, Father Renaldo looked out the window. "Honestly, he scares me, Sister. I do not believe he is a well wrapped man. I do not believe it would take him much to kill everyone in this camp and walk away like nothing happened. He is dangerous, please be careful how far you push him."

Over the next few days, Lieutenant Freeborn carefully worked his way south toward Madang, knowing eventually he would meet up with American Marines establishing a beachhead. However, he had no idea he would be dodging so many angry and dangerous Japanese soldiers along the way. It was as if they were having a killing spree and no one was going to stop them. He watched as they killed native men, women, and children for no reason other than they were on the trail. They killed farm animals and left them to decay as they set fire to the small huts occupied by natives in the foothills. Nothing was safe or sacred to these roaming swarms of killers.

The lieutenant had run out of bullets for his pistol days earlier, and had not been able to find a fresh resupply. Finally, on the fifth day he ran across a dead Japanese soldier no one had attempted to loot. Kneeling down, he removed the soldiers pistol belt and placed it around his waist. Removing the dead soldiers back pack, he found six magazines for the submachine gun that lay on the ground aside of the corpse. Picking up the submachine gun, Lieutenant Freeborn ran for cover as he heard a bunch of screaming soldiers coming in his direction. Now he stood a better chance of survival with a powerful weapon and the three rice cakes that were also in the pack.

As evening fell, Lieutenant Freeborn observed several fires in the foothills about a half mile away. Taking his time, the lieutenant worked his way through the tangled brush until he stood about ten yards from the burned-out village. He listened carefully for any signs of life, but all he could hear was the crackling of the three fires that remained burning. Making his way into the village, he spotted seven bodies that apparently had been lined up in a row before being massacred. There were three more bodies hanging from a tree and several more disemboweled bodies near a small corral where three dead goats lay on the ground.

At the far end of the village, he found a small hut that was partially burned but still usable. Sitting down against the back wall of the hut, Lieutenant Freeborn began eating one of the rice cakes as his ears worked overtime listening for sounds of human activity. As a light rain began to fall, his eyes became heavier and heavier until he could no longer keep them open. Around midnight, he was awakened by the sound of Japanese voices approaching the village. Crawling toward the door of the hut, he could see five soldiers pulling two young native girls into the center of the burned-out huts. One of the soldiers yelled out something to the girls they did not understand. Angered by their sobbing and lack of understanding, the soldier put down his rifle and began tearing at the clothing of the oldest girl as the other soldiers cheered him on.

Taking aim with the submachine gun. Lieutenant Freeborn fired a quick blast at two of the men to the left of the girls. As they fell to the ground, the lieutenant jumped up from the doorway, running forward. He fired a quick blast at another soldier that was about to raise his weapon and return fire. However, three bullets to the chest sent him tumbling backwards. The soldier attempting to tear the clothes off the girl turned to grab his rifle, but was dead before he hit the ground. The fifth man stood frozen in place looking terrified, as he stared down the barrel of the submachine gun.

Slowly, the lieutenant lowered the weapon to his side and smiled. Knowing the soldier did not understand English, he said. "Well, well. Here we are, just you and me. Both of us armed, both of us ready to kill, but who has the guts to move first."

For a moment, the Lieutenant felt like he was in one of those cowboy radio programs he used to listen to as a young boy. The hero and the villain standing on main street, waiting to see who was going to draw first. The Japanese soldier walked a few steps to his right as he snickered and squinted his eyes. He shook his head and said something in Japanese before laughing,

Lieutenant Freeborn nodded his head as he spit in the direction of the soldier. Instantly, the soldier began to raise his heavy rifle as he yelled. Before he could level his weapon to shoot, Lieutenant Freeborn sent a long blast of lead into his body. The man stumbled backward for a moment before dropping to his knees. As he attempted to say something, Lieutenant Freeborn cut lose with a short blast from his machine gun. Instantly, the body fell sideways, ending the standoff.

The oldest of the girls stepped forward, looking up at Lieutenant Freeborn. Half smiling, she said, "Ami GI, you save us. Take us with you, we are now yours."

Realizing that taking two girls through the jungle filled with Japanese soldiers would not be an easy task, he knelt down in front of them. "Tell me, where are your parents, your mom and dad?"

The oldest girl looked at the dead Japanese. "They kill them this night. We alone now, we belong to you now."

Shaking his head, the lieutenant replied. "You belong to no one, you are free." Taking the girls to the hut he had been hiding in, he pointed to the palm mats he had found inside. Then he gave them the last two rice cakes he had. There was no doubt they were hungry as they devoured them in mere minutes.

Sitting down by the door, Lieutenant Freeborn placed his hands under his cheek and closed his eyes for a second. Pointing at the girls he said, "Sleep."

The girls smiled as they cuddled up together. Now there was no way Lieutenant Freeborn was going to fall asleep, knowing he was responsible for the two girls. He listened to the nonstop racket of the nocturnal jungle birds that was interlaced with distant gunshots and explosions from the invasion beach. About 0400hrs, the smallest of the girls stood up and walked over to Lieutenant Freeborn.

Looking at the little child, he could see tears rolling down her soft cheeks. Reaching out to her, the girl came forward and dropped down into his lap. As he placed his arm around her, she finally closed her eyes and drifted off to sleep. If he hadn't hated war before, now it angered him more than anything else ever had in his lifetime. There was no reason on earth these two sweet girls should have been taken from their village, watched their parents being slaughtered and become orphans no one would probably ever want except as servants or slaves. He squeezed the little girl tighter, trying to give her the last bit of adult comfort she would probably ever know.

As dawn broke over the north coast of New Guinea, Lieutenant Freeborn recognized the sound of American tanks coming up from the beachhead. Quickly, he got the girls together and began walking down out of the foothills. Within half an hour they came head-to-head with an advance patrol of Marines.

Smiling Lieutenant Freeborn walked forward to a captain and introduced himself. After shaking hands, the captain signaled for his jeep driver to come forward. "Take the lieutenant and the girls down to the medical tent on the beach. Get back here as soon as you can."

Arriving at the medical tent, Lieutenant Freeborn observed two female nurses having a coffee break by an ambulance. Walking up to them, he said. "I'm Lieutenant Freeborn, United States Navy. These two young ladies have been through hell. Their parents are dead, they have nothing to eat, and all they have left to wear are the rags they have on, but they do speak some broken English. After I'm cleared, I want to return to the fleet, so someone will need to take care of them. What can you do to help me?"

Both nurses stood up and walked over to the girls and introduced themselves. After a short talk the older of the women said. "No problem, Lieutenant, we will take them from here, this is not our first rodeo if you know what I mean."

After giving both girls a good solid hug, Lieutenant Freeborn was taken in to see the doctor. After a major checkup, the doctor said, "Well, you have lost a tremendous amount of weight, you are in the beginning stages of yellow fever, and you are badly dehydrated. I will give you some medication and put you on a plane that is leaving for Melbourne, Australia in about an hour. Once you are fit for flying, we can send you back to the fleet."

Nodding his head Lieutenant Freeborn replied, "All I want to do is get back up there and help end this Godforsaken war. So, whatever it takes, let's do it."

At 1300hrs. a C-47 Dakota loaded with twenty medical patients lifted off from a newly built runway near Madang. Its final stop would be the large allied airbase at Melbourne where a new hospital had been established to treat the wounded. After getting a decent meal and taking his medication, Lieutenant Freeborn slept nearly the entire way. The best sleep he had in nearly six months.

Back at the camp in Bunabufi, things did not change much. On a dark overcast day, a slight rain began falling. Sister Perpetua and Sister Claudia helped Sister Dominique out into the yard for a slow walk that was ordered by Commander Ossani. As usual, he sat on the covered porch sipping iced tea and encouraging the prisoners to walk faster so they could remain in good shape. Each time he called out his sick encouragement, his guards would laugh and clap their hands, joining in on the usual sarcasm.

However, today something was not right. Several times the sergeant that was stationed on the east end of the porch looked nervous as he scanned the sky with his binoculars watching for any signs of Allied aircraft. The prisoners finally realized something big was beginning to happen, as the sound of heavy explosions began echoing off the Owen Stanley Mountains directly behind the camp. Everyone hoped the Allies had indeed landed, and were coming their way.

As two little boys sat down on the wet ground and began making mud pies, one of the officers ran over to them, yelling for them to get back into the circle. Although the prisoners begged the boys to cooperate, they all knew better than to walk over and get involved. When the soldier grabbed at one of the boys, he received a face full of mud.

As the boys laughed, the soldier took a step back, swung his machine gun forward and pulled the trigger. As the machine gun steamed from rain drops falling on the hot barrel, the two boys laid dead as their blood mixed with the mud they had been enjoying.

Suddenly, Sister Perpetua broke from the circle, running over to the boys. Several guards attempted to stop her, but she pushed them out of the way, knocking one man to the ground.

As Sister Perpetua dropped to the ground, pulling the lifeless bodies up to her, the soldier pulled his pistol from its holster. Quickly, Commander Ossani stood up and yelled. "Stop!"

The seething soldier backed away, lowering his weapon as the commander walked out into the rain. He walked over to Sister Perpetua and shook his head. "You tossed a Japanese soldier into the mud. What do you have to say for your actions?"

Sister Perpetua could not answer, as she hadn't heard a word he had said. She simply held onto the boys with all her strength, wailing in grief.

Kicking mud at the grieving sister, Commander Ossani called out. "You have committed a crime, what do you have to say for yourself?"

"My God what have you done? They were innocent boys, just as you were once. What have you done, what have you done?" Sister Perpetua screamed as she was now completely covered with the blood of the dead children.

Shaking with anger, Commander Ossani screamed, "You dare to compare me with the children of an inferior race?"

Before anyone could realize what was going to happen, Commander Ossani pulled his sword from its scabbard and swung it down at Sister Perpetua, who was completely unaware of what was about to happen. A second later, her head rolled across the mud as her body remained in place shaking, for several more seconds before it tumbled forward on top of the boys.

"No!" Sister Dominique screamed, as she raced from the prisoners. After picking up Sister Perpetua's head, she walked over and took hold of her body. As rain washed down across her face she yelled out, "This did not need to happen, she was one of mine, she was one of mine!"

Just as the commander began to raise his sword once more, Father Renaldo and the rest of the sisters ran forward, blocking Sister Dominique from the razor-sharp sword.

Looking over his shoulder, he yelled at his guards. "Push them away, push them away!"

As the soldiers pushed Father Renaldo and the sisters to the side, Sister Dominique laid the lifeless body of Sister Perpetua on the ground and said, "Let me help you with what must be done." Kneeling down, Sister Dominique made the sign of the cross, then pulled her long, wet hair away from her neck and said softly, "Do as you must."

For a moment, it was as if the world quit turning and time stood still, as the rain ended and the wind ceased to exist. Now all that was left in the world was the angry figure of Commander Ossani standing with his sword raised above his head, while Sister Dominique knelt in complete submission before him. Every eye in the camp, including those of the soldiers in the towers, were glued to the actors in the scene in front of them. Father Renaldo closed his eyes and made the sign of the cross, as Sister Claudia buried her face into the chest of Sister Margaret as she wept.

Chapter Thirteen – Decisions

It was evident that the once vaunted and elite Japanese Mountain Troops, were now no more than a starving, sick, worn out, undisciplined mass of humanity, fighting for their lives. They had beat back the cream of the Australian and New Zealand Mountain forces as they ascended the Owen Stanley Mountains, only to be stopped and decimated at the gates to Port Moresby. They no longer faced a ragtag army short on every type of war material that would break and run when the odds were overwhelming.

Now they faced well trained American and Australian Mountain forces that were supplied with the best equipment an army could ask for. Their leaders were no longer green and incompetent men that failed to make decisions until it was too late. Now they had an army of leaders well suited for the job at hand, and led by American General Douglas MacArthur and his Sixth Army.

The skies no longer belonged to the Japanese Zeros. Instead, waves of fighter bombers from aircraft carriers in the Bismark Sea, along with medium ranged bombers based out of Australia, pummeled the Japanese front lines and supply lines with impunity. Whatever the harsh mountain conditions and torrential rains could not hinder was being dealt with by the allied air power completing the job.

Driving up the south track of the Kokoda trail, "H" company of the Second Battalion, Third Division, was running into stiff resistance from the retreating Japanese. Captain Alfred Mayer of Tuscaloosa, Alabama, knelt down next to his new radio man. Picking up the handset, he said, "Golden Goose One, this is Marble Creek Six. We are bogged down and taking heavy casualties, this Jap unit is fighting with every ounce of determination it has left.

Request a mortar strike two clicks north of our position. Fire three rounds and I will give you correction."

Moments later, the three rounds struck exactly where the captain had asked them to be placed. Keying the handset, he said, "Keep them coming and adjust north after twenty rounds."

Giving the handset back to his radio man, the captain said. "Keep your head down Smitty, it's about to get dangerous out there. I lost one radio man already this week, I don't want to lose another."

Corporal Smith grinned and shook his head as he watched the captain take off to his left as bullets continued to fly in every direction with out striking the agile officer.

The well-placed mortar rounds slammed into the side of the Owen Stanley Mountain Range, tearing up trees and heavy vegetation, while killing Japanese that were unable to dig into the hard packed rocky earth of the ancient mountains. Screams could be heard as the hot steel from the exploding shells ripped into soft flesh and tore limbs from bodies. Many of the younger Japanese soldiers ran from the cover they had been using and began running up the mountain, just to be caught in the open as the mortar teams readjusted their fire to the north.

Once the mortar teams ended their barrage, Captain Mayer called out. "H Company, move out, don't let the bastards get away!"

Quickly, the veteran soldiers slammed bayonets onto their rifles and began the job of digging out the Japanese survivors. The Japanese soldiers that survived the attack were shaken and ill prepared to fight on as the Americans came forward. Not one American soldier gave an ounce of pity for the enemy. They were shot or bayoneted wherever they were found. Wounded men simply received a bullet to the brain, as attempting to get them down the mountain to be treated was an impossibility. It did not take long for the narrow Kokoda Trail to run red with blood from the retreating Japanese. As this process of attacking the retreating Japanese had been going on for several days, the stench on the mountain was so overpowering, many American soldiers could barely keep their rations down. At night they could hear nocturnal animals devouring the bodies of the dead, making matters that much worse.

But Captain Mayer was not letting up now that they had the Japanese on the run. There were times where he would outrun his own front line, and have to wait for his men to catch up as he fought his own skirmishes. Many times, the barrel of his Thompson machine gun smoked as he stood over the bodies of Japanese soldiers that were unable to escape his forward charge. He would stand where he was and yell, "Smitty, I need that damn radio again!"

As night would cover the mountain, the captain always set up a perimeter with two defensive rows of men. If the Japanese came with a banzai attack, there was always a chance they could break through one or maybe both lines, then continue on down the mountain until they were all killed. But that always meant heavy casualties to the American reserves.

Many nights the Japanese would start by rolling grenades down the trail, hoping to blow a hole in the defensive line they could attempt to breach. It had turned into a bloody affair, and Captain Mayer knew full well the death and torment caused by the night attacks was going to take a toll on his fine troops. The sooner they could breach the top of the mountain and start the fight down the south slope, the better off they would be. But that was still days or even possibly weeks away.

The jungle was always wet, so his men were constantly getting terrible cases of trench foot. Mosquitoes and other bugs transmitted horrendous cases of dengue fever, jungle rot, dysentery, yellow fever, and malaria. All those illnesses claimed almost as many casualties as the Japanese. Every morning a trail of sick men worked their way down for medical attention as fresh reserves made their way forward. One doctor struggling to keep up with his patient load made the crude comment that at least they were no longer seeing any types of sexually transmitted disease.

Sometimes during the night, entire companies of Japanese infantry would quietly retreat farther up the mountain to a more tenable position and leave behind large numbers of very sick men. None of them could be trusted, as they were known to hide grenades under their bodies and throw them at the Americans as they approached to help. So now, when situations like this were found, the chatter of the thirty-caliber machine gun made it evident none of the sick men were a threat.

It was for the same reason, American forces no longer accepted surrendering Japanese forces. By now it was clear that one or all of them would carry live grenades to use when American forces came near. Still, many Japanese attempted to surrender instead of enduring the harsh and hostile conditions they were being forced to bear. But American heavy weapons units always cut them down before they could approach the front line. It was brutal, no holds barred fighting, something most American troops had initially felt disdain for, but now were beginning to feel comfortable with, after seeing the Japanese soldiers as brutal and barbaric.

It took another several weeks before 'H' Company reached the summit of the Owen Stanley mountains. The Japanese soldiers fought with tenacity, refusing to give up ground that would send them on the downhill side of the mountains where allied air power could easily decimate them. But finally, the tired and outnumbered Japanese army had no choice but to withdraw. When the men of 'H' Company reached the summit, they were taken back by the macabre scene that surrounded them.

Nearly a hundred Japanese soldiers had performed ritual suicide the night before. Some shot themselves, others hugged their friends as they exploded a hand grenade between them, and still others used knives and swords to commit the ancient right of seppuku, otherwise known as Hara Kari. It was a bloody ghastly sight many of the men could never forget.

With the Japanese now in full retreat down the southern face of the mountain, American naval and army fighter bombers were now called in to destroy the enemy. They pummeled the retreating hordes, killing hundreds of them every day. By the end of the first week, most of the Japanese soldiers that remained threw down their weapons and disappeared into the thick dark jungle, hoping to avoid the aerial butchery. Some died of starvation, others eventually killed themselves or were killed by natives, but the lucky ones were able to make their way back to the coastal bases, where they rejoined their army.

However, retreating soldiers reaching the coastal plains suddenly realized things were not much better there. Allied war ships pounded Japanese positions day and night, destroying everything usable and killing their comrades by the thousands.

Starving Japanese soldiers killed anything they could find for food, as the fear of starvation created mass panic. This was not the way it was supposed to be, not according to what the Japanese war lords had promised when the war began. They would simply drive out any non-Asian people from the Pacific

Basin, and create the great East Asian Co-Prosperity Sphere where all Asians could live in peace and harmony with Tokyo as the central government.

But that had all changed after the attack on Pearl Harbor. Now, all the free and determined people of America, Britain and Australia were using their industrial might to drive the Japanese out of the Pacific basin and back to their home islands. Most Japanese soldiers and marines left in New Guinea began to feel their war was lost, but still fought with tenacity to the very end.

General MacArthur's plan to retake New Guinea as a stepping stone to Japan's home islands was unique and well planned. His motto was, hit them where they're not, and starve them out. Starvation would become his ally.

Allied intelligence was now able to give planners a good idea where large concentrations of Japanese forces were being amassed. Those were the spots that the allies would bypass as they made their way along the northern coast of New Guinea.

Such was the coastal plains area near the city of Madang, along the north coastal highway just east of Bunabufi. It could be easily over run and would make a good staging ground to build up supplies for an easterly push farther up the coast.

Immediately, allied ships and aircraft began attacking every Japanese position from Riwo in the east to Kananam in the west.

In Tokyo, the talk of retreat had been considered treasonous since the war began, but by 1944 many top leaders were beginning to see the writing on the wall. During January 1944, members of the high command were already trying to find places to stop the allied movement by removing troops from one battle front in order to strengthen their holds in a more strategic area.

On the tenth of January, war planners met in the office of Prime Minister Hideki Tojo. Unlike the meetings that had been held there just two years ago, today's meeting held a much more solemn tone, as everyone in the room looked somewhat glum.

Tojo stood up from his desk and walked over to a map of New Guinea. Running his left index finger along the northern coast, he said, "We no long control the coast from Lae to Gabun. The allied troops have also forced us to leave Long, Malau, Crown and Umboi Islands, and it appears the United States is looking to make a move near Madang. If we are to save our forces at Madang, we must begin an immediate pull out and move them to Aitape.

We will have to move them cross country, as moving them by sea would be a disaster."

Admiral Kondo walked up to the map, pointing toward Wewak. "We already have nearly twenty thousand troops at Wewak, so that is where we must make our stand. We will be able to drive the Americans back into the sea with few losses."

After he sat down, Admiral Fukudome stood up. "I believe MacArthur will not attempt to take Wewak, instead he will attempt to bypass our strong point and hit Madang as the Prime Minister thinks. MacArthur has been playing it wise over the last six months, attempting to keep down his losses by bypassing our strong points. He will not attempt to take Wewak, so reinforcing it will be a waste of time, energy and equipment. We must begin to use our resources wisely."

Admiral Hara shook his head leaving twenty thousand troops in a vulnerable position to wither and starve makes no sense. I agree we must move everything possible to Aitape, that is where MacArthur will wish to invade next. We can easily stop him there."

After the room was quiet for a moment, General Koiso stood up. "No matter what we do, we must consider what we will do about the POW's and civilian prisoners we have at Bunabufi. If we leave them there, they may all be caught in the middle of a battle and be killed. We must move them at once, before we think about moving our troops."

"Move them? How do we move them at a time like this? We need every ship we have just to move needed supplies while we evacuate islands. We cannot think of POW's and prisoners right now," Admiral Fukudome, replied angrily.

Pacing back and forth, Prime Minister Tojo said, "We may need the POW's and prisoners as a bargaining chip if bad comes to worse for Japan. Admiral Koiso is correct, we need to think about how we can best evacuate them and to where."

Admiral Toyoda slowly stood up. "Honorable Prime Minister, we will need only two transports to make the move. One for military people and one for basic prisoners. We should send the prisoners to the camps near Hiroshima. They were built for large numbers of soldiers so there is plenty of room.

The POW's can go to camps near Tokyo, there is plenty of work for them to do. I believe that would be our best move and cause us less problems."

General Yamashita stood up, shaking his head. "Admiral Toyoda, you have always thought about saving lives of our enemies. Here once again, you put them before the needs of our men and equipment. Tell me, where do we get the ships for all our needs?"

Just as Admiral Toyoda jumped up to face General Yamashita, the Prime Minister spoke up. "We do not have the luxury of time to debate on this issue and that takes us nowhere. You may have your personal arguments once this meeting is over. What I need are constructive decisions!"

As the two officers sat down, Admiral Hara stood back up. "I agree, we must move the prisoners, and they should be moved at once. Then, as I said before, we must reinforce Aitape and be ready when MacArthur arrives."

Although Tojo had called the meeting under the guise of seeking suggestions, everyone understood that all he was really after was a consensus from his leaders to a plan that he had already set down.

Admiral Kondo stood up once more, bowing toward the Prime Minister. "I will withdraw my plan to reinforce Wewak. I believe your plan is sound and should be the plan that we follow."

One by one, the men in the room agreed to begin moving troops to Aitape as the Prime Minister had originally suggested.

Bowing toward his staff, Tojo said. "I will also endorse moving the prisoners to the Hiroshima area and the POW's to Tokyo, where labor is becoming a problem." Turning toward Admiral Toyoda, he said. "Get on the plan as soon as possible. I do not want these people being liberated by the Americans or killed in the fighting. Find ships close by that can be diverted flying a white flag, and notify the camp commanders of a pending date when the move shall take place."

With the American fleet operating nearly at will along the northern coast of New Guinea, it was tough to find any cargo ships operating in the area. The closest ships were at the Island of Mindano in the Philippines. It would be nearly a two-day voyage for the ships to arrive at Bunabufi, but that was the best that could be done.

The day before the ships could arrive, American forces stormed ashore at Madang, after a serious pounding by ships for nearly forty-eight hours. To make matters worse, destroyers would move in close to shore at night and bombard Japanese positions built into the jungle nearly three miles inland. Then, just as dawn crept over the island, medium range B-25 bombers peppered the jungle with tons of high explosive bombs.

The invading soldiers moved inland quickly as the prepared beach defenses were nothing more than piles of smoking rubble. Luckily, the first two landings of marines were handled by veteran men that had already seen the horrors of war, because from the beach to nearly two hundred yards inland, the only Japanese that were found were already dead. Most of them were burned beyond recognition, or were just some of the hundreds of body parts that littered the ground.

The second part of the invading forces turned west immediately into the town of Madang where there was little resistance. By early afternoon, only sporadic sniper fire came out of the jungle, and that was quelled quickly by marine mortar squads.

Early that evening, the commander of the garrison at Madang was captured. He stated he had allowed eight hundred of his men to defect to the west the day before, leaving just another eight hundred to defend the city. With the battle over, only one hundred twelve Japanese soldiers were taken prisoner.

The next morning, Navy Sea Bees landed to begin constructing sea plane piers and metal Marston Mat runways for naval fighter bombers. The mats were interconnecting perforated planking that could be laid down on packed sand for quick runway construction. Once the runways were no longer needed, they could be easily removed and taken to the next island.

The marines constructed a solid perimeter on the west side of Madang to prevent any enemy counter attacks. Large tracked bucket loaders dug pits near the jungle where they could bury all the dead and as well as the body parts that littered the battlefield.

At Bunabufi and the POW camp, Japanese soldiers quickly stockpiled cans of gas that would be used to set all the buildings on fire once they departed. The order from Tojo stated they were to adopt a scorched earth policy, leaving nothing available for the invading forces to reuse.

American carrier pilots and submarine commanders reported the two ships heading toward the coast of New Guinea flying white flags.

Admiral Kinkaid relayed the information to General MacArthur's headquarters, requesting permission to stop the ships and allow his fleet to follow through with the humanitarian rescue, or see if they were attempting to just rescue their own troops.

After much consideration, it was decided to allow the Japanese to move ahead with their plans, but to have photo reconnaissance planes take pictures to verify who was going to be on the ships.

Chapter Fourteen – Move to Japan

Sister Annuncio struggled to break free of Sister Henrietta's grip as tears streamed down her face. For the first time in her life, she felt a sense of anger she had never felt she was capable of. Just as she broke free, a soldier ran out of the Commander's office, yelling something that disturbed Commander Ossani to the core.

Dropping his sword to his side, he yelled at the nearby guards, "Bring her here also!"

Sister Dominique sprung to her feet quickly, while yelling, "She meant no harm, please do not do this!"

One of the soldiers knocked Sister Dominique to the ground as the other took hold of Sister Annuncio and pulled her over to his commander.

Seething with anger, Commander Ossani looked at the soldier with contempt. Grabbing hold of Sister Annuncio, he placed the sharp sword in her hands, pulling her over to where Sister Dominique laid in the dirt.

"Kill her!" Commander Ossani yelled, as he continued holding tightly onto Sister Annuncio's arm.

Attempting to pull free, she yelled "No, I can't do that, please stop. I don't want to do this!"

Laughing loudly, the commander grabbed Sister Annuncios arms, attempting to raise the sword above her head, but Sister Annuncio's powerful will and growing determination to resist made it impossible.

Pulling the sword out of her hand, he shoved her to the ground yelling, "You are a coward! You are all cowards!"

After kicking her in the ribs several times, the commander appeared to settle down. Looking over at the prisoners, he said. "Take a vote, you decide which one will die, do it now!"

Father Renaldo stepped forward. "It is I you should kill, not the sisters."

Before the commander could say a word, every prisoner standing close to Father Renaldo stepped forward, uttering the same words. Reaching down with his left hand, the commander grabbed hold of Sister Dominique's long hair and pulled it straight up. Swinging his sword with his right hand, he brought it down toward Sister Dominique's neck. As everyone closed their eyes, waiting for the worst, the sword sliced through the hair like a hot knife through butter. Holding the hair in his hand, he kicked Sister Dominique in the ribs and backed away.

"You will not be fed tonight or tomorrow. You can blame this one for that," Commander Ossani yelled to them all, as he placed his sword back into its scabbard and walked up to his sergeant.

After Commander Ossani walked into his office, a detail of men, along with Father Renaldo and the sisters, brought the remains of the boys and Sister Perpetua to the ever-growing cemetery.

The following day as one of the guards that usually treated the prisoners decently was taking down the boards that covered the windows at night, Father Renaldo walked up to him.

"Tell me, what did the soldier say that stopped Commander Ossani from cutting off the head of Sister Dominique?"

Looking almost scared, the soldier replied. "Americans just landed at Madang. They may be here in a few days we think. The commander is afraid of being captured by them because he knows they will execute him for things he has done with American prisoners on Choiseul. But this morning he is much better, a ship will be here tomorrow to take all of us off the island. At least that is what we are being told. I hope that it's true."

"Where are we going once we leave?" Father Renaldo asked nervously.

The soldier shook his head and turned to walk away. Becoming angry at the soldier's refusal to answer, Father Renaldo took hold of the soldiers arm and shook him. Glaring at the scared soldier, Father Renaldo demanded, "Where will they be taking us?"

The soldier shook his head again before replying, "We don't know, maybe

Tokyo, maybe another island. We do not know. All I know is we will not be captured, at least not this time."

About eleven o'clock the following morning, the soldiers called everyone together in the courtyard. After taking a head count, they were marched out the front gate of the camp toward the actual town of Bunabufi where the ship pier was located. Commander Ossani rode behind the procession in an old Chrysler for the three-mile trek. At the same time, the POW's from the military stockade were being loaded onto a second ship.

As Sister Dominique reached the top of the gangway, she could see the black smoke rising from what had been their camp. She knew she was lucky to have survived the camp and Commander Ossani. Regrettably, she knew he would still be with them no matter where the ship went.

With the prisoners sealed in the cargo holds, the captains backed their vessels away from the piers, making a course nearly due north across the Philippine Sea.

Sitting in the corner of the dimly lit cargo hold, Sister Dominique ran her hand over her head for the first time since the incident in the yard. She was shaken realizing how close the razor-sharp blade had come to her scalp.

Sister Josephine came over to sit next to her. Giving Sister Dominique a small punch in the arm, she said, "It will grow back you know, but if I were you, I would find a hair dresser as soon as the ship stops, so you can get someone to straighten it out just a bit."

For the first time in a long while Sister Dominique was laughing. She placed her arms around Sister Josephine and said, "Only if you're paying for it, I'm afraid I'm flat broke."

Immediately, both sisters were laughing and crying as they hugged one another. They knew they had cheated death and now it felt good to act like a normal human being, if only for a moment.

Pushing her wheelchair back from the table, Sister Dominique removed the small veil the sisters were now wearing. "You can see my once brown hair has now turned as white as the snow. I never allowed it to grow long again after Commander Ossani sliced it off with his sword. Once we arrived at our new camp, the commander allowed a small barber shop to exist that cut both men's and women's hair. I had them all but shave my head when I arrived, so it all grew back at the same length. For some reason that irritated the commander, so keeping it short felt like the thing to do. Yes, there were times I could be quite devious, and I learned well how to play the games when it was called for."

The students laughed as they saw the twinkle in Sister Dominique's eyes. "But I am afraid I am getting tired, so I will call it quits for today. I feel my soul needs to take a break."

After the students had left, Sister Dominique rolled her chair to her room a short way down the corridor. Sliding open the bottom drawer of her chest of drawers, she removed a plastic bag that held the last war time dress she had worn in the prison camp. Sliding her hand into the left pocket, she retrieved three items. The first was a locket of hair from Sister Perpetua, who had died so bravely in the courtyard holding the bodies of the boys that had been shot.

The second object was a pocket watch with a cracked crystal that had belonged to Pierre Duncan. She smiled as the old watch began to run as she wound the stem. She had seen Pierre check the time of day on this old watch hundreds if not thousands of times since they first met on Nusa Simbo. She could never be sure, but Pierre always said it had been a gift from actor Rudolph Valentino, who had made a movie at his villa in Italy. An inscription on the back of the watch simply said, 'Thanks Pierre, you have been a good friend.'

The third item was a small coral bracelet she had been given by a little Japanese girl before she died of radiation poisoning, after the attack on Hiroshima.

Closing her eyes, Sister Dominique remembered the horrors of what had happened to everyone once they arrived in Japan. This was a period of her life she had never truly spoken about, but now it was time to relive it and tell the world what she had experienced.

Several days later she notified the students that she was once again ready to talk to them. Once young Catherine had the camera and tape recorder running, Sister Dominique took a sip of coffee.

After looking up at the ceiling for a moment to collect her thoughts, Sister Dominique began. "Although we could not see anything from the hold of the ship, we knew we were entering a busy harbor by the sound of all the ship whistles, so we knew we would be free of the darkness very soon."

The transport was pushed up against a massive pier about mid-day. Within minutes, guards unlocked the holds, directing the prisoners up to the main deck. The bright sunlight punished their eyes as they had nothing but a dim light bulb for nearly three straight days.

Sister Dominique and Father Renaldo stood by the railing looking about the busy port. There was every type of warship imaginable. Some sat damaged while waiting for repair, as others sat under huge cranes being loaded with food, fuel and ammunition. Cargo ships bringing in the supplies of war sailed up the harbor where tug boats waited to push them into the pier for unloading. This was the center of the Japanese war in the Pacific, and it looked every bit the part.

Below the cargo ship was an old steam locomotive attached to ten rough looking passenger cars. No one on the ship knew where they were going, but they were sure the train was going to be their method of transportation. With the gangway secured, the soldiers began yelling for everyone to disembark and walk toward the train.

It was evident the military was not taking any chances with the new prisoners. There had to be thirty armed soldiers and several smaller military vehicles with large machine guns covering the train.

Although the windows on the cars were dirty and badly smudged, Sister Dominique took a window seat in the middle of the car, with Sister Claudia beside her, while Pierre Duncan and Father Renaldo took the seats in front of them. Once a car was full, two soldiers took up positions at the front and rear of the car holding submachine guns.

Without wasting time, the engineer began feeding steam to the wheels. Quickly, the old engine was working hard, pulling the train clear of the port area. The busy tracks lead them along the coast to the southwest. They passed through Yokohoma, Shizuoka, Hamamatsu, and Okazaki where the train began to circle Ise Bay toward Nagoya.

The main east bound and west bound tracks flowed through a massive rail yard at Nagoya, before continuing on toward the south. Entering the yard, the engineer slowed the train to about fifteen miles an hour, as an east bound freight train pulling flat cars loaded with tanks, artillery and trucks clamored past the prisoner train heading for the ports of Tokyo.

Suddenly, both trains were thrown from their tracks as explosions tore through the ancient railroad cars, tossing debris and shrapnel in every direction. The trains had come to a screeching metal grinding stop as the tanks from the flat cars broke loose and ripped open the side of the coach directly behind Sister Dominique, crushing several of the prisoners.

The terrified soldier at the front of the car yelled, "American bombers, get off the train!"

In seconds, flames from incendiary bombs were igniting every piece of flammable or explosive material in the rail yard. Massive balls of orange and red flame rose from ruptured oil tankers as clouds of thick black smoke billowed skyward. Cars filled with ammunition and artillery shells disintegrated, throwing massive sections of the cars hundreds of feet into the air.

Several cars from the prisoner train had now been torn lose from their wheels and rolled over, as the heavily loaded flat cars ripped through them with incredible force. Coughing and wheezing, Sister Dominique and Sister Claudia attempted to follow Father Renaldo off the train, but lost him in the heavy smoke. Moments later, Pierre Duncan fought his way back into the car, grabbing hold of Sister Claudia, "It's now or never, we get out of here or we die, follow me!"

It was impossible to believe that Pierre could remember how he had found his way back into the car, but moments later, Father Renaldo was standing at the steps yelling, "Watch your step!"

For a moment, Sister Dominique was unsure if she was in Japan or the bowels of hell. Everywhere she looked, tremendous walls of flame and smoke roared skyward, while the sound of droning engines indicated more airplanes approaching from the east.

The hellish whistle of unseen bombs dropping out of the black sky created sheer panic among the surviving prisoners, as they sought an exit from this manmade hell. With the amount of smoke in the sky, it was clear that the pilots were no longer able to see undamaged targets, so they just released their bombs when they were positive they were over the rail yard. Explosion after explosion rocked the yard as flames rose higher and higher into the darkened afternoon sky.

Finally, after dodging piles of burning debris, Sister Dominique saw what appeared to be a shaft of daylight to her left. Knowing they would eventually be killed where they were, she grabbed Sister Claudia's hand and pulled with all her strength. Moments later, they came out of the smoke by a small bay where the coastal wind was pushing the smoke farther to the west.

Falling down to her knees, Sister Dominique coughed over and over as her lungs began to force out the heavy smoke and toxins she had inhaled. After catching her breath, she sat down on the ground taking a long look around. There were about fifty other passengers coughing and wheezing, including Father Renaldo, Pierre Duncan, Sister Josephine and Sister Henrietta. Standing up, she went looking for Sister Margaret and Sister Annuncio, who were just climbing over a pile of debris that had blocked the door.

Looking back over the rail yard, it was impossible to believe anyone could still be alive inside the massive inferno that roared around her. However, little by little, one or two badly burned survivors made their way toward the bay. No one spoke, as incredibly, they all looked as if they had seen the face of the devil himself.

It was impossible to believe, but all too soon, soldiers arrived in trucks and began gathering up survivors. Those they felt were too badly injured were shot on sight. Sister Dominique watched in horror as a woman pleaded with a soldier not to shoot her husband, but was brushed aside. After a quick shot to the head, the soldier turned and shoved his bayonet into the woman's abdomen.

Sister Claudia grabbed Sister Dominique by the arm. "Stay here, please. The soldiers are enraged, they will kill anyone that resists. Please stay with me."

They were just about to load on a truck when Sergeant Maeda came forward. Grabbing onto Sister Dominique's, arm he yelled, "Come with me, come now!"

Seeing the anger in his eyes, Sister Dominique nodded her head and replied cautiously, "I will come as you ask, I will not resist."

Walking over to a small truck, Sister Dominique observed Commander Ossani laying on a half-burned tarp. It was clear he had been badly burned on his right cheek, arm and chest.

Looking up, he held out his right hand, pointing his pistol toward Sister Dominique. "Woman, come here and bandage me! If you run, I will shoot you."

Reaching into the back of the truck, Sister Dominique placed her hand over the top of the commanders. Carefully, she removed the weapon from his shaky grip and handed it to Sergeant Maeda. "There is no need for that, I will do what I can."

Seeing a black medical bag next to the commander, Sister Dominique climbed into the box of the truck. Opening the bag, she removed sharp bandage scissors and prepared to cut the commanders clothing away from the burns.

Instantly, Sergeant Maeda grabbed a woman that had just come out of the inferno, shoving the barrel of his pistol into her throat. "Take care of him or she will die!"

Placing the scissors down on the commanders chest, Sister Dominique held up her hands. "Do not act the fool here. I must do what must be done to treat your commander. Let her live or you will need to shoot me also!"

Sneering at Sister Dominique, he pushed the woman away allowing her to fall to the ground.

After taking a deep breath, Sister Dominique went back to cutting away the burned uniform. Rolling the officer over onto his back, Sister Dominique shook her head as she looked up at the sergeant that stood nearby.

"He is burned far worse than I thought. He needs plasma and medical supplies that I do not have. He needs to be in a hospital."

Sergeant Maeda picked up the medical bag and shook it. "Here is all you need, fix him!"

After finally removing the balance of the commander's shirt and jacket, she began wrapping gauze bandages around his body, while pouring half the bottle of saline solution that was in the bag over his chest. Sister Dominique then wrapped the balance of the bandages around his neck and cheek while using the balance of the saline solution. Seeing a morphine syrette in the bottom of the bag, she broke it open, jabbing the needle into the commander's thigh.

Looking over at the sergeant, Sister Dominique repeated. "That is all I can do for him. He needs a hospital soon. If he gets an infection, he will surely die."

As Sister Dominique began to crawl down from the truck, the commander said. "No! You will come to the hospital with me. Sit down beside me."

Although unhappy about leaving Father Renaldo and the others, Sister Dominique sat back down beside the commander as the sergeant sat down across from her on the fender. It took about fifteen minutes for the driver to reach a building being used as a medical base. It looked like a former two-story warehouse or industrial plant that had been converted into a makeshift hospital.

As the truck was backed up to the rear door, several men ran from the building. Picking up the commander, they placed him on a gurney and disappeared inside the building. Sergeant Maeda waved his pistol at Sister Dominique and yelled, "Follow him!"

It was evident that the construction work to make the building into a hospital was done haphazardly, and in a real hurry. Some doors did not close properly, and most of the walls were crooked and built from scrap material. Entering a small operating area, Sister Dominique noticed immediately that the doctor was either British or Australian, but had the attention of the people working around him.

Looking over at Sister Dominique who was leaning against the wall, the doctor inquired. "Are you the one who did the quick repair work on this officer?"

Sister Dominique replied. "I used what I had."

The doctor smiled, "You did well, if nothing else you helped prevent infection from setting in. Now, let's see what we can accomplish here." Seconds later, he turned back toward Sister Dominique. "Just for your information, I wouldn't put too much weight against that wall. You're liable to wind up in obstetrics, and I do not believe you need their help."

Smiling, Sister Dominique moved over to an old wooden bench that was sitting against the far wall.

The doctor worked on the commander for about an hour and a half before standing back. Looking over at two soldiers acting as orderlies, he nodded. "Take him to a ward, I'll check on him later. That's all we can do for now."

Sergeant Maeda grabbed Sister Dominique by the arm, "You will stay with the commander."

Just as the orderlies made it to the door, the ambulance drivers arrived with a young girl named Sakura that had been burned in the railyard attack. As Sister Dominique approached the child, she stopped and placed her hand on the girl's forehead. Bowing her head, she said a quick prayer as the girl reached up for her hand.

The child's scared dark brown eyes instantly burned into Sister Dominique's heart. "Stay with me, I am all alone now, my parents and brother are dead, I have no one to care for me. I am so scared."

Before Sister Dominique could respond, the sergeant pushed her forward. "We must go with the commander, we have no time for her."

Quickly, the doctor walked over to the gurney and took Sister Dominique by the arm. Glaring at Sergeant Maeda, he said. "She serves a purpose here, I need her, she stays with me!"

Still shaking with rage, Sergeant Maeda pushed Sister Dominique back against the wall and stormed out of the room, following the gurney with his commander.

Looking up at the surgeon, Sister Dominique said, "I can't thank you enough."

Nodding his head, the doctor said, "What is your name?"

"Dominique, Sister Dominique. I am a Benedictine sister," she replied.

"Alright, nurse Dominique, find a set of whites in the closet and put them on, we have work to do," the doctor replied, as he walked up to the little girl that was already on the surgical table.

Changing quickly, Sister Dominique walked out to the surgical table where a small Japanese nurse handed her a face mask. "What do you want me to do?" she asked the surgeon.

"Talk to her, comfort her as we prepare to put her out," the doctor said, as his Japanese anesthesiologist began to administer the medication.

When the girl was out, the doctor looked over at Sister Dominique, "Her right leg needs to come off at the knee. I think we can save everything above that. She has lost most of her right hand, so we will clean up what we can and give everything a smooth surface so it heals well, if she survives. She has lost a lot of blood and we don't have enough for all patients that will be coming in from the rail yard."

For the next three hours, Sister Dominique worked diligently with the two Japanese nurses as the doctor and his Japanese assistant operated on the girl. Like every other patient, when the doctors were finished, she was taken to a recovery ward so the next patient could be brought in.

It was nearly midnight when the last patient was taken from the surgical room. Removing his mask, the doctor looked at Sister Dominique. "You are good, you made a difference here today. Let's go get some fresh air."

There was a small courtyard behind the hospital with ten-foot high fencing topped with barbed wire surrounding it. As the doctor walked over to a small picnic type table, he sat down. "Not quite the doctors lounge I was used to when I was in Singapore, but here I can see the stars on a clear night."

Sister Dominique smiled. "You know my name, but you never told me yours."

"Ah, you are right. I have been operating here so long everyone in the hospital knows who I am, and I seldom meet strangers anymore. My name is Dr. Walter P. Lewis, Jr., of the Canberra Lewis's. I come from a long line of doctors that lived mostly in the Griffith Park area. My wife's name is Willow. She pretty much runs the obstetrics and pediatric ward you almost collapsed into."

Laughing, Sister Dominique replied, "How did you end up here?"

Looking down at the ground for a moment, Dr. Lewis replied. "The British Government was looking for doctors to work in a new hospital in Singapore. Since Willow and I had no children, we thought answering the request of the Crown was a good idea, so we went. To be bloody honest, we had a marvelous time there at first. We had a nice flat with all types of restaurants and theaters to attend close by. We made many nice friends at the hospital, both from China and England, so our social calendar was rather full and exciting. Sure, we knew of the war in northern China, but never expected Japan to defeat both the Chinese and British Armies. But suddenly, Singapore was surrounded, and the British army under General Percival collapsed, and all non-Chinese or Japanese residents were placed under arrest.

With Marshall law in effect, all foreigners were to report to a Japanese occupation office to register. We heard many Australian and New Zealanders were being repatriated, so we were excited about going home. Well, after we registered, we were told we could go to Japan to work in a hospital, or basically become shark food, so… Japan it was. The first few months we were treated rather badly, but then they learned to trust us as we caused them no problems, and life has become somewhat bearable, although many food items are now becoming scarce, as are medical supplies. The problem is, there is no scarcity of patients, as allied bombing has increased, and soldiers returning from combat in the islands need so much care, but all too often, it is care we can no longer provide. We are most terrified because this old warehouse is not marked with anything on the roof showing it is a hospital. I am afraid one day the warehouse will end up being a target of the American bombers and the end may come quickly. If we do survive the bombings, Willow and I have come to an understanding that when Japan falls, we will disappear from the face of the earth, as will all the other conscripted foreign workers. That's just the way it is, I'm afraid. Even old Winston will not be able to save our behinds."

Sister Dominique was quiet for a moment before looking over at Dr. Lewis. "That would be a tragedy. You are a gifted surgeon and have much to offer the world."

Doctor Lewis smiled as he stood up. "I appreciate that Dominique, but I will be worth nothing to anyone if I don't get some sleep tonight. Come to our quarters tonight. Willow will not mind. She will be happy to meet a woman from Italy, I assure you. Tomorrow, I will talk to Colonel Takeuchi and see if we can get you assigned here, if you don't mind, that is."

For a moment, Sister Dominique thought about Father Renaldo and the sisters, but here she would be able to do something worthwhile and actually help people, and be safe from the likes of Commander Ossani. Standing up, Sister Dominique replied, "I would love to work in your hospital."

The following morning, Dr. Lewis spoke with Colonel Takeuchi, who was happy to assign Sister Dominique to his small staff. After meeting the Colonel, Sister Dominique came to realize that not all the officers in top positions were brutal and uncaring. She was happy to be working in the hospital and enjoyed having the chance to assist the doctor during surgery.

Several days later, a nurse in the recovery unit realized that the little girl, Sakura, had an infection. As they prepared her for another surgery, Sister Dominique sat beside her bed. Sakura looked up at Sister Dominique. "Where did you come from, you look different from Japanese, just like Dr. Lewis."

Running her hands through Sakura's dark hair, she replied. "I come from a place called Italy, about halfway around the world. It is very mountainous, just like Japan, and our people do a lot of fishing just like your people do."

Sakura smiled. "Then we have much in common. Do you wish to go back to this Italy and your family someday?"

"Would you believe me if I told you one of my sisters is here in Japan right now? She is a Catholic sister just like me. We were missionaries on an island before the soldiers brought us here."

Sakura frowned. "I do not know what a Catholic or missionary is. Tell me about them."

"It would take a long time, Sakura, so we will have to save that conversation for another day," Sister Dominique replied, as Dr. Lewis motioned for her.

Looking very lost, Dr. Lewis said. "She's not going to make it and there is nothing more we can do for her but keep her comfortable. She likes you and trusts you. Stay with her, the end is not far away I'm afraid."

Nodding her head, Sister Dominique walked back over to Sakura and sat down. Placing her hand on Sakura's forehead, it was obvious the infection was taking a quick toll on the war-ravaged child. "So, Sakura, tell me about your family, where did you come from?" Sister Dominique inquired.

"We lived in Tokyo with my grandparents. My father was getting afraid of the bombings, and wanted to move us to Kobe where he thought we would be safe." Sakura swallowed hard as Sister Dominique gave her a drink of water. Holding out her good hand, Sakura said, "I'm going to meet my family, aren't I? I do not believe I will see you tomorrow."

Sister Dominique placed a cold compress on Sakura's forehead, and said, "Would you like to see them again?"

Half smiling, Sakura said, "Yes, I think that would be fine, do you think they are happy?"

Nodding her head, Sister Dominique replied. "Oh yes, they are very happy, Sakura, and they will be very happy to see you, too."

"I wish I could see the sky and hear the birds again. They always make me smile," Sakura said, as she struggled to breathe. Closing her little hand tighter on Sister Dominique's hand, Sakura asked, "Is it a far trip to see my family? Which way do I go? Will I know how to get there, or will I get lost?"

As tears rolled down Sister Dominique's face, she replied, "So many questions, sweetheart. You are a very brave little girl."

As tears began to flow down Sakura's face, she struggled to speak. "You need to tell me where my family is, I want to find them soon."

Sister Dominique understood that Sakura was close to death and needed to be told whatever comforted her, regardless of the difference in their religious beliefs. "They are with God, Sakura. A very loving person. He has taken away all their pain and fears and they stand with him waiting for you to join them. They will find you, Sakura. They will find you, don't worry."

"Sister what does this God of yours look like? Does he wear long robes of white and have a face like the sun?" Sakura inquired.

Amazed by what she had just heard, Sister Dominique moved off the chair and knelt down by Sakura's side. "Yes child, that is him, you may go to him. He will lead you home where you will never hurt again."

"But I don't want to leave you, I love you very much. You should come with me. I think it will be a wonderful place, and I no longer fear death as I once did. Everything will be fine, Sister."

Seeing a sudden change come over Sakura's face, making it more beautiful and radiant then ever, Sister Dominique spoke softly. "Go to him, child. This is your time, we will meet again, I promise."

A smile came across Sakura's face as she closed her eyes. Slowly, her head rolled to the right as her spirit left her mortal body forever. For a moment, a bright light energized the room before a strong wind circled about, filling Sister Dominique with peace. A moment later, the room was as if nothing had happened as Sakura's hand slipped from Sister Dominique's grip, sliding down to the bed.

Leaving the room, Sister Dominique walked up to Dr. Lewis. "She's gone, Doctor."

A short time later, soldiers removed Sakura's body so it could be buried in the small field behind the hospital. A field that was filling up fast after the train yard bombing.

Over the next few weeks, Sister Dominique poured herself into her work, helping wherever she could, hoping to find peace after Sakura's death, but nothing appeared to calm her soul. She began to wonder if it was possible to be taken to the prison camp where Father Renaldo and the rest of the sisters were, or would the soldiers just shoot her for becoming a problem.

Several weeks later, several soldiers arrived with a pregnant American woman that had been brought to Japan from the island of Mindanao. She was terrified as she had been separated from her husband without explanation at the pier.

Sister Dominique sat down beside the woman, attempting to calm her fears. Taking hold of her hand, Sister Dominique said, "You are in a hospital, my name is Sister Dominique. I am originally from Italy, where are you from?"

The woman looked into Sister Dominique's eyes and said, "My baby is not supposed to come for another six weeks. Can they take care of us here? I do not want to lose her."

Nodding her head, Sister Dominique replied, "Dr. Lewis is a very good doctor. He will do everything possible to help you, but first you must relax, as raising your blood pressure is not good for the baby. So, tell me where you are from, and what is your name?"

"My name is Martha Evinwood. My husband and I belong to a church in Southern California that has been running a mission and a small hospital on the island of Mindanao. For a long time, the Japanese left us alone, but then about two weeks ago several anti-Japanese guerrillas came into the village where our hospital was. Their leader wanted us to patch up his wounded men and give them food. Our doctors did the best they could with what little supplies we had, but I told them we could not afford to give away our food supplies as the villagers needed it. The leader became angry and told me they would make the village their base, so they could eat the food. We pleaded with them to go, because we knew eventually the Japanese would find them there and we would pay the price. And that is exactly what happened. We tried to reason with the Japanese commander, but he would not listen. They killed many of the natives and took all the Americans to their camp. Several days later we were put on a ship heading to Tokyo."

Sister Dominique nodded her head. "They have been doing that on almost every island they are preparing to leave, it happened to us also."

Martha smiled, "But you are a sister, you are so much stronger than a normal woman. I wish I had your strength."

Wiping the sweat from Martha's forehead, Sister Dominique laughed. "Do not fool yourself, I have been very frightened since we were taken off Nusa Simbo, but I needed to be strong for the ones that were with me. Now, working in this hospital, I have learned that everyone is living in fear."

The following morning, Martha went into labor, so Willow Lewis took over her case, hoping she had the tools and knowledge to save the premature baby.

It was an extremely long labor that sapped Martha's strength, but the tiny baby girl she gave birth to appeared to be strong and a real fighter. Regrettably Martha was not doing very well, and she continued getting weaker every day. Each morning, Sister Dominique would roll the ancient incubator the hospital had over to Martha's bedside for a visit.

After several days, Sister Dominique said, "We do not know what name to put on the incubator, Martha. You have yet to tell us. I think your daughter needs a name."

"Find my husband and tell him he has a daughter named Dominique that needs him." Reaching out, Martha took hold of Sister Dominque's hand and smiled. "You have been an inspiration to me, find my husband, please." With that, Martha's head rolled to the side as she exhaled one last time.

No one spoke a word, but tears flowed freely from Willow Lewis, Sister Dominique and the Japanese nurses that stood nearby.

After rolling the incubator back to the small nursery, Sister Dominique walked out to the courtyard where she sat alone on a concrete bench. Looking up to the heavens, she shook her head. "Tell me Father, how much more am I to endure? I am surrounded by death and misery, and there never seems to be an end to it. Tell me what to do."

As she listened to bombs falling from American bombers somewhere over Tokyo, she said, "Today there will be more death, more innocent people dying. Why will you not stop this war? Why must it continue?"

Before she could say anything else, a Japanese military ambulance pulled up to the door. Quickly soldiers rushed out of the hospital to unload the blood covered victims. Doctor Lewis stood in the doorway, looking at Sister Dominique, already wearing a bloody surgical gown. Holding out his arm he said, "Sister, I need you."

Without saying a word, Sister Dominique stood up and walked toward the surgical ward. She knew she had just been given an answer to her prayers, and she knew her presence made a difference.

It was nearly midnight when Dr. Lewis finished his last surgery. Exhausted and drained, Sister Dominique walked into the obstetrics ward to check on Martha's child.

Standing in the middle of the room was a Japanese sergeant that had blood all over his uniform. He pointed toward the incubator and yelled, "Who's white child is this?"

Sister Dominique replied. "We are trying to find her father, her mother died after delivering the baby."

The soldier looked enraged. "She is taking medical staff and drugs away from Japanese people that need it more, this is wrong. Reaching over for the electrical cord, he pulled it from the outlet. "There, let's see if she is strong enough to survive on her own!"

Without hesitation, Sister Dominique raced forward pushed the angry soldier out of the way, grabbed the power cord and plugged it back into the outlet. Turning toward the sergeant, she yelled, "You have no right to kill that child whether she is White, Chinese or Spanish. She is a living breathing child of God, and you will not touch her.!"

The officer looked at Sister Dominique, and said, "And you have no right to be on Japanese soil, either. You are not one of us, but you will be a slave to our nation when this war is over." Pointing at the incubator, he continued, "But her, she will do nothing but cause a strain on our medical services, and she is nothing to us." Pulling out his sidearm, he aimed it at the incubator.

Sister Dominique lunged forward, attempting to stop the soldier from shooting the baby. But as the soldier side stepped her, he slammed his pistol into the side of her head. As she fell to the floor, Sister Dominique cringed as she heard the sound of two gun shots and the breaking of glass.

Stepping over Sister Dominique, the soldier walked out of the room. Dr. Lewis and Willow came running from the courtyard after hearing the shots. Willow dropped to her knees next to Sister Dominique, and sobbed as her husband disconnected the incubator and wrapped the bloody baby in several towels.

Holding Willow, Sister Dominique said, "It was not to be, you did all you could. We will never understand this war or the people that fight it. This war no longer has a meaning, and no matter how hard we try, death will continue to haunt us no matter how it happens."

Several weeks later as Sister Dominique took a break out in the court yard, she observed Sergeant Maeda pushing Commander Ossani out the door in a wheel chair. Not wanting to speak with the commander, Sister Dominique stood up and began walking toward the door.

However, the commander called out to his sergeant, "Stop her."

Turning toward Sister Dominique, Commander Ossani said, "Come back here, Sister. We need to have a conversation."

Not wanting to create an argument, Sister Dominique returned to her bench, sitting down without saying a word.

Stepping from the wheelchair, the commander walked slowly toward a bench just a few feet away. After sitting down, he said, "I commend you, Sister. I have heard of all the good work you have done in the surgery room for our Japanese people. It is impressive."

Turning to face Commander Ossani, she replied. "Sometimes we may not be able to save them, but we have compassion for human beings, unlike your officers!"

"If you are speaking of the incident with the baby, yes, that was most unfortunate," Commander Ossani replied, as he lit a cigarette.

"Unfortunate? Is that what you call it? He murdered an infant, an innocent infant that had no part in this war. That was—"

Before she could finish, Commander Ossani stood up. "The child was an American, she was an enemy of the Japanese people. Call it what you like, but there was no reason to keep that child alive, as one day she would have struck out against us."

Sister Dominique was about to respond when she felt the ground under her feet tremble and the air around her vibrate. Looking up into the clear blue sky, she screamed, "Oh, dear God!"

Seconds later, the first of several five-hundred-pound bombs slammed into the roof of the hospital. The blast threw Sister Dominique, along with Commander Ossani and Sergeant Maeda, back several feet before falling to the ground. Within seconds, the entire roof and second floor had collapsed onto the first floor, and the southern wall had caved in. Every building in a two-block area was receiving the same treatment, as hunks of concrete and steel shrapnel whistled overhead.

As the planes moved farther toward the west, turning their attention to other targets, Sister Dominique struggled to her feet while clasping her hands over her face. She watched as the east wall crumbled into the rubble pile, sending up a plume of smoke and dust. The heat from the fire was intense as flames rose a hundred feet into the afternoon sky. She remembered Dr. Lewis telling her that one day the makeshift hospital would become a target, as there were no markings on the roof designating it as a medical use building. She knew that Dr. Lewis, Willow and all the patients inside were gone, and was equally sure they never felt a thing as the huge bombs collapsed the building on them in a matter of seconds.

Looking over her shoulder, Sister Dominique was stunned to see the frightened look on the face of Commander Ossani. Quickly, he would look at the inferno in front of him, and then at the decapitated body of Sergeant Maeda laying a few yards away. Sister Dominique knew what had just happened would only increase the anger and hostility inside him for anyone he considered an enemy of Japan.

Knowing there was nothing she could do, Sister Dominique sat back down on the bench she had been using and began to pray for all the victims.

About an hour later, Colonel Takeuchi arrived in a staff car. He walked around the massive fire and shook his head. Walking up to Commander Ossani, he said. "I am sorry for your loss, Commander. I know you and the sergeant have been close for many years. My condolences."

Turning toward Sister Dominique he said. "I have no further use for you. Commander Ossani can have you transferred to the camp you were supposed to go to in the beginning." Turning, he walked back to his staff car, and was driven off in the direction of Tokyo Bay.

Commander Ossani gingerly walked over toward a fire truck and dampened a rag from a fire hose. After wiping blood from his face and uniform, he spoke to several soldiers standing nearby. When he was finished, they walked over to Sister Dominique and said, "There is a convoy with prisoners coming by here shortly. We are to make sure you are loaded on one of the trucks."

Sister Dominique nodded her head. "It is good for me to leave this place."

A half hour later, Sister Dominique was seated on a hard wooden bench in the back of a military vehicle heading toward the prisoner camp. She was not sure where she was going, or if she would be with Father Renaldo and the sisters again, but she was positive of one thing, she knew all too well she would be back in a camp with Commander Ossani, and that was not a good thought.

Chapter Fifteen–Who Lives, Who Dies

From the very beginning of the war with Japan, all the allied planners were certain the only way to end the war was to invade the Japanese home islands. Top military officials named the plan Operation Downfall. It was broken down into two separate invasions, the first was named Operation Olympic and the second, Operation Coronet.

Everyone in the planning department understood that the invasion would be costly beyond what any one wanted to admit. Estimates were that Operation Olympic would create 456,000 allied casualties with 109,000 being killed in action. Operation Coronet would create 1.2 million casualties, with 267,000 projected deaths. That did not include the possibility of the Japanese using poisonous gas as they had in China. If mass amounts of gas were used, casualty rates could be much higher.

President Roosevelt knew America well, and understood they would never accept those casualty numbers, there had to be another way.

Shortly after the war began the president was made aware of a top-secret plan to build a new type of bomb that would be more devastating than any other weapon known to man. After hearing about the weapon, the president authorized funds to continue construction of the first atomic bomb. The code name for the development of the bomb was the Manhattan Project.

It was so secret that even the Vice President was not allowed to know about it. Although research for the project was going on all over the United States, the final headquarters for the operation was located in Alamogordo, New Mexico.

Doctor J. Robert Oppenheimer, an eccentric physicist, was assigned to oversee the entire operation. He recruited geniuses such as Enrico Fermi to direct the operations at Los Alamos. Fermi was also the first man to install a uranium slug into an actual reactor at the Hanford test site in Washington state. Some of the other world-renowned scientists were Leo Szilard, Hans Bethe, Ernest O. Lawrence and Glenn Seaborg.

Roosevelt had been constantly updated on every major advancement with the construction of this new bomb and possible ways to use it. Picking a target for the attack was left up to a committee of scientists and high-ranking officers. They decided the city to be attacked had to fit into three categories. First, it had to be wider than three miles in diameter, with a sizable population. Second, the city needed to have a high strategic value, such as containing large military installations or major war manufacturing plants. Third, the target city must have been spared from the fire bombing raids that had begun on Japanese cities in March of 1945.

Before any cities were selected, the committee stated that the bomb should be dropped over Tokyo Bay to show the power of this new weapon without killing anyone. However, the plan was rejected as top officials wanted to know what the effective killing and destructive ratio of this new weapon actually was. So, the committee went back to the search for a qualified target. Problem was, finding cities to meet those requirements was no longer an easy mission. But in the end, they picked Kyoto, Hiroshima, Kokura and Niigatat. Secretary of War Stimson, who was also on the list of people to receive updates on the Manhattan Project, immediately rejected Kyoto. He argued that the city was a major cultural center with over two thousand Buddhist and Shinto shrines, and their destruction would bring about world condemnation. However, the committee disagreed with Stimson's request and kept Kyoto on the list. It was only after a passionate plea to President Truman by Stimson that Kyoto was eventually taken off the list and Nagasaki added.

During the production period, it was decided there should be two different types of bombs made. The first was to be a bomb using a gun type detonator created out of U235 uranium. It became known as 'Little Boy.' The second type of bomb used plutonium and was named 'Fat Man.' The main difference was that Little Boy would explode, while Fat Man would implode.

Although Oppenheimer realized the plutonium bomb was already going to make the uranium bomb obsolete, his team knew the uranium bomb would be ready before the war ended, so they needed to continue working on it without delay. No one in the scientific community expected progress on Fat Man to move along as quickly as it did.

The island of Tinian was chosen for the location of the 509 composite bomb group that would drop all the atomic bombs. By now, Tinian had become the largest airport in the world with six runways all over two miles long. Plus, if a plane carrying an atomic bomb would go down directly after lift-off, it would automatically fall into the ocean where it may or may not explode, even though it was unarmed. The distance from Tinian to Hiroshima was about 1586 miles, meaning the round trip flight would take roughly twelve hours. That distance to target was shorter than other possible islands in the Mariana Islands that could handle B-29 aircraft. Although the 509 composite bomb group had been picked for this top-secret mission, they were segregated from other bomb groups, and their mail was strictly censored to make sure nothing regarding their training was getting out to the folks back home. Over and over, they practiced take offs with a payload equal to the atomic bomb while learning how to do final arming of the weapon while they were in the air. There was no room for error. None of the men in the group, including Colonel Paul Tibbits, had any idea as to where they would be going, what they would be carrying, or any other pertinent information about the mission. All of that was being withheld until the final hours before the flight.

The United States entered the atomic age on the night of 16 July 1945, at a place named Trinity Site at Alamogordo, New Mexico. A plutonium bomb named, The Gadget, was lifted onto a steel tower one hundred feet high made out of 15,000 pounds of steel. The development scientists estimated the explosive power of the bomb at 19 kilotons.

Exactly at 5:29:45 hrs. local time, The Gadget imploded, sending a never-before-seen mushroom cloud to an altitude of 38,000 feet. After seeing the bomb explode, Oppenheimer said, "Now I am become death, the destroyer of worlds."

There never was a test of Little Boy, as the creation of the bomb used up all the refined U235 that was in the arsenal. However, since there were numerous tests of the gun-type detonator, no one had any doubts the bomb would explode as planned. Dr. Norman Ramsey, a top physicist in the program, argued that the United States should work harder to acquire more U235 because the Little Boy bomb was easier to build and it would take at least fifty bombings before Japan surrendered.

President Roosevelt passed away on April 12, 1945, not knowing if the bomb was going to be ready on time, or if it actually was going to work. After the bomb was tested, America's new President, Harry S. Truman, was told the bomb now actually existed. Although he had been told about the plan, he had not been told of the progress. There were too many people involved in the project that felt Truman could not be trusted, or may in fact stop development of the weapons. It turned out that Truman was all for the project, realizing he had an alternative to sending millions of young Americans onto the beaches of Japan.

After getting permission to move forward with the plan, the last parts of Little Boy including the valuable U235 were loaded on the heavy cruiser U.S.S. Indianapolis. The ship docked at Tinian on July 26, 1945 where scientists began final assembly.

During the months of June and July there were several Japanese diplomats that sought to have the Soviet Union help them negotiate some type of peace settlement. However, the United States had made it clear there would be no negotiated peace treaty. In accordance with the agreement reached at the Potsdam convention between all the Allied Warring partners, only an unconditional surrender would be acceptable. Top Japanese diplomats made it very clear they would never agree to an unconditional surrender.

Finally on July 25, 1945, President Truman was tired of Japan's failure to comply with the directives from the Allied governments. He issued an order that the use of the atomic bombs on Japan be started as soon as possible.

Planners quickly decided that Hiroshima would be the primary target. It had been untouched by fire bombings, it had huge ports that were used to ship war supplies from factories in and around the city, it had a major military headquarters, and photographing the destruction would be easy from the air as there were no nearby mountains. It would also be a good test to find out the destructive power of the weapon, as Hiroshima had 300,000 residents and 45,000 soldiers stationed there.

At 0200hrs. local time, on August 6, 1945, Colonel Paul Tibbits lifted his B-29 named Enola Gay from the massive Tinian airbase. The weather forecast over the target nearly 1600 miles away was mostly sunny with light broken cumulus clouds. Exactly what the planners had hoped for.

Approaching the city of Hiroshima, the bombardier informed Colonel Tibbits he would have no problem zeroing in on the target. At 0815hrs. local time, Colonel Tibbits gave the order to drop the bomb. Forty-five seconds later, Little Boy exploded, 1900 ft. above the city.

Near the explosion site, the temperature climbed to 5,400 degrees. On the ground, fire storms swept through the city and on out into the surrounding countryside, as asphalt buckled and rivers boiled. Two miles from the detonation site, people outside were turned into cinders. Everything within a 4.4-mile radius of the blast was totally incinerated.

The explosion immediately killed 80,000 people, while injuring 35,000 more. Nearly 60,000 more would die over the next year due to radiation poisoning.

Scientists did not expect the radiation levels to be as high as they were, or for residual radiation to cause so many deaths years later. Many survivors reported they had looked up at the sky when they heard the sound of just one B-29 overhead, as there were usually large groups of B29s in staggered formations flying toward there target. Seeing just the one plane, they all felt they were safe for another day. Although the bomb was dropped from 31,000 ft, some survivors reported seeing a large object drop from the bottom of the plane. Most of those that followed the bomb drop until it exploded were blinded for life.

The one thing planners had not taken into consideration, was the amount of POW's and other political prisoners housed in camps around Hiroshima. In the Chugoku Military Police Head Quarters in Hiroshima, were twelve American airman that had survived two B-29's that had been shot down. Eight were killed in the explosion, two were murdered by guards after the blast, and two badly injured airmen were taken to a nearby bridge where they were stoned to death by blast survivors.

Near the city of Zigozen, just 17.3 miles from Hiroshima, were several large camps for political prisoners collected from islands all over the Pacific with more to arrive shortly. Many of them became eye witnesses to what happened over Hiroshima.

Chapter Sixteen – Prisoner Camp

Trucks loaded with civilian prisoners including Sister Dominique, bounced and rumbled down a poorly maintained highway for a day and a half, passing through many industrial cities and the lush countryside. Many of the urban areas already reflected the ability of American bombers to level an entire city with their carpet-bombing tactics. All along the highways were large groups of refugees fleeing the cities that had been bombed, and those that were surely on the list still to be attacked. Many of the people yelled insults at the prisoners, knowing they were going to camps where they would be taken care of, not having to fear the ravages of high level bombing.

Some of the refugees still had cars and trucks to haul the meager possessions they were able to pack into them, while others were using horses and donkeys to pull old squeaking wagons and carts. But Sister Dominique's heart always went out to the small children that were following along, not knowing where they were going, and the crying babies that were tucked into back packs worn by their mothers. At times, she even wondered if all these people knew where they were going. The one thing they all had in common was the look of fear and loss that inhabited their minds and hearts.

What seemed most strange, was that the soldiers driving the trucks or escort vehicles did not attempt to have any type of compassion for their fellow countrymen. When an old woman stepped over to a soldier begging for something to eat, the man pushed her aside, causing her to fall to the ground. Several times when horse drawn carts blocked the road and the owners could not get their scared stubborn animals to comply, soldiers simply shot the animals and dragged them to the side as their owners wept. It was clear to Sister Dominique that she was seeing a losing army in disarray.

During the long ride, Sister Dominique talked a little to the man sitting beside her. He was Dutch and had worked in the oil fields in Java. Once the new wells were producing, the Japanese removed all the foreign workers, sending them to camps at Davao in the Philippines. When the allied forces began to invade, the camps were closed and everyone was sent to Japan. He told her there were people on the trucks from England, France, the United States and Hawaii.

Leaning back against the wooden planking, Sister Dominique closed her eyes. She thought back to the day her father dropped her off at the monastery. It had been a truly sad day for such a little child, and still to this day, she wondered how her parents could have come to that decision. Yet she had learned to give back to the people that needed help without thinking about what happened to her. Now she was once again travelling into the unknown, all alone and unsure whether she would see Father Renaldo and the sisters ever again. Most of all she did not want to lose Sister Claudia, her only true family member. There was no doubt in her mind that Commander Ossani would do whatever he could to make her life a living hell, so separating her from her only family would be a feather in his cap.

Arriving at Kure, the highway began to circle around Hiroshima Bay. The Bay was full of all kinds of ships involved in supplying the hardware of war to the troops all across the Pacific. It was evident there had been no B-29 fire bombings in the area, as everything appeared to be clean and undisturbed. All kinds of vehicles moved about the roads, and in commercial areas, shops and stores were busy with customers that did not appear to have a care in the world. Although, many of them did take a moment to call out insults to the prisoners in the trucks as they shook their heads in disgust.

About forty-five minutes later, the convoy drove into a large camp for political prisoners located just to the north of Zigozen, and stopped aside of what could be called a large viewing stand. It was apparent the buildings had been constructed as needed since the beginning of the war, including the massive towers that encircled the heavy wire fence.

Soldiers came running to drop the tailgates of the trucks, as others stood by pointing automatic weapons at the new prisoners. When everyone was standing together, the trucks were driven off. Moments later a staff car approached the viewing stand. A tall, well-groomed colonel exited the vehicle and climbed the steps of the stand, along with a cadre of officers.

Picking up a microphone he began. "Welcome to prison camp forty-six, my name is Colonel Uchida. Let me make this clear one time, you are not POW's, you are considered political prisoners, so you are not covered by the Geneva Convention as is a combatant. You will be given a list of the camp rules, regulations and feeding schedules. You are expected to follow these rules to the letter. If you do not follow them, disciplinary punishment may be severe, to include a firing squad for serious infractions. We attempt to separate you by nationality so it is easier for you to communicate with your fellow prisoners.

You may not have been aware, but my new Adjutant Commander Ossani accompanied your convoy from Tokyo. He will be in charge of day-to-day operations, and will make sure these rules are followed."

Turning toward the steps, he motioned for Ossani to step forward. After the men shook hands, the Colonel looked at the new prisoners. "Guards will now lead you to your barracks where you can get settled in and read over the rules. We do not wish to have any unfortunate issues.

After the colonel was driven off, soldiers carrying lists of names began assembling people into small groups before leading them away.

Sister Dominique was placed in a group with three other people of Italian descent. As they walked toward two buildings, Sister Dominique recognized Father Renaldo standing next to the building on the left. He stepped forward and bowed to the soldier. After a short conversation, the soldier nodded his head. Turning toward Sister Dominique, he said, "You go with this man. He has room in his barracks for you with some other missionaries."

Bowing graciously, Sister Dominique replied, "Thank you, may the emperor look favorably upon you."

The soldier smiled as he led the other Italians to the building on the right.

Walking up to Father Renaldo, Sister Dominique threw her arms around his neck and cried. "I never thought I would see you or the other sisters ever again. Please tell me they are all with you."

Smiling boldly, he responded. "They are all inside and will be so happy to see you again. Like you, we figured you were lost forever. This is a true miracle."

As she walked inside the barracks, the other sisters charged forward, all taking turns hugging Sister Dominique as they cried. After walking Sister Dominique over to the showers, Sister Margaret handed her a dark brown garment the camp commander wanted all the women clergy to wear.

It was an interesting evening as Father Renaldo and the sisters explained what had all happened to them since they had been separated. They were stunned when Sister Dominique explained to them about the hospital and how everyone inside had been killed during the bombing.

That night as Sister Dominique laid her head on her pillow, she was more thankful than she had been in a long time. She never expected to be reconnected with this special group of people.

The colonel had allowed the sisters to start a small school for any children that wanted to attend. The small building they were using for a school was the perfect size for the thirty American, British, Australian and Dutch children that gladly attended school each day. The colonel provided them a blackboard with lots of chalk, and a large box filled with paper and pencils. In front of the classroom was a large framed photo of Emperor Hirohito with a laurel wreath around it. The colonel made it clear they could teach whatever they felt was necessary, but could not say anything derogatory about Germany or the Japanese Empire. He also insisted that each Friday afternoon he be allowed to speak to the students regarding the glories of the Japanese Empire.

Everything was going well in the small school, and the students were anxious learners as most of them had not been able to attend school for several years. However, one afternoon after school was over, Commander Ossani entered the building. Walking up to Sister Dominique, he bowed slightly.

"It is a good thing you all are doing here. Children need direction and education if they are to succeed. But you must understand the needs of the camp come before your individual needs. Our small hospital is hurting for nurses as there are only three in the camp, and we only have one doctor for over five hundred prisoners. So, starting Monday, the colonel has ordered you to work in the hospital."

Saddened by what she had been told, but realizing the other sisters could continue on without her, Sister Dominique nodded her head. "I shall do what I can do."

About a week later when most of the prisoners were out in the yard for exercise, a large flight of American B-29's flew overhead. Knowing that the taste of war had finally come to the Japanese homelands, a loud cheer went up from the prisoners, as some of them grabbed each other and began to dance. Although the Japanese did not appreciate what they were seeing, the guards did not interfere until one of the prisoners pushed a soldier, knocking him to the ground.

Feeling disgraced by the demonstration, several guards opened fire on the crowd. Screams echoed throughout the camp as bodies fell. Commander Ossani and his security force rushed into the yard, attempting to quell the disturbance that was quickly getting out of control.

By the time peace had been restored, ten bodies lay on the ground as twenty wounded prisoners screamed out in pain. Rushing out into the yard, Sister Dominique began directing soldiers to help the wounded into the hospital, but they refused, and would not allow other prisoners to help Sister Dominique in any way.

Within seconds, voices were raised once again, as prisoners demanded soldiers do something for the wounded, and the soldiers yelled for the prisoners to back up as they fixed bayonets on their rifles. One of the sergeants in charge of the soldiers pushed Sister Dominique to the ground, yelling that this was all her fault.

Angered by the sergeants cursing and false accusations, Sister Dominique jumped up from the ground and grabbed hold of a rifle being held loosely by a soldier, and struck him with the butt of the weapon. Dropping to the ground, the terrified solider cowered in fear as he looked up at Sister Dominique pointing the rifle at his head.

Instantly, a silence fell over the camp as everyone backed away, creating a circle around Sister Dominique and three other soldiers that had fired on the prisoners. No one moved, and it appeared as if no one wanted to take a breath of air, afraid that the very sound would push the scared soldiers to fire.

Father Renaldo rushed into the crowd, pushing everyone out of the way until he stood in front of Sister Dominique. Holding up his hands, he calmly said, "Sister, you need to put down that rifle and let that soldier up. Please put the rifle down."

Shaking her head, Sister Dominique responded, "No, not until they pick up the wounded and take them to the hospital. They are responsible for what has happened here."

"Sister, I realize how you feel, but holding that weapon on a Japanese soldier does nothing to help your case. One wrong move and those men will kill you, me, and possibly many more innocent people. Please put the rifle down," Father Renaldo said, as he took several steps closer.

Seconds later, Commander Ossani broke through the crowd and stopped cold in his tracks. He took a quick glance at Sister Dominique and then at Father Renaldo. Turning to face the three soldiers he said, "Lower your weapons, we've had enough bloodshed here today."

After the soldiers complied, Commander Ossani walked over to Sister Dominique. Holding out his hand he said, "Sister, I know you do not want to take that man's life, that is not who you are. I understand you are angry, but killing this man or any of my soldiers will not change anything. Please hand me the rifle."

As tears ran down her face, Sister Dominique handed the weapon to the commander. Shaking her head, she said, "I would not have killed him, I'm just so tired of all of this."

Before the commander could reply, Sister Dominique reached out for Father Renaldo, threw her arms around his neck and wept.

After Commander Ossani ordered the soldiers to deliver the wounded to the hospital, he stepped forward and took hold of Sister Dominique's arm. "You must come with me, Sister. You will need to be held in solitary confinement until the colonel finishes his investigation. Please do not cause me any more problems."

Nodding her head, Sister Dominique replied. "Do what you must do."

After a week in solitary, the colonel approved a visit from Father Renaldo. Walking into the small damp room, he observed Sister Dominique kneeling by her bed, praying the rosary. When she stopped and looked up, Father Renaldo said, "Continue Sister, I will join you."

Standing up, Sister Dominique replied, "I have been praying many every day. I think the good Lord will allow me to stop where I was. It is better for me to have someone to talk with."

After pacing the cell several times, Father Renaldo stopped and leaned against the wall. "Sister, your anger has become your own worst enemy. You must learn you cannot control the war or the Japanese empire."

Angered by Father Renaldo's comment, Sister Dominique glared at him for a moment. "Father, this war isn't about me, it isn't about you, it isn't about any of us! It's about right, it's about wrong, it's about trying to make a difference." After closing her eyes for a moment and shaking her head, she continued. "Father, it's about living up to what is in our hearts and what we have been taught our entire lives. If we lose that than we lose our individual souls, and we will never get them back, so what does that say about me and what I believe in. Father, what does it say about you, and worst of all, what does it say about humanity! Yes, I may lose my life for what I feel is right, but at least I can stand tall in front of our God and say I tried when others quit."

After pacing the room for several seconds, Sister Dominique walked up in front of Father Renaldo. "I have seen enough and cried enough tears to fill a small ocean, and yet my heart aches for all the people I have seen killed. Let them do as they must because my life has been fulfilled. I cannot change who I am, not for you, not for anyone."

After a moment of silence, Father Renaldo replied, "I have prayed to be strong like you, but have not found it within me. More often, I find myself just trying to survive this damn war. I am not a coward; I just want to survive the war and go on to be a good missionary. That is where I can make a difference. Sister, I just want to live."

Sister Dominique smiled as she reached over, taking Father Renaldo by the hand. "I know you are not a coward. You are now and always have been a brave man, no matter how you see yourself. You must not apologize for your fears, as we all have them. I have faith in you to always do the right thing."

Before Father Renaldo could respond, the guard opened the door and said, "Your time is up."

Placing his hand on Sister Dominique's head, Father Renaldo prayed a blessing and said, "Stay strong, Sister. We both can still come out on the other side of this war."

Several days later, two soldiers arrived to escort Sister Dominique to Commander Ossani's office.

The commander was sitting behind a large wooden desk smoking a cigarette as they walked in. Standing up, he motioned for the soldiers to leave. The commander walked over to the window where he looked out over the yard. He turned and walked around the room without saying a word.

Finally, he stopped and looked directly at Sister Dominique "So, tell me Sister, what am I to do with you now. You took a rifle from one of my men and threatened to shoot him. Everyone in the yard saw it. There would not be one officer in the Japanese military that would not already have executed you for your crimes. Yet, here you are alive and well. You might even say I am your benefactor, because you live and breathe because of me. What do you say to that?"

Looking toward the floor, Sister Dominique did not reply.

"I see," Commander Ossani said, as he backed up against the wall, folding his arms across his chest. "I know you are a smart and brave woman, and I know you have something you wish to say, so I would like to hear what is on your mind."

Raising her head, Sister Dominique starred at her captor as her breathing and pulse rate began to climb, but she felt it was wise to stay still.

Shaking his head, Commander Ossani smiled. "You underestimated me, didn't you. You thought for sure by now I would have ordered a public execution and you would already be dead. Yet, you are not dead. Now we must figure out how to solve this problem. Do you have any suggestions?"

Sister Dominique replied. "None that I can think of at the present. It is in your hands, you must decide."

"Ah," Commander Ossani said with a smile. "You do speak when spoken to, we have made progress. Before we continue, please sit, it will make negotiations much more comfortable."

Sitting down in an old green moth-eaten chair, Sister Dominique stared straight ahead, not knowing what was going to come next. She wished Colonel Uchida was in the room, as it appeared he might be easier to work with.

As Sister Dominique sat quietly, Commander Ossani walked around the room humming a song. The second time he passed behind her, he grabbed her jaw from behind, pulling her head back as far as it would go.

Sister Dominique closed her eyes and placed her hands on top of the Commander's, attempting to break his powerful grip, but to no avail.

"Right now, I could kill you with a quick jerk of your head. Why have you decided to try and make a fool out of me? Do you have a death wish?"

Letting go of Sister Dominique, he pushed her forward out of the chair onto the floor. Gasping for air, she looked up at the angry officer. "As I have told you before, do what you must do to save face, since that is all you are really after."

Stepping forward, Commander Ossani kicked Sister Dominique in the abdomen. Raising his left leg, he stepped over Sister Dominique so his legs straddled her body. "I tell you now, before this is over, you will wish I had shot you right away, so you could remember me for all eternity."

Before Commander Ossani could say another word, the door across from the desk opened up. Colonel Uchida was standing in the doorway with his hands on his hips. "Commander, I think it's best that you go for a walk out in the yard and make sure all is well."

Bowing down to his commanding officer, Commander Ossani replied. "As you wish!"

Reaching down his hand, the colonel said. "Here, let me help you off the floor. We can talk better if you are sitting in a chair."

Sister Dominique refused to take his hand while slowly standing up before taking her place in the chair.

Colonel Uchida walked over to the desk and sat down. "I am aware of your history with the commander, and I must say I am amazed. When you were treating his burns at the hospital in Tokyo, you could have easily killed him, but instead, you let him live. No one would have questioned his death as badly as he was burned. Why didn't you kill him when you had the chance? You knew if he survived, he would continue to torment you."

Sister Dominique replied, "I am a Catholic sister, not an executioner."

Laughing, Colonel Uchida leaned back in his chair. "Yet, you aimed a loaded rifle at the head of one of my men and threatened to kill him."

"I never placed my finger on the trigger of that rifle, and I could not have shot him," Sister Dominique replied, realizing what she had done would make a person think she was capable of murder.

Leaning forward, Colonel Uchida said, "Tell me about your life when you were growing up in Italy. What was it like? I have never been there."

"What difference does it make, that was a long time ago," Sister Dominique replied, not wanting to discuss anything about her life.

The colonel smiled at Sister Dominique, "You mean to tell me you do not wish to talk about your brother Paulo, who has such an important job in the Italian Army. I would think you would want to know everything possible about your family, since you have not seen them in years."

Stunned by what the colonel had just said, Sister Dominique shook her head. "If Paulo is actually still alive, he may live his life as he sees fit. None of that is my concern anymore."

Standing up, the colonel paced back and forth by the windows for a moment before speaking. "Are you not interested in how we know these things?"

"No," Sister Dominique replied.

"Would it interest you that we also know that Sister Claudia is your real sister?" the colonel stated as he looked harshly at Sister Dominique. "You see, the Japanese Kempeitai is much like your American OSS. They are both like an octopus. They have large tentacles that can poke into places that most people can't even imagine. We know your parents gave you up when you were five years old in the middle of the winter. We know about your underground dealings in Italy before you left to be a missionary. Had you stayed there you would be dead already. Does any of this surprise you, Sister?"

Shaking her head, Sister Dominique responded. "None of it matters anymore, It's all water under the bridge as they say."

"Really? Do you truly believe that, Sister? How do think the Italian government would feel if they knew one of their top officers had a sister that was a loyal member of the Italian underground? What do you think they might do to Paulo if they suspected him of treason? Have you given that any thought?"

Sister Dominique shook her head as she smiled. "No doubt they would kill him, but there is nothing I can do to stop it, so what does it matter?"

Sitting back down in his chair, Colonel Uchida smiled. "Oh, it matters, Sister. If I send a cable to Italy telling them I have captured a former spy that is a sister to a senior officer in the Italian Army, they will jump for joy and arrange for your pick up within days. They will have a national holiday when they execute both of you side by side. In fact, I can send Sister Claudia along so they can have a threesome as you Americans say. Would not that be cozy?"

For the first time since she left Italy, Sister Dominique was afraid for her family. She knew very well that the colonel would do exactly what he promised and think nothing of it. Now she had to decide what was the right course of action, and not do anything she would be sorry for later.

Looking over at the colonel who had a sly smile on his face, Sister Dominique replied. "Do what you must do. If we are to die together, so be it. I have no power in this world, only God does."

Slamming his fist on the desk, Colonel Uchida yelled. "There is no God other than our Emperor. You will see him sitting on a great throne governing all the nations in the Greater East-Asia co-prosperity sphere, and dictating to the rest of the world. You will see, it will come to pass."

Laughing, Sister Dominique replied, "If that is so, why are your forces being withdrawn from islands all across the Pacific, why are American B-29 bombers destroying your cities? Again, do what you must do and let's quit this silly game."

After a moment of silence, Colonel Uchida said, "So be it." Pushing a button on an intercom system, he said, "Find me Commander Ossani and bring him here."

Several minutes later, the commander entered the room. After saluting, Colonel Uchida said, "Go to the school, grab two of the sisters and tie their hands behind their backs. Assemble a firing squad and have them prepared for my order."

After the commander left, Colonel Uchida said, "You told me to do as I wish, and so I wish to shoot one of your sisters for your sins. Then we shall go on living as always. What do you think of that idea?"

Kneeling down, Sister Dominique removed a Rosary from her pocket and began to pray.

"That will do you no good, Sister Dominique!" the colonel yelled as he pulled the Rosary from her hands, tearing it apart, sending the beads all across the floor. Pulling her up by the neck, the colonel slammed her against the brick wall. "You think this is a joke, you think you can intimidate me with that string of beads. Well, I am sorry, Sister. I have no more time for you. I will have my men shoot one of your friends in fifteen minutes, then send you back to solitary where you can pray to your God to have mercy on your soul!"

Shaking her head, Sister Dominique looked up at the colonel. "Nothing is in my hands now or has it been, you are in control, and you will do what you want to do. There is no difference between you and Commander Ossani from what I am seeing."

After slapping Sister Dominique across the face, he grabbed her by the arm, dragging her to the window behind his desk. "See? There are your two sisters and the firing squad, just waiting for my command. Let me show you what your failure to cooperate has cost you."

As he pulled the shade part way down, the firing squad opened fire. Instantly Sister Henrietta's body dropped to the ground as six bullets tore her chest apart. Sister Dominique turned her head away from the scene in the courtyard, as tears ran down her face. Grabbing Sister Dominique by the jaw, the colonel turned her face back to the macabre sight as blood continued to cover the ground. This was your fault, and I have three more sisters that may have to die for your sins. What do you think of that?"

Before Sister Dominique could respond, he called for the soldiers that had posted just outside his office. "Take her back to solitary confinement, I think we have reached a compromise."

As the soldiers began removing her from the room, the colonel called out, "Wait!" Taking Sister Dominique back over to the window, he said,

"By now you should have had a few minutes to think as to how you are going to act in this camp when I release you from solitary. If you look out in the yard, you will see another friend of yours is still standing with her hands tied. Her life is also in your hands. Or do you wish me to have Sister Claudia brought out instead."

"No, please do not harm those women, I beg of you. What kind of animal have you become with this war? Have you forgotten that you will need to answer to God and man for what you have done here today?"

Laughing, Colonel Uchida grabbed hold of Sister Dominique, slapping her across the face as hard as he could. "From now on you must think before you act in this camp because you are wrong about one thing. I will never answer to this God you speak so highly of, and from now on only you have the power of life and death, not me. Choose well, Sister!"

After taking a deep breath and being totally scared, Sister Dominique inquired, "What do your parents think of what you are doing in this war?"

"My parents!" Colonel Uchida said loudly, with a tone of disgust in his voice. "They were nothing but dirt farmers that could not even raise a family decently. They taught me nothing, because they knew nothing. No, I ran away when I was thirteen and joined the army. They sent me to Germany and Austria to learn the ways of the Third Reich and learn from them and I did. I made something of myself, whether they ever accept it or not."

Some how feeling a bit bolder again, Sister Dominique pressed forward. "So, your parents are still alive? Did you have brothers and sisters?"

Sitting down in the desk chair, the colonel smiled. "I see what you are trying to do here, but creating a relationship with me will not change anything. I will never feel guilty for shooting your friend or anything else I have done in this war. Unlike you, I have no conscience. But you will need to suffer for what you were responsible for today. I feel sorry for you."

Sister Dominique suddenly felt very empty inside, the colonel had finally beaten her. "Colonel, may I help bury my friend before going back into solitary. It would mean a lot to me."

After laughing, the colonel leaned forward in his chair. "For your information, my parents are both dead. They died during the cold winter of 1937, and I had nothing to do with their burials and neither shall you."

Signaling the soldiers, the colonel said, "Take her back to solitary for another week."

Sitting down on her bunk, Sister Dominique could not fully comprehend what had just happened. First Sister Veronica died, then Sister Perpetua and now Sister Henrietta, and she feared none of them may survive this war with people like Colonel Uchida and Commander Ossani in charge.

One week later, the colonel ordered Sister Dominique released from solitary. In one respect she was happy to be leaving, but now she would have to face the other sisters and explain to them what happened to Sister Henrietta. It would be a huge challenge, as she still felt totally guilty.

She was surprised when the guard at the door handed her a sealed envelope containing all the beads from her Rosary. Looking at the guard, she said. "Thank you, this means a lot to me."

The soldier bowed slightly before asking. "The colonel said you use them for praying. How do you pray with those beads, and who is on that cross?"

Seeing several other soldiers standing nearby, watching what was going on, Sister Dominique said, "Come to my barracks one evening, we will teach you about it."

Standing by the door of the barracks, Sister Dominique took a deep breath. She knew Father Renaldo and the other sisters were expecting her tonight. She just couldn't be sure of the reception she was going to get. Slowly she pulled the door open and walked inside.

Chapter Seventeen – A Bright Light

The sixth day of August in 1945 began as any other day in Prisoner Camp 46. The doors to the barracks were unlocked, roll call had been taken and breakfast was served. There was no doubt the Japanese were quickly becoming short on rations, as nearly every day the amount of food given to the prisoners became less and less. All of the prisoners in Camp 46 were beginning to lose weight rapidly, and many were becoming quite sick. Deaths were on the rise as many older people died in their sleep each night. Soldiers began to help dig graves as most of the men in the camp no longer had the ability to dig into the hard ground.

Flyovers of B-29 bombers was now a daily occurrence, but no one cheered them on ever again. Colonel Uchida had given prisoners cans of white paint and brushes, so they could paint the letters POW on the roofs of every building. Even though Camp 46 was located in an open area seventeen miles from Hiroshima, Colonel Uchida wanted to make sure they were not bombed by accident. The prisoners enjoyed painting the letters on each building because they knew the camp would be photographed from the air, allowing rescuers to find them quickly when the war ended. That was if the guards did not kill them before leaving the camp.

No longer did Red Cross inspectors arrive to inspect the camp, which was tough on the moral of the prisoners. They always provided tidbits of information as to what was happening in Europe and out in the Pacific. Everyone knew since the war was over in Europe, the might of the allied armies was going to fall on the heads of the Japanese military and the war would come to an end much more quickly, but when was the question. Another thing the prisoners were upset about was that Red Cross packages were no longer handed out to each prisoner. Everyone in the camp knew the packages were arriving, but since they always contained some type of candy or food product, the guards were stealing them for their families.

The death of Sister Henrietta had taken a severe toll on the mental well-being of Sister Dominique. She had become more withdrawn, and spent extra hours in the hospital so she wouldn't have to spend time with anyone from the barracks. Although no one was blaming her for what happened, Sister Dominique totally blamed herself, and searched her soul for peace that just never seemed to appear.

At 0800hrs. local time, Sister Dominique looked out the window toward the school. She watched as the three remaining sisters went inside to prepare for the children. She jumped as Doctor Jacques Phillips walked up behind her and spoke. "Well, Sister, do you think we will survive this day, or is this the day the Japanese decide to kill us before the Allies arrive."

Turning to face the doctor, she said, "I do not think our time has come to die. I have faith we shall survive."

Doctor Phillips shook his head, "Faith, what the hell is that? The Japanese took all that away from me, and I know we shall all perish on this stinking island. You best prepare yourself, look what they did to me."

Sister Dominique knew he was referring to what had happened to him before he came to Camp 46. He had been one of the top doctors working in the Dutch East Indies for a large petroleum company. After the Japanese invasion, he was treated rather well and given many privileges other foreign workers were not. The night the Japanese decided to send all foreign workers to Japan, many people attempted to run. Several Japanese soldiers were killed and their weapons used on other soldiers that arrived to quell the uprising. Soon it was a major battle that the foreign workers were never going to win. As the battle began to subside, the commandant of the camp took retribution. Every nurse that had worked with Dr. Phillips in the hospital, along with their families, and the families of many oil field workers, were lined up and shot. Dr. Phillips was spared to take care of the wounded Japanese soldiers. From that day on he had become a very dour individual, seeing nothing but the worst in everything that happened in the camp.

Wanting to get away from the doctor for a few minutes, Sister Dominique picked up a pail of water she had used to scrub the floor. She walked out the back door of the hospital and dumped it onto the hard packed ground. Taking in a deep breath of fresh air, she looked up into the bright morning sky where a lazy pattern of light clouds passed along the coast line.

But something appeared odd this morning, as usually one or two flights of shiny B-29 bombers typically would have flown over by now, on the way to their assigned targets. Nevertheless, today the sky was eerily empty in every direction. Even the screeching sea gulls were nowhere to be seen. A shiver rolled down her spine as she realized something was wrong, something in the universe was out of place and it appeared as if even God himself was holding his breath.

Walking away from the bucket, Sister Dominique walked over to the corner of the hospital to take a long look around the camp. The door to the school was open and the shutters over the windows were pushed up. A group of workers were preparing to put roofs on several new barracks that were being built, and the workers that kept the barracks clean were already hard at it. Even the guards in the towers were leaning back against the wooden railings, soaking up the warm morning sun as if they hadn't a care in the world.

Shaking her head and smiling, Sister Dominique mumbled to herself, "I guess maybe I've been locked up too long, and I need to quit listening to the doctor."

After flying above the city of Hiroshima, Major Charles W. Sweeney, pilot of the B-29 named *The Great Artiste*, dropped scientific instruments over the city before radioing Colonel Tibbits in the *Enola Gay* that the target was clear with only light scattered clouds. That was the last bit of information Colonel Tibbits required before releasing his bomb. At 0915hrs. local time, the bombardier informed Colonel Tibbits that they were directly over the Aioi Bridge, their assigned aim point. Instantly, the atomic bomb known as Little Boy was released from the bomb bay of the *Enola Gay*, causing the aircraft to rise ten feet after the massive loss of weight.

Immediately, Colonel Tibbits threw the *Enola Gay* into a sharply banked turn of 155 degrees, which was supposed to get him out of the way of the bomb blast. Many scientists did not believe the aircraft could survive the blast, no matter how hard the pilot attempted to escape. The *Enola Gay* shook violently, making control of the plane all but impossible. When the *Enola*

Gay was nearly twelve miles away, once again the plane was violently shaken. What the crew at first though was enemy flak, turned out to be a shock wave that reverberated up from the ground. As co-pilot Captain Robert Lewis looked back at the billowing mushroom cloud, he said, "My God what have we done!" By this time, nine out of ten people within a half mile or less from the blast site were dead.

Just as Sister Dominique reached down for the handle of the bucket at 0915hrs local time, she saw a bright light flash over Hiroshima. Instantly, a low rumble reverberated across the land, becoming louder by the second. She had heard explosions before, but she understood this rumble was like nothing she had ever heard before. It did not die away, and instead grew in intensity of both tone and volume, causing the earth to tremble under her feet, and it terrified her.

Quickly, a massive ugly dark cloud appeared in the sky where the bright flash had been. The base of the dark gray-green cloud reached down to the earth, while the top continued rising ever higher up into the heavens. All around the edges of the gathering cloud, tremendous bursts of lightening roared up and down the churning black monster.

Standing frozen in place, Sister Dominique and other prisoners that had gathered outside stood speechless as they watched the shape of the cloud form and reform as it rose ever higher.

Then something odd caught the attention of Sister Dominique's eye. It was a lone B-29 bomber flying overhead, circling the gigantic cloud. As the plane circled, a strong wind began to blow across the camp, carrying an awful, frightening smell with it. Over the next minute or so the temperature in the camp went up nearly forty degrees, and still the B-29 circled.

By now the top of the cloud over Hiroshima had ceased to grow, but was higher than the plane that was circling it, and still the roar continued.

Suddenly, Sister Margaret and Sister Claudia were standing beside Sister Dominique. Taking hold of her arm, Sister Margaret said, "Tell me, is this the end of the world?"

Putting her arms around the terrified sisters, she replied, "I do not believe so, but whatever it was has opened the gates of hell upon mankind."

The soldier that Sister Dominique had taken the rifle away from walked up to the sisters. "My wife and children live in Hiroshima. They are gone now

I feel. I could feel my wife's spirit pass by me in the wind. I fear everyone is gone. What was this weapon that stares down upon us? It scares me to the core."

Before Sister Dominique could answer the soldier, he turned and walked off as tears streamed down his sun tanned face.

Father Renaldo and Pierre Duncan soon joined the sisters near the hospital. Looking more scared and unsure of himself than Sister Dominique had ever witnessed, Father Renaldo said, "Whatever it was that fell from that plane will change the world forever. God help us!"

In the camp office, Colonel Uchida attempted to call his commanding officer at the military barracks in Hiroshima, but the lines were simply dead. He then attempted to call other friends of his that lived in the city, but found all those lines dead as well. Turning to look out the window at the great cloud once more, he hung his head. Slowly he mumbled, "For sure, now all is lost."

The *Enola Gay* and its escort aircraft, *The Great Artiste* continued flying back toward Tinian without any damage. The third B-29 of the group, *Necessary Evil*, held back, circling the city three times as Russell Gackenback, the cameraman on board, photographed the cloud and whatever he could see on the ground. Captain George Marquardt, the pilot of *Necessary Evil* changed course slightly as he had been instructed by scientists not to attempt to fly through any part of the atomic cloud.

Commander Ossani had been given a few days off to attend a training exercise at the Hiroshima Army Base. He rose at four-thirty to take in a five-mile run before preparing himself for a busy interesting day. Wanting to make a good impression on the instructors, Ossani put on a brand new, well starched uniform he had just purchased a few days ago.

As Ossani and several other officers approached the building where the class was to be held, he looked at his watch. "We have some time, I'm going to the tea shop in the basement to get a cup of tea. Anyone wish to join me?"

The other men decided to go straight to the classroom and find a favorable seat near the lectern. Just as Commander Ossani entered the tea shop, the building began to twist and shake. Parts of the ceiling began to fall as the electricity cut out.

Seeing a large heavy table in front of him, Ossani grabbed hold of a terrified young woman and pulled her to the floor. Ducking under the table, he laid on top of her saying, "We will be safe here, do not try and run."

Suddenly, the room became black as night as the sun no longer came through the windows. The temperature climbed higher than the commander had ever experienced before, and a wind more

ferocious than a typhoon roared around the building as if it were reaching out to grab him.

Suddenly, every wall crumbled as the floor above caved in all around them. The young woman screamed, attempting to fight off the commander as she wanted to run, but he kept telling her there was no place to run to.

Neither the commander or the woman could tell anyone how long the destructive force of the bomb ravaged the city, but the hands on the commanders watch clearly said 0955 when the roar had subsided and light could be seen through the rubble overhead.

Both the commander and the woman yelled for help, but it was clear there was no one to answer their pleas. Rolling slightly to his right, the commander could see a large piece of concrete that was being held up by the table. There was a large void under it that appeared to lead back toward the stairway he had just come down.

After getting himself turned around, he told the woman he was going to check out the space and she should remain there. Terrified of what was going on she refused, and crawled along with him. They had to try and maneuver several pieces of concrete and steel out of the way in order to get to the stairwell, hopefully without dropping the rest of the building down on top of them.

Finally, the commander was able to kneel aside of the fifth step where he could see the entry way. Carefully, he helped the woman onto what was left of the stairs, allowing her to crawl toward freedom. Crawling behind the woman, the commander was positive the building had been hit by either a five-hundred or thousand-pound bomb. Nothing else besides a large naval gun would collapse a building like this.

However, as he stood up on what was left of the sidewalk, he knew he was wrong. Everything around the military base was gone. Every tree was broken off near the base, and every car and truck that had been parked in the huge parking lot across the street had melted down to the pavement below.

An eerie gray green cloud of dust hung over the army base, but not another human being was anywhere in sight. Looking at the terrified woman, he said. "We shall walk west, that is where my base is located, we can get help there."

As they walked westward, they ran into a few people that no longer wore clothing and were horribly burned. They stumbled along not saying a word as blood oozed from every part of their bodies. Some people were missing arms or hands, and some appeared as if their faces were half melted away. But these strange looking creatures were few and far between. For the most part the city was nothing more than an incinerated landscape, void of any human or animal life.

Walking past the Ota River, Commander Ossani could not believe his eyes. Steam rose from the water as bodies that appeared to have been boiled alive floated on the surface. The young woman screamed and backed away as she threw her hands over her eyes. Dropping to the ground, she yelled repeatedly, "Get me out of her, get me out of here, I want to go home!"

Reaching down to take the woman by the hand, she pulled away. "I have seen too much, I don't want to see anymore!"

Grabbing hold of her wrist, Ossani said. "You can come with me to safety, or you can stay here by yourself and figure out what you want to do. But there is nothing left here for anyone."

Slowly, the woman stood back up and began walking west, trying not to look at the horror around her. They had walked about four miles when they began running into buildings that were only slightly damaged, and cars that had been rolled over on their sides by the tremendous wind. About a half mile further, Commander Ossani observed a car sitting next to a brick building that appeared to be mostly intact. Opening the door, he noticed the keys hanging in the ignition. On the second attempt, the engine sprang to life.

Without being told, the woman crawled into the passenger seat, slamming the door shut. "Please take me away, I do not wish to see any more of this," she said, as she wept.

Driving down the highway they met large groups of people walking west. Some were dressed normally, while others had their clothing burned off. One thing they all had in common were large burns or their hand and faces, and many with fingers totally burned off. Hearing the car coming toward them, some stepped out into the road begging for a ride, but most just continued walking west until they fell over in the ditch and died.

Arriving back at Camp 46, Commander Ossani waved his hand for the guards to open the gates. He immediately drove up to the colonel's office and ran inside with the woman.

Colonel Uchida stood up from his desk and took a deep breath. "Commander, are you a ghost, I have heard no one survived the attack."

Commander Ossani bowed. "I assure you Colonel, we are not ghosts. We were in the basement of the school when the blast hit. We were able to dig our way out, but life in Hiroshima is all but wiped out. You cannot imagine what we have seen as we walked through the city to the edge of the blast zone. The city is gone, I have never seen anything like it."

The colonel walked around the desk and looked at his shaking commander. "You must not tell anyone what you experienced. Neither the guards or the prisoners must know. Headquarters does not know what kind of weapon was used, but surely the Americans will use it again if they decide it was successful. We must not flinch, as we still have our duty to perform our jobs.

By the morning of August 8, small groups of survivors from Hiroshima began arriving at the gate of Camp 46. All of them had terrific burns, and some of them were near death. They begged and pleaded for water, food, medicine and clean bandages.

Sister Dominique and Doctor Phillips urged Colonel Uchida to let them treat the wounded and set up a burial team to bury those that were beginning to die, lest disease spread through the camp. As there was little food and medical supplies left in the camp to begin with, all the sisters could do was tear up sheets and other clean white cloth to bandage the horrific burns. The problem was the burns were so deep, that in just a short period of time, the bandages were completely soaked. Dehydration became a major problem for the burned victims very quickly.

On the morning of August 9, Colonel Uchida called his officers together. Once they were assembled, he said. "Headquarters told me just a short while ago that another new bomb was dropped on Nagasaki. They say this one appears to be worse than the one dropped on Hiroshima. Headquarters says the high command is looking into some sort of surrender agreement with the allies. If in fact that happens, we will abandon the camp and go home. We will open the gates and let the prisoners go where they want. We will do them no harm."

On the morning of August 10, Sister Dominique and Father Renaldo asked for a meeting with Colonel Uchida. Arriving in his office, the Colonel bowed down to them. "You have done much to help the people of my country, and I am very appreciative. What can I do for you today?"

Sister Dominique replied. "We hear from the survivors that there are many more in Hiroshima that cannot travel but need help. We would like to go to Hiroshima and help those that we can. Can you help us with our request?"

Shaking his head, Colonel Uchida replied. "I have orders to not let anyone go to Hiroshima or anywhere else. According to headquarters, there is nothing you can do, the city is now a ghost town of ashes. You can still work with the ones that can make it to the camp, but I'm afraid there is nothing more you can do in the city."

"Have you found a source for food for these people, they need food and medicine if they are going to survive," Father Renaldo pleaded respectfully.

Looking rather forlorn, Colonel Uchida responded. "Our food supply here is all but gone, and we will not be getting any more. When it is gone, it is gone. I have checked around the countryside and many of the people are already starving. Headquarters says our medical people have never seen burns like this before. Nothing we have appears to be working. Whatever kind of weapon the American's used against our cities is brand new. There is nothing anyone can do to help."

After walking around the office and looking out the window, the colonel turned to face them. "I believe the war will end any day now. I believe neither the emperor or those in the high command wish to see anymore of our cities destroyed."

Feeling very concerned, Sister Dominique looked at Colonel Uchida. "And what shall become of us? Have you given that any thought?"

The colonel walked back to his desk and sat down. "I have heard nothing from headquarters as of yet. I am sure they will give me orders."

Father Renaldo leaned forward in his chair. "People are worried, Colonel. They are afraid we will be—"

Before he could finish, Colonel Uchida cut him off. "As I have said, headquarters will tell us what to do. Until then, nothing is going to happen. I beg of you to keep the peace."

Knowing further bartering with the colonel was not going to accomplish anything, Father Renaldo looked sternly at the forlorn officer. "I do not wish to threaten you, but you must understand the allies will hold anyone accountable for mistreating prisoners, whether they be soldiers or civilians. I beg of you to keep that in mind."

Angered by Father Renaldo's comments, the colonel kicked his chair back and stood up. "I do not appreciate your threats, Father. Sometimes one has no decision on how things work out in the end. We all must do what we must do and consider the consequences later. Now, it's time for you to leave!"

Walking out into the camp, Father Renaldo looked at Sister Dominique, "Do you believe they will kill us all?"

After a moment of thought, Sister Dominique replied. "No Father, I do not. I believe the Colonel is already worried about some of the things he has done, and does not want to be blamed for more. I think when the end comes, he will do what is right. At least I hope that is accurate."

Although Emperor Hirohito announced that Japan was willing to surrender on August 10, no one in the camp was informed of his speech. All the prisoners waited to hear which city was going to be bombed next, and hoped the Japanese would not take it out on the prisoners.

Although Colonel Uchida had firmly said he would surrender the camp when the allies arrived, it became clear on the night of the twelfth, that was not going to be the case. Throughout the night, Japanese soldiers were planting mines on the fence, on the main gate, and out in the main yard.

On the morning of the thirteenth, the prisoners were herded out into the yard where they were assembled inside a circle of land mines. Colonel Uchida and his aides sat in the middle of the group wearing civilian clothing so they could not be easily spotted from outside the circle. Soldiers in the watch towers kept a close eye on the road for any vehicles approaching the camp. Since Colonel Uchida had ordered there be no water for the prisoners, many of the older people passed out from the oppressive heat caused by the midday sun.

During the day, several low flying American C-47 Dakota cargo planes flew over the camp. Although the side drop doors were open, nothing was dropped down into the camp, as crew members were unsure of what to do.

Load Masters stood in the open doorways staring at the scene below, knowing something was very wrong. After making two more circles over the camp, the planes flew off toward the south.

As darkness came over the camp, Colonel Uchida ordered all the prisoners back to their barracks. The bodies of five people that were not able to survive the heat were piled near the main gate. With the barracks secured, guards dug up mines and replanted them in different spots, so no one would have any idea where they were the next day.

At 0700hrs. the following morning, the prisoners once more were marched out into the circle under the hot unforgiving sun. Once again, only the colonel and his staff had canteens of water.

Some three hours later, a convoy of American trucks rolled up to the main gate of the camp. A tough looking sergeant holding a Thompson sub machine gun stepped out of the lead jeep and looked up to the Japanese soldier in the tower.

"We mean you no harm. We are here to liberate the camp and remove the prisoners. Can you tell me who is in charge here?"

One of the soldiers pointed to the circle of bodies in the middle of the camp.

Seeing the mines on the main gate, the sergeant was leery about walking any closer. Instead, he called out to the second truck. "I need a mine detector and an engineer here!"

Quickly, two men came forward carrying heavy mine detectors, as the .50 machine gun operator in the rear of the truck kept his weapon pointed at the soldiers in the tower. In a matter of minutes, the soldiers had cleared the road leading to the front gates. Standing near the entrance, it was clear to see that the four mines on the fence were wired in sequence, so if one went off, they all went off. A detonation cord ran from the gate to the main tower, where a soldier stood with a detonator in his hands.

Holding his hands out to his side, the sergeant stopped two feet from the gate. "I am Sergeant Kranz of the United States Army. I would like to speak to whoever is in charge."

After being prompted by the colonel, one of the soldiers yelled back. "We are here in the middle of the prisoners. If you attempt to kill us, we will explode all the mines around us. We wish to surrender under our own terms."

Before the sergeant could respond, another jeep drove up by the gate containing Captain Parcel. Walking up to the fence, the captain looked at the mines and shook his head. We need to end this now before someone gets cock-eyed and blows everyone to kingdom come."

Nodding in agreement, the sergeant said, "Welcome to Japan, sir. I'm thinking this is your call. You tell me what you want done, and we'll do it, but I'm afraid Tojo there may have his own ideas."

Once again, the soldier in the middle of the yard called out. "We do not want anyone else to die today. Please help us end this."

Angered by what was happening, Sister Dominique looked at the colonel. "The war is over and your emperor asked all of you to surrender. What is it you're trying to prove?"

Colonel Uchida looked harshly at Sister Dominique. "You must stay quiet so we can work this out. We will not surrender under their terms."

Without warning, Sister Dominique stood up and threw up her arms. "Captain, these men wish to surrender under their own terms. You must work with them to ensure no more innocent people die."

Captain Parcel shook his head. "Sister, the emperor has agreed to unconditional surrender and my orders from MacArthur clearly state there are no deals to be made. Now, we can back away and let the tanks that are at the end of my column deal with this gate, and I have no problem doing that. But if that jackass decides to blow you all to bits, there is nothing I can do about it. But I'm not going to have my brave men die after the war is already over. You talk to the commander quickly, because I'm calling up my tanks."

Captain Parcel stepped back to his jeep and ordered the driver to send up three tanks. Sister Dominique looked down at Colonel Uchida. "Colonel, I have a feeling this man has been through hell fighting his way to Japan. He's not going to kid around with you, and he will blow that gate, mark my words. What happens after that will be your responsibility, like it or not."

One of the soldiers in the group looked at the Colonel. "Sir, I do not wish to die by their hands or by my own. I have a wife and baby in Kyoto to go back to. Please do not do this!"

As the tanks rolled up to the gate, Captain Parcel climbed up on the lead Sherman and pointed out the mines, and the wire leading up to the tower.

After a brief discussion, Captain Parcel stood and faced the camp. "Colonel, you have thirty seconds to make up your mind before my tanks open fire.

Sitting down next to the turret again, the captain turned his attention to the second hand on his watch.

Quickly, Sister Dominique took several steps toward the gate as everyone in the circle yelled for her to stop. She looked over her shoulder at the trembling Colonel. "Now you must act or we all die!"

When captain Parcel's watch had ticked off thirty seconds, he nodded at the tank commander. Instantly, the turret machine gun operator fired a short blast into the soldiers in the tower. With the detonator disabled, the second Sherman tank rolled forward, busting through the main gate where the operator brought the speed down to a bare crawl, inching closer to the circle of prisoners.

Sweat poured down the face of the colonel as he watched the steel behemoth closing in on the first row of mines. Standing up, the colonel raised his hands. "Do not come any closer, you are ten feet away from the mines, we will surrender"

Without being told, the soldiers sitting next to the colonel stepped forward and began disarming the mines. When they were finished, they placed their sidearms on the ground and knelt down with their hands outstretched behind them. American soldiers quickly tied their hands and led them to a waiting truck.

Captain Parcel leaned on the front of the tank that had broken through the gate with his arms crossed as he glared at the colonel. "Sir, I respect your rank, but you will come to me and surrender your weapon as required by the Geneva Convention."

Sister Dominique shook her head. "Captain, don't you think this is taking things a bit too far. Just have your men come forward and take him into custody. We do not need any melodramatics here."

Placing his hands on his hips, Captain Parcel glared at Colonel Uchida. "You have heard my terms, Colonel. I have gone through hell the last three years, losing way too many good men to win this war. If you think for one minute that I'm coming to you for a surrender, you are completely wrong. I would just as soon put a bullet through your head." As he finished speaking, Captain Parcel pulled his sidearm, aiming it at the colonel.

"For heaven's sake, Captain, the war is over, there does not need to be any more bloodshed. Please do not do this!" Sister Dominique called out as Sergeant Kranz held her back.

Sister Dominique jumped as Captain Parcel fired a shot that struck the ground inches from the colonel's feet. "Next one goes in your brain Colonel, your call," the captain explained, standing solid as a rock. Smiling, he added, "You started this war, now it's time to be a man and surrender."

Holding up his hands, the colonel slowly walked forward until he was about three feet in front of the captain. Removing his sidearm, he handed it to the captain and graciously bowed.

Refusing to look the captain eye to eye he said. "We were the worst of enemies, let us now find a way to be civil toward one another."

After handing the pistol to the corporal that was standing behind him, Captain Parcel replied. "You are right, Colonel, The United States and Japan were the worst of enemies since Pearl Harbor. And because of that we have littered the islands of the South Pacific with thousands of your country men. Countless civilians have been killed, and thousands of American boys died crushing your evil empire. So, to be honest I have no desire to be civil to you or any other Japanese officer I have the need and pleasure to arrest. All you have earned is my disdain and contempt. My job now is to deliver you to allied headquarters in Tokyo, where you will be processed as a war criminal. May God have mercy on your soul."

Grabbing the colonel by the arm, he pushed him toward Sergeant Kranz. "Cuff him and place him in my jeep. I want to make sure he doesn't cheat the hangman."

As the colonel was led away, Sister Dominique approached the captain. "Was any of that necessary, Captain? I would have expected better from an officer of the United States Marines. You treated that man disgracefully. Enemy or not, he is still a human being!"

After placing his pistol back in its holster, Captain Parcel looked coldly at Sister Dominique. "Have you heard of Guadalcanal, Okinawa or Iwo Jima, Sister? I fought on each of those islands and saw exactly what the Japanese are capable of. Don't lecture me, not after I saw hundreds of good young men die because of the likes of him. Gladly, the son-of-a-bitch still has the worst to come."

Climbing back into his jeep, Captain Parcel smiled at Sister Dominique. "Don't worry, Sister, he'll make it back to Tokyo where he'll get a fair trial and a fair hanging. I can damn well guarantee you that!"

As trucks arrived, the prisoners were loaded for the short drive to Hiroshima where three United States amphibious landing ships were anchored in Hiroshima Bay. Medical staff had already set up a line near the hastily erected military hospital, checking incoming prisoners for any diseases or parasite infestations. On August 30, the first load of prisoners left the cramped barracks they were being held in. People cried and hugged each other as they prepared to leave the medical facility. They had been together a long time and had endured enough fear to last them a lifetime.

Sister Dominique, Father Renaldo and the rest of the sisters approached a marine major named Whitmore that was in charge of the embarkation procedures. He was standing by his jeep checking over paperwork for the next group to board one of the ships. He smiled at Sister Dominique as he placed the papers in a folder. "What can I do for you, Sister?"

"Well Major, we were wondering if there was any possibility for us to go into Hiroshima and help out where we can? Several of us have some nursing experience, and would be willing to do what can be done for the survivors."

Removing his helmet and wiping the sweat from his forehead, he shook his head. "I've heard it's bad, Sister, real bad. The navy unloaded several ships here in the harbor full of medical and scientific equipment, so scientists and doctors could begin the process of helping survivors. From what I have been told, most of those that survived have horrendous burns that can't be treated. I don't think you want to go there."

Father Renaldo smiled at the Major. "Those are the places we are best suited for. We can give piece and comfort to the dying and help the doctors any way we can. We would appreciate anything you can do to help us get there."

Placing his helmet back on his head, the major nodded. "There is a check point about six miles from here where a command center is located. Let me run up there and see what they have to say. I should be back within an hour."

After climbing back into his jeep, the driver spun the vehicle around and charged up the road toward the center of Hiroshima. About forty-five minutes later, the major returned. Jumping out of the jeep, he called out, "Alright, gather around. I have paper work authorizing you to go to Hiroshima to help with medical problems. You will report to a Captain Ozgood at the hospital tent. You each need to sign and print your names. One copy stays at the check point, one goes to the captain. There will be a truck here at 0800hrs tomorrow morning." Looking over at Pierre Duncan, he inquired, "And who is this man? He was not with you before."

Father Renaldo threw up his hands, "He was busy trying to sort out a problem between some of the prisoners when you were here. This is Father Duncan, he was with us on the island of Nusa Simbo."

The major shook his head and smiled. "If you say so, Father, but I recall hearing about a Pierre Duncan that was a wealthy plantation owner in the Solomon's before the war. Any relation Father Duncan?"

Pierre shook his head. "My father had many relatives on his side of the family, perhaps there was another Pierre, but this I do not know. You see I grew up in Belgium and joined—"

"Yeah, yeah, I got the picture," the major said, as he handed Pierre the pen. Just sign like the rest of them and make sure you put father in front of your name."

"But of course," Pierre said, as he took the pen in his hand.

After returning the pen, the major looked at Pierre. "You know, I just happen to be a catholic from Pittsburgh with ten years of religious schooling to my credit. So, let me ask you, what are the seven sacraments."

Pierre Duncan shook his head and responded. "Oh, you of little faith. Of course, the first one is Baptism. That is followed by the sacrament of Penance and Holy Communion. Then—"

The major laughed, "Alright Pierre, I'll give you a passing grade. Stay safe while you are there, I have heard there are strange illness's floating around since the bombing. After handing the paper work to Father Renaldo, the major and his driver sped down the highway.

Sister Margaret looked over at Pierre Duncan and smiled. "When we were on Nusa Simbo, you told me you were far too busy to worry about God and religion. So, where did you learn about the seven sacraments?"

Folding his hands in front of him, Pierre bowed slightly and smiled. "Strange are the ways of the Lord, my daughter, one must just have faith."

Slapping Pierre on the shoulder, Sister Dominique said, "Welcome to the club, Father."

The following morning at 0800hrs., a navy truck arrived at the pier. After checking over the paperwork, the driver helped everyone climb aboard. Since the canvas tarp that usually covers the back of the truck had been removed, everyone on board was able to see the destruction as the driver made his way through rubble covered streets. He drove them up to a marine armored vehicle that was doubling as part of Captain Ozgood's command center.

After crushing out the cigarette he had just finished, Captain Ozgood took a deep breath. "There is nothing here we can use, the bomb destroyed everything. When you arrive at the operation center you will see we have set up three tent hospitals near what used to be the center of the city. We have a group of doctors and nurses working there to help the sick and wounded. The problem is, most of them die within a few hours. One of the scientists told me radiation poisoning is the major cause of death, and there is no way to treat it."

Father Renaldo looked strangely at the officer. "Radiation poisoning, what would cause that?"

The captain looked strangely at the group in front of him, then nodded his head. "Well, being in the prison camp I suppose you didn't hear President Truman's statement about the bomb. That B-29 dropped a new kind of weapon, called an atom bomb. They also dropped one on Nagasaki two days later. It appears that no one knows much about the bombs or the radiation that is killing so many people. But the heat must have been intense, just look at how the cranes along the dock were warped and melted. Those blobs across the street used to be truck tractors. Now they are melted junk."

Turning to Father Renaldo, the captain finished. "Jump back on the truck, he'll drive you to our hospital where you can go to work."

As the truck made its way toward the makeshift hospitals, Sister Dominique called out for the driver to stop. Near the Aioi Bridge stood a large structure, nearly intact. "What is that building?" she inquired.

"That was the Hiroshima Prefectural Products Exhibition Hall, commonly called the Genbakku Dome. No one understands why it survived the bombing. But it was full of people at the time. There were bodies in there that were torn apart and literally melted together. I'll never forget what I saw in there. It was ghoulish."

Arriving at the tents, Father Renaldo introduced himself to Dr. Tim Stansfield, a naval doctor. Walking outside the tent, the doctor said, "We're saving a few, Father, but I'm not so sure they'll survive very long. Their hair is falling out, they have severe diarrhea, bleeding of the gums, and they cannot keep food down very well. One scientist said it was exposure to high amounts of gamma rays, another scientist said neutron rays or something called beta rays were the reasons for the severe radiation. Hell, I'm not sure anyone here has a damn clue. We take a lot of blood tests and put them in lead lined boxes and write a report on the condition of the victim before sending it off to Hawaii. In fact, what we have here is a large guinea pig factory, and everyone is just guessing."

Over the next several weeks, the sisters worked as nurses during amputations, dressing massive burns, and attempting to console the victims before they died. The worst was when little children were brought to the tent and they would scream as their skin rolled off their bodies when anyone attempted to touch them. Not even a strong injection of morphine would sooth their pain. All anyone could do was sit with them until they died.

Tears ran down the face of Sister Dominique as she rolled her wheelchair back from the table. "I have never seen so much suffering and pain. And still, young mothers attempted to nurse their dying children even though their lips and noses had been burned off. They never gave up until they also died. Sailors and soldiers would walk through the tents gathering up the dead. Some were taken to bomb shelters that had been dug in the hills around Hiroshima and sealed with an explosive. In some places huge pits were dug and filled with bodies. Then different types of petroleum products were poured over them so they would be cremated, and sometimes the pits would burn for days. Some soldiers laid bodies on straw mats two or three high, and when the pile was big enough, they would set them on fire using the same method as in the pits. It was awful, horrible work for those boys. I never thought I would get that smell out of my nose ever again." After looking over at the clock, Sister Dominique smiled at the students who sat motionless, hanging on every word she was saying.

"It is time we take a break and let the spirits of Hiroshima rest wherever they are, and as for us, we can resume tomorrow at ten o'clock," Sister Dominique said, as she turned her chair to leave.

However, Steven, one of the boys in the group, asked quickly, "Sister, did you ever return to Hiroshima? Or were the memories so bad you could not return?"

Nodding her head, Sister Dominique replied. "That is a good question to end the day with. Yes, I have been back there. Twice in fact. Once in 1960, and the last time in 1999. It's an amazing city that has been built out of the total destruction of the atomic bomb. It is a beautiful city with many parks and gardens. The Genbakku Dome is the center of the peace garden today, and is constantly being preserved to make sure it stands as long as mankind exists. You all must go there and see it for yourself. The first time I went back, I did it to honor all the dead and people that still suffer today from the radiation. The last time I went back was to allow my soul to have peace. I found it in an old woman that I had treated as a child. It was a miracle she survived at the time. Today, she is rather crippled and lives in a type of government run nursing home for radiation victims. We talked for hours, and her love and forgiveness has given me the peace I needed. But it is impossible to ever forget what the city was like when we first arrived there."

Chapter Eighteen – Camp 45

Paulo was working near the tall wire fence with several other prisoners when he observed a tremendous burst of light in the direction of Hiroshima. Everyone stopped working as they watched the cloud build until it stretched out from the ground to thousands of feet into the atmosphere. Moments later, they were struck by a tremendous sound wave far louder than any thunder Paulo had ever heard before.

The Japanese guards assigned to cover the work crew were frightened and ran off in the direction of the commander's office. The soldiers in the towers were similarly terrified and began pointing their machine guns in the direction of work crews.

Seeing all that was happening, Paulo yelled out, "Sit down, put your hands over your heads and don't move. Do not give them any reason to open fire!"

Nearly a half hour later, a young lieutenant arrived back with the guards to escort the prisoners back to their barracks. As they collected their tools, Paulo could not help staring at the mushroom cloud that appeared to take on a life of its own. Having not seen the planes overhead, Paulo wondered what could have happened in Hiroshima to create that type of powerful explosion. Several of the prisoners stated it must have been some new type of Japanese weapon that had accidentally exploded. They all agreed if this terrible new weapon was released against the allies, Japan would certainly win the war and their lives would matter little now.

The following morning at roll call, several officers came walking through the ranks, asking them to sign documents relieving them of any and all wrong doings against the prisoners. That was the first indication anyone had that the weapon that had exploded over Hiroshima was an allied creation. The soldiers would not talk about what had happened in the city, but it was evident the effects of the weapon scared them to the core.

As at Camp 46, by late afternoon many survivors of the blast were at the gate of the camp seeking food, water and medical help. The commander of the camp gave strict orders that the gates were to remain closed, so whatever illness the people had would not be transferred to the guards or his prisoners.

On the afternoon of August 9 Captain Chiba called a formation in the yard. Looking ashen gray, he walked up to the large wooden podium in the middle of the yard. It was the first time the prisoners had seen him without his customary sword, pistol and well-shined combat helmet. Looking over the prisoners, he said, "This morning, the city of Nagasaki was removed from the face of the earth in a similar attack as what happened to Hiroshima. We do not know what kind of weapon it was, but the results of the explosion are beyond anything you can imagine. I expect our war ministers to seek some type of a surrender proposal to the allies in order to prevent another such attack. I promise you we will follow through with all directions to surrender, and there will be no type of retribution by my staff. This may take days or weeks, but I promise you we will treat you well and make sure no harm comes to you."

As Captain Chiba left the podium, a massive cheer went up from the prisoners. Paulo quickly looked around the yard to see what kind of reaction might come from the guards. He was surprised to see them hang their heads and follow their commander back toward his office.

On the eleventh, several American C-47 Dakota aircraft flew low over the camp dropping pallets of food and medical supplies. It was a welcomed site as food rations had been cut several times over the last few months.

On the fourteenth, all the prisoners were surprised to see a convoy of American military trucks and tanks drive past before stopping at the gate of Camp 46. They could not tell what was happening, but were sure that all was not well with the surrender. The following morning a convoy of marine trucks pulled up to the front gate of Camp 45. As a lieutenant stepped from the lead jeep, two Sherman tanks positioned themselves aside of the jeep. Captain Chiba, wearing all his military regalia walked toward the gate. He bowed to the lieutenant before handing over his samurai sword and personal pistol. After a quick discussion the gates were opened wide and the convoy drove straight to the center of the camp with the tanks in the lead. Immediately, all the Japanese soldiers laid down their weapons and the tower guards tossed their machine guns out the windows.

After all the Japanese were rounded up and removed, the lieutenant in charge of the operation walked up to the podium. "My name is Lieutenant Oscar Warren, United States Marine Corp. We will be setting up several stations here in the base to begin identifying and working with resettlement plans. As there are over four hundred of you here, it will take a few days. Work with us and we'll get you out of here as soon as possible."

On the second day of processing, Paulo walked up to a marine sergeant. "My name is Captain Paulo Trevisiani, a deserter from the Italian Army. I wish to speak with Lieutenant Warren."

The sergeant looked at Paulo with contempt. "A deserter and you wish to speak with my commander? I don't think so. You'll be turned over to allied intelligence in Tokyo to see if there are any warrants for your arrest. Captain, you just became a POW."

Paulo's heart sank, as he knew Dominique was somewhere in Japan and he had come this far to find her, and now all his progress was being taken away. After being placed in a smaller barracks used to house problem prisoners, Paulo sought out the sergeant in charge of security. He explained everything that he had gone through to find his sister and pleaded to see Lieutenant Warren.

After hearing Paulo's request, Lieutenant Warren looked at the sergeant. "I'm sorry, but every one of these people have some sort of extenuating circumstances. If we don't follow the plan that was set up by allied command, we'll still be here in 1950 trying to sort out each individual case. Tell him I'm sorry, but he's going to Tokyo."

At a former Japanese military base outside of Tokyo, Paulo was placed in a barracks holding Chinese, German and Australian soldiers. One by one the men were taken to a registration building where a file was created and interviews were conducted. As Paulo sat down across the table from American Army Warrant Officer Darin Wilfred, he began to plead. "You now have my name and all pertinent information about me. All I want to do is find my sister and take her back to Italy. The longer I am held here the farther apart we may become. You need to help me find my sister, I beg of you!"

Warrant Officer Wilfred shook his head. "Everyone coming through here has some type of emergency to deal with and you're all in a hurry to get out. Well, the allied government is not in a hurry to release military prisoners until we declassify them and decide whether or not you should be set free. Being you are an Italian it may take a while longer, as we don't have all the files of the Italian military like we do with Germany."

"She is a Benedictine Sister. She should be in a camp here in Japan from what I have been told. Please just let me meet her and I will be happy. We can arrange another meeting down the road when things are settled. I haven't seen her since she was five years old," Paulo pleaded.

"Yeah, and my mother secretly baked goodies for the emperor of Japan, no matter how much time it took away from our family. Sorry Captain, but I'm not buying your sob story. Like I said, everybody has one." Looking over at the military police officer that had brought Paulo into the building, he said. "Label him category five and put him back in the barracks."

Arriving back at the barracks, Paulo looked at the M.P. "What is a category five?"

The officer shook his head. "It means we are waiting for paper work from a belligerent warring nation that may be hard to come by. Just kick back and relax, you may be here for a while."

Nearly six weeks later, Paulo was called back to see Warrant Officer Wilfred. He looked at Paulo. "It seems the new Italian government has dropped all charges against you for desertion and will allow you to return free and clear. There have also been no documents filed against you for war crimes with the Supreme Headquarters Allied Expeditionary Force. That means you are free and clear to return to Italy as soon as travel arrangements can be made. There is a British ship leaving from here on Monday, and I have scheduled you on the manifest. Congratulations Captain, you're going home."

Paulo shook his head. "No, you don't understand. I wish to stay here in Japan to find my sister. As I have said, she is a Benedictine sister and so it's likely she's known as Sister Dominique. She could be helping out in a hospital, or orphanage. With your record keeping you should be able to find her and point me in the right direction."

Warrant Officer Wilfred shook his head. "Allied command does not want former soldiers of warring nations running around in countries they do not belong in. Captain, you are going back to Italy and that is final. You can go voluntarily and do as you wish once you land in Italy, or we can put you on a ship with prisoners listed as belligerent, and be placed in a stockade when you get there. That is your choice, but either way you're going back!"

Feeling defeated, Paulo nodded his head. "I will not cause you any more problems, just send me back home. I will find my sister on my own."

Sensing Paulo was being truthful, Wilfred reached into his desk. "Look Captain, when you get to Italy contact this address in Rome or Milan. They are registration offices for the displaced persons office in Italy. They have all the records for people that have been displaced that we know of so far. There is a good chance your sister might be on one of their lists. But do not attempt to come back here to Japan or you'll end up in a stockade and be charged with a crime by the allied government. Best of luck, Captain."

Monday morning, Paulo walked up the gang plank to the British Transport HMS Regal. He was sharing a small cabin with an Italian business man named Andrea that had been in Japanese custody since the fall of Singapore in 1942. As the two men talked, Andrea talked about the scary end to his confinement in Camp 46. He talked about Colonel Uchida's last stand and the tanks busting through the front gates.

After Andrea finished his story, Paulo inquired, "Did you have any Benedictine priests and sisters in your camp?"

Nodding his head Andrea replied. "Yes, they really were a big help to all of us in so many ways. They taught school, worked in our small hospital and of course said mass and helped all of us deal with the torments of being in the camp."

Beginning to shake inside Paulo asked. "By any chance, did you have a sister by the name of Sister Dominique that would have been from Italy?"

Andrea nodded his head. "Yes, she really went through hell. The colonel did not like her one bit so he tortured and beat her. She was very important to all of us. And yes, the entire group was from Italy, including Sister Henrietta who was murdered by the colonel. I hope the bastard hangs!"

Paulo hung his head as his stomach felt like it was going to rip itself apart. He knew Camp 46 and Camp 45 were just a few miles apart. He had come so close, and now he was on his way back to Italy with no way of changing course.

Arriving in Naples, Paulo was taken to a former Italian army base that was now used by the allies to detain, sort out and identify Italian soldiers wanted for war crimes. As it was near 2000hrs., all the offices on base were closed, so Paulo was taken to a barracks for the night.

The following morning, Paulo walked into a building marked new arrivals. Approaching the registration desk, he handed his file over to a tough looking British sergeant.

After looking over the file, the sergeant said. "Japan, huh? How did you ever manage to get to Japan? I say, it rather looks like you ran right into the mouth of the beast."

Paulo decided to keep things simple and get off the base as quickly as he could. "A very long story, but I was cleared in Tokyo of any warrants by the allied government."

"Why yes, yes you were," the sergeant said, as he flipped through the last pages of the file. "So, tell me Captain, where do you wish to go here in Italy. I'm sorry, I can't let you go to another country as Italy was part of the axis alliance."

"Naples, I would like to stay in Naples for the time being. There is someone here I need to see before I do anything else," Paulo replied.

"Ah, Naples you say. That is a simple assignment as the port is very big and very busy and we need men like you that have had experience dealing with maritime issues. When you arrive in Naples, report to an American Major by the name of Hollister. He will be your commanding officer and assign you to a barracks and get you the appropriate uniforms. However, there is one more issue I need to tell you about. Everyone leaving this base gets a free railroad pass to a final destination in Italy of their choice, but since you are staying here in Naples, I can authorize you to use the pass anytime in the next two years. How does that sound, Captain?"

Paulo nodded his head. "That would be wonderful, Sergeant. Thank you very much. But I have one more favor to ask of you. Can you tell me where the Displaced Persons Office is here in Naples?"

"Certainly Captain. Go to the main gate, catch bus 302 toward the wharf. Get off at Giovani Street, it's right about there."

After leaving the military base, Paulo took the 302 bus to Giovani Street. Walking up to a British lieutenant that was directing traffic, Paulo asked, "Sir, can you tell me where the Allied Government Displaced Persons Office is located?"

Turning to his left, the officer pointed at a brown brick building across the street. "You're in luck, my friend, you won't need to walk far. It's right there on the corner, and the building next to it offers a swell cup of tea for a mid-morning break I dare say."

Smiling, Paulo walked off, finally feeling like a free man. With so many people searching for friends or loved ones, Paulo had to wait nearly three hours before he could work his way up to a desk. A young American lieutenant looked up from her desk. "Can I help you, sir?"

Paulo sat down and began. "My sister was in the Pacific as a missionary on some island before the Japanese over ran it. She ended up in a prison camp, simply called Camp 46. I was in Camp 45 just a few miles away. Camp 46 was liberated before my camp was, so I wasn't able to find her when I was set free. Her name is Sister Dominique, she is a Benedictine sister. She went over there with a group of sisters from Naples. That's about all I can tell you."

The lieutenant walked over to a cabinet and picked up a large ledger and brought it to her desk. As she flipped through the pages she looked up at Paulo. "Camp 46, you say?"

Nodding his head, Paulo replied, "Yes ma'am."

A moment later she stopped turning pages. "Yes, here it is. Quite a lengthy list, well over 400 names." Turning to the third page, she stopped. "Yes, here it is. Sister Dominique, Sister Margaret, Sister Claudia, Sister Annuncio, Sister Josephine, Father Renaldo and Father Duncan."

Paulo smiled as he felt his heart beat nearly out of his chest. "Tell me, where did they go?"

"According to the book, they all went to Hiroshima to help the military with patients from the bombing. We have not had any updates, so they would still be there," the lieutenant replied, smiling.

Paulo shook his head. "To be honest, I'm a former Italian Army officer, so it appears that will keep me from going to Japan to visit her, is that correct?"

"That is absolutely correct, Captain. You are not allowed to travel out of Italy for any purposes for at least a year from the date you arrived in Naples.

Only then can a change be made to your travel status." The lieutenant replied quite firmly.

Feeling frustrated, Paulo asked, "Can I send her a letter at least? How can I do that?"

The lieutenant shook her head. "Captain, we are lucky to have these records, and sometimes we have a hard time updating them. Right now, the only mail going to Japan must be authorized by the Allied military post office in England. I'm afraid your letter would not meet those requirements. The best thing you can do is to continue checking with our office every month or so to see if she leaves Japan. Then maybe something can be worked out."

Taking another bus down toward the naval station near the pier, Paulo looked up Major Hollister. Within an hour, he had received his new uniforms and was assigned to a barracks of about twenty men. The next day, Paulo began his new job checking documents for freight and passengers leaving the port for countries all over the world. It didn't take long for Paulo to have some major arguments with passengers, as they attempted to ship items that were not allowed to leave Italy by the new allied government. Although most people eventually capitulated to the strict allied rules, a few did not. That forced Paulo to arrest them and turn them over for a hearing with the local Provost Marshal, who was not happy to deal with people that did not choose to cooperate, or with officers in his command that could not handle problems on their own. But Paulo continued following the guide lines he was given, not knowing what kind of a problem he was causing for himself.

Chapter Nineteen – Vengeance

The following day, all the students were waiting at the table when Sister Dominique was rolled into the room by one of the novitiates. With Sister Dominique setting down a full cup of coffee, she looked at Novice Loretta. "I have asked Mother Superior to allow you to stay here with me today, Loretta. There should be a lesson here for you today, so you might want to stay. I will even share my coffee with you."

As the novice took a seat by the table, Sister Dominique shook her head. "I fear I might not be so clear today. Many of the ghosts of Hiroshima invaded my dreams last night. Many still ask why, many wonder if their deaths ever made a difference in today's world. Sadly, I am not sure their deaths made a difference. If it had, no one would ever want to possess such a weapon of destruction, or even contemplate using it. However, it's like Pandora's box. Once the Genie escaped, it can't be put back in the box ever again.

Reaching into her pocket, Sister Dominique removed a well-worn photo of a young Japanese couple with a small child. As I told you, the dying man in the ditch in New Guinea asked if I could return his billfold to his family in Nagasaki. Of course, at that time no one knew that city would be obliterated by an atomic bomb. But since we were preparing to leave and had nothing else to do, I asked our lieutenant if I could go to Nagasaki to return the billfold.

Lieutenant Carmichael nearly laughed out loud at Sister Dominique. "You want to go to Nagasaki to return a billfold? Sister, you have seen Hiroshima, and Nagasaki was much worse. Who in hell do you intend to return it to?"

Sister Dominique was angered by the Lieutenant's attitude. "We can try, there may be someone that would have known him, we must try. If you do not wish to help me, maybe General MacArthur might wish to try. Can I get permission to see him?"

Lt. Carmichael laughed as he shook his head. "I heard you were one determined individual before you arrived, but I never thought it would come to this. But the last thing I want is a problem that could lead to the occupation government getting involved. So, I'll find a truck, and tomorrow morning I will get you and two of your friends to Nagasaki. But orders are all trucks are to be off the road before dark, and there are no exceptions to MacArthur's orders, so we must be back before 1700hrs. Will that work for you?"

Smiling, Sister Dominique replied, "I can see the Holy Spirit working within you, Lieutenant. I look forward to driving to Nagasaki with you in the morning." Father Renaldo and Sister Claudia quickly volunteered to take the trip.

It was hard to tell whether Nagasaki was any worse than Hiroshima when they arrived, but it was evident the bomb had created complete destruction. Arriving at the make shift headquarters, Sister Dominique walked up to an army sergeant that had small drawers filled with three by five cards used for holding information of identified survivors and where they may be.

Sister Dominique handed the billfold to the sergeant. "There is an identification card inside. Can you tell me if you have any record of that name?"

After looking over the name, the sergeant swung his chair around and went toward a cabinet. After fumbling through the well-worn cards, he brought out two. "The first card is for a Sori Kinoshita, she is eighty years old and has gone to a refuge center near Konpira Park. It does not list any family. The second belongs to an Asahi Kinoshita. She is thirty years old and has moved to Nishiki. She says she had a brother that is missing in the war, but has not given a name. I'm sorry, but that is all I have on record for that name."

After thanking the sergeant, everyone returned to the truck. After checking the allied map of the Nagasaki area, the driver drove to the small town of Nishiki. Sister Dominique was getting restless as the day was passing quickly, and this would be her only chance of finding a living relative of the man that died in the ditch with her. After circling around several streets, the driver stopped by a building that had a sign hanging outside the front door that read, "Kinoshita Building."

Walking into the front door of a small fabric shop, Father Renaldo approached a woman wearing an apron. Bowing graciously, he said, "Can you tell me where I can find an Asahi Kinoshita?"

The woman nodded her head and pointed toward a set of narrow steps leading toward the second floor. "She is there, but not feeling well today."

Walking up the steps, Sister Dominique took a deep breath before knocking on the door. Moments later a very slender woman wrapped in a brightly colored kimono opened the door. Looking strangely at Sister Dominique, she said. "What can I do for you? I have told all the people in Nagasaki all that I know. There is nothing left to tell, but you may come in."

Once everyone was seated, Sister Dominique handed the photo of the young couple to Asahi. "Do you know this man, his name was—"

Before Sister Dominique could finish, the woman spoke. "His name is Aoki Kinoshita, he is my younger brother. He was a sergeant in the Imperial Army. I have not seen him in several years. Last time he wrote me he was somewhere in New Guinea. Where did you get this photo?"

Sister Dominique relayed the tragic story of the battleship attack and how brave Aoki had been before he died.

As tears rolled down Asahi's face, she held the photo to her chest. "I feared he was dead, but I had no proof. I asked the army many times, but they always told me they had no idea where he was. Now I know why they said that. I believe he died for nothing, like every other Japanese soldier."

Father Renaldo asked. "Do you know where his wife and child are?"

Nodding her head, she replied. "She took the train into Nagasaki the morning of the bombing to visit my parents. It was my mother's birthday and they were going to celebrate at a restaurant she enjoyed. I was supposed to meet them, but business kept me busy that day. The building shook when the bomb exploded. I ran outside to see what was happening and there was this cloud like I have never seen before rising from the ground to the heavens. It was green and gray and it appeared to snarl as bolts of lightning ran up and down the sides as it grew. It appeared as if the monster was looking for things to devour. I have never been so scared, but I knew my family had been devoured by the monster and I would never see them again. Now I am all alone with just my memories, and I have no cemetery to go to so I can honor them. It was all so tragic."

Sister Dominique stopped talking to the students as she looked up toward the ceiling for a moment. With a frown on her face, she said, "Actually, going to Nagasaki to seek out the soldiers family was the only reason for me to extend my stay. Everything else that happened to me along the way was what all you students call extra credit."

After the students laughed, Sister Dominique drank some coffee and continued.

"So, by the fall of 1946, it was decided by the Benedictine order that we were needed elsewhere, so we packed up to leave, all except Pierre Duncan. Using his resources, he helped set up a clinic dedicated to working with radiation illness. He hired many good doctors and scientists to help find solutions for the growing number of people suffering from cancer and other radiation related illnesses."

After taking a deep breath she continued. "We were already in Adachi, just north of Tokyo, waiting for our military orders to arrive so we could leave Japan. We were staying in a small undamaged hotel, when a team of military attorneys and investigators came looking for us. Every day there were stories in the press regarding the military tribunals and the hunt for remaining war criminals. It was something I had hoped to avoid, but soon it was at my front door."

On a clear Saturday afternoon, as Sister Dominique and Sister Claudia sat under a large Banion tree sipping tea, four men walked up to them and sat down. The leader of the team was a Colonel Walter Bretmann. He wasted no time as he looked at Sister Dominique. "You have been pointed out to me as a person that knows much about several men we are looking for. So, tell me about Commander Ossani and Colonel Uchida."

Shaking her head, Sister Dominique replied, "Colonel, the war is over now. I have read much about the Nazi war tribunals as far as they have gone, and I wish not to be part of any such process here in Japan. We are scheduled to fly out of here in two days, and I intend to leave the war here when I board that plane."

Smiling, the colonel reached into his briefcase, handing Sister Dominique several documents. "I am afraid your departure has been postponed indefinitely, as you and the rest of your group have been listed as material witnesses in at least three cases. We have captured two of the criminals already, and are still looking for the third.

The trial for Colonel Uchida is scheduled to begin next Monday. We are moving you to the military base at Yokohama where the trial will be held. General MacArthur has ordered your assistance with these cases, it shall not take too long."

On Monday morning, tensions around the military base were running high, as there had been rumors of a pending attack by Japanese loyalists to set the colonel and other prisoners free. Military police officers and American infantry men with tanks had all but shut down the large base in preparation for a battle.

At 0900hrs., Colonel Uchida was walked into the courtroom wearing a clean well-fitting uniform. When he was asked if he would swear to tell the truth and nothing but the truth, he replied. "You tell me, what is the truth?"

After the judge demanded he answer the question, the colonel stood silent, looking out the window. Knowing it would make no difference to the colonel, the judge told him he could be found in contempt of court for failing to answer. Laughing, Colonel Uchida replied, "That is fine, I have nothing but contempt for you, this court proceeding, and the allied government."

Motioning to the bailiff, the judge ordered the colonel to take a seat at the defense table. Over the next two days, the prosecution delivered nearly twenty witnesses that gave vivid descriptions of criminal incidents the colonel had been involved in. Finally, Colonel Bretmann called Sister Dominique to the stand. "Could you please explain to the court what happened on February 3rd of last year, and I remind you, Sister, you are under oath.

Sister Dominique looked harshly at the attorney that was glaring right back at her. "Things were not good in the camp, and the prisoners cheered when a group of B-29's flew overhead. The guards became increasingly angry and shots were fired. Ten prisoners were killed and twenty were wounded."

Walking toward the prosecution table to pick up a paper, the colonel continued. "When that happened was the colonel out in the yard?"

She replied, "I do not know."

Nodding his head, the colonel said. "Was Commander Ossani in charge of the men that did the shooting."

"Yes, he was," Sister Dominique responded.

"Sister, be honest now, who was responsible for stopping anymore violence in the camp?" Colonel Bretmann asked as he glared intensely at Sister Dominique on the witness stand.

"I took a rifle away from a soldier and pointed it at the man. Commander Ossani came forward and talked me down so I would not shoot him. When I relinquished the rifle, everyone in the camp backed away," Sister Dominique replied.

So, what you're saying is neither Commander Ossani or Colonel Uchida were in control of the soldiers in the camp. The colonel never responded even after ten prisoners were murdered, did he?"

Looking over at Colonel Uchida, she responded. "No. He never left his office."

Feeling confident, Colonel Bretmann continued. "Tell me what happened several weeks later when the colonel had you delivered from the stockade to his office."

"Actually, Commander Ossani had me delivered to the office. But his interrogation was interrupted by the colonel who took over," Sister Dominique replied.

"Interesting that you used the word interrogation. Were you not beaten and choked by both the commander and the colonel?" Colonel Bretmann asked, as he moved closer to the stand.

"Look Colonel, what happened in the office has no bearing on this trial. If you want to build your case, go on to what happened out in the yard. That is where the crime is you're searching for so badly occurred," Sister Dominique stated loudly.

The judge turned toward Sister Dominique. "It is not your job as a witness to tell the prosecuting attorney how to handle his case. You will tell him what he wants to know, or I will find you in contempt."

Sister Dominique nodded her head. "I'm sorry, your honor, it will not happen again."

Colonel Bretmann looked down at Sister Dominique and said, "Please tell the court about the colonel's part in the death of Sister Henrietta."

Tears that began as a small stream running down the face of Sister Dominique, rapidly turned into a torrent as she related the entire story.

After giving Sister Dominique a moment to compose herself, the colonel continued. "Sister, did Colonel Uchida hesitate for a moment before authorizing the death of Sister Henrietta?"

Shaking her head and looking over to the table where Colonel Uchida sat, she responded. "No, he just matter-of-factly gave the order to have her shot. There was no hesitation, he just ordered his firing squad to shoot."

"Who was in command of the firing squad?" Colonel Bretmann asked, as he stood looking down at Colonel Uchida.

"It was Commander Ossani. The colonel ordered him to get two sisters from the school and form a firing squad, he did so without question.

Colonel Uchida stood up from the table and said, "I alone take responsibility for anything that happened in my camp. The commander was just following orders, you cannot put blame on him!"

Once the military police officers had pushed the colonel back into his chair, the judge said. "Colonel, if you do not stay quiet until you are called to testify, we will continue this trial with you listening by speaker in another room."

When the trial ended two days later, the jury found Colonel Uchida guilty of murder and crimes against humanity. He was sentenced to death by hanging.

Since Commander Ossani had still not been found, the allied government did not want to try him in absentia. They decided to hold off on his trial until he could be arrested.

As Sister Dominique packed her bags in preparation to finally leave Japan, Colonel Bretmann arrived in her quarters. "Colonel Uchida is asking to see you before you depart. I did not promise you would come to see him, I just agreed to deliver the message. You may do as you wish."

After a restless night, on Christmas Eve day, Sister Dominique walked over to the stockade where the colonel was being held. Reaching the front door of the stockade, Sister Dominique felt like turning back, but some invisible force drove her forward. Once inside, a sergeant walked her over to the colonel's cell, placing a chair about ten feet from the bars.

The colonel was sitting on his bed looking up toward the small window on the back wall of his cell. Without looking at Sister Dominique, he said, "It is cold out there today."

Sister Dominique did not respond, instead she stood behind the chair, feeling empty and angry.

Turning to face Sister Dominique, the colonel, looking much older and worn out said, "Tell me, Sister, how did we get here?"

Shaking her head, Sister Dominique said. "Good bye, Colonel."

As she turned to leave, the colonel stood up and walked up to the bars. "I apologize, Sister Dominique. That was a terrible comment to make. We all know how we ended up here. The reason I asked to see you is simple. Christmas is the most holy day of your religion. I have read that this man you call Jesus came to earth to save the world. How did he save it? We have been killing one another since 1937. It makes no sense to me."

Sister Dominique replied. "I will find you a bible if you like, then you can read more about him."

The colonel laughed as he slammed his fist against the bars. "I am to die in three days, so what more can I learn on this earth? All I ask is this. Since the day you call Christmas is tomorrow, will you forgive me for what I have done?"

Sister Dominique was caught off guard by the colonel's request. After a moment of thought, she replied. "What happened cannot be undone, and so I am bound by my faith to forgive you, and so I have. But there is a difference in forgetting, and that is something I shall never be able to do. I wish you peace, colonel."

As Sister Dominique turned to go, Colonel Uchida yelled. "Sister, do not leave me like this. Please stay and help me, I cannot face death by myself. Please have pity on my soul!"

After knocking on the door for the sergeant, she turned and looked back at the colonel. "I have no pity, Colonel. My heart has been drained of all emotion. You must face your destiny by yourself. Pray to God that he will give you the strength you need. I'm sorry, there is nothing more I can do."

Even after the sergeant closed the heavy door to the cell block, everyone could hear the colonel yelling, "Sister, do not leave me like this. You must come back."

As she exited the stockade, she ran into Colonel Bretmann. "Merry Christmas, Sister. How was your visit?"

Shaking her head, Sister Dominique replied. "It was a mistake. A terrible mistake, I should never have come here. I don't know what I was thinking or expecting."

Colonel Bretmann stood silently for a moment before replying. "Like all men he has come to grips with the reality that he is about to die. The clock is ticking and there will be no reprieve. He is scared and cannot find any peace in his heart. I have seen this in several other Japanese trials since the war ended. For that reason, I have given orders that you will not be allowed to be at the execution. He will not die with dignity and it will be shameful to witness."

Sister Dominique nodded her head. "None of them expected the whirlwind to turn back upon them. They believed in their cause, and believed they truly were a master race destined for glory. Sadly, the colonel will continue to believe that myth, even as he climbs the steps to the gallows."

Chapter Twenty – Uncertainty

Although there were many Japanese military officials still to be located, the bulk of the trials had been completed by March of 1947, so the military tribunal released all potential witnesses, allowing them to leave Japan, subject to possible recall.

Calling everyone together, Father Renaldo read the letter from the tribunal. He looked over at the weary sisters and shook his head. "You have all been through so much, it's hard to believe we have survived. However, there is one more item we will need to accomplish before we can head back to Italy. Since we all spent so much time in Hiroshima, there is a medical team in Hawaii that would like to give us a large battery of tests. I do not know how long we will be there, but it is important that we do this."

After all they had been through, Sister Dominique stood and looked at the DC-4 passenger plane standing on the tarmac in front of her. "I shall never step aboard that thing. Find me a ship, I do not wish to fall out of the sky."

Both Father Renaldo and a frustrated army pilot talked with her for nearly an hour before she reluctantly decided to climb aboard. Having to land at Clark Field in the Philippines to refuel bothered her even more, as a steady rain fell while the pilot brought the aircraft down through the clouds.

After departing the plane in Honolulu, Sister Dominique turned toward Father Renaldo. "You either find me a ship to return to the United States, or here is where I shall spend the rest of my life. I will never climb aboard that contraption ever again!"

The staff at Fort Shafter in Hawaii treated Father Renaldo and the sisters like they were war heroes, putting up a huge dinner buffet their first night on the base. None of them had seen so much food in one place for many years. Even Sister Dominique forgot about her flight experience long enough to sample some of the food they were served.

The following day they were taken to Tripler Army Hospital where they were admitted to begin their testing. Doctors and scientists drew blood, took x-rays, and ran tests no one had ever heard of before. Each person was quarantined in separate rooms throughout the tests. They could not talk with one another about what was going on, so test results could be tracked more efficiently.

After a week, doctors informed Father Renaldo that Sister Annuncio had a small tumor that appeared to be cancerous growing in her right lung. Sister Josephine had several small tumors growing near her spine, and a sore on her right leg that was caused by radiation poisoning. Finally, Sister Dominique had a tumor growing in her left lung. Doctors were well aware that these tumors were most likely caused by some type of radiation they had come in contact with while in Hiroshima, but they were not sure the sisters could get the best treatment in Hawaii. It was recommended they be flown to a specialized hospital in New York called Sloan Kettering. They had been researching and working with cancer patients for nearly two years, and had made some significant advancements.

That evening, Father Renaldo took each of the woman aside to tell them what the doctors had found. Sister Dominique looked at Father Renaldo. "What are our chances of survival if we have the surgery, compared to if we refuse?"

Pulling no punches, Father Renaldo replied. "Without surgery, you will be dead within a year as the cancer will spread quickly through your blood system.. The doctors say your tumor is small so it should easily be removed, and you will recover beautifully. But you need to act as soon as possible, so getting back on that plane is a must this time."

Several days later, the DC-4 left Honolulu bound for San Diego where it would refuel before flying on to New York.

At the hospital, many of the tests done in Hawaii were repeated, and many new ones conducted. With everything completed, a Doctor John Smithmore walked into Sister Dominique's room.

"Sister, you certainly have used up several lives over the past few years. I truly cannot even begin to imagine what you have been through. However, now you have a new fight to win. We can easily remove your tumor, but that is just the start. Then you will need to go through a new type of cancer treatment called chemotherapy. It's rough on your body, you will lose your hair, and you will fight to keep food in your system, but it appears to have the best results over other treatments we have tried. It is still relatively new, but again, results have been good."

Shaking her head, Sister Dominique replied. "We did all we could for the people in Hiroshima. We never thought we would get sick because we were not there during the blast. Tell me, how are Sisters Annuncio and Josephine doing, I need to know!"

"I understand," Dr. Smithmore replied. "Sister Annuncio is in about the same position as you are, but Sister Josephine would appear to be in worse shape, as she has had more radiation poisoning in her system. We would like to schedule your surgery for tomorrow morning at 0600hrs., followed by Sister Annuncio at about 1300hrs. and Sister Josephine after that. Will you sign off on that?"

Before signing the paperwork, Sister Dominique asked, "What about Sister Claudia? She is my blood sister, how is she?"

Smiling, Dr. Smithmore replied. "Not a trace of tumors or cancer anywhere. She is in good health and has volunteered to give blood if you need it."

Smiling, Sister Dominique said, "Give me the papers."

It had been nearly six weeks since Paulo had checked on the whereabouts of his sister, so after work he went over to the Displaced Persons Office. As he entered the room, a sergeant he had spoken to several times stood up and waved him over.

"I received paperwork that your sister is in New York in the United States. According to the documents, she is in a hospital called Sloan Kettering. She contracted some type of illness after working in Hiroshima. I think our colonel would relax your restrictions to travel to the United States in a case like this. I have already informed him you would be coming in some time soon."

After a conversation with the colonel, all the necessary documents were completed allowing Paulo to fly to New York. The ticket was paid for by the Resettlement Office, since he was working for the Italian government.

Arriving at the hospital, Paulo was not sure who to talk to, so he told the woman at the front desk about Father Renaldo and the sisters. She quickly made some phone calls and found Father Renaldo.

Several minutes later, Father Renaldo and Sister Claudia arrived in the lobby. Before anything could be said, Sister Claudia ran across the room, throwing her arms around her brother. The two of them cried as they held each other tight. Finally, Paulo looked at Father Renaldo and shook hands with him. "I want to thank you for keeping my sisters alive through all you went through. I can never repay you."

Father Renaldo laughed slightly. "To be honest, it was Sister Dominique that battled us out of many bad situations. She is a remarkable woman to say the least."

"I searched for her day after day, night after night, vowing to not give up. She was my little sister, someone had to care about her. I still do not understand how my parents did what they did and why they couldn't tell us. Yes, it would have been tough to deal with, but at least we would have known she was alive and well.

Claudia hugged Paulo. "You must forgive them, Paulo. They did what they thought was best so we could live. Look at us now! We are alive and our little sister is just upstairs. Don't dwell on the past, Paulo, think about our future down the road."

Nodding his head, Paulo said, "Tell me, how is Dominique doing?"

Father Renaldo replied. "The surgery went very well, and now she is on a new type of therapy that is supposed to kill cancer cells. She has had two treatments so far and is very weak. But she is still a fighter, so I believe she will be alright."

Going up to the third floor of the hospital and arriving outside the door to Sister Dominique's room, Paulo's hands began to tremble. Looking at Claudia, he said, "What do I say to her? Perhaps you

should come in and introduce me first."

Claudia smiled. "Do not be so scared, Paulo. You need to walk in that room and deal with your pain, fears, and the emptiness that has ruled your life all these years. I will come in later, but this you must do by yourself."

After taking a deep breath, Paulo slowly entered the dimly lit room and stopped. He looked at the woman lying in the bed and could not believe it was the same Dominique he had searched for, so many years earlier. As he took a few steps toward the bed, Dominique gasped. "Paulo, Paulo is that really you or are you an apparition?"

Half smiling and half crying, Paulo replied. "It is I, little sister."

Holding out her hand, Dominique called out, "Don't stand there, come to me."

A moment later, Paulo sat down on the edge of the bed, pulling his little sister into his arms as he wept. "Baby sister, I searched so hard for you. Day after day, until the winter storms came. Papa said you were lost forever, but I could not accept it. You were never lost to me, I loved you so much."

As Dominique sobbed, she kissed Paulo on the cheek. "Never let go, please never let go, Paulo. I have missed you so much Where have you been all these years? I never understood why you, Claudia and Giana did not look for me or come to visit me in the Abbey. It broke my heart for many years, I never dreamed Papa and Mama would tell you I was lost in the forest." Crying even harder, Dominique laid her head against her brother's heaving chest.

It was impossible for Paulo to respond, as he cried harder than he had ever cried before in his life. He just kept repeating, "Dom, I've missed you so much, I've missed you so much."

Finally, Dominique said. "Enough of that now, no more tears." Pushing Paulo back a little, she said, "Let me look at you, let me see the man you have become." After taking a long look at her brother, she continued. "You have father's high cheek bones and his dark brown eyes. You look so much like him. That is why I asked if you were an apparition when I first saw you. I thought Papa had come back from the grave to see me one more time. Oh Paulo, you are the best medicine I have had in a very long time. Tell me you can stay and visit with me for at least a few days. We have so much to share with one another. Have you seen Claudia? She is here as well."

Hearing her name mentioned, Claudia walked into the room. Approaching the bed, she began to cry. "We are once again whole. We are a family."

Putting her arm around Paulo, then laying her head against Dominique's shoulder, she said, "It would be so good to have Giana here with us."

As Paulo drew his sister in tighter, he said, "I believe she is here, Claudia. As you say we are whole again, and Giana needs to be part of that, we must include her. We will turn Sicily upside down so we may find her someday, and then we will be completely whole."

The doctors had to agree with Dominique that Paulo was the best medicine she could have. Almost immediately after his visit, she began to get better and took on an entirely new attitude. Although Paulo was supposed to have reported back to his job in Italy, Father Renaldo requested he stay with Dominique for a few more weeks, as every day she appeared to improve with Paulo and Claudia at her side.

When the hospital was ready to discharge Dominique, she had a tearful good bye with Paulo, knowing they would see each other again. The hardest decision she had to make was which monastery she wanted to go to. Even though both Claudia and Paulo decided they were going to return to Italy, Dominique was unsure whether or not she was ready to return to her home country, where her war time experiences had caused her so much pain. She felt it was best if she stayed away from Italy for a while longer, giving her emotional wounds more time to heal. After checking on monastery options in the United States, Father Renaldo spoke to her about a quiet Benedictine Monastery in Minnesota he had heard about that was surrounded by forests, lakes and lots of fresh air, and it would only be a two-day train ride.

Arriving at the train station in St. Joseph, Minnesota, Sister Dominique and one other new sister, were met by several sisters from the convent that was about a mile away.

There was no doubt that news of Sister Dominique's exploits during the war had preceded her halfway across the country. No matter which sister she met in the Abbey, every one of them had questions for her. She became an instant hero to the sisters as well as many of the students that were looking into joining the convent.

Within six months, Sister Dominique began teaching Italian in the high school and college programs, and from time to time lectured in the history program regarding her experiences in the Pacific and Hiroshima.

It was at that time a reporter named Madeline Provost from the New York Record sought her out. Miss Provost was working on a story regarding the atomic bomb attacks on Japan, and had heard about Sister Dominique work among the survivors. After two days of questions and answers, Miss Provost sat back in her chair. She looked intently at Sister Dominique, and said, "After all your experiences, how do you feel about the Vatican Ratline?"

Looking confused, Sister Dominique replied. "I have no idea what you are talking about. You will need to be more explicit."

Understanding that Sister Dominique had been out of the country for some time, Miss Provost said, "When things began to go bad for the German Wehrmacht, an unknown quantity of German gold was deposited in the Vatican with several important Cardinals. The gold was to be used to help high ranking German officials and S.S. members escape from Germany after the war. It has been exposed by the Israeli Mossad and other Nazi hunters."

After a moment of silence, Sister Dominique replied, "I cannot believe that is accurate. The Pope would never allow such an operation to take place, knowing what the Nazi's had done. There must be some mistake!"

Digging into her briefcase, Miss Provost removed a translated newspaper article regarding the ratline that had been published in a Paris paper. After reading the articles, Sister Dominique said, "If this is in fact all truthful, then everyone involved should be treated like a war criminal and brought to justice. Nothing like this should ever be allowed to happen. The world needs to be cleansed of the Nazi's and everything they stand for with no exceptions."

Smiling, Miss Provost said, "Sister, may I quote you on this issue in my article?"

Nodding her head, Sister Dominique replied, "Yes, of course you may quote me. If this situation is going on as it appears to be, it must be stopped, and the world needs to know what is going on. I stand by what I said and will continue to speak out on the issue. You can be guaranteed of that."

Finally in 1960, Sister Dominique felt her heart being pulled back to Italy where her life in the convent began. She had never planned to stay away permanently, so now she asked permission to return home and it was granted.

Chapter Twenty-One – Devastated

Working on the docks in Naples, Paulo enjoyed getting pats on the back from Major Hollister for his strict interpretation of the allied government rules. It was one place the major felt comfortable with, so he could turn his attention to other matters.

However, one morning a tall blonde man of about sixty arrived at the dock preparing to sail for Canada on a one-way ticket. The man said nothing as he handed his papers to Paulo. After looking over the documents, Paulo saw some inconsistencies that bothered him. Turning to the man, he said, "Can I see your ID papers?"

Angrily, the man produced what appeared to be a brand-new ID card from his suit coat, without saying a word.

"So, you are Gianmarco Ricci from Varcaturo, is that correct?" Paulo inquired of the nervous man.

Appearing to get angrier by the minute, the man called out. "There is nothing wrong with these documents, just stamp them and allow me on the ship and everything will be just fine!"

Hearing the solid German accent, Paulo knew something was amiss. Taking a step back, Paulo drew his weapon and said, "Well, Mr. Ricci, put down your bag, put your hands in the air and come with me. We need to get this checked out before I can allow you to board."

Mr. Ricci glared at Paulo, "You know where these papers came from, what are you trying to do to me? You must let me on the ship quickly."

Paulo was even more confused after listening to Mr. Ricci's comment.

Shaking his head, Paulo replied. "Let's go, we need to check with my supervisor."

After locking Ricci in a detention cell, Paulo called Major Hollister and explained the strange circumstances. After hearing everything Paulo had said, the major replied. "Quickly release the man and get him on the ship. Do not ask questions, do not make any calls, just do as I say. When your shift is over, come to my office at once."

Hanging up the phone, Paulo was not so sure he wanted to release Mr. Ricci. He knew something was not quite right, and he wanted to know what was going on. Walking into Ricci's cell, Paulo sat down on a chair.

"I have orders to release you and let you go on the ship, but I know your name is not Ricci, and I know for a fact you did not come from Varcaturo. You best tell me your name if you wish to leave on this ship."

Ricci stood up from his chair. "You have no idea who you are messing with and what you are getting yourself into. My name is Ricci and that is all you need to know. Now get me on that ship!"

Paulo smiled, as he stared at Mr. Ricci. "So, you are a criminal attempting to escape from either Italian or allied justice?"

"You are going to pay for what you are doing to me, I can assure you of that. For your own health, it would be wise of you to let me go," Ricci said, kicking over the chair he had been sitting on.

Before Paulo could reply, his assistant, Sergeant Cataldi, entered the room. "Captain, there is a man to see you, and I think you need to speak with him right away."

Walking out of the interrogation room, Paulo saw a man in a black suit, with a black rain coat over the top of it standing by his desk. Before Paulo could say a word, the man said, "Captain Trevisiani, what are you trying to prove? Release Mr. Ricci at once and let him board this ship!"

Paulo's interest was growing by the second. "And who might you be?"

"Your worst nightmare if Mr. Ricci misses this ship. Now do as I say and release Ricci this minute!" The man yelled as he glared at Paulo.

As the man moved his hand back toward a semi-automatic pistol on his belt, Paulo quickly pulled his weapon and pointed it at the man. "Remove your weapon carefully, and lay it on the floor. You are under arrest!"

Before the visitor could remove his weapon, Major Hollister walked into the office. Pointing at Paulo, he said, "Put your weapon away, release Ricci and do not say another word!"

Realizing something was totally amiss, Paulo nodded his head. Several minutes later, Ricci and the man in the black suit left the office and walked up the boarding gangway.

Taking Paulo into the interrogation room, the major explained about the Vatican Ratline and the organization called Odessa that was responsible for getting Nazi war criminals out of Europe. Paulo was stunned by what he was hearing, and was warned for his own safety, never to interfere again.

That evening, as Paulo walked back toward his barracks, a black French Citroen pulled up beside him. A man holding a German Schmeisser stepped out. "Get inside, Captain," the man said, as he pointed the weapon at Paulo's chest.

With the door almost closed, the driver sped away, leaving the base behind. Paulo sat quietly as the city of Naples slowly disappeared behind them. Stopping in an abandoned farm yard, the man next to Paulo told him to get out.

Stepping from the vehicle, Paulo observed three men walking toward him. Before he could say a word, two of the men grabbed him and began working him over with their fists and rubber truncheons. As he fell to the ground, the third man kicked him in the ribs before speaking.

"You highly upset things today, Captain. You have no idea how close we came to having Mr. Ricci being arrested by the allied government. That would have been a disaster we cannot afford now or ever again!" Pulling Paulo up from the ground, the man threw him back up against the Peugeot.

Pushing a riding crop up under Paulo's chin, the man continued. "Captain, we know you have a sister by the name of Dominique that was part of the underground in Italy before leaving for the Pacific. She still owes us a debt she can never repay. We know where she is right now, and we will always know where she is. If you want to see her and your other sister Claudia stay alive, just do as you are told. Otherwise, they will disappear under rather ugly circumstances. Your major has found out the hard way already, just ask him where his daughter is. So, now you have been told what your job is and what will happen to you if you do not comply."

As the man that had done all the talking turned to walk away, the other two men took turns slugging Paulo and striking him once again with their truncheons until he passed out.

Waking up, Paulo could barely make it to his feet before falling forward and striking his head on the side of a burned-out car. Looking inside the car, Paulo gasped. The bodies of two people sat erect in the front seat, exactly as they had been when they were consumed by the flames.

As Paulo turned to walk away, a young woman walked up behind him. "Captain Trevisiani, I have an envelope for you."

Turning around quickly, he observed a woman in her twenties standing a few feet away from him, holding a German Luger in her right hand. Reaching out with her left hand, she thrust an envelope into his chest. "Read it, Captain."

Opening the envelope, Paulo removed a sheet of paper. Unfolding it, he read the words. "Never forget, Odessa does exist!"

"So, how do I get back to Naples?" Paulo asked as he carefully watched the woman.

Start walking, someone will pick you up," the woman replied, before walking back to a battered old pickup truck being driven by an elderly man.

Paulo walked about a mile before a farmer pulled over in a truck filled with fire wood. The driver looked at Paulo. "I think you are one of the lucky ones. Get in, be quiet, and I will drive you back to the naval base."

Walking into Major Hollister's office, Paulo grabbed the major by the throat. "Do you mean to tell me the Nazi's still run roughshod over the Italian government?"

Raising his arms in the air, the Major replied. "I get photos of my daughter about every two weeks. If you cross Odessa, bad things will happen to your loved ones. Do not cross or question anything to do with the Vatican Ratline. I want my daughter back alive!"

Paulo walked back to his barracks where he took a long hot shower and put on clean clothes. He was shocked to see a copy of the New York Record laying on his bunk. It had been opened to page three where the reporter had written Sister Dominique's comments about the Vatican Ratline. In the margin were the words. "Stop this or she dies!"

Before travelling to Milan where Sister Claudia was doing research work, Sister Dominique stopped in London to visit Sister Josephine. It was a very heartwarming experience to visit with her old friend. However, it was in London where she learned the war was not entirely over.

The second night she was there, Sister Josephine and several other sisters took her to see a popular play in an outside amphitheater. Throughout the entire performance, Sister Dominique could not get over the feeling that she was being watched by someone, and it was most uncomfortable. After the show, they walked over to a small outdoor coffee shop. Once again, Sister Dominique felt as if she were being watched by someone, but everything appeared to be normal. Slowly, she gazed around the patio but could see no one she knew, or anyone that appeared to be taking an interest in her or the other sisters.

Leaving the coffee shop, the sisters laughed and joked as they walked back to the small van they had driven from the Abbey. As Sister Josephine climbed behind the wheel, Sister Dominique called out. "Josephine, get out of the van and don't try to start it!"

Sister Josephine looked strangely at Sister Dominique and smiled. "Sister, did that play get to you? Are you seeing bad people behind every rock now?"

By now, Sister Dominique was standing directly by Sister Josephine. Reaching over, she placed her hand on the top of Sister Josephine's. "Please do not turn this key, step out and walk away, and do not close the door."

Listening to Sister Dominique's tone of voice, and seeing the expression on her face, Sister Josephine nodded her head and slowly slid out of the van.

Walking over to a pub, Sister Dominique called the local police station and told them she thought there was a bomb in their van.

About a half hour later, several police cars and a large van arrived in front of the pub. After Sister Dominique explained about her connections with the Italian underground and the feelings she had in the theater and coffee shop, the investigators decided to take her complaint seriously. Nearly twenty minutes went by before several specialized bomb disposal members removed a bomb from under the hood of the van. They took the van back to the police garage to be checked over more thoroughly, and gave the sister's a ride back to the Abbey.

The following day, an agent Smythe from British MI6 came to visit Sister Dominique. Sitting down over a cup of tea, Smythe asked a tremendous number of questions regarding Sister Dominique's activities with the underground and her trip from Italy to Nusa Simbo.

When he was finished with his questions, he opened his briefcase, bringing out a small stack of photos. "Sister, these are former German gestapo and S.S. officers still on the loose. We know some of them have been here in England, and some float around the continent working with members of Odessa. Go through these photos and see if you recognize anyone."

Sister Dominique laughed. "Agent Smythe, do you really believe any of these people would still want me dead after all these years? I mean this is 1960, who cares anymore?"

Agent Smythe took out a small book from his brief case. "Take a look at the names in this book, Sister, then look at the dates behind their names. All of these people have been killed over the last ten years by Nazi sympathizers or former gestapo or S.S. officers, and believe me, this is for real. We at MI6 have been working diligently with Mossad and the CIA to help find these bastards, but they are not easily tracked."

Feeling her skin crawl, Sister Dominique began going through the stack of photos one at a time, studying each face carefully. About halfway through the stack, she came upon the photo of Captain Rochefort from Mumbai. "Yes, I know this man. He was a gestapo man in Mumbai when we stopped there on our way to Nusa Simbo. He was an angry man that scared me very much. He had an assistant named Sergeant Albrecht. I would consider him a dangerous man as well, but at least he allowed me to get on the ship before the captain changed his mind. I would not like to meet up with either of those men again."

Agent Smythe looked at the photo for a moment before scribbling some notes on his pad. "We have not had anyone identify this man so far. Mumbai you say. I wonder where he may be now?"

As agent Smythe was talking, Sister Dominique continued going through the photos. Quickly, she stopped again, handing the agent another photo. "This is Sergeant Albrecht."

Turning the photo over, he replied. "We know him as Lieutenant Albrecht. A very bad man that is wanted for several crimes. You are right, turning your back on him would be a bad thing to do. He has been connected to the Vatican Ratline for some time."

Sister Dominique shook her head. "There is that term again. I was told about the Vatican Ratline when I did an interview with a Madeline Provost from the New York Record when I was recuperating, but she never explained much about it."

"Yes, we are well aware of your interview, as is everyone working for Odessa. It would take me all day to explain what is all involved with the Ratline. But keeping it short, it's a group of people in the Vatican that are helping former Nazi officials to escape from Germany. They are helping to plant them all over the world. It is a very dangerous bunch that will go to any lengths to complete their mission," Agent Smythe explained as he repacked his briefcase."

"Am I in danger?" Sister Dominique inquired, as she felt her stomach tightening into a knot.

"I would have to say yes, but to what point I cannot say." Handing Sister Dominique a piece of paper, he said, "These are former members of the Italian underground near Milan that survived the war. When you get to Milan, it might be a good idea to contact them for assistance. I guarantee you they will be willing to help you no matter what. While you are in England, my office will keep an eye on you the best we can."

Feeling very uncomfortable in England, Sister Dominique left for Italy three days later. Both Sister Margaret and Sister Claudia met her at the airport and drove her to a convent in Milan where Claudia was working.

When Paulo was told that Dominique had arrived in Milan, he went to Major Hollister asking for time off to visit her, and to warn her to keep quiet regarding anything to do with Odessa or the Vatican Ratline. Without question, the major told Paulo to take all the time he needed. The minute Paulo left the office, Major Hollister called former gestapo agent Rochefort, who was now working for Odessa. He informed him of Paulo's trip to Milan the following morning and that Sister Dominique was already there.

As it was late when the train arrived in Milan, Paulo took a taxi to a small hotel where he was going to spend the night before meeting his sisters in the morning. He kept a wary eye on everyone he came in contact with, evaluating each of them as to whether or not they may be working for Odessa.

Arriving in his third-floor room, Paulo sat down at the window, holding his semi-automatic pistol as he watched the parking lot and driveway to see who was coming or going. By 0100hrs., he fell asleep in the chair feeling confident no one had followed him.

The following morning, he took a taxi to the convent where his sisters were staying. He had the driver circle around Milan and stop in several locations so he could watch out the back window for any suspicious vehicles.

What neither Paulo or Captain Rochefort could have known, was that Detective Smythe from England's MI6 had contacted Mossad and the CIA regarding Sister Dominique's plans. He was sure she was being watched by Odessa, so this might be an opportunity to capture some wanted war criminals. He joined Mossad in Milan, hoping to be in on any good arrests.

Wanting to be honest and open with everyone, after breakfast Sister Dominique explained everything that happened to her in England. Paulo felt his stomach turn after listening to his sister, but chose to keep quiet on what had happened to him. He was now caught in the middle between Odessa and the safety of his sisters, but decided that if he did what he was told, no harm would come to his family.

In the afternoon, Renzo Conti, a former member of the Italian underground, and now a member of the provincial police, drove the three sisters, Paulo, and Romano Altero, another former underground member, to the convent at Acqualagna. They also visited what had been the Trevisiani farm site that Dominique had last seen when she was five years old. Most of the buildings were either in bad shape or had been destroyed during the war, so the new owner was in the process of tearing everything down.

But it gave Dominique a sense of peace as she walked along the stream that flowed behind the barn. She and Claudia laughed when they discussed all the times they played in the cool water during the long hot summers.

That evening as they visited late into the night, Sister Margaret explained that Abbey di San Vincenzo was in the process of being rebuilt after all the damage it received during the war. She stated she had lined up permission to take everyone to the Abbey the next day if they all still wanted to go.

There was nothing more that Sister Dominique wanted than to show Paulo and Claudia where her life in the convent had started, so she happily agreed to go. She felt having security from former members of the underground was unnecessary, but Paulo knew it was a very good move, so the two men agreed to join them.

The following morning the sky was a brilliant blue, with just a few low hanging cirrus clouds floating over the Abbazia di San Vincenzo, which sat high above the Furlo Pass, as if clinging to the very side of the mountain. About 0800hrs., Sister Dominique, Sister Margaret, Sister Claudia, Paulo and the two body guards climbed into the convent van for a trip up the mountain.

Sister Dominique sat frozen in place as she remembered the ride up the road with her father forty years earlier. It had seemed to be a great adventure as the horses snorted, creating great clouds of steam that rolled from their nostrils as they struggled to dig their hooves into the nearly frozen ground on the steep road that led to the Abbey. She shivered slightly, remembering the cold wind that circulated around the heavy blanket that covered her. She remembered every twist and turn in the road along with the towering pines that swayed and creaked while their swirling branches covered the road with evil looking monsters.

Arriving in the driveway near the Abbey, it was a shame to see the huge old wooden overly varnished doors pock marked with bullet holes from machine guns. They used to be a welcoming sight to anyone arriving at the Abbey, as the morning sun glimmered off the well-oiled finish. The majestic stained-glass windows that circled the vestibule were shattered, and the huge stone cross that topped the front of the building lay on the ground near the front doors with part of the circular bottom blown away.

Sister Dominique was heartbroken as she led everyone through the front door. No matter where they looked, bullet holes were everywhere. Much of the centuries old marble was chipped or broken from explosions. Walking up to the second floor, Sister Dominique was saddened to see the giant fresco of St. Joseph gone, as the painted plaster now laid crumbled on the floor. Even the long wooden table where the sisters ate their meals was gone. All that remained of it was a small pile of wood stacked near one of the fire places. Many of the ornate bronze light fixtures that hung along the corridors either lay broken or had disappeared completely.

The chapel was probably in the worse shape of any part of the monastery. Both altars had been torn apart and all the paintings on the walls were damaged one way or another. The nearly eight foot ceramic tile picture of St. Benedict had been torn from the wall. Tiles that had not been smashed were strewn throughout the chapel. The corner that had been used as the baptismal font was now the location for a hanging gallows. Two ropes containing hangman nooses still hung from the open beams overhead.

The Germans had not only destroyed much of the ornate old monastery, but they had also done their best to desecrate every aspect of the structure.

The foreman of one of the construction crews walked up to Sister Margaret. "The third floor is under heavy construction right now. We are covering bullet holes, replacing plaster and repainting each of the rooms. All the wooden trim was removed for firewood, so we are in the process of staining new wood, and repairing all the broken windows. We should be done up there in about six months, then we shall drop down one floor at a time. Some of the upper floors were left untouched, except for the balconies where they placed machine guns. Other than art work, we hope to finish the entire project in about three years, if the money continues to come in."

Sister Dominique sat down on what was left of one of the chapel's pews that had been riddled with bullet holes. She wept after seeing the destruction to the magnificent old monastery she had called home for so many years. Sister Claudia sat next to her and held her tight.

Renzo and Romano had stayed in the main entrance, keeping an eye on the road outside. Seeing three black Mercedes sedans and a van drive up to the front of the monastery, they began running up the staircase. All the contractors except one ran for cover, as they knew there was going to be trouble. The one remaining worker pulled a pistol from his tool box and began firing in the direction of Renzo. Quickly, Romano dropped to one knee on the stairs and fired back from between the marble railing supports. As the bullets tore into the workers chest, several men dressed in black entered through the front door and began firing back at Romano. Attempting to spin away and take cover behind the next set of marble supports, two bullets struck him in the left leg. He slid part way down the marble steps as bullets continued to strike all around him. Realizing there was nothing he could do to escape the relentless attackers, Romano grabbed the railing, stood up and returned fire. One of the attackers went down as bullets struck him in the head, and a second spun around as a bullet struck his shoulder. The third man cut lose with a long blast of his submachine gun, striking Romano several times. Taking a last breath, Romano fell over the railing, falling twenty feet to his death.

Renzo raced toward Sister Dominique and the rest of the group. "Odessa is here, there are a lot of them, we have no way out."

Hoping to keep anyone else from being killed, Sister Dominique led everyone to a large room that used to be a library filled with ancient books, but now contained nothing but empty shelves. With everyone in, Sister Dominique slammed the huge steel bar down that secured the door. Seconds later a stream of machine gun bullets ripped through the weaker panels of the door.

When the shooting stopped, a voice Sister Dominique remembered well from Mumbai spoke up. "You are all trapped and have nowhere to go. The best thing you can do is open this door and surrender right now. Those that are not wanted by Odessa will be set free. Sister Dominique, we all know this is your fault, so we will not let anyone else suffer because of you!"

Sister Claudia grabbed hold of Sister Dominique's arm. "Do not listen to anything he has to say, they will kill all of us without question."

Looking around the room, Renzo spoke softly. "Sister, are there any secret exits from this room that you know of? I heard construction workers found several secret passages during the renovation."

Shaking her head, Sister Dominique replied. "This room was very sacred when I was here. I read many of the books, but always took them to my room to read. I know there is a door on the balcony that leads to the third-floor corridor, but that will not help us much."

As Renzo and Paulo began pulling on book cases trying to find a secret way out, several more cars arrived in front of the Abbey. Detective Smythe and four Mossad agents ran into the front of the building, firing at two Odessa men that were standing near the stair case. Both of them dropped immediately as a man on the top of the staircase fired a long blast from his machine gun, causing Detective Smythe and the Mossad agents to seek cover.

Captain Rochefort turned and looked down the corridor. "What is it, what's going on?"

The man with the machine gun replied. "It must be Mossad, it sounds like they're calling out to one another in Hebrew."

Stomping his foot on the floor, Rochefort placed the barrel of his pistol under the chin of the construction foreman. "Is there another way into this room? Tell me now or die!"

Shaking like a leaf, the foreman explained about the door on the third floor, and a large ventilator shaft on the north wall of the balcony that can be accessed from the fourth floor.

Quickly, Rochefort and two of his men ran up to the fourth floor with the foreman and found the shaft. After solidly securing the door from the inside, the foreman led Rochefort and his men to the heavy vent screen. Moments later, Rochefort kicked in the screen from the shaft and crawled out onto the balcony floor with his two men behind him.

Everyone in the library screamed, as they observed Captain Rochefort and his men appear so quickly on the balcony. As one of the men turned his machine gun toward the sisters, Paulo jumped out from behind one of the book cases, firing his pistol at the man, but missing. Seconds later, Paulo laid on the floor in a pool of blood as the man with the machine gun fired a massive volley in his direction.

Sister Dominique screamed in horror as she watched her brother collapse onto the floor. Both Sister Dominique and Sister Claudia ran to the aid of their dying brother. "Why Paulo, why did you do such a thing? Sister Dominique screamed as she placed her hand over one of the bullet holes, attempting to stop the bleeding.

Looking up at his sisters, Paulo said, "I knew they would be coming here looking for you. All of this is my fault. I had to do something to try and stop it."

Claudia shook her head. "Paulo, none of this is your fault. The fault lies with the people that have hate in their hearts and will not let go of it."

Attempting to smile, Paulo raised his hand, placing it on Dominique's cheek. "I have found you at last, and know that my search so many years ago was not in vain. You were alive, I knew you were, and now we will be together forever. I will never leave you."

As tears rolled down Dominique's face, she nodded her head. "Yes Paulo, I was alive, and I always believed we would find one another and we have."

Realizing his life was about to end, Paulo took hold of Dominique's hand and drew in a long breath of air. I love you both so much, remember me."

As Paulo's head dropped off to the side, Dominique pulled his blood covered body into her arms and wept. Claudia leaned over against Dominique, sobbing as she held on to Paulo's arm. Looking up toward the balcony where the man with the machine gun stood, Sister Dominique said, "There is no place you can ever hide, I will find you, and I will bring you to justice for what you have done. May God have mercy on your wretched soul."

Turning toward Rochefort, she said. "You are no more than a dead man."

Rochefort looked down at Sister Dominique. "I do not scare easily, and your intimidation attempts do not bother me. But you may wish to think about your own life, not mine."

After reaching the second floor of the monastery, Detective Smythe realized he was involved in a major standoff and there was no way to enter the library without getting all the hostages killed. Standing outside of the library door, Detective Smythe called out, "Rochefort, we know you are in there, and we are not going to let you escape. It's time to face the hangman and finally do what's right."

Rochefort laughed. "I am not going to allow you or Mossad to take me prisoner and embarrass me in a public court of humiliation. Many people will die before that happens. I suggest you leave the monastery and allow us to do so as well. A standoff will earn you nothing."

One of the Mossad agents stepped up beside Detective Smythe. "We can blow the balcony doors up on the third floor and throw in gas. Then we can rush them and get the prisoners out. How do you feel about that?"

Detective Smythe shook his head. "That is a rather large room. They would have a chance to kill everyone before the gas does what it's supposed to do. No, we need a better plan than that."

Realizing the men had been looking for an escape tunnel behind the book cases, Rochefort told his men to continue looking. Within fifteen minutes, they found an escape tunnel on the east wall of the library behind a heavy book case, that had been well used to take out the books while the monastery was occupied during the war. One of Rochefort's men went through the adjoining tunnel lighting all the lanterns that hung from the walls. Returning, the man smiled. It goes down into the sub-basement where there is a large door that leads outside to the back of the monastery. We should be able to find a vehicle rather quickly from that point."

Rochefort smiled. "Take everyone from the main floor of the library down there now so we do not have to worry about them later. If they cause you problems, shoot them. One of you find us a truck or van and bring it up to the large doors. When I come down the tunnel be ready to go. We will take

Sister Dominique with us and leave the others tied up in the basement."

After a long argument with Detective Smythe, Rochefort said. "Listen to me. This man named Paulo was wounded when we came in here and he is getting worse. Call for an ambulance so he can get treatment. When the ambulance arrives, let us know."

As soon as he was done speaking, Rochefort ran to the tunnel, pulled the book shelf back against the wall with the attached rope, and ran down into the basement. Sitting by the big door was a delivery style truck with all five Odessa men and Sister Dominique onboard. When Rochefort climbed into the cab, the driver headed south away from the monastery.

Detective Smythe pounded several times on the door once the ambulance had arrived. Getting no response, he looked at the Mossad agent. "Blow it!"

When the doors swung open, they were all surprised to see the room empty except for the body of Paulo. It became evident to Smythe there had been an escape tunnel somewhere in the massive room. As they began to search, they found a lot of dirt on the floor by the bookshelf that led to the tunnel. Pulling it open, they followed the tunnel to the basement and the large doors where the truck had been parked. Quickly, they untied everyone, attempting to get information as to the whereabouts of Rochefort and his men.

Detective Smythe was angrier than he had been in a long time. He had Rochefort and some of his cronies right in his grasp, and they had escaped with a hostage he had sworn to keep safe. Now they would need to start all over again, and no one could say how much time Sister Dominique had left to live.

Driving a top-heavy delivery van on the twisting mountain roads in broad day light was always a challenge. But driving one in the dark at high speed with a light rain falling was a recipe for disaster. Several times the van fish tailed as the driver attempted to maneuver the van through the tight curves, but he never attempted to slow down even as the rain intensified into a full down pour. With water now standing on the highway, the driver put the van into a slide that he could not control. As the vehicle began to roll over, Sister Dominique grabbed onto the back of the driver's seat, pulling her legs up into a fetal position. The van sat up on two wheels for several seconds before ripping through a guard rail and plunging off the road. The vehicle rolled twice before landing on its side, partially submerged in a small river.

Suddenly everything inside the van was completely quiet, and the bodies of the Odessa men had stopped flying around the truck. Luckily, Sister Dominique was on the side of the van that was sitting on the ground. Letting go of the back of the seat, she noticed her hands were covered in a sticky substance. Sitting up, she looked into the seat she had been holding onto. The steel post from a road sign had been sheared off and had impaled the driver's chest. She noticed the windshield was gone, and Captain Rochefort was missing from the passenger seat.

After washing her hands off in the water, Sister Dominique pulled herself up into the small drivers compartment and rolled out of the van through the windshield opening. Although her legs were a bit wobbly, Sister Dominique realized she did not have any serious injuries. Looking down at the ground, she found a flashlight that had been thrown from the van. She knew turning it on meant giving away her location, but in her heart, she understood that everyone in the van was a human being that may need her help.

In the back of the van she found one man that was in serious condition but was still breathing. It appeared the other four were all dead. After pulling the injured man out through the windshield opening, she began looking for Captain Rochefort. There was no way to tell if he was under the van or down in the deep part of the river, but she could not find any sign of him. Returning to the man she had pulled from the van; it was evident he had now passed on.

Cold, wet and sore, Sister Dominique did not wish to seek cover inside the van with four dead men. She knew the driver had made many turns before ending up on the road they were now travelling on, so she had no idea where they might be. But by the light from the lightning flashes, she knew they were in a narrow mountain canyon.

After walking about a half mile, a bright bolt of lightning illuminated a building about twenty yards from the left side of the road. Approaching the structure, it was clear the building had been abandoned for some time. Pushing open the front door, Sister Dominique used the beam of the flash light to search the building for any signs of life. The one thing she saw that brightened her spirits was a wood burning stove with a pile of wood stacked neatly in the corner, and a box of matches still sitting on a shelf. After building a fire in the stove, Sister Dominique barricaded the door with a large old wooden table. Feeling safe, she pulled an old worn overstuffed chair near the stove and sat down. The warmth of the fire was a welcome relief. After stoking the fire several times, Sister Dominique curled up in a comfortable position on the chair and fell asleep around midnight.

A loud clap of thunder awoke Sister Dominique as dawn was just arriving in the valley. Heavy rain continued to fall in torrents as a strong wind made the old structure creak and moan. After piling more wood into the old stove, Sister Dominique took time to look around the abandoned building. In what had been a small kitchen, she found a sealed can of peas. Picking up a hammer and screw driver she went about ripping the cover from the can. After setting the can on top of the stove for about ten minutes, the juice began to boil. Sitting back on the chair she poured some of the peas into her mouth. They tasted fine, but she thought a little salt and pepper would go a long way to improving the taste. Suddenly she found herself laughing. Here she was in an abandoned building in the middle of nowhere, not knowing how she would find her way back to the Abbey, and unsure if Captain Rochefort was out there looking for her, and she was thinking about condiments to improve the taste of her peas.

After finishing her breakfast, she sat erect in the chair. She thought she heard someone outside, but was afraid to look out the window. After hearing the scraping sound again, Sister Dominique picked up the hammer and slowly made her way to a window. She was stunned to see a bloody and battered Captain Rochefort leaning against an old fifty-five-gallon drum, just ten feet from the door. Moments later, the captain called out.

"I see the smoke from your fire and I need your help. Can you please let me in?"

After using the house to dry off, warm up and find something to eat, the last thing Sister Dominique wanted to do was let the man that had been trying to kill her into the building that had offered her refuge throughout the night.

But after the captain begged for help a second time, Sister Dominique pushed the table away from the door and opened it. Looking out at the captain, it was clear to see he was in no shape to offer any resistance. Rushing out into the rain, Sister Dominique grabbed the captain and pulled him into the building. Laying him on the floor next to the stove, she quickly removed his sidearm from its holster.

Taking a longer look at the captain, she was surprised he was still alive. He had a large piece of wood protruding from an abdominal wound and his left leg was crooked and appeared to be badly broken. There also was a large cut on the top of his head that continued sending small trickles of blood down over his face.

Looking up at Sister Dominique, he said, "Today I fear I will meet this being you call God. Who is he and what will he do with me. Sister, I am frightened. I have led a horrible life."

Sister Dominique looked down at the dying man and said, "Like you, many people in this world find death to be a frightening experience. None of us know for sure what is beyond the veil that separates life from death. But we believe God is waiting there and will reward those that have led a good life and ask for forgiveness."

"Sister that is not me, I have killed many people, and sent many more to concentration camps. My life has been filled with evil, and I have never attempted to walk away from it. What does that way about me?" The Captain asked as tears ran down his cheeks.

"Now is the time you must ask the Lord for forgiveness for all you have done. I will pray with you." Sister Dominique stated as she made the sign of the cross.

As the captain coughed, a large amount of blood drooled down his chin. "I think it's too late for that, Sister. But I am glad you let me in, I did not want to die alone out in that storm."

Feeling a sense of pity, Sister Dominique responded, " Captain, no matter how or where we die, we all die alone in some respects with our own thoughts and fears. We must have faith."

The captain shook his head slightly, "What is faith and who is this God you keep talking about? What do I say to him? Where will I meet him? I have never thought he was real, now you say to pray to him. How do I do that, how can this God hear me?"

Sister Dominique smiled at the Captain as she brushed some mud from his face. "Just ask for forgiveness and God will hear you, believe me Captain, he will hear you."

"After all the wrong I have done, why will this God have pity on me. Please tell me I do not understand. I am scared Sister, more than I have ever been before in my life, I do not want to die like this, please tell me what to do. What shall become of me?" Slowly the captain reached out his right hand as he gasped for air. Looking up at Sister Dominique with fear in his eyes he said, "Sister I do not wish to go." As he exhaled one last time, his tortured body became still.

Sister Dominique knelt down beside the captain's body, closing his eyes as she began to pray for him. When she stood up, she dragged the body into the room in the back of the building so she wouldn't have to look at it.

After spending another long night in the old chair, Sister Dominique was happy to hear the rain had stopped the following morning. The sun was breaking through the lower layer of clouds as the high-level winds were pushing the storm clouds off to the east.

Picking up the captains pistol, Sister Dominique placed it in a basket along with the box of matches, the hammer and the screwdriver. Opening the door, she walked out to the road and began walking north.

Coming to a tee in the road, Sister Dominique stared in every direction. She could not remember which turns the driver had made before ending up where they did, so she turned east and continued walking. Late in the afternoon, she could hear the sound of a vehicle coming toward her. She was not sure whether she should run for cover or take her chances and see who it was. As the old truck rounded the curve in front of her, Sister Dominique waved her hands at the driver, but he just passed her by, disappearing off to the west.

As the sun was beginning to set, Sister Dominique saw a light off in the distance on the north side of the road. Walking toward the light, she realized she had found an active farm where people lived and livestock roamed the pastures. Walking up to the house, she knocked on the door.

To her surprise, a little girl of about four or five opened the heavy wooden door. Sister Dominique smiled and said, "Is your mommy or daddy here?"

The girl screamed and ran back into the house, just as a middle aged woman arrived. Gasping, she said, "My God are you alright, Sister? Come in, please!"

For the first time, Sister Dominique looked down at her tattered habit. It was torn in many places and covered in the blood of the man she had pulled out of the truck, along with the blood from Captain Rochefort's body.

The woman's husband came walking in from the kitchen. Taking a long look at her, he said, "Were you in the truck accident on road 391?"

Nodding her head, Sister Dominique responded, "Yes, I was, I am the only survivor. My name is Sister Dominique, and I am trying to find my way back to the Abbey at Acqualagna. Can you help me?"

The man looked at the pistol in the basket and said, "We don't want any trouble, please. We will help you with whatever you want."

Removing the pistol from the basket, she handed it to the young farmer. "Here, you may have it. It may come in handy to kill rodents or other vermin. I have no need of it."

A few minutes later, the woman walked up to Sister Dominique, handing her a brown dress. "It is not exactly a religious habit, but you can have it, as yours needs to be burned. It will never come clean, and it is to torn to mend."

After Sister Dominique changed clothes and washed up, she explained about everything that had happened to her over the last forty-eight hours, and who the men in the truck were.

The following morning, the man drove Sister Dominique back to Acqualagna where everyone was happy to see her again. They took her to a new grave in the local cemetery where they had buried Paulo the day before. It broke her heart knowing her brother that had been lost for so long was now dead. But at least she would always know where he was buried.

After walking in the courtyard of the convent with Claudia for several minutes, Sister Dominique led her over to an old bench. After they were situated, Claudia said, "You have been through so much over the past few years, you need a long rest. What are your plans now that Captain Rochefort is dead.? You should be free to do as you wish without fear."

Sister Dominique shook her head. "Every time I think I have life figured out, something new jumps out in front of me that sends my life into turmoil. True, the captain is dead, but Odessa still lives on and if they want me, they will never quit looking. Actually, all I want out of life now is to find a peaceful corner of the world where I can do God's work and never have to live in fear again. But in reality, does such a place really exist?"

Claudia looked over at the rose bushes for a moment before answering. I cannot answer that question, but I pray there is. If anyone deserves it, you do."

Chapter Twenty-Two – The Past is Present

After several days in the convent, Mother Superior called Sister Dominique into her office. After they were seated, Mother Superior shook her head and smiled. "Sister, you have been through so much. I do not know if I would have had the strength to survive all you have been through. I know you have major ties to the Abbey, so if you would like to be reassigned there and begin creating a new monastic group, I can take care of that promptly."

Sister Dominique slowly stood up and walked to the large window overlooking the convent courtyard. As the rain drops splattered against the glass, Sister Dominique said, "On days like this, Commander Ossani would make us march in circles around the parade yard. He would sit on the covered porch of his office and drink iced tea as he yelled insults at us. I often wondered what kind of enjoyment he could possibly have derived from acting that way. What sense did it make?"

Mother Superior leaned back in her chair. "He was a sadist, pure and simple."

Nodding her head, Sister Dominique said, "Yes, there is no doubt about that, he was a very evil man. At times I wonder where he went, and then I am glad I have no idea. If there ever was a man I could have killed and felt no guilt, it would be Commander Ossani."

Sitting back down in the comfortable red leather chair, Sister Dominique smiled. "But back to your question, Mother Superior. The Abbey was my home for many years after I was dropped off by my father. While I was in the prison camps, all I could ever think of doing was returning to that wonderful place where I would spend the rest of my life in true peace. But now I saw my home torn up by hate and bullets once again, and my brother Paulo died there attempting to be an honest hero. Sadly, the peace of the Abbey has been destroyed, and I do not think I would like to live there anymore. In fact, I have been thinking about going back to the United States if that is possible. I think it would give me a new piece of mind that Italy can no longer do."

Surprised by Sister Dominique's response, Mother Superior said, "The United States? What would you do there? Where would you go?"

Sister Dominique smiled. "I think I would like to teach at the Catholic University in Washington D.C. I have read much about it and think it would be a good fit for me. I could teach, I could write about my war experiences, and maybe even help in the Smithsonian with war time documents. I believe I could make a difference there and it would be a good fit for me."

After some discussion, Mother Superior said she would begin the paperwork to make the transfer possible.

Three months later, Sister Dominique arrived at the Catholic University. After being assigned to her quarters, she was given a tour of the sixty-six-acre campus. She was totally excited when she learned she would be teaching Italian three days a week, and two days a week she would be working in the library and resource center, where crates of unread documents from World War Two were still waiting to be read and cataloged.

After several months of filing and categorizing documents, Sister Dominique ran across a box with a label that said "POW's New Guinea." Placing the box on a table, Sister Dominique slowly sorted through the box, creating several stacks of documents. Some files were just basic military records regarding troop movements, bombing missions and coordinated ship attacks.

But one thick file toward the bottom of the box was exactly what she was hoping to find. Documents in the file had dates and numbers regarding how many civilian and military prisoners were being held in the stockades. Another file had names of high-ranking Japanese officers that ran the camps and what happened to them after the war. Slowly, Sister Dominique read through each page looking for any information on Commander Ossani. On a document dated 3 August 1970, was a notation by a Captain King that said, "Both leads in England turned out to be unproductive."

Taking the file to Helen Straight, the head of the research department,

Sister Dominique laid out all her reasons she should be allowed to reopen the investigation regarding Commander Ossani. Miss Straight shook her head, "Sister, do you see how large that file is? There has been search after search, but it's apparent that the commander wants to remain in hiding, as he has done a very good job of it since 1945."

Sister Dominique nodded her head in agreement. "There is no doubt the commander has gone to great lengths to remain hidden. But I believe if the proper team is put together, this man can finally be brought to justice. His file of war crimes is hideous, and I watched him smile when one of his soldiers killed the two boys. Then he mercilessly behead Sister Perpetua, and followed through with orders to shoot Sister Henrietta. This man is evil and must be brought to justice!"

After a moment of serious thought, Miss Straight leaned forward from her black leather chair. "Sister, have you ever heard of a man named Reverend Henry Baker from London?"

Smiling, Sister Dominique responded. "I knew him quite well. He and his late wife were captives with us for some time in New Guinea."

Standing up and pacing the room, Miss Straight looked out the window of her office. Turning to face Sister Dominique, she said, "Reverend Baker is in the United States right now working with retired General Robert Cannon on the whereabouts of Commander Ossani. General Cannon worked with General Krueger in command of MacArthur's Sixth Army in the Pacific. They are down in Florida at the General's home, working on the latest information. I do not know if they wish to be disturbed or have anyone else involved in their work, but I could call Reverend Baker if you would like me to."

The following day, Miss Straight walked into the archive office handing Sister Dominique an airline ticket to Orlando, Florida. "Both men would be delighted to have you join their team. You leave in the morning."

Arriving in Orlando, Sister Dominique recognized Reverend Baker immediately after she claimed her luggage. They drove to a large country estate a few miles out of town, where the general and three other people were working in a large garage that had been converted into an efficient office.

Over dinner that evening, General Cannon filled Sister Dominique in on everything the group had done over the last two months. The next morning,

Sister Dominique joined the team processing documents and making notations on large maps that filled the side walls of the garage.

Late one evening, Sister Dominique was looking through photos that someone had sent to the general the day before, from all places, Washington D.C. The photos included a coffee shop where Sister Dominique and her co-workers often went first thing in the morning, and several photos of a park on the campus of the Catholic University. Taking a large magnifying glass, Sister Dominique was able to pick out a man that certainly could be the commander. The one photo that made her skin crawl the most was of an art gallery in Georgetown she enjoyed. In the photo, she saw herself with one of her co-workers having a cup of coffee, as a man resembling the commander, peered through a window as if watching their every move.

Without giving thought to the time of day, Sister Dominique called Reverend Baker and General Cannon immediately. When they arrived, Sister Dominique handed them the photos with a red circle around the face of the oriental man, and her face on the photo from the art gallery.

General Cannon looked at Sister Dominique. "This is unreal! Did you have any idea you were being followed or watched?"

Shaking her head as her hands shook, Sister Dominique replied. "You are in crowds all the time in Washington, and you only see a small percentage of the people around you on any given day. But I still cannot believe I never saw him or felt his presence."

The following day, the general and his staff moved to an office in the Pentagon where they could continue their work in safety. The photo analysis office enhanced the photos and compared them to Commander Ossani's original military ID photo. The study came back affirming that the man on both photos were one in the same. Now the team had to find out where he could be hiding in plain sight. If there is one thing Washington D.C. is known for, it is the sheer number of news photographs that are snapped in any one given day. Over the next week, the team sorted through thousands of photos in the Washington Post's photo archives. Late on a Friday afternoon, Henry Baker yelled out, "Got him!"

Everyone jumped from their chairs to take a look at three photos that lay on the table in front of Reverend Baker. They were stunned to clearly see

Commander Ossani standing for a group photo with a delegation from the Chinese Embassy and visiting Cuban officials.

After getting copies of the photos, Henry Baker went to find the photographer who took the photos, while the general and the balance of the team headed back to the pentagon to speak with their people on far east affairs. The woman in charge of the office identified everyone except Commander Ossani and one other oriental man. She was totally aware of who the two men from Cuba were.

When Henry arrived back at the pentagon, he was smiling. "The photo was taken after several new North Korean delegates to the United Nations in New York arrived for talks. The two men he pointed at were the two the woman from far eastern affairs could not recognize.

So now it was clear that Commander Ossani was working with the North Korean government and was part of their United Nations delegation. Pulling up the files on the North Korean delegation at the pentagon, they clearly found Ossani's face with a small beard and the name Kyong Gwan underneath it.

Calling the North Korean United Nations office, Reverend Baker asked to speak with Mr. Gwan. He was told Gwan was in Washington D.C., staying at the Chinese Embassy until the following Tuesday when he was to fly to North Korea for a high-level meeting.

General Cannon called for an emergency meeting of Washington security operations. At the meeting, he laid out that Commander Ossani, a wanted war criminal, was working with the North Koreans and visiting the communist Chinese embassy, and was freely walking the streets of the city, and trailing a United States citizen. Everyone in the meeting was interested in taking down Ossani, but wanted to make sure they did not spook him prematurely and send him running.

The following day, Sister Dominique returned to her job at the university, following her old schedule as much as possible, but Ossani never appeared. The following weekend, Sister Dominique and Miss Straight decided to attend the opening of a Japanese art exhibit in a gallery in Georgetown.

Sister Dominique and Miss Straight walked slowly through the gallery, speaking with several of the artists, while keeping their eyes open, but it did not appear Ossani was anywhere to be found.

After enjoying a cup of espresso in the coffee shop, the two women began walking toward the bus that would take them back to the university. Suddenly, Ossani stepped out from between two parked buses. He pointed a pistol at Sister Dominique and said, "My life has been good, but now you are trying to destroy everything I have worked to build. I cannot allow you to do that." Turning toward Miss Straight, he continued. "Walk, both of you, toward that blue van. If you yell or cause a commotion of any kind, you will both die here in this parking lot!"

Understanding that he was going to kill them no matter what, Sister Dominique spun around and struck Ossani on the side of the head with the palm of her hand. Looking at Miss Straight, she yelled, "Run, run, get out of here!"

Dropping down to the pavement, Sister Dominique struggled to get the pistol away from the commander before he could kill her or anyone else. Just as Henry Baker and two secret service agents came running, the weapon discharged. Commander Ossani jumped to his feet, attempting to run as Sister Dominique lay on the parking lot with blood streaming from a bullet wound.

One of the secret service officers dropped to his knee, firing several shots at Ossani. Seconds later, Ossani screamed out in pain as he stumbled forward on his right leg as a large stream of blood ran down his left leg.

Henry Baker and the second secret service agent knelt down beside Sister Dominique. "Looking at the wound, the agent nodded his head. "It's what we call a through and through. The bullet went through the muscle by your shoulder and out the back side. You'll heal just fine, Sister."

Within minutes, two ambulance crews arrived, one taking Sister Dominique to a nearby hospital, while the other took Ossani to an army hospital at Fort Mead, Maryland, where he could be placed under tight security.

The students sitting across the table from Sister Dominique sat in utter shock after hearing she had been shot. After a moment, Donald finally said, "Sister, what went through your mind when you realized you had been shot?"

Shaking her head, Sister Dominique replied. "First off, I could not believe I had been stupid enough to tackle a man with a gun, and then there was that moment of fear that the wound was serious enough that I may die. You cannot believe the amount of blood that was on the pavement. But when the agent worked to control the bleeding and told me I would be alright, a sense of calm came over my entire body. I realized that I would not have to look over my shoulder the rest of my life to see if the commander was standing there, and I knew now he would have to finally pay for his sins. Although I was in tremendous pain, I felt a sense of peace."

Looking dead serious, Catherine asked, "Sister, what would you have done with the pistol had you been able to wrestle it away from the commander?"

Smiling at Catherine Sister Dominique replied. "Actually, I had not given that a whole lot of thought when I struck him. I hoped that help would arrive before it got to that point, but for the next several weeks I replayed that scenario over and over in my mind. I believed I could not shoot an unarmed man, but then this was the very soldier that beheaded Sister Perpetua right in front of me. This was the man that had killed countless innocent people and was planning to kill me. To be honest, I went through a period of self-doubt that was very real. Even in my dreams, my mind replayed the incident over and over, and sometimes I could see myself shooting him. I guess today you call it PTSD, but I can tell you, it was very real at the time. It took me months to put it all to rest."

Nodding her head, Catherine asked, "Would you say the trial gave you complete closure?"

"Closure. That is a term our society uses a lot these days. But what may be this so-called closure for one person, may just open the wounds for another. I do not know if a person actually finds this so-called closure, as much as one makes peace within their own heart. For me, I don't know what closure is. I lived through the war and went through many horrible things as you have all heard. Time has helped to dull the pain and anguish, but the memories of those that suffered and those that died are still vivid in my mind. I do not know how to close the door on them, or if in fact I want to. I do not know how to set them free and feel at peace. All I can tell you is that with prayer and by helping others, I have come to a point where I have finally accepted the fact that these memories and feelings are part of me and always will be. I cannot escape them, I cannot run from them, I can only accept my part in making those memories good or bad, because I cannot go back and change what I did or didn't do. To be totally honest, I do not understand or accept the present psychological concept of closure. I believe if you ask any World War Two veteran if they have found closure for all they went through, they will tell you no. If you ask them if revisiting the battlefield years later gave them closure, they will say no, it just gave me a new perspective. And perspective is everything, it is what keeps you sane." Sister Dominique replied knowing her experiences would live within her forever.

Taking a deep breath, Sister Dominique sat back in her chair as she once again smiled. "Surprisingly, none of you asked if getting shot hurt. I can tell you it does, it hurts like hell!"

Everyone in the room laughed as Sister Dominique nodded her head and pointed at each one of them. "I highly recommend none of you ever try it. So, let's get back to the story."

Taking a sip from the cup in front of her, she continued. "

Well, over the next few days complaints were filed by the Chinese Embassy and the North Korean Government, who refused to admit that Ossani was a Japanese war criminal. They called him a diplomat and a problem solver, but the allied nations continually referred to him as a war criminal.

Several weeks later, after being released from the hospital, Sister Dominique requested the opportunity to visit Commander Ossani, but he refused to see her.

Japanese officials made it quite clear that they did not wish to have the trial take place in Japan, so it was moved to the Hague in the Netherlands, where many high profile Nazi officials had been tried.

The trial went off with little fanfare and had very little news coverage from the world press. The night before Sister Dominique was to testify, her dreams were filled with the brutality of Commander Ossani. She could remember picking up the head of Sister Perpetua and holding it in her arms as she screamed in total horror. Several times during the night, she woke up screaming as she relived every minute of her time with the commander. By the time she crawled out of bed in the morning, her sheets and other bedding were soaked with sweat.

Arriving at the courthouse for the first time since the trial began six days earlier, Sister Dominique was taken to a small room with two chairs and a small table. About five minutes later, a tall man with graying hair walked into the room. Bowing slightly, the man began speaking with a deep British accent. "I am William T. Rathbone, barrister for the Crown's Supreme Court. I was given the job of prosecuting Commander Ossani. I have prosecuted two

Nazi war criminals and have won both cases, so you see I am experienced in this sort of matter."

Sister Dominique nodded her head. "Sir, I never had any doubts about your qualifications to try this case. I do not know where you got that idea."

Smiling, the barrister replied, "You are Italian and I am British, and there has always been a, shall I say, a lack of understanding between our nations when it comes to legal niceties."

Throwing up her hands, Sister Dominique replied. "I am a Catholic sister and do not care about the politics of England or Italy. Right now, I'm working in the United States and plan to be there for some time. Let's just try this case and put politics out of it completely if you don't mind."

"Awe, that sounds all well and good, Sister, but were you not a member of the Italian underground early on in the war? Did your group not take part in the destruction of a rail bridge, the murder of five German officers, and several less, shall I say, less dramatic episodes?" Barrister Rathbone stated boldly, as he glared at Sister Dominique. "All of that had to do with politics, and quite deadly politics if you ask me."

Leaning against the back wall of the room, Sister Dominique took a deep breath. "So, I am on trial here, is that what you are trying to say? Because if that's the case, I have not had time to hire an attorney or prepare a defense for the charges you appear to have against me. So, I am asking you to leave, as I do not wish to say a word to you that you may choose to use against me in a court of law, and furthermore, I wish to have a lawyer here with me before I speak in court.

Mr. Rathbone smiled. "No Sister, you are not on trial here, nor is anyone looking to arrest you for crimes you may or may not have been a part of when you were with the underground. I was simply trying to see how you might react if the defense attorney chooses to throw that all in your face. I don't know that he will, but there is always that possibility."

Sister Dominique nearly shook with rage when the barrister sat down at the table and opened his brief case. "If the defense attorney wishes to dig up my past then he may do so. Yes, I was involved with the underground, and probably should not have been, but I cannot change any of that today. I will not perjure myself in court if that is what you are concerned about."

Looking up at Sister Dominique, the barrister pointed toward the other chair. "Please sit, Sister, we have some things to go over before you take the stand."

About an hour later, the barrister left the room with a slight bow. Sister Dominique had to laugh. Barrister Rathbone was correct about one thing. Like most European people, she did have a certain amount of contempt for the always God righteous people that served in the British Queen's Government.

About a half hour later a bailiff came to the room to escort Sister Dominique to the courtroom. She was surprised to see Commander Ossani sitting in a glass enclosed booth with two armed guards standing by the exit door. Ossani was wearing a dark gray suit with a white shirt and a lilac-colored tie. He looked the part of any business man, but she knew what he was actually capable of.

Barrister Rathbone treated her with full respect during questioning, and several times told her to just take her time and not to rush. Everything went fine until Rathbone walked over to the evidence table and picked up the samurai sword that belonged to Ossani. After sliding the sword out of the case, he looked at Sister Dominique.

"Is this the sword the defendant used to decapitate Sister Perpetua?"

Before she could say a word, a torrent of tears gushed forward as she placed her hands over her face and wept. She could see the scene unfolding in her head, in slow motion so every detail was as clear as if it happened the day before. She could hear the sound of the blade slicing through the bone and tissue before Sister Perpetua's head rolled across the ground. She could see the decapitated body shaking, arms still holding on to the two dead boys the commander's man had shot moments earlier. Then slowly, Sister Perpetua's body rolled over and blood gushed from the arteries, soaking into the ground.

Since that horrific day, Sister Dominique had endured many dreams about the incident, but seeing the actual sword being waved through the air again right in front of her crushed her soul. No matter how hard she tried, she could not stop crying and everything around her began to spin. As she gasped for air, her eyes rolled back into her head and she slowly rolled off the chair onto the floor where she passed out.

Waking up in the hospital, Sister Dominique felt like she had been run through a washing machine and hung out to dry. Although she was alone in the room, she could feel Commander Ossani's eyes peering down at her as he threatened to cut her head off with the same sword. After all he had put her through, she was not sure she could retake the stand and testify about the horrors he created.

While Sister Dominique was in the hospital, the trial continued with other witnesses Sister Dominique knew very well. She heard that Father Renaldo, Sister Margaret and Sister Claudia had all been brought to the Netherlands to testify, and she was told they had done a very good job. When the court adjourned for the weekend, the judge ordered prosecutor Rathbone to have Sister Dominique ready on Monday or drop her from the witness list.

On Monday morning, after a long hot shower and a good breakfast, Sister Dominique was determined to finish her testimony and see Commander Ossani punished for his deeds. With Sister Dominique once more settled in the witness booth, Barrister Rathbone picked up Commander Ossani's sword, pulling it from its case.

"Sister Dominique, you testified last week that this sword belonged to the commander, is that not correct?"

Nodding her head, Sister Dominique replied, "It is."

As Barrister Rathbone laid the sword down in front of Sister Dominique, she felt like she was going to vomit as sweat poured down her forehead. A moment later, the barrister leaned forward against the witness box and asked. "Is this the weapon Commander Ossani used when he cut off Sister Perpetua's head?"

While still staring at the sword, Sister Dominique struggled to control her breathing and anger. Finally, turning toward glass box where Commander Ossani sat with a smug look on his face, waiting for her to fall apart again, she sternly replied, "Yes, it is."

Picking up the sword and raising it into the air, Barrister Rathbone said, "Did Commander Ossani not threaten to behead you with this same sword just minutes after killing Sister Perpetua?"

As the anger inside her built, Sister Dominique began to shake. After taking several large breaths of air, she replied, "That is correct."

"Please tell the court what stopped the commander from killing you," Barrister Rathbone inquired, as he placed the sword back in its sheath.

"A sergeant ran out of his office to tell him that American marines had landed at Madang and were moving toward the north. The news totally startled the commander, and actually appeared to take him off guard. He looked around in every direction for a moment, then ran as fast as he could for his office. That was the last we saw of him that day," Sister Dominique replied, hoping this would be the end of the questioning.

Barrister Rathbone stood calmly in front of the glass box where commander Commander Ossani was seated. "Tell us, Sister, why were ten prisoners killed in Camp 46."

"A flight of B-29 bombers flew over the camp. Everyone was happy to see that the allies were coming closer to Japan. Just about everyone in the camp cheered and danced around at the sight of the bombers. Angered by the outburst, the guards started shooting prisoners. When it was over, ten were dead and twenty were wounded. We tried to help the wounded but did not have the medical supplies we needed. We begged the guards to get supplies, but they all refused to help us," Sister Dominique stated, as tears ran down her face. "It was all so unnecessary, they all died for nothing."

After a moment of silence, Barrister Rathbone said, "When Camp 46 was liberated, Colonel Uchida and several soldiers sat in a circle of prisoners refusing to surrender. Why did the prisoners sit so calmly and not walk away from them?"

"The guards had planted mines all around the area where we were seated during the night. They led us out of the barracks and placed us in that circle before walking away. We were told some of them were hooked in unison, so that if one went off, more would detonate. We were all terrified to be so close to freedom and then get blown up when the war was already over."

Walking up to the box where Sister Dominique was seated, the barrister placed his hands down on the wooden ledge in front of her again, and said, "Do you mean to tell me that after the war was over, mines were being placed around prisoners?"

Nodding her head, Sister Dominique replied, "That is the sad truth, yes."

That evening the case went to the jury. They deliberated a total of eight hours before finding the commander guilty of crimes against humanity and 125 counts of murder. The next day he was sentenced to fifty years in prison.

Before heading back to Washington D.C, Sister Dominique inquired as to whether or not she could see the commander for a short visit. When the visit was approved, Sister Dominique was escorted to the his cell.

"I was amazed that you would want to visit me," the commander said, as he smoked a cigarette. "I was sure you would fly back to Washington and go on with your life and forget about me."

Sister Dominique laughed slightly. "Forget you? I don't think so. Sadly, you will always be a part of my life no matter where I go or what I do. You are a brutal man that took the lives of many innocent people for no reason. No commander, I will never forget you, but I am working hard on forgiving you. It will take time, but God says we must forgive everyone, and so in time I will also forgive you."

Walking toward the bars, Commander Ossani replied. "So, your religion teaches that your God forgives everyone if they just ask for forgiveness. Do you believe that also?"

Nodding her head, Sister Dominique simply responded, "Yes."

Laughing loudly, the commander crushed out his cigarette. "I believe your religion is a joke. If this God forgives men like me, he is a fool. If he forgives me, then there is no reason to put me in prison for fifty years. I should be free if I am forgiven by your God."

Taking a deep breath, Sister Dominique responded. "There is a difference between the laws of God and the laws of man, and I am not the one to cast judgment as to how those laws should intertwine." Turning to leave, Sister Dominique stopped and looked back at the commander. "But may God have mercy on your eternal soul."

The commander smiled as he nodded his head. "Fair enough, Sister Dominique, fair enough."

Returning to the visitor quarters, Sister Dominique ran into Father Renaldo. He was ashen gray and had lost a tremendous amount of weight since she had last seen him. After exchanging a hug, Father Renaldo led Sister Dominique toward a small lounge.

Sitting down, Sister Dominique said, "Father, have you been sick?"

Smiling, he replied. "Yes, the doctors think it had something to do with the radiation I inhaled while we were in Hiroshima, but they don't know what is going on inside of me. I actually feel better than I look, so I continue to work every day, although I believe my days are now numbered. Someday scientists will figure out everything the radiation affects, but it will be too late for me."

Sister Dominique shook her head. "It was such a shame what all happened after the Australian pilot shot down that Japanese float plane. Everything on the island was still running so smoothly. Maybe the Japanese would still have removed us from the island and set up bases there, but we will never know."

Father Renaldo nodded his head. "Yes, we will never know. But I just wanted to talk with you for a minute before my plane leaves. Sister, you were such a joy to work with, and you taught me a lot about myself. You gave me courage when I was lost, and you gave me strength when mine was gone. And more than that, you helped me realize many times just why I became a priest. Meeting you has been a blessing I will never forget, but now I must get on the bus for the airport."

Standing up, Sister Dominique and Father Renaldo hugged each other tightly. As tears ran down Sister Dominique's face, she watched the valiant priest walk out the door with several other passengers. In her heart, she knew she would never see Father Renaldo again.

After returning to work at the university, Sister Dominique began feeling more relaxed, realizing she had successfully closed the door on Commander Ossani. What happened to him in prison would have nothing to do with her.

However, late one evening as Sister Dominique sat alone in the records office sorting through some documents, one of the security guards approached her. "Sister, there is a Henry Baker outside that says he is a friend of yours, and that he had worked here for a while. Can we let him in?"

Smiling at the officer, she responded, "Indeed, you can. I know him well."

As Henry walked into the document room, Sister Dominique walked over to him and gave him a big hug. "After we brought Ossani to justice, I heard you quit. I always enjoyed working with you."

Henry smiled as he sat down in a large desk chair near where Sister Dominique was working. After looking up at the ceiling for a moment, he said, "Capturing the commander brought everything back to life. While I've been away, I've been trying to seek peace for killing my wife. I know she would have allowed the Japanese to kill Lieutenant Freeborn, when he had done nothing wrong. But what gave me the right to play God?"

Sister Dominique sat down and wondered how she could answer that question. She knew what her religious training had taught her about murder, and she fully understood why Mr. Baker had committed the act, but the words she needed to console the hurting man right now totally escaped her.

"Your silence speaks volumes, Sister. I know you have not condemned me, but still you know what I did was wrong. Tell me, how do I find peace, because absolution in confession with a priest will not take away the grief, anger or depression that is tormenting me. Evelyn was a good person in most respects and she always meant well, and I believe we did a lot of good at our mission. But poor Evelyn had an angry streak that ran through her that was incurable, even to God. She cared only about herself no matter the situation. I knew when we came out there, she would suffer some type of tragedy, but I never dreamed it would be at my hands."

After hearing everything Henry had to say, Sister Dominique replied. "There is no doubt in my mind you are sorry for what you have done, and I truly believe you need forgiveness much greater than any that I can offer you. If you like, I could walk you over to the church where Father Donovan is on duty tonight. He is a very compassionate and understanding man and priest. I think you should speak with him. Would you like to walk with me, Henry?"

"Yes, I would like to meet this Father Donovan," Henry replied, as he stood up.

They had walked to within fifty yards of the church when Henry stopped. "No, I can't do this tonight. Maybe another time, but not tonight."

Sister Dominique was about to speak when Henry walked toward the edge of the road, hailed a cab and left without saying another word.

The following morning as Sister Dominique finished her Italian class she noticed two men in suits standing outside her classroom. After her last student left, she motioned for the men to enter.

Feeling something was terribly wrong, Sister Dominique sat down behind her desk and said, "Can I help you, gentlemen?"

The older of the two men took out a leather folder from his pocket and said, "I am Sergeant Pemmill from the Washington Metro Police Department, and this is my partner, Detective Brown. We are looking into what appears to be a mugging gone bad last night near the Lincoln Memorial. Two young thugs tried to rob a couple at gun point that were out for a late-night walk with their dog. A Mr. Henry Baker appeared out of nowhere and knocked one of the attackers to the ground. He then grabbed the second man and fought over the gun, while yelling at the couple to run. Mr. Baker was hit in the head with the pistol and fell to the ground, where the punk fired two rounds into his head. The couple saw a police car, told the officers what was happening, and they arrived just as the shooting ended. Regrettably, it was too late for Mr. Baker, and he died at the scene. In his jacket pocket we found his billfold and identification papers, along with a small bible and your business card. What can you tell us about Mr. Baker? Did you see him last night?"

As tears ran down her cheeks, Sister Dominique said, "Yes, that would have been Henry, no doubt in my mind." After pouring each of them a cup of coffee, she explained everything that had happened with Henry since they were in the camp in New Guinea."

Detective Brown shook his head. "Yeah, how do you live with that? But it appears to me he went out of his way to make up for it last night." Finishing their coffee, the detectives stood up. We have notified his daughter and she is on her way here to make proper identification and claim his remains. Would you like to speak with her when she gets here? Now that you have told us the entire story, I'm guessing she may want to talk to you about all that happened between her parents."

After a moment of thought, Sister Dominique replied, "If she wishes to speak with me, I'll certainly meet with her."

The next afternoon, Detective Brown brought Sister Dominique to the police station. As they walked toward an interview room, the detective said, "She knows nothing about her mother's death. She is really confused right now and wants answers, but I don't think what you have to tell her are the answers she is looking for."

Sister Dominique stopped and leaned back against the wall. Looking at Detective Brown, she said, "That young lady is suffering right now and I do not intend to pile hurt upon hurt. She heard from you that her father died a hero, and we certainly don't need to take that from her."

Stepping into the room with Henry Baker's daughter, Sister Dominique walked over and gave the woman a gentle hug. "My name is Sister Dominique. What is your name?"

As the woman prepared to sit down, she said, "Olivia, Olivia Baker. I was told you knew my parents when they were in the Solomon Islands. What can you tell me about them? About what happened to my mother?"

Sister Dominique nodded her head, "Yes, I knew your parents, but it was after they were removed from the Solomon's, as I was. They were working out of a mission quite a distance from the island of Nusa Simbo where I was working. Once the Japanese began collecting every person of non-Japanese descent from the islands, we were shipped off to many different camps. Sometimes during transfers, we would stay together, other times we were split up, never to see each other again. I was in several Japanese prisoner camps with your parents, and got to know them fairly well, about as well as anyone could under those circumstances."

Olivia leaned forward and said, "When the war was over and father began helping people in Japan, he wrote me a letter saying that mother had passed sometime back while they were in New Guinea. He never told me how she died, and I was looking forward to talking to him about it someday, but now that will never happen."

"Many people died in those awful camps. From typhus, dysentery, yellow fever, jungle fever, rat bites and from the brutality of the guards. Your parents were with a group of people that were attempting to escape from a camp when bombers destroyed the fence. Everyone was running trying to find the best place to hide as bullets flew in every direction. People were screaming, guards were yelling, exploding hand grenades were sending shards of shrapnel through the air. People were falling, some of them badly hurt, some of them dead. I saw your mother and father on the ground for a few moments, then your father got up, stumbled forward and continued running, until he was recaptured like the rest of us. A burial detail was assigned to bury all the dead near the jungle in a common grave."

Olivia was quiet for a moment before looking up at Sister Dominique. "My mother loved my father very much and helped him in his ministry where she could, but in many ways was not happy with her life. She wanted to do something grand, something she could tell the world about, but that was not dad's way. It was her idea to take up a mission in the Solomon Islands. There were many arguments about it before father gave in. I am all too sure their life in the jungles of the South Pacific was not all happy and exhilarating. I was not sure what you could tell me about mother's passing, but you have given me enough to know that they were together in a hopeless situation when it happened, and that means a lot to me."

Sister Dominique smiled. "Now, go and make arrangements for your father's funeral. It does not matter where your mother is buried, they are still together."

Standing up from her chair, Olivia shook hands with Sister Dominique. "You have done me a wonderful service, and I will always be proud of my parents for what they attempted to do."

As Olivia left, Detective Brown walked into the room. Looking down at Sister Dominique, he said, "I was listening through the intercom system. You handled that well, better than I could have. She will be at peace now. Thank you."

Sister Dominique stood up and looked at Detective Brown. "Although I can deal with what I told her, I will be having a long conversation with God about it. But yes, she will be at peace and that's what matters in the long run."

After a moment of silence, Sister Dominique added, "Unless a person experienced the horror we were subjected to they simply cannot understand. Evelyn Baker was a scared and fearful woman, and she was deteriorating a little more each day. It may well be possible that Henry saved her in ways we will never understand."

Chapter Twenty-Three – Italy Once More

With the completion of the war documents project, Sister Dominique once more asked to be transferred back to the Abbazia di San Vincenzo in Italy. Arriving back at the Abbey that was still under reconstruction, Sister Dominique once more settled into the small room she had first lived in back when she was five years old. She was sorry to hear that Sister Claudia had moved permanently to Rome, but she enjoyed being back with Sister Margaret and Sister Josephine.

Although the Abbey was once more beginning to look as it had when Sister Dominique left for the Pacific, the smell of paint and new construction materials lingered throughout the entire structure. The room she hated the most was the library. She could still see Paulo's body lying on the floor in a pool of blood.

The narrow tunnel she had used as a child to escape was now filled in, and Brother John's words and etchings were lost to history. No matter how much work had been completed to bring the Abbey back to life, there were still scars from bullets and shrapnel on the marble staircase, and stone pillars in the foyer that could never be repaired.

Obviously, much of the centuries-old art pieces could never be replaced, as the German's had hidden them or sold them to wealthy collectors. However, Sister Dominique was determined to find a way to help bring the art back to the Abbey where it belonged.

About sixth months after arriving at the monastery, an old man driving a rusted-out pickup arrived at the front door of the Abbey. Looking curiously at Sister Josephine, he said, "Is there anyone here that was here when the

German's took over? I have something that needs to be identified that may have come from here.

When Sister Dominique and Mother Superior walked into the foyer, the man placed a wooden box on top of a table. Opening the box, he removed a chalice that was wrapped in cloth. Handing it to Mother Superior, he said, "Does this belong to the Abbey?"

Turning the chalice over and over in her hands, she looked toward Sister Dominique while pointing at the inscription on the bottom of the vessel. Taking the gold chalice in her hand, Sister Dominique replied, "Yes, it belonged to a Franciscan Monk named St. Humillis of Bisignano that died in 1637. It had been locked in the chapel sacristy with many other chalices and relics. Where did you find it? Do you have more artifacts?"

The man shook his head. "I found it in an old cave on my property. Someone had blown the entrance closed during the war. My son and I decided to reopen it and see what might be sitting in the cave. There was a German truck with two bodies in it, some tools, and this box sitting against the wall of the cave. Some papers in the truck mentioned the Abbey, so we thought it might have been looted from here. We removed the box before we notified the officials of what was in the cave. It is home now, and for that I am glad." The sisters hugged the old man and fed him a nice lunch before he left.

Late that evening, as Sister Dominique sat in the chapel holding the chalice, she heard a scraping noise behind her. Turning to see who was there, she was surprised to see no one. A few moments later she heard the same sound coming from the far rear corner of the chapel. Standing up, she said, "Who's there, what do you want?"

In the reflection of the candles, she could see an old hunched over man standing near a votive candle rack. Slowly walking toward the man, she said, "Who are you, how did you get in here?"

Smiling, the old man slowly sat down on the last pew. Sister, you ask questions you already have answers for, why is that?"

Confused by his reply, Sister Dominique said, "I do not know what you are talking about. Now, who are you and where did you come from?"

The man looked up at the ceiling and said, "It's good to be free and back where I belong. You hold the truth in your hands."

Looking down at her hands, Sister Dominique began to shake. "You are…"

"Yes Sister, I am Humillis of Bisignano. I have lived in this monastery with my chalice since it was delivered here by my friends. Will you be placing my chalice back in the sacristy?"

Nodding her head, Sister Dominique replied. "That is where I was going when I decided to sit down and look it over one more time."

"Ah, that is a good thing, we were quite comfortable there," the old man replied, as he looked down at the floor. There are others that are still missing. They were placed on trucks and driven to Germany and then sold or buried as plunder, and many may never be found." Sister Dominique, you must find them, you must look and bring them home."

Slowly, the figure of the man began to fade away until he was gone. Walking into the sacristy, Sister Dominique opened the reliquary and placed the chalice back where it had been. After locking the door, she heard the voice of the old man echo throughout the chapel. "You must look for them!"

The following morning, seeing Mother Superior standing by a window overlooking the courtyard, Sister Dominique knocked on the door frame of her office. Before she could say a word, Mother Superior turned to face her. "Come in, Sister Dominique, I believe I know why you are here. Last night I heard you talking in the chapel with an old man. I was about to come in, but the door would not open, so I thought I would go around to the side door near the kitchen. When I arrived, there was an old man in tattered clothing leaning against the wall. He stared at me for a moment before saying. "She must try, let her go." He then disappeared. I have never had an experience like that in my life. Tell me, what are you to do?"

"Humillis told me to go out and find the missing relics from the Abbey, but I haven't a clue where I would begin to look," Sister Dominique replied, as she leaned up against the wall.

"Take Sister Margaret and go look wherever you think they could be, start in Berlin. Please bring them back," Mother Superior replied, as she placed her hands upon Sister Dominique's shoulders.

Several days later, Sister Dominique and Sister Margaret boarded a train for Bonn, Germany. They spoke with several people regarding the artifacts taken from the Abbey. Each person gave them a long and complicated answer that in the end led nowhere. It was clear that either no one actually knew, or they possibly possessed the items and were not willing to release them.

Nearly six weeks into the search and still no luck, Sister Dominique was considering giving up the search and calling it quits. However, that evening as she and Sister Margaret sat outside a small hofbrau in Frankfurt, an old man approached their table. "Sisters, may I join you? I know what you are looking for, and you will not find it here. What you are looking for could kill you, and no one will care."

Motioning toward a chair, Sister Dominique replied, "Please sit and tell us more."

After ordering a dark beer, the man said, "Most of what was taken from your Abbey was sold off to collectors for cash. Most gold and silver items were melted down into bullion bars and sent back to Italy in 1945 and 1946 to help fund the escape of high-level Nazi officials. I doubt any of that exists anymore. If it does, it would belong to Odessa and be in vaults in South America with the rest of their riches."

Sister Dominique looked at the old man. "How do you know all this, and why should we believe you?"

The old man smiled, "It's good to be wary of strangers, especially in a situation such as this. My name is Trach, Stefan Trach. I was convicted of war crimes and spent eight years in Spandau Prison. You can easily verify that. I was in the Abbey when Goering cleaned it out, and helped melt down the gold and silver in a workshop in Berlin. The Third Reich had their own gemologist that examined each chalice to assure all precious gems and stones were removed before they were melted. It was such a shame, but Goering had more chalices than one man could ever enjoy. We photographed the art work and logged each piece before re-casing them. Some of the cases went to caves in Austria, some went to three caves in Bavaria. Regrettably, two trucks were incinerated by allied bombers near Bonn. In 1966, I went to the caves in Austria and found them to be empty. Two of the caves in Bavaria were caved in during bombing raids. When they were re-opened by Goering, whatever was damaged was burned, and the rest was sent to the third cave that was still intact. Early in 1945, Goering conducted an auction and sold everything from the third cave for escape cash, which we know today he never had the chance to use.

One of the biggest buyers was an American that was wintering in Grindelwald, Switzerland at the time. The man spent millions of American dollars for many of the paintings that came from your Abbey. As you can suspect, no transaction records of the sales were kept. But I do know a man here in Germany that had six paintings before he passed away. I think his family may still own them. I will tell you where the people live, and who the American is, but I will not be involved more than that."

Sister Dominique looked coldly at the man. "Tell me, why are you getting involved at all?"

"I am an old man, Sister. I am looking for some type of redemption for what I did to help the Nazi bastards. When I heard you were here in Frankfort poking around and getting nowhere, I felt it was my duty to step forward and finally do something right. My wife died about a year ago and always asked me to repent and give back what was taken. She would be proud that I am helping you."

After retrieving the names of the two men, Sister Dominique went to the German government and asked for their help. At first, they refused, stating they had broken down too many doors over the years to find nothing, and they did not trust Stefan Trach.

Traveling to NATO Headquarters in Brussels, Belgium, the sisters explained the entire story to General Walter Amdahl in Supreme Headquarters Allied Powers in Europe. He had a detail of men in his agency that still searched for Nazi treasure. He was able to confirm much of what Trach had told them, but was not aware of the clandestine auction. However, several other sources had testified that many artifacts had in fact disappeared through Switzerland. After approaching several legal officers and judges in the Headquarters Operation, General Amdahl was given a warrant to search the estate of former German General Kurt Kaufman.

The large estate was settled in a valley near the Bavarian National Forest. Ernst Kaufman, the General's son, was very unhappy regarding the intrusion, and even more unhappy when art work began disappearing from the walls of the mansion. In all, fifteen paintings and two sculptures were removed from the house. Young Kaufman demanded they be reimbursed for the pieces, but was silenced when General Amdahl's team told him he and his mother could still be tried for war crimes if they chose to be a problem.

After each item was inspected and prepared for shipping, Sister Dominique and Sister Margaret escorted the art work back to the Abbey. It was a joyous day for the sisters when the art work arrived. Everything was carefully rehung exactly where it had been prior to 1943. The value of the recovered art was estimated at slightly more than five million dollars. Sister Dominique knew that getting permission to chase down the missing art work in the United States was going to be much more of a problem.

Although the United States Attorney General's office gave their permission, the state of New York was not ready to allow the mansion of a prominent businessman and supporter of the Governor to be raided.

The third night the sisters and their associates from Supreme Headquarters Allied Powers in Europe were settled into their rooms for the night, their van was fire bombed. That just told Sister Dominique that they were on the right track. The following day as they were waiting for a judge's ruling, Sister Dominique and Sister Margaret went for a walk in Brighton Park with a Corporal Erika Anderson from the Brussels office. They had walked about a mile when several men wearing dark suits approached them. One of the men looked directly at Sister Dominique. "Sister, the war has been over for a long time, there is no reason to hassle my client this way. Go back to Italy and be happy with your life."

"Your so-called client was dealing with the Nazi's and providing them money before the war was over. That means he can be tried as a war criminal. I don't care what happens to him, we just want the art work back," Sister Dominique stated boldly, as she glared at the Odessa agent.

Shaking his head, the man replied. "It will never happen. Not now or twenty years from now. My client purchased art work from an auction and had no dealings with Goering or any other Nazi. You go after my client and it will cost you dearly!"

As Sister Dominique took Sister Margaret by the arm to begin walking around the men, the smaller man of the three, pulled out his pistol. Before he could say a word, Corporal Anderson pulled a pistol from the waistband of her pants and fired one shot.

The man with the gun let out a scream as blood poured from his right wrist. Corporal Anderson yelled, "Get on your knees and do it now, the next shot won't be so well placed." Reaching for a two-way radio under her jacket, she called for back up from the local Coast Guard Station Security Team located nearby.

The man that had done all the speaking looked angrily toward Corporal Anderson. "Do you really think that was necessary? What do you think you accomplished by shooting my security agent?"

Continuing to point her weapon in the direction of the three men, she replied. "Damn straight it was necessary, and my superiors will have zero problems with it. That's all that matters!"

Two days later, a judge in the Second Judicial District authorized legal authorities to proceed with a search warrant of the mansion belonging to one Alphonse Moeller on Long Island.

When the caravan of federal vehicles pulled up to the front of the mansion, it was clear to see a large bonfire had been started on the beach behind the house. Running from the car, Sister Dominique yelled, "No, no, stop them, they're burning the paintings!"

She was just in time to see a five by six-foot painting that had hung on the third floor being tossed into the fire. The centuries old canvas immediately burst into flames as the wooden frame collapsed into the raging fire. Lying next to the fire were three hand carved busts that had been smashed with a heavy mall. As tears rolled down her face, she turned toward Mr. Moeller. "Tell me why? Why would you do such a horrible thing? Do you not realize much of that art work was several hundred years old?"

"Ja, I understand all that, Sister. But they were mine. I paid for them, and you were going to take away the art work that I so enjoyed without giving me a penny. They were mine to do as I pleased with, not yours, and I did what I had to do. Now, go ahead, search the house. You will see there is nothing left from the monastery," Alphonse Moeller replied, as tears rolled down his craggy wind worn face.

Falling to her knees, Sister Dominique wept as she held pieces of the smashed busts in her hands. Looking up at Mr. Moeller, she said, "Did you not know some of these were done by the masters of the Renaissance period, did you not realize they were priceless?"

"Ja, Ja, I understood all of that. But as Goering told me when I bought them, now everyone that comes to my home will be able to enjoy the richness of this art work, they will not be locked up in some old dusty monastery where no one can enjoy them. And I did as Goering said, I showed them to everyone that came to visit, they were loved by everyone. Now they will no longer be locked away, I made sure of that!" Moeller replied, with a smirk on his face.

Moments later, an FBI Agent walked up to Moeller. "Sir, I am placing you under arrest for the purchase and destruction of illegally obtained Nazi treasures."

Before the agent could walk him away, Moeller called out, "Please stop!"

Looking over at Sister Dominique and Sister Margaret he said. "Go back to your monastery and mourn for your lost art work. Tell your Mother Superior that in the end, Herman Goering won this battle for the Third Reich."

Walking up to Moeller, Sister Dominique said. "It's people like you that will never allow that war to be over. I do not understand the hatred that exists in your hearts."

Laughing, Moeller shook his head. "What I believe in or what I do is not for you to understand. But know there are many more like me around the world that will be more than happy to rekindle the work of the Third Reich, and there is nothing anyone like you can do to stop it. A few burned paintings are nothing to us, that is the difference between you and us."

Sister Margaret looked angrily at Moeller. "I hope you rot in prison so you can never again spread your vile hatred."

Laughing once again, Moeller replied "Ja Sister, I may die in prison as I am a sick old man. But I will die happy knowing I helped the Third Reich in my own way. That is more priceless to me than all the art work I destroyed."

It made Sister Dominique physically sick as she listened to Moeller continue laughing as several FBI agents walked him to the waiting car.

Returning to the Abbey, the sisters explained everything that happened to the rest of the congregation. Sister Dominique decided she was finished chasing down stolen art work, after dealing face to face with an ardent Nazi.

Six months later, Sister Dominique read a news story stating Moeller was sentenced to three years in prison, with a chance for parole after completing two years of the sentence. After tossing the news magazine to the floor, Sister Dominique felt she could hear the arrogant Nazi laughing all the way to his prison cell.

With the mission to find the missing art work completed, Sister Margaret wanted nothing more than to return to the Abbey in Italy, however, Sister Dominique did not have the same desires. After Sister Margaret departed New York, Sister Dominique applied for an open position at a Canisius College in Buffalo, teaching Italian and working in the history department.

Nearly a year passed before she was contacted by a man named David Katsman. He had also been on the Japanese transport *Koshiro Maru*, when it was sunk by the American submarine. He inquired three times as to whether or not Sister Dominique would tell her story regarding the sinking, but each time she flatly turned him down. That was one part of her life in the Pacific she did not wish to relive.

Frustrated by the refusals, Mr. Katsman traveled to Canisius College with the hopes of convincing Sister Dominique to tell her story. At first, Sister Dominique refused to see Katsman when she was told of his arrival, but a professor in the history department wanted to hear the entire story and asked Sister Dominique to speak with him.

Walking into an interview room in the library, Katsman stood up from the table to shake hands with Sister Dominique and Professor Friedmann. Taking a deep breath, Katsman said, "Sister, I apologize for pushing myself onto you, but there is no way I can complete my effort to tell the whole story of that awful night without speaking with you. So please forgive me."

Professor Friedmann smiled. "Oh, she forgives you and is ready to cooperate with your manuscript any way she can."

Sister Dominique laughed as she lightly punched the professor in the shoulder. "I told you it was fine if you listened in, I did not say you could speak for me."

"I am speaking for history, Sister, and you were part of it. The world needs to know all that happened that night and who was responsible. So now you must speak," Professor Friedmann stated as he smiled kindly at Sister Dominique.

Nodding her head, Sister Dominique smiled, "Professor, somehow you always manage to get in the last word, but you are the best history professor I have ever met. So, I am here and I will tell what happened. Just please be patient as this is not easy to talk about." Before saying any more, Sister Dominique rolled up her left sleeve, uncovering the terrible scars from the shark attack. "I was lucky, the men in the raft saved me from being pulled under by the creature. I still have nightmares about the size of that shark and the pain it's razor-sharp teeth inflicted on my body. The thought of being eaten alive by one of God's creations still terrifies me. No one can ever imagine what goes through your mind at a moment like that."

After being seated, Mr. Katsman turned on his recorder and took short hand notes to capture every word of Sister Dominique's amazing story. He worked his way down a well prepared list of questions. When he asked Sister Dominique if she had spoken to Commander Sakurai, skipper of the transport, she shook her head.

"I saw him twice. First, when we left Nusa Simbo. He was standing on a platform above the well of the ship, yelling at the soldiers to hurry up with the loading. The second time I saw him was when I was in the water. He was standing on the floor of one of the life boats, watching the passengers struggling in the water. He turned his back, sat down on a bench and never looked back despite all the screaming. He was a coward and an evil man," Sister Dominique replied, as tears ran down her face. "I still don't understand how a man could turn away and do nothing to help as innocent women and children were being torn apart by ravenous sharks. How can a person live with themselves after that?"

After nearly two full days of testimony, along with additional question and answer sessions, Mr. Katsman said, "Now I know how you feel about the incident and Commander Sakurai. But I need to ask you a question. How would you feel about meeting him?"

Sister Dominique sat frozen in place as she stared at Mr. Katsman for a moment. "I don't know if I can, the thought of seeing him makes my stomach ache. Where is he?"

"Surprisingly, not far from here, he is in a nursing home in Rochester. He was never tried for his actions that night, so he lived freely in Japan and San Diego. When his daughter took a job in Rochester, she had him brought to a nursing home nearby. He is in poor health but his mind is still very active and clear. I asked him last week if he would like to see you and he said yes. So, now it's up to you. I will drive you and the professor there and make all the arrangements if you decide to go."

The professor did not say a word, he just looked at Sister Dominique and nodded his head. After a moment of thought, Sister Dominique agreed to the visit.

Two weeks later, Sister Dominique stood outside Commander Sakuri's bedroom door. One part of her wanted to walk in the room and scream at him for what he had allowed to happen, and the other part of her hoped for a quiet conversation ending with a solemn apology and a plea for forgiveness.

Taking a deep breath, Sister Dominique pushed open the door and stepped inside. Instead of seeing the tall Japanese officer with a stern condemning look on his face, she found a frail old man that could barely pick up a glass of water while lying in bed.

Bowing his head slightly he said. "Welcome, Sister Dominique. I personally do not remember you, as I do not remember anyone from that ship. My job was to transport you, not to get to know you, and I failed in that respect. My ship was going down and I had no help nearby to save all of you. It was a terrible experience for everyone involved. I shall never forgive myself for what happened to all of you. You must remember, in that war there were many times we left American survivors and our own men behind to fend for themselves in shark filled waters in order to save our ships. It was nothing we liked to do, but something we had to do. No officer, regardless of rank, truly accepted those orders, but we did what was expected of a loyal officer of the Imperial Japanese Navy." The commander stated as he looked up at Sister Dominique with the same cold eyes she had seen the night of the attack.

It became very clear there was not going to be any heart felt apology or act of contrition from this aging officer. He was still a staunch believer in the ways of the Japanese warrior code and that was not going to change by a visit from anyone.

No longer wishing to share her story, or hear anything else the arrogant officer had to say, Sister Dominique took a step back and bowed slightly. "Commander, in these few minutes we have been together it's clear we have totally different points of view as to what happened with the *Koshiro Maru*. There is no doubt in my mind that we will never agree to anything about that night. I give Mr. Katsman credit for trying to find the truth of what all happened that night, but I leave here now giving you my contempt for your arrogance and stalwart belief in the Bushido code. May God have mercy on your soul!"

Before another word could be said, Sister Dominique left the room and walked back out to the car. Arriving back at the convent, she said goodbye to Mr. Katsman, telling him she did not wish to be involved in any more of his research. It may have seemed petty to some sisters in the convent, but Sister Dominique no longer wanted to live so close to the man that had left her out in the ocean to die. He displayed no remorse and probably would do the same thing today. It ate away at her until one day she read a memo stating the convent in St. Joseph, Minnesota was once more looking for a full time Italian teacher. She remembered how much she had enjoyed life there, so she asked to be reassigned.

Mother Superior of the Buffalo convent was not totally happy with Sister Dominique's reasons for wanting to leave, but in the end agreed to the transfer, but telling Sister Dominique she herself would most likely spend the rest of her years as a sister right there, because as far as she was concerned, the war was long over and people needed to forgive, forget and move on.

Two weeks later, Sister Dominique boarded a train for Minnesota and never looked back.

Chapter Twenty-Four – Lt. Charles Freeborn

Two months after arriving in the hospital in Melbourne, Australia, Lieutenant Freeborn was declared fit to return to active duty. Several days later he walked up the gangplank of the heavy cruiser U.S.S. Birmingham that was preparing to sail for Pearl Harbor. He knew it would be a long fifteen-day cruise, but there were no carriers scheduled to dock in Melbourne for nearly six weeks. The trip to Pearl Harbor went without any major incidents and the weather was acceptable. It gave the lieutenant added time to get his body back in shape to deal with the rigors of aerial combat.

Sailing into Pearl Harbor, Lieutenant Freeborn observed two carriers tied up to the 1010 dock. They were the fleet carrier U.S.S. Intrepid, and the light carrier U.S.S. Princeton. Both ships had been sent to the harbor to repair battle damage, and were now preparing to rejoin the fleet on its march across the Pacific. The long steel deck of the Intrepid was an inviting site. It was exactly the home he had been looking for since he was shot down. But he would gladly take the small Princeton before being assigned to an island post. In the end, a carrier was a carrier and he was ready to get back to war.

Entering the Bureau of Personnel, the lieutenant had a mountain of paperwork to fill out as he had been listed as missing in action for so long. After he had all of the paperwork squared away, he was sent to see the bases top flight surgeon.

Dr. Warner looked over all the paperwork from Melbourne and nodded his head. "Well lieutenant, it appears to me you have done your share for the war effort. I think we'll just send you back home for a visit with your family, and then you can test fly new aircraft coming off the production lines. How does that sound to you?"

"That sounds like hell, Doctor. I want to climb into the cockpit of a fighter and get back into this damn war," Lieutenant Freeborn replied angrily.

While flipping through the pages of his file, Dr. Warner smiled. "You have already flown twenty-nine sorties, shot down three Japanese aircraft, and been given an assist in sinking one light Japanese destroyer. You hid out with missionaries and escaped from a prisoner camp. I really think you have done your share, son. Why push your luck, we have many new pilots coming up that haven't had a chance to accomplish what you have."

Feeling sick, Lieutenant Freeborn replied. "Sir, I don't want to go back home. I want to finish doing my part for the war effort. My younger brother is over in Europe fighting the Nazi's, and my sister is a nurse on a hospital ship. You just can't send me home to test new planes, sir. Please give me a break and let me get back into the war."

Closing the file, Doctor Warner removed his glasses. "Every time I come up against a pilot like you that has a remarkable war record and wants to get back in the fight so badly, I get scared. I know by signing on the dotted line I could be sending you to your death. Early on in the war I didn't have much choice, as we didn't have the number of pilots we do now. So today I try and let you guys that have earned veteran status get the hell out of here, and all I get is arguments."

Smiling, Lieutenant Freeborn replied, "That's because we know we have what it takes to finish this war, and keep some of those young guys from getting their asses blown off out there."

Laughing, Doctor Warner picked up his pen. After signing the forms, he looked at Lieutenant Freeborn. "This signature says you are medically ready to return to combat. Now you'll have to prove it to a fitness board. Be at Ford Island by 0830hrs. tomorrow morning.

With his papers in hand, Lieutenant Freeborn arrived by ferry on Ford Island at 0810hrs. After reporting in to the fitness office he and two other pilots were taken out to the flight line where ten F4U Corsair fighters sat ready to go. After completing a ground inspection, the pilots crawled into their assigned planes. To Lieutenant Freeborn, it was as if he had never left the cockpit. He remembered where every switch was and how to adjust his fuel mixture for the different altitudes he could be flying at. He was back home.

Roaring down the runway, Lieutenant Freeborn pulled back on the stick, taking his corsair into the clear cool morning air. He followed the directions he was given by the tower, and completed each assignment as if he had never been shot down. He enjoyed looking down at the ships moving back and forth outside Pearl Harbor as he glided along at three thousand feet.

Bringing his aircraft up to six thousand feet, he flew towards a naval tugboat pulling a target rack. When he was given permission to attack, he dropped down the nose of his corsair and dove toward the rack. When he had the rack in his sights, he pushed the button on the stick that engaged the six fifty-caliber machine guns. Instantly, the plane shuddered as the heavy machine guns threw their bullets toward the target rack. Finishing his run, Lieutenant Freeborn climbed back to sixty-five hundred feet and rolled the plane over on its side. Diving at a high rate of speed, once again he bore down on the target rack that was now being pulled in a zigzag pattern by the tug. After making a slight adjustment, the six machine guns roared to life once more. From this angle, he could see his bullets striking the target and he was hitting it perfectly.

With all his ammunition expended, Lieutenant Freeborn set his corsair down gently on Ford Island, idling up to the flight line. As he climbed down from the cockpit, one of the training officers walked up to him. "Well done, Lieutenant, you scored an eighty-nine on the target rack. We were especially interested in your second attack. Who taught you to roll the plane over like that and drop the nose down for a second run so quickly?"

Removing his gloves, Lieutenant Freeborn replied, "Captain Clark Stevens taught me that. Sorry to say he was killed when his corsair was hit by a flak burst over Guadalcanal. He was a hell of a pilot."

The officer shook his head. "That was tough, how did you get shot down, Lieutenant?"

"I wasn't shot down. I started a machine gun attack from about four thousand feet, when I lost all my oil pressure and my engine seized. Before that happened, the Japs on that patrol boat didn't even see my coming. I jumped off the port wing at about 1600ft and landed in the jungle. I was rescued by some missionaries. From there it's a long story.

The officer laughed as he scribbled his name on the paperwork. "Head over to the bureau of personnel to be assigned. Both carriers are still looking for pilots."

Lieutenant Freeborn was totally hoping he could be assigned to the *Intrepid*, as it had seen a lot of action and he was sure Admiral Halsey would use her whenever possible.

However, that was not to be the case. The captain at the assignment desk made it clear that the *Intrepid* was only taking pilots that had seen recent action and were prepared for heavy combat, so Lieutenant Freeborn would be assigned to the *Princeton*.

There were no aircraft on the *Princeton* when the lieutenant arrived. All the planes were sitting at either Ford Island or Hickam Field. They would be flown onto the ship once it cleared the harbor and was underway. Lieutenant Freeborn was stunned to find that a friend of his from the *Enterprise* was going to be his squadron commander. Commander Ustice Markham was a graduate of Annapolis and a fourth-generation naval man in his family. He was aiming for a top position like his grandfather, Admiral Ustice P. Markham, that had served in the Spanish American War. There was no one better at spit and polish than Ustice.

After listening to what Lieutenant Freeborn had been through after jumping from his disabled aircraft, Ustice said, "I have not found a man in this squadron I would rather have be my XO. You have three kills and a lot of other experience. I know the captain will allow your assignment if you agree to it."

Suddenly, Lieutenant Freeborn realized his assignment to the *Princeton* was exactly what his career needed.

The day the carriers sailed from Pearl Harbor, Lieutenant Freeborn and half of third squadron were taken by bus to Ford Island to pick up their planes. Commander Markham took the rest of third squadron to Hickam Field where their aircraft awaited them.

The newer F6F Hellcat fighters were a sturdy aircraft with a 2000 horsepower radial engine capable of speeds exceeding 375mph. It had six machine guns like the Corsair, but it also had three air to ground rockets on each wing that were proving to be a devastating weapon. In order to keep the pilots safer, the F6F included an armor-plated seat that kept the pilot from getting shot in the back during dog fights. It was the first American carrier-based fighter the Japanese pilots came to fear.

As Lieutenant Freeborn took to the air, he fell in love with his Hellcat immediately. It handled better than his old Corsair and felt much more solid. He was anxious to take his squadron up against the Japanese as soon as possible.

The two carriers joined up with a massive task force heading west across the Pacific. From the air it was impressive to see how far the convoy of ships were spread out across the ocean.

Nearing Midway Island, the task force both the *Princeton* and *Intrepid* were assigned to turned off toward the southwest. The Princeton was patrolling the far-left side of the task force as it sailed toward the Philippine Islands. As the task force neared the island of Palau, Lieutenant Freeborn was patrolling with third squadron, when a group of ten Japanese Zero's decided to take a run at the task force.

Immediately, third squadron broke into two attack formations and went after the Zeros. Rolling his Hellcat hard over to starboard, Lieutenant Freeborn found himself dropping down on top of a Zero that was attempting to make a run back toward Palau. Immediately, he pressed his trigger, sending a string of machine gun bullets into the top of the plane, ripping off the canopy. He watched the pilot slump over in his seat as the aircraft raced straight into the ocean below. By the time the battle was over, just two Zeroes were able to climb into a cloud bank and disappear. Only two planes from third squadron received any damage, and it was light and could easily be repaired on the carrier.

Once the fleet entered the waters around the Philippine's, the *Princeton* and several other smaller carriers sailed from the Sulu Sea into the Bohol Sea where they were to take up a position near Surigao Straits.

During the night of October 23, 1944, a major Japanese task force was expected to come down Surigao Straits and attempt to attack the landing fleet in Leyte Gulf. Just at the crack of dawn a large segment of the Japanese task force broke out into the open sea. Nearly every attack aircraft on the smaller escort carriers, including the *Princeton*, were launched to strike at the approaching fleet.

Third squadron had barely been launched when a large flight of Japanese bombers and torpedo bombers broke through the thick cloud laden sky. Immediately, dive bombers dropped several five-hundred-pound bombs that tore through the flight deck, exploding inside the ship. Several other hits turned the *Princeton* in to a raging inferno.

From four thousand feet, Lieutenant Freeborn could see the naval battle taking place. It was evident at this point that the American surface fleet was having the better of the fight. Seeing a Japanese light cruiser retiring toward the north, trailing a column of smoke, Lieutenant Freeborn decided that would be his target with the five-hundred-pound bombs attached to the belly of his aircraft. A small amount of flak came skyward, as he and his wing man dropped down out of the sky. Seconds later, he released both bombs as he pulled back on the stick, attempting to regain altitude. Looking back out of his canopy he could see one bomb slamming into a five-inch gun turret, completely destroying it. His second bomb missed the ship, but exploded right next to the hull, causing several steel plates to buckle. Water immediately began rushing into the ship. His wing man, Lieutenant Mark Ozissky from Wisconsin, fared much better. One of his bombs struck the top of the control bridge, killing all the top officers of the ship. His second bomb struck the forecastle of the ship, blowing a large hole in the deck and starting several huge fires.

Not wanting the ship to get away, Lieutenant Freeborn swung around and placed all six of his rockets into the forward hull of the ship. Large sections of steel were torn away, causing massive amounts of water to flood the forward decks. Immediately, the ship began to slow as the bow began settling in the water. Lieutenant Ozissky fired his rockets into the stern of the ship, shearing off one of the massive rudders and bending a second, while shredding two of the props. As massive flames roared out of the foredeck, the stern of the cruiser began raising out of the water. Fifteen minutes later, the ship rolled over on its starboard side and began to sink. For the pilots, it was payback for the loss of the *Princeton*. Low on fuel and ammunition, the men sought out the *Intrepid,* currently about a hundred miles to the northeast. After getting permission to land, the planes were refueled and given another set of rockets, but no bombs. Their mission was to take on the Japanese planes that were attacking the fleet.

Just minutes after taking off, Lieutenant Freeborn spotted a Japanese dive bomber going after an American battleship. Making a quick turn to port, he poured all the power he could to his radial engine as he dropped down into a dive. Coming up behind the aircraft, he let go a barrage of machine gun bullets. As the bullets ripped up the port wing root of the dive bomber, the plane swung out of control and began twisting wildly toward the surface of the ocean. The plane exploded a good hundred yards from the battleship. After regaining altitude, Lieutenant Freeborn observed a Japanese airbase about a mile inland from the sea. Four Zeros were beginning to line up to rejoin the fight after refueling. Dropping down to a thousand feet, Lieutenant Freeborn fired his rockets. Two zeroes exploded instantly, while the third plane in line had part of the right wing torn off.

On the way back to the Intrepid, Lieutenant Freeman observed a Japanese plane circling around an ammunition ship that was waiting to go ashore and unload. It was evident that the Japanese pilot never saw the F6F bearing down on him, as he made no evasive maneuvers. Lieutenant Freeborn cut loose with the last of his machine gun bullets, ripping the cockpit to shreds. The plane rolled over on its back and dove into the sea.

As Lieutenant Freeborn set his Hellcat down on the deck of the *Intrepid*, he was very happy. Today he got his fourth and fifth kills. He would now be considered an Ace fighter pilot. He knew full well that the cream of the Japanese Naval Air Corp had been slaughtered during operations in the Mariana Islands, but a kill was a kill, and that meant one less Japanese plane to deal with.

The following morning after getting his sixth kill, Lieutenant Freeborn went down to strafe a Japanese destroyer when a wall of flak went up from ten different ships. Lieutenant Ozissky was hit, immediately tearing off his right wing. The plane spun out of control, smashing into the sea, not allowing the lieutenant the opportunity to jump clear.

Moments later, the canopy of Lieutenant Freeborn's F6F exploded as an anti-aircraft shell exploded just feet above his left wing. Shrapnel tore into the his chest, left arm and left leg, making it nearly impossible to move the rudder controls. Pieces of glass from the damaged canopy stuck out of his face and neck. Pulling back on his stick and pouring fuel to the engine, Lieutenant Freeborn began making a wide turn away from the Japanese fleet, while hoping to find the *Intrepid* close to where it had been when he took off. Smoke poured from under the instrument panel as small flames began emanating from his engine bonnet. The lieutenant knew his plane was all but doomed, and his life jacket shredded by shrapnel. The last thing he wanted to do right now was jump out into shark-infested waters, unable to swim and covered in blood.

However, he was also well aware that there were two live bombs hanging from the undercarriage of his Hellcat. He knew he would have to drop his bombs before being allowed to land on the carrier, or attempt a crash landing at sea. Although jettisoning his bombs into the sea made perfect sense in order to land on the carrier and save his life, he was angered at the thought of wasting two good bombs. Looking over his shoulder, he could see a small Japanese carrier about the size of the *Princeton* under attack by American fighter bombers. After taking a quick breath, he rolled his plane over to the right and dropped it down into a dive. The problem was, now he wasn't sure he could pull the damaged aircraft out of the dive before he slammed into the ocean. Immediately, flack bursts began exploding all around him, with some of the shrapnel entering the cockpit from the damaged canopy. His engine sputtered several times which meant it was being starved for fuel from either a leak or a failing fuel pump.

Nevertheless, he was in the dive now and he was not going to pull out, as he was sure the damaged aircraft might break apart attempting such a maneuver. At seven hundred feet, he released both his bombs as he pulled back on the stick, applying full right rudder. He could tell either the rudder or control cables were damaged, as the plane did not respond as it was supposed to. Now he knew he had another problem that could keep him from landing on the carrier.

Looking back over his shoulder, he could see one of his bombs had struck the rear ramp of the carrier deck, making it impossible for a plane to attempt a landing. His second bomb must have missed the carrier, striking the water just aft of the ship. Leveling off at two hundred feet, he began flying evasive action as best he could with a badly damaged plane until he was clear of the flack.

Once he was away from the enemy fleet, he slowly brought his suffering hellcat up to five hundred feet. Even with the plane weighing two hundred pounds less, it was handling worse, and the smell of aviation fuel began to fill the cockpit.

Watching his fuel gauge dropping quickly, he knew he had suffered a major fuel leak, and that was going to put him in the water long before he had planned on it. Looking off to the horizon, Lieutenant Freeborn observed the silhouette of an aircraft carrier heading straight west into the wind, which is what he needed to set his damaged aircraft down on the rolling deck.

When he was five miles out, Lieutenant Freeborn dropped his landing gear and called the carrier.

"Home base, this is Princeton Cat 223, coming in with heavy battle damage, and badly wounded, request clear deck.

The Landing Officer replied. "Can't take a chance 223, put her in the water near a destroyer, will pick you up."

Shaking his head, Lieutenant Freeborn replied. "Home base, wounded badly, not sure I can get out before she sinks, need to have your deck."

Once again, the Landing Officer replied, "Negative 223, I have an entire ship and crew to think about. I can't take a chance of you starting a massive fire, you need to take a water landing, and do it now!"

"Commander, I'm just about out of fuel, I have no ammunition left, my left leg is shattered and I'm bleeding badly. My canopy has been partially blown away and I may not be able to slide it open with one arm, as I think my left arm may be broken, and who knows how this cat may break apart when I crash. Need your deck, sir."

After a moment of silence, the Landing Officer replied. "Alright 223, bring her in slow, we'll get you down."

Remembering how optimistic Sister Dominique had always been in New Guinea, he said to himself. "Alright Sister, if you can hear me, I need your help, and I need it quick. Please get me down on that carrier in one piece, please get me down."

Making one more adjustment to his alignment, Lieutenant Freeborn said, "Power cut, air speed 110 knots, final fuel jettisoned, bring me home, Sister Dominique."

"Sister Dominique? What the hell is Freeborn talking about now?" the landing officer said to the ensign standing aside of him.

The ensign shook his head. "Maybe he's delirious from loss of blood, or maybe he's having hallucinations from being under pressure, I've heard about things like that."

The landing officer looked at the young ensign and shook his head as he mumbled, "Hallucinations, what the hell? I sure hope you didn't learn about that in the naval academy."

Moments later, the wheels of Cat 223 slammed down hard on the deck of the *Intrepid*. Immediately, his damaged right wheel broke away, sending the plane into a skid. With the crash barrier rigged across the deck, the careening hellcat came to a sudden stop as part of the damaged right wing snapped off, dropping to the deck.

Emergency crews quickly descended on the smoking aircraft, cutting Lieutenant Freeborn out of the wreckage before pushing the remains of the smoldering aircraft overboard.

Doctors in the surgical department worked carefully, removing the thick shards of steel from Lieutenant Freeborn's chest, arm, leg and abdominal area. After the glass was removed from his face, he was packaged to be sent to a hospital ship nearby.

This time he knew his war was over no matter how much he argued, but he would go out as an ace and that meant a lot to him. It was something many good pilots attempted to do, but ended up getting killed in the process.

Lieutenant Freeborn spent the next four months recuperating from his injuries in Hawaii. When he was discharged, he returned to San Diego where he taught new pilots the art of combat flying and how to judge the pitching deck of a carrier. He was amazed at the quality of pilots America was still sending into the fight, compared to the poorly trained pilots the Japanese were now deploying to the South Pacific. It was clear to every pilot that the Japanese were losing the war, as they no longer were able to design newer, better aircraft. They were still relying on the Zero fighters that had been redesigned nearly eighteen months earlier. More importantly, the Japanese were no longer capable of matching replacement aircraft production as the United States was.

With the war ending, the navy decided they no longer needed Lieutenant Freeborn, as his injuries banned him from combat flying for the rest of his life. However, that did not stop him from being a test pilot for Boeing aircraft. For the next forty years, Chuck Freeborn flew every type of military aircraft Boeing produced. During that time, he was married to the love of his life Catherine, and together they raised two daughters.

Sadly, in 1997, Catherine died from cancer. Although Chuck was still in pretty good shape for his seventy-seven years, he decided to move into an assisted living apartment complex that was the home for many former naval veterans and retirees.

Over the years, Chuck wrote several papers for Boeing and the navy on planes he had tested. He always enjoyed it when people arrived at his apartment to complete interviews on his experiences with aircraft.

Chapter Twenty-Five –
Reunions and Good byes

In 2007, Chuck Freeborn was sitting with one of his friends reading the Seattle morning paper. His friend Ralph said, "You got to see this, Chuck. There's a Benedictine sister in Minnesota that's turning ninety-two years old. During the war she had been a prisoner of the Japanese on several islands and witnessed the bombing of Hiroshima. Sounds like she's led quite the life."

As he began to tremble, Chuck looked over at Ralph. "Does it say her name?"

Rereading the story, Ralph replied, "Let me see, yeah here it is, it says her name is Sister Dominique."

Tears flowed down Chuck's face as he walked over to read the story. "I knew her in New Guinea, she was one tough woman. I have always wondered what happened to her and to the other sisters that were with her. And there was a priest, darn, what was his name? Oh yeah, Father Renaldo. They were all from Italy."

Finishing the story, he folded the newspaper and said, "I need to call my daughter, Cynthia. We're going to Minnesota, one way or the other."

By the end of the day, Cynthia had made all the arrangements and called the monastery to see if she and her father would be allowed to visit Sister Dominique. She was happy to hear Sister Dominique's memory was still sharp as a pin and that she was looking forward to seeing the lieutenant whenever he could get there.

Being eighty-seven years old and using a cane for stability due to battle damage to his right leg, Chuck Freeborn was ready to go the minute his flight arrived in Minneapolis. He had so many questions for Sister Dominique, and he wondered how many of the other sisters were still alive.

Chuck made sure that Cynthia kept the story quiet, as he did not want any press or reporters to interrupt the reunion. He wanted it to be personal with no fanfare.

After spending the night in a motel in St. Cloud, Chuck awoke feeling very apprehensive about making the trip. Cynthia assured him at least a dozen times that he was doing the right thing.

As Chuck put on his World War Two uniform that still fit like a glove, she said. "Look Dad, what have you got to lose by meeting Sister Dominique again. I don't think you will ever regret it."

Kissing his daughter on the cheek, Chuck said, "Honey, when you turn 87 you actually hope you might do something you'll regret, because you don't have long to think about it anymore."

Cynthia laughed as she made sure all the medals on her father's uniform were straight and in the proper order.

As Cynthia parked their car near the Benedictine monastery in St. Joseph, Minnesota, Chuck had to smile. Above the door where an ROTC welcoming party stood, was a banner that read 'WELCOME LIEUTENANT CHARLES FREEBORN.'

As a tear ran down his strong weathered face, Lieutenant Freeborn climbed out of the car, placed his cap on his head, took hold of his cane and walked straight as an arrow toward the greeting party that awaited him. Giving them a perfect salute, he said, "Lieutenant Freeborn, United States Navy, reporting as requested!"

A captain in charge of the college ROTC members stepped forward, returning the salute. "Sir, it's a pleasure to meet you, and Sister Dominique is most anxious to see you again."

Nodding his head, Chuck replied. "Very good Captain, lead me forward."

Entering the building, Chuck and Cynthia were greeted by Mother Superior and many other sisters living at the convent. When they had reached the end of the greeting line, Mother Superior smiled.

"She's waiting in the lounge, follow me."

When Chuck reached out for Cynthia's hand, she said, "No Dad, I will meet her later. This needs to be just the two of you. You can do this."

As Chuck walked through the door, Sister Dominique stood up from her wheelchair and reached out her arms. Chuck moved forward, quickly taking hold of Sister Dominique. They both wept as they held each other tightly.

After several minutes, Chuck helped Sister Dominique settle in her chair. He wheeled her over toward a sofa where he sat down and took hold of her hands. "I would have recognized you anywhere, Sister. You still have that smile that can warm the heart of any soul on this earth."

Sister Dominique laughed as she looked over the medals on his uniform. "You were a busy man, Lieutenant. I hear you almost did not return from your last mission."

Nodding his head, Charles responded. "Yes, Sister, and I was definitely not alone in the cockpit that day. In fact, I don't know if you heard me, but I was calling out for you to pray for me so I wouldn't be killed when I crash landed. It was all pretty ugly and some days I'm still surprised I survived that landing. But the prayers paid off and here I am."

Clapping her hands, Sister Dominique said, "That is a wonderful story and I am so proud you made it back to the navy. I knew you wanted to get back and fight so badly, although I did not understand why when you were safe and away from the killing. I guess I didn't understand all of that back then."

The conversation went on for most of the day, with Cynthia and Mother Superior joining them after lunch. Sister Dominique was most interested in his story about saving the two native girls. She looked at him and said, "I always thought you had the makings of a true hero." She then reached over for a book that was laying on a table next to her. Opening the book, she took out the Roman collar he had worn when he was disguised as a priest. "After you left us in the jungle, I felt that one day I would see you again. How I did not know, but I just had a feeling. So, I dug down under the leaves to retrieve your collar, I did not feel right to leave it buried where you left it. So, today it goes back to you, a souvenir from a war long over."

Holding on to the collar, Chuck smiled, "Believe me, it came out better than the shirt it went with. By the time I was rescued, it was in tatters. After they gave me a shower and a shave, I think someone tossed it in the burn barrel."

Late that afternoon, Chuck looked intently at Sister Dominique. "So, tell me, where are Sister Margaret, Sister Claudia, Sister Josephine, Sister Perpetua, Father Renaldo and Pierre Duncan. I always wondered what happened to all of you."

Taking hold of Chucks hands, she began, "Commander Ossani beheaded Sister Perpetua. His men shot two little boys that tossed mud on a soldier. When Sister Perpetua ran over to hold them, he drew his sword and killed her."

Chuck cried for several moments, as he shook his head. "She was such a wonderful person, she did not deserve that."

"Father Renaldo died in 1975 from a radiation illness the doctors could not cure. I don't know what happened to Pierre Duncan. I always hoped he went back to his beloved plantation, but I don't know. Sister Margaret and Sister Josephine went back to the Abbazia di San Vincenzo on the mountain where I grew up. They both died there. Sister Josephine's Cancer came back with a vengeance, but she was a real trooper up until the day she passed. My real sister, Sister Claudia was also at the Abbey for many years before she took a position in Rome. She passed away in 2000 from a bad strain of the flu that killed many Italians that year. So, now your question has been answered."

"So, you and I are the last members of the group that I knew. I always wondered what might have happened if I had not shot that Japanese guard. Would I have survived pretending to be Father Martin, or would the Japanese have found out who I really was? That would have been the end of it for me. I have always been grateful to all of you for saving my life. It was not easy leaving all of you after knowing the sacrifices you made to keep me alive" Chuck said, feeling very grateful.

"It was hard on all of us to see you leave. You gave us so much strength, and I think most of us knew you were not a priest to begin with, but we were all in the same boat, so what did it matter," Sister Dominique said with a broad smile. Continuing, she said, "After I was back in the camp, I would laugh to myself many times, wondering what Commander Ossani would have felt if he knew he had an American fighter pilot right under his nose."

Laughing loudly, Chuck said, "Actually, I've thought about that myself many times. It would have been fun to see him after the war and tell him that right to his face."

Cynthia looked intently at Sister Dominique. "Why didn't you go with my father when he went to find the American's?"

Sister Dominique smiled. "Believe me, that was a decision that had to be made in a split second. I knew if anyone could make it through the jungle, it would be the lieutenant. But I also knew I would slow him down and possibly get him captured. Plus, I did not want to desert Father Renaldo and the rest of the sisters. We had come so far together I felt I had a responsibility to stay with them. But I will be honest with all of you, that night before I fell asleep, I cried, wishing I would have run with the lieutenant, I knew in my heart he had what it took to make it, and I know now I was right. However, by staying I was able to witness the atomic attack on Hiroshima, something most people on earth have never experienced. I was able to nurse many of them and actually witness the devastation of the bomb. It was a marvelous experience mixed in with the evil I endured." Laughing, Sister Dominique added, "As the war was coming to a close, we saw many American fighters fly over the camps. I always wondered if you were up there, Lieutenant. Sometimes, the planes would fly so low you could see the pilots faces. I always stopped what I was doing so I could see if one of those gallant pilots was you. Even though I never knew, I believed you were my guardian angel up there."

Cynthia laughed as she looked at her father. "Sister thought you were up there as her guardian angel, and you prayed to her to help you land on the carrier. Why didn't you seek each other out long before today?"

Sister Dominique said, "Life went on after the war, and you never knew who made it and who did not. You never forgot about them, but life kept us all busy and we never took the time we should have to find those that were important during those difficult times. Maybe it was better that way, because we never knew who didn't make it. That way we could believe they were all out there doing well, and someday we might just run into them."

Chuck nodded his head. "Cynthia, for me there was you and your sister to raise, the long hours my job took, overseas missions to teach pilots, and eventually your mother's cancer to deal with. As the saying goes, there is never enough time in a day, or when it comes down to it, in a lifetime, to do what should be done. But in your heart, you never forget them, and it keeps their memory alive, and sometimes that's all you have to cling to, but in the end it's all worthwhile."

Taking a deep breath, Sister Dominique looked at her history students and said, "Now you know my story and everything there is to know about me. Sometimes it seems like my life was played out on a huge movie screen, with characters jumping in and out of the story when they had a part to play in the next scene. It has all gone so quickly, and it was nothing that I thought my life would ever be like when I was five years old. All I had was my family, the animals, and a small house where we lived a quiet life. I was not sure what my future would be, after all, how many young five year old children ever think of that? But all of that was uprooted and it forced me to change everything I was expecting. While hurtful and traumatic, the change allowed me to visit places I had never heard of, and I have seen things most people have never seen or could have imagined. And now here I am, 100 years old, and the world has turned over many times, and some of it I shall never understand or attempt to. I have asked myself over and over, why me? Why have I survived this long while all the others have died one way or another? I think back to the day my father dropped me off at the monastery and left. I can still see that little girl throwing the horrible tantrum until reality set in, at least as much as it was going to. Now memories are all I have left of a life that I hope was well lived. Only God will be able to answer that question when we meet. But for now, you have my story to write and I look forward to reading it."

Donald smiled as he looked at Sister Dominique. "There is one thing you have not spoken about. Do you have any regrets about your life?"

"Oh Donald, that is a question that haunts me every day. People I loved very much died and I question myself over and over as to what I could have done differently to save their lives. Of course, today everything is in hind sight, and I now know many things I did not know at the time. I guess keeping all that in mind, I have come to some realizations. One of them is that people die in war for no good reason, and there is nothing we can do to predict it, or change it. Secondly, people do horrible things during war they otherwise may not ever do. What sparks these outrages is also something we may never understand. And I learned very early on that human beings are a strange animal in every respect. I still do not know what makes them function. But we all get caught up in matters that leave us wondering that age old question, what could I have done to change the outcome. Most often, the answer is nothing. So, Donald, I have come to the conclusion that a life well lived to the best of our abilities, is about the best we can ask for. We make mistakes we can never change, and we say things we can never take back. It's all a part of life. Man is an imperfect being, Donald, and we can only hope we are doing our best."

After being quiet for a minute, Sister Dominique said, "I was just thinking, there was a song that was very famous when I was a young woman. The singer said, 'Regrets I've had a few, but then, too few to mention.' After one hundred years, I guess that fits me very well, so that's where I will leave the answer to your question."

Catherine looked warmly at Sister Dominique. "If you could go back and change one thing in your life, what would it be?"

Smiling, Sister Dominique replied, "Not being removed from my family is the first thing that comes to my mind, but then, where would I be today? Certainly not talking with all of you. I would have never experienced life in the South Pacific, I would not have experienced parts of World War Two the way I did, and I would not have met all the interesting people I have known throughout my life. I think we can all look at little things in our life we totally dislike and wish we could change them. But in the end, that one small insignificant change could lead us in a totally different direction, changing the outcome of our lives forever. It comes back to the old adage, 'Be careful what you wish for.' So no, Catherine, there is nothing I would change. It has been a remarkable life, and I have out lived nearly everyone I've known over the years. That is even more remarkable."

Sandra, a history major that helped line up the interview, asked, "Becoming a sister was pretty much inevitable after living in the Abbey for nearly fifteen years. Do you ever wish you could have had a different vocation?"

Laughing slightly, Dominique replied. "There was a day when Mother Superior came to me and told me I would need to make a decision as to whether I wanted to continue on with becoming a Benedictine sister, or would I rather leave the convent and go out on my own. I was stunned by the question, thinking I must have done something wrong. But Mother Superior said that was not the case, I simply had to decide which path in life I wanted to take. I thought about it for nearly a week, wondering what life would be like outside the walls of the Abbey. Where would I go? What would I do? Could I reconnect with my family again? All very scary questions for a young girl back then. But in my heart, I knew that becoming a sister was all I really wanted to do. The only time I questioned it was when I received that tongue lashing in Buffalo from Mother Superior, that this transfer may be my last, and I had to get past all that had happened to me. I was angry with her for a while, but it made no difference because I found peace here and wish to go nowhere else anyway, not even back to my blessed Abbey in Italy."

Sitting by the warm fireplace in the monastery that evening, Sister Dominique looked over at Sister Lucinda. "You sat through most of the interview, so tell me, did any of it make any sense? Did we accomplish anything worthwhile?"

Sister Lucinda smiled. "I learned you were a stronger woman than I had ever expected. I learned you were capable of more things than I ever thought a person could be. I learned that when everything seems at its worst, there is always a way out, even though you may not like the consequences. I came to understand we actually never know ourselves completely until we have to make some God-awful decisions, and that is when we are at our best. Yes, Sister, I think everything you told the students was spot on and will make a remarkable story for students in the future."

Looking over at the window as a light snow continued to fall, Sister Dominique said, "But I question why I am still here. What more do I have to offer to this wonderful Abbey and to the world. Each day I wake up I'm excited, but I always ponder those questions. Like most people I wonder what is out there beyond this life. Where will I go? What will I do? What will I see? Will I experience it with my family and friends that have already passed? So many questions. But I know if it compares to the incredible life I have had here on this earth, it will be a wonderful marvelous experience.

Epilogue

*Sister Santina, the first sister to meet Dominique's father at the door. She died at the age of 85 in the Abbey.

* Novice Agnesia. During the winter after taking her final vows, Agnesia came down with virulent strain of pneumonia and passed away. She was just 25.

*Lorenzo Seneca leader of the Milan underground was captured in February 1945 and hung in Milan by the Nazi Government.

*Lieutenant Sam Kirksy commanded the U.S.S. *Rockfish* that torpedoed the landing ship after it left Nusa Simbo. In February of 1945, he was promoted to commander and assigned to submarine tactical command at Pearl Harbor where he finished the war. He retired from the navy in 1960, living the rest of his life near Boston, Massachusetts. He never knew there were prisoners on that ship. He passed away in 1985.

*Ensign Dave Collins was the executive officer on the U.S.S. *Rockfish* when it sank the landing ship after it left Nusa Simbo. He was killed when the submarine he commanded in June of 1944 was sunk near the Aleutian Islands.

*Sister Magdalene, Mother Superior at the convent that assigned the sisters to Nusa Simbo, remained in the Abbey with the rest of her congregation until the Nazis removed them in November of 1943. They moved to a smaller convent in Acqualagna, hoping to return to the Abbey after the war. She died at the convent in Acqualagna in 1970 at the age of ninety.

*Japanese Colonel Mizawa, who first warned Sister Dominique on Nusa Simbo, was killed in the battle for Okinawa in June, 1945.

*Japanese Major Ouichi, who removed the sisters from Nusa Simbo, was tortured and hung by Filipino guerrillas on the island of Mindoro, November, 1944.

*Captain Kimura at Rabaul. Rabaul, on the island of New Britain was referred to as the fortress of the Pacific by the American High Command. Although it was bombed and shelled repeatedly, the base was never captured until after the war was over. However, Captain Kimura was not so lucky. He was transferred to Iwo Jima in December of 1944 to help bolster its defenses. On February 6, 1945, the captain ordered nearly two hundred tough Japanese marines into a cave to prepare for a night time Banzai charge against American lines. Several American combat engineers, seeing what was happening, rolled three fifty-five-gallon drums of diesel fuel into the cave, and then tossed in several hand grenades. A massive fire ball ripped out of the cave opening collapsing the roof. Tons of rock and dirt sealed the mass grave and the fate of all of those men, along with Captain Kimura.

*Commander Ossani died one year to the day after he began his sentence. Guards found him dead laying on his bed. He had died during the night from taking cyanide. It was never determined how he was able to get the capsule.

*General Robert Cannon actually was in MacArthur's sixth army headquarters in the South Pacific. After the war he served in several eastern commands. He passed away in 1967.

*Lt. Charles Freeborn died from pneumonia in 2008. He and his wife Catherine are buried in the Tahoma National Veteran's Cemetery near Tacoma, Washington. His youngest daughter Cynthia and her husband frank are retired teachers and still live in the Seattle area. His oldest daughter Charlotte is still alive and lives with her husband Edward in Astoria, Oregon where he retired from the Coast Guard.

*Colonel Takeuchi, the commander of the hospital in Tokyo. He hid out in the mountains for nearly two years after the war ended. He was eventually captured by an American patrol. He was found guilty of crimes against humanity and sentenced to thirty years in prison. His sentence was commuted by General MacArthur before he left Japan. The Colonel died in 1978.

*Asahi Kinoshita the sister of the soldier that gave Sister Dominique his billfold. She began having problems with radiation poisoning in 1950. She passed away from cancer in 1952.

*Lieutenant Earl Stoneman from PT 262 was severely injured during an attack on a Japanese convoy after transferring to the Philippine Islands. He spent several months recuperating in Tripler Naval Hospital in Hawaii. After several surgeries, doctors were able to save his left arm, but he lost most of his hand after gangrene set in. Returning home to Huntsville, Alabama, he became a car salesman at a Hudson dealer. He married his high school sweetheart and had two daughters. He died in 2001.

*Pierre Duncan left Hiroshima in 1947, and returned to Nusa Simbo where his banana plantation had been rebuilt and enlarged. He returned to Hiroshima once a year for the rest of his life to work in a medical clinic he helped to support, that worked with patients suffering from radiation poisoning. He died on Nusa Simbo in 1999 from a major heart attack while sitting on the veranda at the home of his daughter.

*Father Renaldo returned to Rome for just a short period of time. As his health once more improved, he was assigned to Germany where he worked with the ongoing resettlement program, and helped find funds to rebuild the Catholic churches destroyed in the war. After he once again became very sick with radiation poisoning, he returned to Rome where he taught young seminarians. Although he and Sister Dominique exchanged letters several times a year, the only time they met face to face again was at Commander Ossani's trial. Father Renaldo passed away in his sleep, Christmas Day 1975.

*Sister Margaret spent the rest of her life living and working in the Abbazia di San Vincenzo. She passed away in 1998.

*Sister Josephine split her time between the Abbazia di San Vincenzo and Rome where she worked on several Papal projects. She passed away in the Abbey in 2002.

*Sister Claudia moved from the Abbey to Rome in 1985, where she worked with several Papal organizations that funded missions all around the world. She passed away in 2000 from a serious bronchial infection brought on by the flu.

*Commander Sakurai, skipper of the *Koshiro Maru*, died of cancer several months after Sister Dominique's visit. To his death he never believed he was guilty of any wrong doing after the sinking of his ship. He believed saving his crew was all that mattered.

*Captain John Studdard led the attack to liberate the Abbey. He survived the war despite being seriously wounded during fighting along the Rhine River in Germany. He returned home and married his high school sweetheart, had three children and worked as a crane operator in the New York City Sea Port. He died in 2006.

*Colonel Joseph Winslow, commander of the Australian forces on the Island of Ranongga. His men fought for three more days after Sister Dominique and Pierre Duncan departed. With just twenty men left alive and most of them wounded, Colonel Winslow surrendered to the Japanese commander. For all his efforts, Colonel Winslow was immediately sentenced to death by the Japanese commander for war crimes, as he did not surrender earlier. He was sentenced to death and hung on Ranongga the same day. His men were taken away to a POW camp on Rabaul. Only one of them survived the war. Two Australian Coast Watchers that had been high in the mountains managed to escape by submarine a month after the island fell. They testified to the colonel's fate.

*German Major Gerhardt Young who took over the Abbey became a prisoner of war. He was transferred to a POW camp in North Africa. He was repatriated to Germany after the war, where he went to work in his father's print shop. He took over the business after his father passed away. He died in 2001.

*Lieutenant Hans Vogel, aide to Major Young, was also transferred to a POW camp in North Africa. After the war he was repatriated to Germany. He was killed in 1946 by American military police while attempting to smuggle stolen art work out of Germany.

*General Mark W. Clark commander of the fifth army in Italy. Was the youngest four star general in the United States Army. He went on to serve in Korea. He died in April of 1984 at the age of 87 in Charleston, South Carolina.

*Captain Bironi the friend of Paulo in Naples. His wife testified in 1998 that he was uncomfortable about Paulos questions and attitude during their visit. He reported Paulo to the Gestapo. Although Captain Bironi had given the Gestapo much information during the war, he and his wife disappeared in 1946.

*Barrister William T. Rathbone worked in the Allied military government in Germany until 1951. He then returned to England and was elected to Parliament. He was killed in a boating accident on the river Thames in 1968.

*Stefan Trach, who helped recover some of the art work for the Abbey, continued his search for stolen Nazi artwork until 1989. He and his wife lived in a small home near Lucerne, Switzerland, until he passed away in 1993 from a freak mountain climbing accident. Rumors still say he was murdered by members of Odessa.

*Corporal Erika Anderson, who was instrumental in chasing down stolen art work in New York, spent thirty years in the Army, retiring with the rank of Command Sergeant Major. She and her husband had two children and lived in Burlington, Vermont where they ran an art gallery. She passed away in 2009.

*Alphonse Moeller returned to his mansion in New York after being released from prison. After his death in 1990, the new owners of the mansion did extensive remodeling. They found several pieces of art work from the Abbey in a secret room in the basement. They were returned to the Abbey six months later. The pieces were valued at over four million dollars.

*Colonel Paul J. Tibbits piloted the B-29 Enola Gay that dropped the Atomic Bomb on Hiroshima. He retired from the army in 1966 at the rank of Brigadier General. He was married twice and was survived by three children. He wrote several books about his Army Career before passing away in November of 2007.

*Russell Gackenbach did the photography work from the Necessary Evil as it flew around the atomic bomb cloud. After discharge, he entered Lehigh University in Bethlehem, Pa, and in 1950 received a B.S. In Metallurgical Engineering. He was employed as a materials-corrosion engineer for a large chemical-pharmaceutical firm in New Jersey for 35 years, retiring in 1985 as principal materials engineer. He served as a consultant for 10 years before moving to Florida. He passed away in November of 2019 at the age of 89.

*Captain George Marquardt flew the B-29 Necessary Evil around the Atomic Bomb cloud at Hiroshima. He was also on the bombing mission to Nagasaki. He passed away in 2003 at the age of 84. He was in a retirement center in Murray, Utah for several years suffering from Parkinson's disease.

*Captain James Parcel that was in command of liberating camp 45. He was a career soldier that also served in the Korean War. He retired from the

Marine Corp in 1953 after thirty years of service. He and his wife Marilyn had two children. The Captain worked part time as a reserve police officer for the city of Tulsa, Oklahoma for ten years. He died in 1985 at the age of 80 from a major heart attack.

*Sister Dominique spent the rest of her life in the monastery in St. Joseph, Minnesota. Before dementia became a problem in 2016, she wrote a book of poetry and did many historical interviews about the war. She died peacefully in her sleep at the age of 102 in 2017. She is buried in the monastery cemetery in St. Joseph, Minnesota.

*All the islands, names of cities or towns in the Pacific, and the locations where the Japanese had prisoner camps are accurate. Nusa Simbo is located on the far southwest side of Wilson Passage, about forty miles south of Ranongga Island. It is under the control of the Solomon Island Government. In 2007 is was struck by a major earth quake that caused the Ove volcano to become active again.

*The treacherous Kokoda Trail over the Owen Stanley Mountains still exists today. Climbers that have followed the dangerous trail report seeing many war artifacts strewn about the jungle floor. Unexploded ordnance still claims lives of islanders and nosy hikers to this day.

www.ingramcontent.com/pod-product-compliance
Lightning Source LLC
Chambersburg PA
CBHW031232290426
44109CB00012B/256